Studies in Contemporary European History

Editors:

Konrad Jarausch, Lurcy Professor of European Civilization, University of North Carolina, Chapel Hill, and a Director of the Zentrum für Zeithistorische Studien, Potsdam, Germany

Henry Rousso, Senior Fellow at the Institut d'historie du temps present (Centre national de la recherché scientifique, Paris) and co-founder of the European network "EURHISTXX"

VISIONS OF THE END OF THE COLD WAR

VISIONS OF THE END OF THE COLD WAR IN EUROPE, 1945–1990

Edited by
Frédéric Bozo, Marie-Pierre Rey,
Bernd Rother and N. Piers Ludlow

Berghahn Books
NEW YORK • OXFORD

First published in 2012 by

Berghahn Books

www.berghahnbooks.com

Library of Congress Cataloging-in-Publication Data
Visions of the end of the Cold War / edited by Frederic Bozo ... [et al.].
  p. cm. – (Studies in contemporary European history ; v. 11)
  Includes bibliographical references and index.
  ISBN 978-0-85745-288-7 (hardcover: alk. paper) – ISBN 978-0-85745-370-9
(ebook)
  1. Cold War. 2. World politics–1945-1989. 3. Balance of power. I. Bozo,
Frédéric.
  D843.V527 2012
  909.82′5–dc23

2011039175

British Library Cataloguing in Publication Data

A catalogue record for this book is available from the British Library.

Printed in the United States on acid-free paper

ISBN 978-0-85745-288-7 (hardback)
ISBN 978-0-85745-370-9 (ebook)

CONTENTS

INTRODUCTION

Frédéric Bozo, Marie-Pierre Rey,
Bernd Rother and N. Piers Ludlow

The fall of the Berlin Wall on 9 November 1989 quickly came to symbolize the end of the Cold War as a whole, including the liberation of Eastern Europe from Soviet rule in 1989, the unification of Germany in 1990 and the break-up of the Soviet Union in 1991. Its twentieth anniversary in autumn 2009 was therefore an opportunity to celebrate not just that particular event – however meaningful – but an extraordinary period that in barely two years led from the dismantling of the Iron Curtain to the liquidation of the whole 'Yalta' order. Yet the celebrations were not only a commemorative moment but also a historiographical one, marking the culmination of almost twenty years of ceaseless scholarly production on the end of the Cold War. Innumerable academic events were held on the anniversary itself in order to revisit the period, and a wealth of new works predictably came to enrich an already considerable literature. Furthermore, this clearly is not the end: as historical evidence continues to become accessible as a result of the regular opening of archives after the standard twenty to thirty years, the end of the Cold War is likely to keep historians busy for quite some time to come.

There are numerous explanations for the infatuation that continues to prevail among scholars and the general public with the end of the Cold War. The sheer historical importance of the period ranks high amongst them: the events of the late 1980s and early 1990s – often described as the 'revolutions of 1989' – were hugely momentous because they terminated four decades of East-West conflict, of the division of Germany, and of the domination of communism in Eastern Europe, all of which had defined the second half of the twentieth century on the continent. In a sense, the 1989–91 period even marked the definitive end of the 'short' twentieth century itself – an era of total conflicts and totalitarian ideologies.

But another reason for the fascination aroused by these events is their unexpected and, indeed, their unpredicted character. To be sure, by the

Notes for this chapter begin on page 13.

late 1980s the notion that the Cold War would end someday was generally recognized, but usually more as a theoretical point than as a definite prediction – in fact, the longer the Cold War lasted, the more it was perceived as likely to last for an indefinite period of time. In truth, those individuals – whether decision-makers or thinkers – who had effectively foreseen the end of the Cold War as it happened were few and far between. Even less numerous, in particular, were those who had sensed that the process could be both as rapid *and* as orderly as it turned out to be, a combination that certainly remains to this day the most remarkable characteristic of the events of 1989–91.[1]

And yet the end of the Cold War had been a constant and recurrent theme throughout the whole duration of the Cold War itself. Ever since its inception in the second half of the 1940s, statesmen, diplomats, politicians, academics and others had reflected on ways of ending the East-West conflict and overcoming its undesirable consequences. As the Cold War settled in – most clearly by the late 1960s – the East-West status quo no doubt increasingly came to be seen by most contemporaries as an enduring reality. Yet the situation was, arguably, never considered to be irreversible in the long term: even at times when the established order appeared to have become all but perennial, the need to overcome it and the ways to do so were more or less openly or more or less intensely and passionately discussed.

It is remarkable, therefore, that recent historiography has not more systematically sought to explore and investigate the visions of the end of the Cold War that were articulated and offered *before* the end of the Cold War took place. This is precisely the subject of this volume. The following collection of essays, then, is not an umpteenth book on the end of the Cold War itself.[2] Rather, it is an attempt at envisaging the entire Cold War through a prism that has arguably not been used systematically by historians or international relations specialists before: the retrospective analysis of the conceptions of the demise of the 'Yalta' system that emerged in the course of the four decades of Cold War.

The lack of a systematic exploration of those visions is not entirely surprising. The multifaceted character of the subject matter is one possible explanation. Many different types of actors may indeed be considered in one way or another to have offered, or to have been associated with, a particular vision of the end of the Cold War. The most identifiable case is of course that of the statesman: there are numerous instances of prominent figures – mostly decision-makers or political leaders – whose careers have been marked by their articulation of a clear, explicit vision of ending the Cold War. George Kennan, Charles de Gaulle, Willy Brandt, Mikhail Gorbachev, François Mitterrand and – with strong nuances, as seen below

– Ronald Reagan (all studied in this volume) are classic examples. Within civil societies, groups of individuals may also have entertained visions of ending the Cold War: consider, for example, the role of experts (e.g., the Bilderberg Group, studied in this volume) or scientists on both sides of the Iron Curtain (Pugwash naturally comes to mind, but the case of Soviet scientists, studied in this volume, is also of interest), or the role of dissidents in Eastern Europe (studied in several contributions to this volume). But such visions may also have been associated with processes rather than actors: for example, recent historiography (reflected in some of the contributions) has brought to the fore the importance of the Helsinki process or that of European integration as providers of at least implicit visions of surmounting 'Yalta' and the division of Europe, and the same is of course true of concepts of security and disarmament (some of which are again discussed in the book) that were developed during the Cold War, particularly in the 1970s and 1980s. In short, the visions of the end of the Cold War were just as numerous and diversified as their possible vectors.

Another difficulty that comes with the topic is the diversity that also prevails with regard to the nature of these visions. Some may be qualified as truly visionary, daringly sketching out a clear exit path from the Cold War situation: this was certainly the case for a Kennan or a de Gaulle in the first half of the Cold War. Others, in the second half of the Cold War in particular, may be seen as more evolutionary, taking into account existing realities and building on them in order to gradually assuage the strictures of 'Yalta': this was very much the case for Brandt and more generally for those inspired by Ostpolitik and its various correlates, whether 'change through rapprochement', the liberal peace concept or 'common security' (analysed in two contributions). It was also the case, with variants, for Mitterrand, Gorbachev and, in general, the many proponents of a pan-European, Helsinki-centred process to overcome the Iron Curtain, including some Eastern European dissidents (typically Jiří Hájek and his Charter 77, the subject of one of the contributions). In some instances, one may have doubts – despite the claims – that there really was a vision of overcoming the status quo: this was the case for Margaret Thatcher and, to some extent, in spite of later reconstructions, Reagan (both analysed in the volume). Finally, instances in which the need for a vision of overcoming the Cold War was altogether dismissed in the name of the need to manage it (no doubt the case of Henry Kissinger, analysed in one of the contributions) also deserve scrutiny.

Beyond the difficulty raised by the diversity of the matter and the heterogeneity of the material involved, some methodological precautions are in order when historically appraising visions of the end of the Cold War. First, contextualization is of the essence: discussing the need or the ways and means to overcome the Iron Curtain has different meanings depending on the circumstances in which it is done. For example, it makes a difference whether this was done at a time when the Cold War was still a fresh and perhaps a transitory state of affairs (as was the case when Kennan and, although less so, de Gaulle discussed it) or at a time when the Cold War had settled in (typically, Brandt). When analysing visions of the end of the Cold War, it is therefore essential to keep in mind that it was never the immobile reality that the convenient label suggests. Second, and as a consequence, those visions should be analysed not just as anticipations, but also as political expressions. Ending the Cold War was – from its start and increasingly so as it settled in – a long-term prospect, whereas discourses on overcoming the Iron Curtain were necessarily influenced by shorter-term considerations: for example, de Gaulle's advancing the need to transform East-West relations and to overcome 'Yalta', while no doubt sincere, was also a way to challenge American domination and transform West-West relations. Visions of the end of the Cold War, in other words, must also be seen as instruments of policy and not necessarily taken at face value; therefore a healthy dose of scepticism is in order when analysing them, as shown by the authors in this volume. This is all the more so because, finally, one must avoid the risk of retrospective determinism: because the Cold War eventually ended, it is all too tempting to give the credit to those who had expressed strong views on this, irrespective of their actual influence – the case of Reagan and of the myth of a 'Reagan victory' is quite illustrative.

In spite of all the foregoing caveats, we believe that exploring visions of the end of the Cold War can in many ways help us better reflect on, and understand, the Cold War itself and its historically complex reality. They help us understand its essence: what was the Cold War about? There are as many answers to that question as there were visions of ending it. To choose only one example from the 1980s: for Eastern European dissidents, ending the Cold War meant restoring individual liberties; for most Western European social democrats, it meant strengthening common security. These contrasting visions speak volumes about the diversity of the Cold War and the situations and perceptions within it. Reviewing them, as hinted above, also helps us better contextualize the 'long' Cold War: because they were shaped in specific situations and in specific circumstances, they tell us something about not only the aspirations that they expressed, but also these situations and circumstances. Hence de Gaulle's vision in the 1960s was very much the reflection of the fluidity – perceived or actual – that characterized the situation in Europe, particularly Eastern Europe, at least before the backlash of 1968 and the confirmation of the status quo that it brought about. By contrast, Brandt's vision in the 1970s and 1980s was evidently influenced by the then prevailing perception of the durability of that same status quo. This is a reminder that the Cold War was not a uniform, unchanging reality but, as is the case for all historical periods, a succession of changing dynamics.

Finally, examining visions of the end of the Cold War make us reflect on its durability. For four decades, these visions were of little, if any, help in overcoming the realities of the Cold War. Why? This fascinating question surely has many valid answers, but we suspect that one of the most decisive explanations is simply that many, and at many junctures, saw the Cold War as a lesser evil. For example, it is reasonably clear that in many instances (the disengagement debates of the late 1950s, studied in this volume, provide a good example), exploring possibilities of assuaging the East-West conflict by engaging in disarmament or other security steps with the Soviet bloc was seen as running the risk of unravelling the Western institutions such as NATO or the European Community that, having been set up in response to the Cold War, had become keystones of Western security, both external (against the Soviet threat) and internal (against a resurgent Germany). Similarly, Soviet offers to end the Cold War, in particular in the late Stalin era or in the period immediately after Stalin's death (as studied in one of the contributions), were never entirely sincere because they could have led to the reunification of Germany in the Western sphere, something Moscow would likely not have accepted. The bottom line is that the Cold War situation lasted as long as it did because it was most often seen as less a problem than a satisfactory arrangement – one that offered a solution to even more daunting problems, such as the German question.

But of course the Cold War eventually ended. Examining what the visions of its end had been during its existence and how they relate to its actual ending is therefore a crucial step in understanding why and how it ended, the focus of much of the current historiography of the Cold War. Eventually there was a convergence between the visions and the reality, even if the latter did not coincide with the vast majority of the former: would events have unfolded so rapidly and so peacefully in 1989–91 if so many people had not, during the previous four decades, desired, envisaged and pondered possible exits from the Cold War? Again, this volume is not in and of itself a study of the end of the Cold War, but we believe that it can contribute at least indirectly to our understanding of why the Cold War did end and how it actually ended peacefully and rapidly.

The volume begins with two contributions focusing on the period during which the East-West division crystallized. The early 1950s were a time when to articulate a vision of the end of the Cold War became a destabilizing, almost subversive act. This becomes evident from the forceful reactions to George Kennan's ideas. The first of the two chapters, that by John Harper, reveals Kennan's misgivings about the emerging architecture of the Cold War during that very period when, as director of the State Department's Policy Planning Staff, he was at the heart of U.S. decision-making. The author of the Long Telegram was thus unwilling to accept an enduring division of Europe or of Germany, sceptical about the long-term strength of the Soviet Union's hold over Eastern Europe and deeply uncomfortable with the possible consequences of a lasting American involvement in Western European affairs. His views, however, were out of step with those of both his own government and America's main European allies; as a result Kennan's radical plans, such as the 1948 Program A for German reunification never made it off the drawing board. Despite having left government service in 1950, partly out of disillusionment with his declining influence, Kennan retained an ability to speak with authority on Cold War matters. This helps explain the extraordinary impact of his 1957 Reith Lecture series for the BBC, in which he advocated a programme of superpower disengagement from Europe.

As Thomas Gijswijt shows in his contribution, however, few of the influential Western politicians and decision-makers who met regularly within the 'Bilderberg Group' were won over by Kennan's ideas. On the contrary, the Bilderberg network became just one of the mechanisms through which a forceful counter-attack against Kennan's heresies was concerted – a counter-attack that would see other leading figures from the Truman administration, such as Kennan's former boss Dean Acheson, strongly repudiating the notion of disengagement and highlighting the serious dangers that such a course would entail. Multiple European leaders, from German Christian Democrats to French Socialists, also rejected Kennan's vision, drawing attention to the damage it might do to Western Europe's impressive but still fragile recovery. In the end, however, it would be Soviet actions, and in particular Nikita Khrushchev's provocative diplomacy over Berlin, that would do most to douse Western support for the idea of disengagement.

The next three chapters ask whether there were missed opportunities to end the Cold War in the period immediately prior to and soon after Stalin's death. Geoffrey Roberts examines Soviet policymaking in the late 1940s and early 1950s. Controversially, he suggests that Moscow's offers to reconsider the division of Germany in particular and to explore ways in which the Cold War divide could be undone before it had hardened were more sincere than was believed in the West at the time. In both Stalin's final years and in the period immediately following his death, many in the Soviet leadership were prepared to hold substantive negotiations with the West about the Cold War division of Europe and would have gone into such talks willing to make major changes to the Soviet Union's position in Eastern Europe. These overtures met with little Western response, and eventually Khrushchev lost patience with those like Vyacheslav Molotov, who had long advocated negotiation with the West. But a strand of such 'peace' diplomacy would remain alive in the form of Soviet advocacy of an international conference on European collective security – a vision that would eventually lead to the Conference on Security and Cooperation in Europe (CSCE) in the 1970s.

Jaclyn Stanke returns to the period immediately after Stalin's death in 1953 and asks whether the West missed an opportunity to bring about an end to the Cold War. Her chapter focuses upon three differing Western reactions to this potential window of opportunity. The first set of views examined are those of the psychological warfare specialists within the Eisenhower administration, notably C. D. Jackson, who strongly argued that Stalin's demise represented a unique opportunity for the West to destabilize the Soviet system and bring about its collapse. President Eisenhower, her second subject, was not prepared, however, to engage fully with the programme of action Jackson proposed. He did make a presidential address calling for peace, but he failed to follow it up with any diplomatic action and flanked his peaceful rhetoric with the decision to authorize a number of covert actions designed to subvert the Soviet bloc. This half-hearted response disappointed not only the psychological warriors but also Winston Churchill. The British prime minister's belief that Stalin's death should be followed by a major summit meeting between the new leaders of the Soviet Union and their Western counterparts is the third reaction Stanke examines. This vision too would fail, betrayed by internal divisions in London and Washington and by Churchill's failing health.

Vladislav Zubok's chapter reviews dissident voices amongst Soviet intellectuals about the course of the Cold War. Chess prodigy Mikhail Botvinnik and the nuclear physicists Lev Landau and Andrei Sakharov acted separately from one another and with rather different motivations. Their critique of Soviet strategy and their warnings about the dangers of nuclear war had little immediate impact on Moscow's actions. But in the longer term, Zubok argues, such contrary views did matter, for the same dissatisfaction Botvinnik, Landau and Sakharov had shared regarding the risks and costs of nuclear war would later lie at the heart of the 'new thinking' associated with Mikhail Gorbachev and his generation of Soviet leaders in the second half of the 1980s. The three intellectuals thus foreshadowed ideas that would contribute significantly to the end of the Cold War.

The next section returns the focus to Western debates and looks at two European critics of the Cold War order during the 1960s. The views of Charles de Gaulle caused huge consternation at the time, both amongst his fellow European leaders and in Washington. But as Garret Martin demonstrates, the French leader was not simply motivated by anti-American sentiment. Instead his rejection of the Cold War status quo reflected a view of world politics formed well before the East-West divide came to dominate the international scene, combined with a close examination of global developments during the 1960s. These last led de Gaulle to believe that both blocs were becoming less cohesive and less firmly tied to their respective superpowers. This meant that an escape from the Cold War framework could be possible – although de Gaulle was always very imprecise as to the time frame he envisaged for such a transformation – with Soviet and American domination of Eastern and Western Europe giving way to a new Concert of Europe based upon the triangular relationship between France, Russia and a reunified Germany.

Franz Josef Strauß, the subject of Ronald Granieri's chapter, developed a similar view of a Europe emancipated from superpower control. Although sometimes dubbed a German 'Gaullist', the Christian Democratic politician had a rather different vision from that of the French leader. Thus Strauß's Europe was to be much more integrated than that foreseen by de Gaulle: it was a Europe that could include the United Kingdom, a country the French president would twice debar from entering the European Community, and it was a Europe that would remain in an Atlantic partnership with the United States, albeit a partnership based on a much greater degree of equality than that which actually existed between the U.S. and its European allies. Neither vision would ultimately succeed, but both strikingly illustrate the dissatisfaction with the Cold War status quo that afflicted Western Europe in the 1960s.

The next section looks at whether or not there was ever a prospect of overcoming this status quo through that landmark of East-West multilateral dialogue, the CSCE. Martin Brown's chapter analyses Britain's approach to the CSCE process, an episode that many historians have identified as being important in hastening the end of the Cold War. The United Kingdom had no such vision, Brown asserts. Rather its approach was low-key and tactical, with London viewing the Helsinki process as something with which it had to engage so as to keep its allies happy and to respond to public opinion, but from which it expected to profit relatively little. This cautious approach did not, of course, preclude some useful gains being made in the negotiations – indeed British diplomats did achieve results in Helsinki and Geneva – but it does put in perspective the rather inflated retrospective claims that have been made about the human rights dimension of the Helsinki process in particular.

Angela Romano by contrast has a rather more positive view of the CSCE. Her assessment, however, has less to do with the ultimate outcomes of the European conference itself than with the way in which the Helsinki and Geneva talks represented a first, and successful, testing ground for the newly launched mechanism for coordinating the foreign policy approaches of the nine European Community (EC) member states, European Political Cooperation (EPC). The EC Nine did, in other words, approach the talks with a degree of vision, but rather than this being a shared view of how the Cold War could be brought to an end, it was a common desire to see the EC speaking with one voice and thereby proving a more effective actor on the international stage.

The next section addresses the ideas of two statesmen and one dissident, all of whom squarely envisaged the possibility of overcoming the East-West divide. The first contribution, by Gottfried Niedhart, concentrates on Willy Brandt. Germany's Ostpolitik from 1969 onwards was intended to transform the Cold War, Niedhart makes clear. The German chancellor was cautious in his public pronouncements about his ultimate ambitions, highly aware of the disquiet that some of his ideas provoked on both sides of the Iron Curtain. While a gradualist strategy based on change through rapprochement rather than confrontation, Brandt's Ostpolitik had the long-term goal of significantly altering Eastern Europe (including East Germany) and the Soviet Union itself. Indeed, in Brandt's view German reunification could only come about as part of a wider process bringing the division of Europe to an end. Recognizing and coming to terms with the status quo, the process that dominated the first stages of Brandt's new Eastern policy, was thus not an end in itself but instead only the first stage of a much longer transformation that would bring about an end to the Cold War.

The Italian Communist leader Enrico Berlinguer also had a vision of a post–Cold War world, Laura Fasanaro explains in her chapter. The leading figure in the move towards Eurocommunism during the 1970s, the Italian politician foresaw an end to the East-West conflict without the victory of either side over the other. Rather, the ongoing process of détente would serve to transform both the internal politics of countries like Italy and weaken the militarized blocs of NATO and the Warsaw Pact. Both East and West, he believed, were undergoing deep structural crises, but each retained the potential to scale down their rivalry and move peacefully towards a more multipolar world. Such was the hold of this vision that it was one Berlinguer continued to believe in, even when the events of the late 1970s and early 1980s began to cast doubt on the viability of the détente process that he hoped would bring about this inexorable change.

Christian Domnitz's chapter traces the career of another visionary, Jiří Hájek. As foreign minister of the Prague Spring government, Hájek played a key role in formulating a view of how a more liberal Czechoslovakia might survive in a Europe still divided into antagonistic blocs. But it was as a member of the dissident movement Charter 77 that he was able to think most creatively about how to overcome the Cold War. His recipe for doing so attached great importance to the CSCE process – an institution that would remain at the centre of his vision until his death a few years after the Cold War had actually come to an end – as well as human rights protection and pressure for disarmament. Still more fundamentally it was a vision that centred on the possibility of overcoming the Cold War through pressure from below, from civil society, rather than remaining reliant on interstate relations and negotiations. It thus anticipated crucial features of the revolutions of 1989.

By way of contrast, the following section turns to two figures who did not adopt a visionary approach to the Cold War, the first being U.S. National Security Advisor and then Secretary of State Henry Kissinger. As Jussi Hanhimäki explains, Kissinger was intent on managing the Cold War rather than ending it. Détente and negotiation with the Soviets were thus tools used to secure certain American national interests, not a process designed to end the Cold War. The opening to China and triangular diplomacy served similarly utilitarian purposes. And Kissinger was highly dismissive of those who maintained that either Ostpolitik or the CSCE process could radically transform the East-West status quo. Paradoxically, however, Kissinger contributed to several changes to the Cold War system that in the end helped to hasten the end of the bipolar confrontation. That they did so, Hanhimäki asserts, was the result of accident rather than design.

For his part, French President Valéry Giscard d'Estaing recoiled from anything other than slow, evolutionary change in the Cold War, Georges-Henri Soutou explains in his chapter. In part such caution was tactical: Giscard believed strongly that the type of confrontational tactics over human rights adopted by U.S. President Jimmy Carter, for instance, would be counterproductive. Too aggressive a line with Moscow would also endanger the spread of contacts and trade between the blocs that Giscard believed would ultimately serve to undermine the Soviet Union and loosen the grip of communism. Giscard's own dealings with the Soviet leadership were hence marked by an attempt to limit ideological clashes between East and West. But at a more profound level, the French were also aware of the possible deleterious consequences the end of the Cold War might bring. After all, it was the Cold War that kept Germany divided – thus helping France aspire to equality with its Eastern neighbour – secured the U.S. presence in Europe and allowed France to play a distinctive role in East-West relations.

The final section looks at the 1980s and the extraordinary diversity of visions of the Cold War's end that were to flourish in the course of the decade. Some of these were marked by a degree of caution comparable to that displayed by Giscard. As Gregory Domber makes clear in his chapter on a group of Polish intellectuals whose dissident ideas would go on to influence the course taken by Solidarnosc, many Eastern European opponents of communist rule were extremely careful about how far they took their critique of their own government and the Soviet Union. So many earlier attempts at change had been brutally suppressed that Leszek Kołakowski, Jacek Kuroń and Adam Michnik agreed on the need for self-limitation in their protests. They were also highly sceptical that wider changes in the international system, let alone an end to the Cold War, were the best method to improve the position of the Polish people. Instead they preferred to focus on gradual, low-level change designed to address the material grievances of ordinary Poles and cautiously liberalize the political system and civil society. And they held little or no faith in Gorbachev as a Soviet leader who might be prepared to act differently from his predecessors. Their role, and that of the Solidarity trade union in helping to spark the dramatic events of 1989, was hence as much as a surprise to them as it was to global opinion.

Bernd Rother's chapter concentrates on the activities of Willy Brandt in the 1980s. The former chancellor, he explains, became deeply concerned at the decline of the détente process that his own earlier policies had helped foster. In particular, Brandt worried greatly about the intensification of the arms race. He therefore sought to use his prestige and position, within German left-wing politics but also more widely within the Socialist International, in efforts to keep interbloc dialogue alive. This would lead him to pioneer an extensive range of contacts between the German opposition SPD and the ruling East German SED from which a detailed blueprint for a new European security architecture would emerge. The blueprint involved not merely the establishment of nuclear-free zones through much of Central Europe, but also a series of pledges on the part of the SED to begin the process of liberalizing East Germany. Brandt admittedly had little success in selling such a vision to his own side – neither the government of Helmut Kohl nor, still less, that of Ronald Reagan was interested. And ultimately such designs would be overtaken by a very different ending of the Cold War. But their radical nature does highlight the extent to which Brandt and many others on the European left continued to place their trust in gradual change through rapprochement rather than confrontation.

A rather different account of the European left's trajectory in the 1980s is presented in the chapter by Marie-Pierre Rey. Her focus is the reaction of the French Communist Party and of French Socialists to the emergence of Gorbachev as a reforming Soviet leader. She demonstrates very clearly how the French communists initially reacted with some enthusiasm but were ultimately to be profoundly discomforted as the changes brought about by the Soviet leader became ever more far-reaching. The Socialists, by contrast, acted in the entirely opposite fashion, initially manifesting both caution and scepticism towards perestroika and glasnost but then evolving into ardent supporters of Gorbachev's reforms. There was thus great complementarity between Gorbachev's notion of a 'Common European Home' and Mitterrand's own ideas of a wider European confederation, although ultimately neither materialized.

The next two chapters look at two of the key Western European leaders in power when the Cold War came to an end: Margaret Thatcher and François Mitterrand. Ilaria Poggiolini seeks to demonstrate that Prime Minister Thatcher's Britain did have an active Ostpolitik. British diplomats hence kept a close watch on the evolving situation east of the Iron Curtain, the prime minister and her ministers made a succession of visits to the region, in the course of which they met both government figures and dissidents, and the United Kingdom sought to increase its economic and other contacts with Eastern Europe. Such activity was, however, premised on the idea that any change in the Cold War status quo would be gradual and controlled. Britain in general and Thatcher in particular were thus badly wrong-footed by the acceleration of history in 1989, and the prime minister lost both prestige and influence in an ill-fated attempt to slow, if not arrest entirely, Germany's movement towards unity. Yet this undignified end should not, Poggiolini argues, obscure the earlier years of more constructive British policy towards Eastern Europe.

Frédéric Bozo meanwhile suggests that while France too was initially taken aback by the speed of developments in 1989 and 1990, Mitterrand recovered his footing and his touch rather more quickly than his British counterpart. In so doing he was helped by the fact that he and the French foreign policy establishment had long held a vision of overcoming the Cold War (inherited of course from de Gaulle) that made France much better prepared for the revolutions of 1989 than many other Western nations. Admittedly, neither the timing nor the speed of the change was predicted in Paris – nor was it elsewhere. But once the initial shock had been overcome, the French president was able to draw upon a vision of a united Europe and take advantage of relative superpower disengagement, which appeared more relevant than ever as the Cold War came to its end.

The final pair of chapters look at Ronald Reagan's contribution to the end of the Cold War and take issue with suggestions that the collapse of the Soviet Union in 1991 constituted a premeditated U.S. victory. Beth Fischer's contribution is particularly critical of what she describes as the 'triumphalist' school of historiography. Reagan, she acknowledges, did exhibit a strong degree of scepticism about communism's ability to endure even before becoming president. Once in power, however, neither the aggressive military build-up of the early years of his tenure nor the turn towards engagement and negotiation with the Soviets in the period after 1984 was designed to bankrupt the Soviet Union or bring about its collapse. On the contrary, the former reflected a genuine belief in U.S. strategic vulnerability, and the latter a desire to lessen dangerous levels of tension through arms control talks. These last did contribute to the ending of the Cold War, but they were not a consistent attempt to engineer the Soviet Union's downfall.

Marilena Gala's chapter, which focuses on the arms control issue, reinforces this message. Reagan, Gala shows, did have highly distinctive attitudes towards nuclear weapons that flew in the face of orthodox U.S. policy. The Strategic Defense Initiative in particular was something to which he attached a degree of importance entirely unmatched amongst most of his entourage. But this gap between Reagan and his advisors, not to mention his allies, significantly lessened the radical impact that some of the president's own ideas might have had. Reagan's nuclear vision, and especially the change in the language used about atomic war that he helped bring about, did contribute, Gala asserts, to the end of the East-West conflict. But this could only happen because the U.S. president found a Soviet interlocutor who shared some of his own unorthodox views as to the usability and utility of nuclear weapons.

This volume is the result of an international conference held at the Sorbonne and organized by the Universities of Paris I Panthéon Sorbonne and Paris III Sorbonne Nouvelle in cooperation with the Bundeskanzler-Willy-Brandt-Stiftung (Berlin), the London School of Economics, the Machiavelli Center for Cold War Studies (CIMA, Florence) and the Paul H. Nitze School of Advanced International Studies (SAIS) Bologna Center.[3] The editors wish to thank all those involved, most of all the contributors and authors, for having made the event and the publication possible.

Notes

1. See M. Cox. 2009. 'Why Did We Get the End of the Cold War Wrong?', *British Journal of Politics and International Relations*, 11, 161–176. (This article is part of a special section on 'Political Science and the end of the Cold War', edited by Erik Jones and Marco Cesa. The papers included in the section were presented as part of a separate IR panel at the international conference mentioned below.)

2. A recent attempt at investigating the end of the Cold War in light of new sources and renewed problematics may be found in F. Bozo, M.-P. Rey, N.P. Ludlow and L. Nuti. 2008. *Europe and the End of the Cold War: A Reappraisal*, London, Routledge.

3. See also above, note 1.

Section I

CRYSTALLIZING THE COLD WAR

Chapter 1

GEORGE KENNAN'S COURSE, 1947–1949
A Gaullist before de Gaulle

John L. Harper

In February 1994, the Council on Foreign Relations held a dinner to mark the ninetieth birthday of its most distinguished member. In his remarks, the guest of honour took no credit for recent developments. Instead, George F. Kennan rebuked the triumphalism of contemporaries who believed that the United States had been correct to pursue a policy that amounted to seeking the 'unconditional surrender' of the Soviet Union in Europe and who thought victory in the Cold War had been costless. Following the initial phase of containment, Kennan argued, the United States should have entered into serious negotiations with Moscow. Echoing the point made years earlier in his memoirs, he suggested that the Cold War might have been called off or rendered far less risky and harmful: 'We will never know who was right and who was wrong. One course was tried. Its consequences, good and bad, are visible. The other remained hypothetical. Its results will never be known.'[1]

Why, after having helped to define containment and U.S. objectives in the Cold War, did Kennan find himself in disagreement with U.S policy? What was his alternative course, and why did it remain hypothetical? What kind of assessment does his approach deserve?

Kennan's Perspective

Kennan's signal contribution to early postwar U.S. policy was to help to bury what he considered the 'entire complex of illusions and calculations and expectations' constituting 'the Rooseveltian dream'.[2] The 'dream' had

Notes for this chapter begin on page 27.

foreseen a collaborative relationship with Stalin's Soviet Union and assumed that Moscow's longing for security would be satisfied on the basis
of its domination of Eastern Europe and the end of the German threat.
Roosevelt had opposed schemes for European regional cooperation that
might have alarmed Moscow and/or become a vehicle for American en-
tanglement. He had taken for granted a rapid withdrawal from Europe
and a redirection of American attention toward the western hemisphere
and Far East.

In sharp contrast, the Truman administration adopted the view that
Stalin's regime was a 'political force committed fanatically to the belief
that with [the] US there can be no permanent modus vivendi and that
it is desirable and necessary that the internal harmony of our society be
disrupted, our traditional way of life be destroyed, the international authority of our state be broken, if Soviet power is to be secure'.[3] The Truman
administration put into practice Kennan's recommendation of 'a policy of
firm containment'[4] by opposing Soviet pressure along the 'Northern Tier'
of the Middle East and taking responsibility for the rehabilitation of Europe. As head of the Policy Planning Staff (PPS), Kennan was instrumental
in the launching of the Marshall Plan.

Kennan's parting of the ways with the administration was the result of
his opposition to policies that served to consolidate what Charles de Gaulle
and his followers called '*le système de Yalta*'. Kennan believed strongly, even
passionately, that the division of Europe was pernicious and unnecessary.
It was pernicious because it robbed the Eastern European states of their
independence. It also made war more likely. As Kennan put it in mid-1948:
'it can be argued with considerable logic that the long-term danger of war
will inevitably be greater if Europe remains split along the present lines
than it will be if Russian power is peacefully withdrawn in good time.' A
permanent East-West division implied an unnatural and harmful transatlantic relationship. The nations of Western Europe would become dependent on the United States, and to defend them the United States would rely
on the 'first use' of nuclear weapons. 'Such a weapon', he later wrote, 'is
simply not one … with which one readily springs to the defense of one's
friends'.[5] As a Europeanized professional diplomat, moreover, Kennan
found it hard to believe that those same proud nations, including a sullen,
and (in his view) still strongly nationalistic Germany, might acknowledge
America's moral authority.[6] Visiting Germany after the war, he felt an 'almost neurotic distaste' for its American occupiers, 'setting an example of
empty materialism and cultural poverty'.[7] For Kennan, the possibility that
the United States might dominate Europe over the long run was literally
unthinkable.[8] European and America civilizations were distinct in character and destiny – *Et vive la différence!*

As an American raised in the Midwestern heartland, Kennan was equally preoccupied by the implications of an imperial policy for his own country: 'The present "bi-polarity" will, in the long run, be beyond our resources.'[9] The United States was unsuited institutionally or temperamentally for anything but transitional leadership. Its political system was too unwieldy and its politicians too provincial and attached to universalistic, escapist approaches to international problems – witness FDR.[10] America, finally, had its own unfinished business. Kennan was haunted by what he saw as the breakdown of a sense of community wrought by urbanization, and the passivity and loss of a sense of responsibility on the part of individuals subject to the centralized 'media of psychological influence (press, radio, television, movies)'.[11] Even in the Long Telegram, his dramatic call to confront the Soviet Union, he observed: 'Every courageous and incisive measure to solve [the] internal problems of our own society, to improve self-confidence, discipline, morale and community spirit of our own people, is a diplomatic victory over Moscow worth a thousand diplomatic notes and joint communiqués.' In 1949, he asked, 'not being the masters of our own soul, are we justified in regarding ourselves as fit for the leadership of others?'[12]

Fortunately, Kennan's instincts told him, the division of Europe was reversible. True, at the time of Yalta he wrote a disgruntled letter to his colleague Charles Bohlen arguing that the continent should be divided 'frankly into spheres of influence'.[13] The Allies had missed the opportunity to provoke a 'full-fledged and realistic political showdown' with Moscow during the 1944 Warsaw uprising. Drawing a line was a regrettable necessity. But this did not mean recognition of Soviet control in the east. It was a way to limit the spread of Soviet influence further west.

He also saw reasons for optimism. Practically alone among U.S. officials, he had visited Nazi-occupied Europe and studied the techniques of German control in the 1939–41 period.[14] The experience had confirmed Edward Gibbon's observation that 'there is nothing more contrary to nature than the attempt to hold in obedience distant provinces'. Like the Germans, the Russians lacked a positive ideological message and would have to contend with the force of nationalism.[15] 'It should not be forgotten', moreover, 'that the absorption of areas in the west beyond the Great Russian, White Russian, and Ukrainian ethnological boundaries is something at which Russia has already tried and failed'. The western provinces of the tsarist empire had become 'the hotbed out of which there grew the greater part of the Russian Social Democratic Party which bore Lenin to power'. The loss of those territories had facilitated Stalin's consolidation of power, but Moscow was now saddled with them again. Kennan raised the possibility that

> The seeds of a new convulsion are already being sown, as the seeds of the Russian revolution were planted by the condemned Decembrists ... And if the same telescoping of time continues, another five or ten years should find Russia overshadowed by the clouds of civil disintegration which darkened the Russian sky at the outset of this century. Will this process be hastened and brought to maturity by the germs of social and political ferment from the restless conquered provinces of the West?

If the United States and Britain were able to 'muster up the political manliness to deny Russia either the moral or material support for the consolidation of Russian power throughout Eastern and Central Europe, Russia would probably not be able to maintain its hold successfully for any length of time over all the territory over which it has today staked a claim. In this case, the lines would have to be withdrawn somewhat.'[16]

As this May 1945 analysis indicates, Kennan's major statements contained a two-part message. The first part, aimed at residual Rooseveltians, was that 'the semi-myth of implacable foreign hostility'[17] was profoundly rooted in Russian history and Marxist-Leninist ideology. It was not possible to have normal relations with people who would not sleep soundly until Western civilization had been destroyed. This was the part of the message that hit home in Washington in 1946. The second part, aimed at those resigned either to war or to an indefinite stalemate, was that the Bolshevik hold on Eastern Europe, and on Russia itself, was vulnerable to pressure. Drawing a key distinction, the author of the Long Telegram observed that Soviet power, 'unlike that of Hitlerite Germany, is neither schematic nor adventuristic ... It does not take unnecessary risks. Impervious to the logic of reason, it is highly sensitive to the logic of force.' 'By virtue of recent territorial expansion' it faced strains that had 'once proved a severe tax on Tsardom'. Not only that, the Soviet system had yet to prove itself 'as a form of internal power'.[18]

Nearly half of 'The Sources of Soviet Conduct' was dedicated to this theme. There was the 'terrible cost' of forced industrialization, to which the war had added 'its tremendous toll'. Kennan was one of few U.S. officials who had observed the Russian people between mid-1944 and early 1946. The experience convinced him that '[t]he mass of people are disillusioned, skeptical and no longer as accessible as they once were to the magical attraction which Soviet power still radiates to its followers abroad.' Finally, the 'little self-perpetuating clique of men at the top' would sooner or later have to transfer power to younger, perhaps disaffected cadres of the party, a process that might trigger a serious crisis of the regime. Under the circumstances, the United States had it in its power 'to increase enormously the strains under which Soviet policy must operate ... and in this way to promote tendencies which must eventually find their outlet in either the breakup or the gradual mellowing of Soviet power. For no mystical, messianic movement – and particularly not that of the Kremlin – can face frustration indefinitely without eventually adjusting itself in one way or another to the logic of that state of affairs.' Kennan indicated a time frame of ten to fifteen years.[19] The least that could be said was that Stalin was unlikely to try to conquer Western Europe. 'Further military advances in the West could only increase responsibilities already beyond the Russian capacity to meet.'[20] The threat to Western Europe was political, residing in the strength of the local Communist parties. Compared to the West as a whole, the Soviets were 'still by far the weaker force'.[21]

It would be mistaken to think that the second part of Kennan's message was entirely ignored or dismissed. Indeed, when Defense Secretary James Forrestal requested a comprehensive statement of policy toward the Soviet Union, Kennan responded that U.S. objectives should be 'a. To reduce the power and influence of Moscow to limits in which they will no longer constitute a threat to the peace and stability of international society; and b. To bring about a basic change in the theory and practice of international relations observed by the government in power in Russia.' With respect to 'the satellite area', the U.S. aim in time of peace should be 'to place the greatest possible strain on the structure of relationships by which Soviet domination of this area is maintained and gradually, with the aid of the natural and legitimate forces of Europe, to maneuver the Russians out of their position of primacy.'[22] These general objectives and specific aims were incorporated into National Security Council NSC 20/4 (23 November 1948), the basic statement of the Truman administration's objectives in the Cold War.[23]

But few embraced the objective of 'rollback' with the same conviction and intensity as did the head of the PPS. Moreover, for those who lacked Kennan's expert 'feel' for Soviet reality, the two parts of his message could only appear inconsistent. The view that the Soviet Union was implacably hostile yet a giant with feet of clay could not be readily embraced by those whose image of the threat was based not on deep study and first-hand experience, but on the epic performance of the Red Army, the Russians' brutal record in Eastern Europe and Germany, and the fact of Stalinism's 'magical attraction' to millions in France and Italy. In effect, Kennan had been behind what he thought was the Potemkin village – the rickety façade – of Soviet power. His audience had not.

Kennan's Course, 1947–1949

Kennan's unique perspective gave rise to an idiosyncratic recipe of policy positions. A pattern emerged whereby Kennan inspired or supported some of the Truman administration's major initiatives, although not always for the same reasons as his colleagues. Other initiatives he opposed and attempted to replace with his own. What lends a basic consistency to his positions is the aim to prevent the division of Europe and hasten an end to the Cold War.

In 1947, Kennan supported aid to Greece on the grounds that a Communist defeat might set in motion the sort of reverse domino effect he had suggested in May 1945. If Western European Communists were 'to start on the backward slide', it was possible to imagine 'a general crumbling of Russian influence and prestige which would carry beyond those countries, and into the heart of the Soviet Union itself'.[24] Kennan was intimately involved in the launching of the Marshall Plan, in particular 'in the decisive emphasis placed on the rehabilitation of the German economy and the introduction of the concept of German recovery as a vital component of the recovery of Europe as a whole'.[25] Nearly as important for Kennan was breaking down the East-West division. Offering aid to the Russians and Eastern Europeans was a way of forcing Moscow either to accept the opening up of the satellite economies to Western influence, or (in the more likely scenario) to face the resentment of those denied the benefits of the plan. After Russia's refusal the plan remained a means of 'building up the hope and vigor of western Europe to a point where it comes to exercise the maximum attraction to the peoples of the east'.[26]

Kennan's alternative took clear shape in 1948. In February, he discussed the possibility of 'a new situation' in which the Russians might be prepared 'to do business seriously with us about Germany and about Western Europe in general'. If so, he recommended secret discussions with Stalin to reach 'a sort of background understanding'. As for the substance, the U.S. side must be able to show the Russians that it would 'be worth their while (a) to reduce communist pressure elsewhere in Europe and the Middle East to a point where we can afford to withdraw all our armed forces from the continent and the Mediterranean; and b) to acquiesce thereafter in a prolonged period of stability in Europe'. The credentials required on the part of the U.S. envoy to such talks bore a remarkable resemblance to his own.[27]

This suggestion came after a famous attack on 'Mr. X' in September 1947, and raises the question of whether Kennan's was not really Walter Lippmann's course. Lippmann had rebuked Kennan for seeming to rule out a diplomatic solution to the division of Germany and the presence of the Red Army in Europe. 'The history of diplomacy was the history of relations among rival powers, which did not enjoy political intimacy … Nevertheless there [had] been settlements … There would be little for diplomats to do if the world consisted of partners, enjoying political intimacy, and responding to common appeals.'[28] There is evidence that Kennan had *not* ruled out negotiations and had invited misinterpretation by appearing to do so.[29] But there is little doubt that Lippmann's critique prompted him to move beyond the view that the Soviets were simply 'impervious to reason'. Above all, Kennan was now persuaded that negotiations were promising and urgent. The victory of the pro-Western parties in the Italian elections of 18 April 1948 heralded something like the 'new situation' he had imagined. Negotiations became urgent because the blocs were rapidly congealing. As a reaction to the European Recovery Program (ERP), or Marshall Plan, Moscow had tightened its control over Czechoslovakia in February 1948. Simultaneously, negotiations were underway in London with a view to creating a separate West German state.

Most troubling was that the fear of war gripping Western Europe fed support for a transatlantic alliance. Kennan recommended 'realistic staff talks' and informal guarantees to reassure the Europeans but regarded their anxieties as 'a little silly'.[30] The Czech move was in his view purely defensive. He had written: 'The Soviet Government neither wants nor expects war with us in the foreseeable future.'[31] Why did the Europeans 'wish to divert attention from a thoroughly justified and promising program of economic recovery by emphasizing a danger which did not actually exist but which might indeed be brought into existence by too much discussion of the military balance and by the ostentatious stimulation of a military rivalry?'[32] He could only oppose actions that tended 'to fix, and make unchangeable by peaceful means, the present line of east-west division'.[33]

A pair of developments in May–June 1948 had an important impact on Kennan's course. Marshall decided to make a secret approach to the Kremlin, but not of the kind Kennan had originally suggested. Rather than talks with Stalin, the approach consisted of two meetings between U.S. Ambassador to Moscow Walter Bedell Smith and Foreign Minister Vyacheslav Molotov. Smith reaffirmed U.S. determination to hold the line against Soviet encroachment but stated that the door was 'always wide open for full discussion and the composing of our differences'. Rather than keep the exchange secret, Moscow publicly accepted the U.S. 'proposal' for negotiations, thereby eliminating the possibility that secret contacts might develop. It seemed obvious that Moscow was either in no mood to negotiate or did not take Washington's 'offer' seriously. Not only that, the release produced an embarrassing incident: British Foreign Secretary Ernest Bevin, who feared few things more than Soviet flexibility, was indignant and let Marshall know it. The administration's approach and Moscow's reaction raised doubts about Kennan's course.[34]

Kennan seized on another unexpected event – Belgrade's break with Moscow – as a reason for optimism. He was one of the architects of a policy of patient cultivation of Tito and of trying to promote 'Communist heresy' elsewhere.[35] The Tito break also encouraged him to embrace a tactic to which he had already devoted some attention. Impressed by the apparent success of CIA efforts in Italy, he had called for 'a "directorate" for overt and covert political warfare'. NSC 10/2 (18 June 1948) created the Office of Special Projects. Renamed the Office of Policy Coordination (OPC), the body began operations in September 1948. As head of the PPS, Kennan helped to inspire and supervise OPC activities including the recruitment of Eastern European refugees for intelligence gathering and paramilitary activities, and the launch of Radio Free Europe and Radio Liberty.[36] Kennan's support of 'plausibly deniable' political warfare grew logically out of his view that the communist threat was essentially political and that Soviet control in the East was fragile. Whereas an overt military alliance was unnecessary and counterproductive, fighting fire with fire made perfect sense.

But the OPC was a complement, not an alternative, to negotiations. Indeed the Tito break, together with the London Programme and the Soviet blockade of Berlin, reinforced his view that negotiations were possible and urgent. After extensive consultations, the PPS completed 'Program A'. The plan foresaw a reunited, democratic Germany that would participate in the ERP but be demilitarized, with the Ruhr under continuing international control. A key feature of the plan was the reduction and withdrawal of the forces of the four occupying powers to peripheral garrison areas.[37] Program A was not a 180-degree turn on Kennan's part.[38] It was true, he had argued earlier, that it would be easier to bring the segments of a *partitioned* Germany into a European federation than it would a united Germany, but no such federation existed. He probably also believed that reunification would force the Western Europeans to transcend the 'weariness and timidity and lack of leadership' that prevented them from building the true federation he favoured.[39] He did not exclude the possibility that a united Germany would make deals with Moscow, or even be taken over by the communists.[40] But he was sure that the Germans themselves were strongly opposed to partition. Forcing them to accept it would play into the hands of the Russians, and/or 'place a premium on the emergence of a new Bismarck and a new 1870'.[41] Naturally, uniting Germany was a way of pursuing his broader aim – the withdrawal of foreign forces and prevention of a permanent division of Europe. Uniting and demilitarizing Germany through agreement with the Russians would give the Red Army a graceful exit from Central Europe just as, he believed, the virus of Titoism was making its presence there problematical.[42] The possibility could not be ruled out that without a graceful exit, Moscow might provoke a war. It would also give the West a graceful exit from its precarious position in Berlin.

Nearly everyone who counted rejected Program A. The head of the U.S. occupation, General Lucius Clay, had invested too much effort in the project of a separate West Germany. The National Military Establishment believed the troop withdrawals would put U.S. and British forces in jeopardy. In May 1949, shortly before a meeting of the Council of Foreign Ministers (CFM), the *New York Times* revealed that Washington was still considering German reunification and the disengagement of foreign armies. The article, and the hostile reactions of the British and French governments, constituted 'a spectacular *coup de grace*' for Program A.[43] Kennan, as he later put it, 'clung desperately to the hope of getting the Russians to retire' from the centre of Europe.[44] Most of the rest of the world did not share his hope.

Kennan's final efforts to influence U.S. policy were connected to his vision of a Europe reunited and in control of its destiny. In PPS 55, he argued that Washington should support two allied but separate federal groupings, one Anglo-Saxon (the United States, Canada and Britain), the other continental, with France and Germany at its core. Britain's membership in a European entity would only create a 'ceiling' to integration. A European grouping excluding Britain could go further, and provide a home for the satellites that Moscow (presumably) would be readier to give up if the Anglo-Saxons had withdrawn. Kennan's U.S. colleagues rejected his vision of 'three worlds instead of two' on the grounds that Britain must be in Europe and France must not feel abandoned. Kennan claimed that the French officials with whom he discussed his conception were simply unable to understand it. He added: 'There was a certain irony in this fact, because before too many years those same French officials would be serving as instruments of a great Frenchman [Charles de Gaulle] who understood these things very well.'[45]

His opposition to the hydrogen bomb and a U.S. strategy relying on the 'first use' of suicidal weapons only reinforced his support for a deal to bring about a retraction of Soviet forces.[46] As for NSC 68, what better way to give Moscow the enemy it needed, freeze the blocs, and heighten the risk of war than a huge peacetime rearmament? NSC 68 incorporated the objectives of NSC 20/4, but in its analysis and recommendations it departed radically from Kennan's views.[47] The reckless, schematic Soviet Union it portrayed (a regime that might well launch a nuclear strike on the United States once it had the capacity to do so) represented the confusion of Stalin with Hitler that he had warned against. A build-up premised on the Soviet Union's presumed capabilities rather than its real intentions and carried out for the purpose of soothing European anxieties was counterproductive in the extreme.

Conclusion

Let us concede that we can never really know, as Kennan said, which course was right and which was wrong. We *can* know why his attempt to prevent the division of Europe from congealing was probably doomed to fail. The answer, as political scientists are fond of saying, is 'overdetermined'. As Kennan saw at the time, he was fighting a losing war on at least two fronts. The Western European governments did not see the communist threat as solely political and did not want the kind of self-reliant European federation Kennan thought they should want. Kennan's view of Germany was too rooted in history to be able to capture the novelty of the situation. Like Stalin, Kennan overestimated the strength of pan-German nationalism in postwar Germany and failed to see how resistance to the Berlin blockade helped to produce a kind of bonding between West Germans and the United States.[48] In the end, Kennan had few if any European interlocutors who shared his outlook or measured up to his expectations. De Gaulle himself at the time would have had limited sympathy for Kennan's views.

A second problem was that most of Kennan's U.S. colleagues did not fully share his convictions that Stalin's Soviet Union (unlike Hitler's Germany) was cautious and vulnerable, that the division of Europe was unnatural and unsustainable and that Western European preferences should not heavily condition U.S. choices.[49] Nor did they share his deep aversion to nuclear weapons or consider U.S. hegemony over Western Europe unthinkable. Many came to take the U.S. role as Europe's protector and pacifier for granted. Needless to say, they were encouraged to do so by the Europeans, who in general accepted America's moral authority far more readily than Kennan had imagined they would do.

Finally, there are the questions of how willing the Soviets were to compromise and whether Kennan's course was properly conceived to achieve that objective. Let us assume that Kennan's assessment was basically accurate on three points: (a) Stalin did not intend to launch war on Western Europe, (b) Eastern European nationalism made Soviet control tenuous, and (c) before 1953, Moscow had not ruled out a deal for a reunited Germany. If so, Kennan was correct to see that the Atlantic pact initiative and the London Programme contributed to what in 1952 he called 'a sort of cosmic misunderstanding': the West's mistaken assumption of a Soviet military threat led it to take steps that convinced Moscow that the West was planning aggressive war, prompting Moscow to behave accordingly.[50] There would seem to be little mystery in Stalin's decision to begin a military build-up. What more evidence did he need of Western intentions than what the West was doing in 1948? It may well be, however, that it was the launching of the Marshall Plan in 1947, the centrepiece of Kennan's rollback strategy, that confirmed an irreversible consolidation of the blocs. By the time Kennan had begun to advance his alternative in earnest in 1948, the Cominform had been created and the Soviets were scrambling to counter the effects of the ERP in Eastern

Europe. And one can only wonder what effect the publication of the 'Sources of Soviet Conduct' had on Moscow. The Russians did not need to read between the lines to see that the United States apparently aimed not only to reverse their hard-won position in Eastern and Central Europe but to change the Soviet regime itself.

By the same token, the encouragement of heretical communism and the intensification of covert action were probably counterproductive. If, as Kennan claimed, Tito's break 'was as important for Communism as Martin Luther's proclamation was for the Roman Catholic Church', then Stalin was sure to be at the head of a ruthless counter-reformation.[51] On balance, chances for the evolution of the Soviet bloc in the direction Kennan desired might have been better if the Tito break had not happened when it did. Kennan knew the weaknesses in the Soviet position and was determined to exploit them. But Stalin knew them even better and was in a position to neutralize Western pressure. If, as Kennan wrote years later, the results of statesmanship never 'bear anything other than an ironic relation to what the statesman in question intended to achieve and thought he was achieving', the statement would seem to apply to his own approach.[52]

In late 1952, the Truman administration revised its official picture of the Soviet Union in ways reflecting the views of Charles Bohlen.[53] Bohlen's Soviet Union was more prudent than Paul Nitze's (as depicted in NSC 68) but more resilient than Kennan's (as depicted in 'The Sources'). As Bohlen had written to Kennan at the time of Yalta: '[W]hat is clear is that the Soyuz [Soviet Union] is here to stay, as one of the major factors in the world.'[54] For most of the rest of the Cold War it was Bohlen who had the 'final word'.

Notes

1. G. Kennan, 'America's Duty to the Wide World Starts at Home', excerpt published in the *International Herald Tribune*, 14 Mar. 1994, 4. See also G. Kennan. 1967. *Memoirs*, vol. 1, Boston: Little, Brown, 365.
2. G. Kennan lecture in Geneva, 'The Shattering of the Rooseveltian Dream', 1 May 1965, George Kennan Papers (hereafter GKP), Seeley G. Mudd Library, Princeton University, box 21. See also his lecture, 'The Roosevelt Error', 12 Oct. 1955, GKP, box 19.
3. See the Long Telegram, Part 5, Kennan to Sec. of State, 20 Mar. 1946, *Foreign Relations of the United States* (hereafter *FRUS*) 1946, vol. 6, 696–709.
4. See G. Kennan. 1947. 'The Sources of Soviet Conduct', *Foreign Affairs*, 25(4), 566–582.
5. See 'A Sterile and Hopeless Weapon' (1958), reprinted in G. Kennan. 1983. *The Nuclear Delusion*, New York: Pantheon, 7. See also 'International Control of Atomic Energy', 20 Jan. 1950, *FRUS* 1950, vol. 1, 39.
6. See PPS 23, 24 Feb. 1948, in *FRUS* 1948, vol. 1, 517.

7. Kennan, *Memoirs,* vol. 1, 428–429.
8. In 1948, he wrote that in the long run there could only be three possibilities for Western and Central Europe: 'One is German domination. Another is Russian domination. The third is a federated Europe, into which the parts of Germany are absorbed.' Kennan memo, 24 Feb. 1948, *FRUS* 1948, vol. 1, 515.
9. Kennan, PPS 13, 6 Nov. 1947, *FRUS* 1947, vol. 1, 771.
10. On this point, see ibid., 526.
11. Kennan to Hooker, 17 Oct. 1949, *FRUS* 1949, vol. 1, 403–405.
12. The Long Telegram, part 5; Kennan to Hooker, quoted in previous note.
13. Quoted in C. Bohlen. 1973. *Witness to History,* New York: Norton, 175.
14. Kennan spoke fluent German and was a member of the staff of the U.S. embassy in Berlin, returning to the U.S. only in spring 1942.
15. Gibbon quoted in Kennan, *Memoirs,* vol. 1, 129–130. See also his 'Résumé of World Situation', 6 Nov. 1947, *FRUS* 1947, vol. 1, 774.
16. Kennan, 'Russia's International Position at the Close of the War with Germany', May 1945, *Memoirs,* vol. 1, 545–546.
17. Kennan, 'The Sources of Soviet Conduct', part one.
18. The Long Telegram, part 5.
19. Kennan, 'The Sources of Soviet Conduct'.
20. Kennan, 'Russia's International Position'.
21. The Long Telegram, part 5.
22. Kennan, PPS 38, later designated NSC 20/1, 18 Aug. 1948.
23. NSC 20/4, 23 Nov. 1948, *FRUS* 1948, vol. 1, 663–669. On the importance of this document and Kennan's role in its preparation, see G. Mitrovich. 2000. *Undermining the Kremlin,* Ithaca: Cornell University Press, 34–36.
24. Kennan lecture, 'Russia's National Objectives', 10 Apr. 1947, GKP, box 17.
25. Kennan, *Memoirs,* vol. 1, 343.
26. PPS 38, 50. See also W.D. Miscamble. 1992. *George F. Kennan and the Making of American Foreign Policy, 1947–1950,* Princeton, NJ: Princeton University Press, 198.
27. Ibid., 522.
28. W. Lippmann. 1947. *The Cold War,* New York: Harper and Bros.
29. In the Long Telegram itself, Kennan had noted: 'I for one am reluctant to believe that Stalin himself receives anything like an objective picture of the outside world' – suggesting that he must be open to reason. Kennan also noted that it was impossible to deny that 'useful things have been accomplished in the past and can be accomplished in the future by direct contact with Stalin'. GK to Sec. of State, 20 Mar. 1946, *FRUS* 1946, vol. 6, 722.
30. Kennan, *Memoirs,* vol. 1, 399.
31. Kennan, 'Résumé of World Situation', 6 Nov. 1947, *FRUS* 1947, vol. 1, 770–771.
32. Kennan, *Memoirs,* vol. 1, 408–409.
33. Kennan memo, 24 Nov. 1948, enclosing PPS/43 (concerning the North Atlantic Treaty), *FRUS* 1948, vol. 3, 283–289. Cited in Miscamble, *George F. Kennan,* 134.
34. For documentation, see *FRUS* 1948, vol. 4, 834–864. Bevin had written Marshall shortly before Smith's démarche: 'Russia may suddenly become conciliatory and this would be the most dangerous phase.' Ibid., 844.
35. PPS 59, quoted in Miscamble, *George F. Kennan,* 206.
36. See ibid., 106–111, 199–205; Mitrovich, *Undermining the Kremlin,* 18–23.
37. See *FRUS* 1948, vol. 2, 1324–1338.
38. Such is basically the view of Miscamble, *George F. Kennan,* 145 and A. Stephanson. 1989. *Kennan and the Art of Foreign Policy,* Cambridge, MA: Harvard University Press, 114–115, 144.

39. Kennan memo, 28 Aug. 1948, *FRUS* 1948, vol. 2, 1296.
40. Ibid., 1293.
41. 'If we did not have the Russians and the German communists prepared to take advantage politically of any movement on our part toward partition we could proceed to partition Germany regardless of the will of the inhabitants, and to force the respective segments to take their place in a federated Europe. But in the circumstances prevailing today, we cannot do this without throwing the German people into the arms of the communists.' Kennan, PPS 23, 24 Feb. 1948, *FRUS* 1948, vol. 1, 516. He recalled later: 'The idea of partition – of breaking the country up once again into a multiplicity of small sovereign entities, no longer seemed to me realistic. It had appealed to me in 1942; but I had been obliged to recognize that the experience of Hitlerism and the war, horrible and tragic as they were, had probably deepened the sense of national community, and that the attempt to keep the country partitioned in a Europe where most other linguistic and ethnic bodies would be unified would only be to re-create the aspirations and compulsions of the mid-nineteenth century, and to place a premium on the emergence of a new Bismarck and a new 1870.' Kennan, *Memoirs,* vol. 1, 416.
42. He noted that the 'the Soviet satellite area is troubled with serious dissension, uncertainty and disaffection'. Kennan memo, 28 Aug. 1948, *FRUS* 1948, vol. 2, 1295.
43. Kennan, *Memoirs,* vol. 1, 444.
44. Ibid., 447.
45. Ibid., 457. On PPS 55 and the hostile reactions of Kennan's colleagues, including Bohlen, see J. L. Harper. 1994. *American Visions of Europe,* Cambridge: Cambridge University Press, 213–222.
46. 'If the Atlantic pact nations wish to address the present disbalance in the power of conventional armaments, as between east and west, they must find means first and foremost to get the Russians out of the center of Europe'. Kennan memo, 20 Jan. 1950, *FRUS* 1950, vol. 1, 34.
47. For an account stressing the continuity between NSC 20/4 and NSC 68, see Mitrovich, *Undermining the Kremlin,* 48–59.
48. On this point, see V.M. Zubok. 2007. *A Failed Empire: The Soviet Union in the Cold War from Stalin to Gorbachev,* Chapel Hill: University of North Carolina Press, 76–77.
49. Ironically, since Kennan was forced to leave the Foreign Service in early 1953, the Eisenhower administration contained more officials in tune with his basic views than Truman's. Eisenhower's adviser C.D. Jackson favoured the convening of a CFM to take up the questions of the reunification of Germany and Austria (combined with an aggressive political offensive against the USSR) following Stalin's death in March 1953. Dulles himself advanced the idea of a general negotiated settlement with the USSR in Sept. 1953. See Mitrovich, *Undermining the Kremlin,* 129–132, 151; see also Stanke's chapter in this volume.
50. See Kennan's Sept. 1952 dispatch, 'The Soviet Union and the Atlantic Pact', *Memoirs,* vol. 2, 336.
51. Kennan, in fact, called his sponsorship of the OPC 'the greatest mistake' he ever made. Miscamble, *Undermining the Kremlin,* 109. For Kennan's 1949 statement on Tito, see ibid., 195–96.
52. Kennan, 'The Gorbychev Prospect', *The New York Review of Books,* 21 Jan. 1988.
53. On this see Mitrovich, *Undermining the Kremlin,* chap. 3.
54. Bohlen, *Witness to History,* 176.

Chapter 2

THE BILDERBERG GROUP AND THE END OF THE COLD WAR

The Disengagement Debates of the 1950s

Thomas W. Gijswijt

In November and December 1957, George F. Kennan gave the prestigious Reith Lectures, broadcast live on BBC Radio.[1] These lectures contained little that was new for those familiar with Kennan's thinking, but they triggered an intense public debate on the nature of the Cold War in Europe and the question whether a military disengagement of the United States and the Soviet Union was either feasible or desirable. One of the primary transatlantic venues for this disengagement debate was the Bilderberg group, a network bringing together leading members of the foreign policy elite from virtually the whole political spectrum in Western Europe and the United States.[2] The Bilderberg discussions indicate that a decade after Walter Lippmann coined the phrase, a majority of the transatlantic foreign policy elite continued to see the Cold War as 'a necessary evil' despite powerful arguments in favour of reaching a settlement with the Soviet Union.

Essentially, the disengagement debate of the late 1950s revolved around the question whether the dangers of the status quo in a divided Europe were greater than the risks of a negotiated end to the Cold War. Kennan and other advocates of disengagement, who could be found mainly in the British Labour Party and the German social democratic SPD, argued that the only solution to the division of Germany – without doubt the most dangerous and intractable problem underlying the East-West conflict – was a mutual military withdrawal by the two superpowers. Such a withdrawal was needed, they said, not only to solve the German conundrum, but also to weaken the hold of Moscow on the satellite countries of Eastern Europe. Opponents of disengagement countered that risking the two major

Western Cold War accomplishments – NATO and European integration – was irresponsible. This was not only because the fundamental reorganization of military, political and economic relations within the Atlantic Alliance and within Europe was still at an early and precarious stage, but also because the Soviet Union could not be trusted to seek a real end to the Cold War. While the United States would all too willingly pull back its forces from Germany and Europe, the Soviet Union would be tempted to reassert its influence over Eastern Europe and draw a reunited Germany into its sphere of influence. The combined fears of another Rapallo, an American return to isolationism and an expansionist Russia dominated the thinking of the majority of the Bilderberg members and contributed to the hardening of the Cold War fronts in Europe.

George Kennan was by no means the first to suggest a military disengagement. Walter Lippmann, one of America's most influential columnists, had long advocated a neutral, reunified Germany. Throughout 1957, moreover, Western diplomats, politicians and experts discussed different disengagement proposals. In fact, Kennan may have acquired some of his ideas for the Reith lectures at the February 1957 Bilderberg meeting at St. Simon's Island in the United States. At this meeting, Denis Healey, a Labour Party expert on foreign affairs, made the case for some form of disengagement in Central Europe. Kennan was one of the few present who supported him. Healey based his argument on a critical assessment of the state of the Atlantic Alliance. He argued that the Suez crisis, the lack of a common Western response to the violent Soviet repression of the Hungarian uprising, and the excessive reliance of NATO on (American) nuclear weapons for its defence had exposed the fundamental weakness of the alliance. Unless NATO could devise a way to reach a settlement with the Soviet Union in Europe, Healey said, European publics would fall into the trap of neutralism. A tendency in public opinion in Western Europe to 'write off N.A.T.O.'s defence effort as something which does not really concern [Europe]' was already discernible, Healey argued. '[A]n attempt to negotiate a military disengagement on the continent of Europe', he added, 'is the only way of helping the satellite peoples and making Hungary's sacrifice worth while.'[3]

No doubt, Healey saw the Bilderberg meeting in the United States as an opportunity to win American support for disengagement and to test the international waters. And although ideas about a neutral zone in Germany or Central Europe had been around for a long time, the link between disengagement and the defects of NATO's nuclear strategy represented an important new element in Healey's proposal – which, he was the first to admit, still lacked many details a real plan would require. Still, this was a potentially powerful issue in view of the widespread public concern about nuclear weapons. An additional reason for putting disengagement on the agenda at this particular time was the fact that elections in the Federal Republic were scheduled for September 1957.[4] The West German Social Democrats were hoping to exploit Chancellor Konrad Adenauer's rigid policy with respect to NATO and reunification in order to win extra votes. In this respect, electoral 'brain trusting' from the British Labour Party, as C.D. Jackson, a Republican publisher close to the Eisenhower administration, called it, could help the SPD case.[5] Domestic British politics, of course, also played a role. If Healey remarked that public opinion in Europe more and more tended to regard NATO as 'the last bastion of the Cold War, increasingly remote from the desires and expectations of its member countries', then this was a development the Labour Party could use for its own political purposes.[6]

Whatever the exact motives of the Labour Party, Healey's plan – which C.D. Jackson immediately dubbed the Healey Doctrine – caused a fierce debate at St. Simons Island. Many participants were clearly worried about the prospect of a strong move towards disengagement supported by both Labour and the SPD. Though Healey emphasized that such a move only made sense if NATO stood united, the potential for divisive debate was undeniable. C.D. Jackson was perhaps overreacting when he talked of the SPD's 'eagerness to Munichize NATO', but there was no denying the Social Democrats' willingness to sacrifice NATO for the reunification of Germany.[7] The SPD leader Erich Ollenhauer contributed a paper for the Bilderberg conference in which he summarized his standpoint: if the Soviet Union agreed to the reunification of a free Germany and the creation of a European security system, Germany need not remain a member of NATO. At the same time, Ollenhauer attempted to make the SPD position more palatable to Western opinion by arguing that his party was no longer fundamentally opposed to NATO or to West German armed forces. The SPD, in other words, would not quit NATO if elected in September, at least not until the moment a European security system made Germany's NATO membership superfluous.[8]

A clear majority of participants at the February 1957 Bilderberg meeting expressed their opposition to Healey's plan and worried about its impact on NATO. The only unqualified backing came from German Socialist Fritz Erler, with former Belgian Prime Minister Paul van Zeeland and George Kennan acting the roles of more reserved but sympathetic supporting actors. The first to respond to Healey was a Bilderberg newcomer, Henry L. Roberts, director of the Russian Institute at Columbia University. In 1956, Roberts had published a much-noted book on American-Russian relations – the result of a prestigious Council on Foreign Relations project – and he was considered one of the foremost academic experts on the Cold War.

Roberts identified two flaws in Healey's argument. First, he very much doubted that the Soviets would be willing to withdraw from Eastern Europe, primarily because of the recent upheaval in Hungary and Poland. The Soviet leaders realized that they risked losing their sphere of influence if they pulled back their forces. Perhaps even more important was the ideological implication. A Soviet withdrawal would be tantamount to conceding the failure of communism in Eastern Europe. Roberts's second point concerned the Soviet reaction to a Western disengagement proposal. Roberts disagreed with Healey that the West risked little, even if Moscow rejected it. Experience showed that the Soviet leaders would not immediately reject the proposal; they would make a counterproposal and try to prolong any resulting negotiations. In the meantime, NATO governments would have an even harder time than at present strengthening their defence efforts.[9]

Kurt-Georg Kiesinger, a leading CDU parliamentarian, defended the established line of the Adenauer government on German reunification.[10] The guiding principle, Kiesinger said, remained simple: 'no unification at the price of our freedom'. He shared Roberts's doubts about Moscow's willingness to disengage. 'Certainly the prospect of the [Soviets] withdrawing their troops behind the eastern frontiers of Poland is a tempting picture. But it seems to me not very likely that the [Soviets] will do that, at least under present circumstances. They certainly know that they can't depend on the loyalty of the one hundred million people living in the satellite area, especially not in the case of a crisis.' Instead of advancing proposals with possibly dangerous implications for NATO, it might be wiser, Kiesinger said, to allow the developments in the Soviet orbit to run their course. 'It may well be that we will find there some day the key to solve some of our most difficult problems. Up to now nobody can tell what really may happen.'[11]

In the meantime, Kiesinger clearly thought that the most important factor for Europe's security remained the United States. 'This dependence', Kiesinger acknowledged, 'is a very bitter truth only reluctantly accepted by many Europeans who still think in the terms of a past and obsolete Europe-centred world policy. But even if we have realistically abandoned this notion and confined ourselves to maintain a modest but dignified existence as smaller powers, we must – with or without a unified western Europe – recognise the fact that even this modest existence depends largely on the interest the United States – their government and their public opinion – take in western Europe's freedom and independence.' Everything should be done, Kiesinger concluded, to 'try to maintain and strengthen this American interest and to maintain and strengthen our bonds and alliance with them'.[12]

It is interesting to note that, despite the British and German socialist support for disengagement, some of the strongest opposition to Healey's suggestions came from fellow European socialists. The Norwegian Socialist Jens Christian Hauge flatly rejected Healey's proposal. Hauge argued that it was impossible to limit the neutralization of Central Europe to that area. It would inevitably extend to the North and the South, thus fatally endangering NATO's future. Healey's proposal, Hauge argued, amounted to 'gambling with the security of our countries'.[13] Hauge received strong support from, among others, the French Socialist Pierre Commin, who had been sent by Prime Minister Guy Mollet, a founding member of Bilderberg.[14] This reflected not only the fact that among Germany's neighbours the prospect of a reunified and neutralized Germany – with all the connotations of a German *Schaukelpolitik* – was not regarded as desirable. Just as important was that Healey's proposal could undermine the Common Market and Euratom Treaties, which were finally nearing completion in early 1957. Instead of risking the complete neutralization of Europe, Commin said, a united and prosperous Europe should be built. In the long run such a Europe would constitute a powerful attraction for the satellite countries.[15]

Healey skilfully defended his proposal, but he could only rely on Fritz Erler for active support. The two overriding aims for the West, Erler said, were security for themselves and freedom for the oppressed peoples in Eastern Europe. The first aim might be reached by a defensive policy. 'But to obtain the second aim, we must have a dynamic policy, a forward strategy in the political field.' With respect to the division of Germany, such a dynamic policy necessitated a real discussion of proposals that might be acceptable to Moscow. Erler argued that in the final analysis the Soviets were concerned mostly about their own security. The Soviets feared the combination of German manpower and American technology. 'Let us try if we cannot obtain substantial concessions for all of us if we deliver them from that fear.' A reunified Germany would need a limited army, effectively controlled, for its own protection. In fact, Erler argued, this would not be all too different from the existing WEU construction. However, a reunified Germany could not be a member of NATO – this was clearly, and for understandable reasons, unacceptable to the Soviet leadership. In all other fields – cultural, economic, political – Germany would be free to remain 'a member of the Western family of nations and fulfil her task in the European community.' A Western policy of waiting until 'the Soviet Empire' fell apart was not enough, Erler said. 'This might take a pretty long time, longer than the suppressed people in Europe can afford.'[16] Ever since the Stalin Note of March 1952, which had suggested that Moscow was willing to accept a united, independent Germany, the West German

Social Democrats had been in favour of negotiating with the Soviets. The question no one was able to answer, however, was what would satisfy the Soviet need for 'security'. Given his somewhat naïve argument that a united Germany would be allowed to remain part of the European community, Erler clearly thought that German rearmament and NATO were the key issues. Adenauer and his ruling coalition, on the other hand, were convinced that Moscow's ultimate aim was a complete neutralization, followed by the communization of Germany. The only way to prevent this from happening, the chancellor argued, was to embed the FRG as strongly as possible in the West.

In early 1957, the disengagement debate was fought out mainly in foreign policy elite circles such as Bilderberg. Attempts by Denis Healey and other Labour politicians to make it a major public issue were largely unsuccessful. Judging by the February 1957 Bilderberg meeting, most members of the Western foreign policy elite rejected a superpower settlement based on a mutual withdrawal from Central Europe and the neutralization of Germany. The West German electorate seemed to share this view, if the devastating SPD defeat in the September 1957 parliamentary elections was any indication. How, then, to explain that only a few months later Kennan's Reith Lectures on the same subject became what the *New York Times* called 'a veritable journalistic and ideological triumph' – in Walter Lippmann's words, 'a public debate which has so many of the characteristics of an historic event'?[17]

Part of the explanation had to do with the author of the lectures. The fact that one of the founding fathers of containment now seemed to acknowledge the failure of this strategy was bound to attract attention.[18] Kennan's literary talents, moreover, added considerably to the force of his arguments. Still, the most important change was the launch of the Soviet Sputnik in October 1957 and its impact on Western publics. In Lippmann's words, 'a profound reappraisal of the balance of military power' had taken place.[19] American superiority in the field of nuclear weapons and technology suddenly seemed an illusion, and NATO's heavy reliance on nuclear weapons for its defence appeared reckless. The Polish proposal for a zone free of nuclear weapons in Central Europe – the Rapacki Plan, first announced in October 1957 – was therefore received with much interest in many European countries, particularly Great Britain.[20]

Kennan's basic argument in the BBC lectures remained that the status quo in Europe was unacceptable and highly dangerous. The situation in the satellite areas was unstable. On the other hand, if the Soviet Union managed to reassert full control, the consequences would be far-reaching. 'If the taste or even the hope for independence once dies out in the hearts of these peoples', Kennan said, 'then there will be no recovering it; then

Moscow's victory will be complete. Eastern Europe will then be permanently lost to Europe proper and to the possibility of any normal participation in international life.' The only solution for the satellite countries, Kennan argued, would be a departure of Soviet forces.[21]

The second reason for the need to change the status quo, Kennan said, was the division of Germany. Any Soviet withdrawal from Eastern Europe was impossible as long as American and British forces remained in West Germany. And any reunification of Germany remained impossible as long as the West insisted upon the freedom of choice for a reunited Germany to remain a member of NATO. True, there were those in Western Europe who saw advantages to the presence of American forces in West Germany. 'But there is danger in permitting it to harden into a permanent attitude. It expects too much, and for too long a time, of the United States, which is not a European Power.'[22] Moreover, the exposed position of West Berlin was so dangerous that a change in the status quo was urgent. To those who said that Moscow would never agree to reunification, Kennan answered: how would we know until we really try? To those who brought forward military reasons for doubting the wisdom of a military withdrawal from Germany, Kennan replied that he did not think the Soviet Union was likely to attack Western Europe. 'We must get over this obsession that the Russians are yearning to attack and occupy Western Europe, and that this is the principal danger.' Kennan argued that strong and internally healthy European societies with paramilitary forces would be capable of resisting any Soviet coercion.[23]

A third reason for the need for positive action concerned the nuclearization of NATO. Kennan warned explicitly against arming continental European countries with nuclear weapons in response to the launch of Sputnik. This would dangerously increase tensions with Soviet Russia. Moreover, it would make any arms control agreement in the future much more difficult to achieve. Kennan strongly criticized U.S. and NATO reliance on nuclear deterrence. 'A defence posture built around a weapon suicidal in its implications can serve in the long run only to paralyze national policy, to undermine alliances, and to drive everyone deeper and deeper into the hopeless exertions of the weapons race.' The recent suggestions that tactical atomic weapons might provide an answer, Kennan argued, should also be rejected. 'That it would prove possible, in the event of an atomic war, to arrive at some tacit and workable understanding with the adversary as to the degree of destructiveness of the weapons that would be used and the sort of target to which they would be directed, seems to me a very slender and wishful hope indeed.'[24]

The most notable reaction to the Reith Lectures came from Kennan's former boss at the State Department, Dean Acheson. In January 1958, Acheson published a highly critical 'Reply to Kennan'. Christopher Emmett of the American Council on Germany – an organization with an aim similar to Bilderberg's, but operating bilaterally to improve American-German relations – had asked Acheson to counteract the impact Kennan was having in West Germany, where many thought he spoke for the Democratic Party. Emmet took care of the distribution of Acheson's article, making sure that it appeared in many major European newspapers.[25] In his reply, Acheson denied that Kennan's ideas represented the views of the Democratic Party and went on to attack Kennan's arguments for disengagement. 'Mr. Kennan has never, in my judgment, grasped the realities of power relationships, but takes a rather mystical attitude toward them.' Acheson thought it was wishful thinking to expect that Western Europe would be able to withstand Soviet pressure without the presence of American and British power. By the same token, American power would not be able to deter the Soviet Union in Europe 'if the United States and Western Europe are separated and stand alone'.[26] During a press conference one week later, Acheson called Kennan's Reith Lectures 'nothing but "isolationism" dressed up in fine words'.[27]

Acheson had felt compelled to react because of the enormous popular response to Kennan's lectures. As the former secretary of state told Joseph Harsch, European correspondent of the *Christian Science Monitor*: 'An appeal to the lotus-eating spirit in mankind, which urges him to relax just at the time when real effort might possibly cause a great improvement, could be disastrous – at any rate, I believe so, and the people whose judgment I respect most both in America and Europe believe so. I decided to let him have it, and the reports which come to me from the continent indicate that it was well worthwhile.'[28] It was important that Acheson, who was highly respected in Europe, and not Secretary of State John Foster Dulles, who was not, led the attack on Kennan. Still, Harsch informed Acheson, 'All of Western Europe is presently suffering a deep inclination to go lotus eating, and George is primarily responsible for articulating the idea.'[29]

The Bilderberg organizers – among them Chairman Prince Bernhard of the Netherlands and Honorary Secretary General Joseph Retinger – shared Acheson's concern about widespread European support for Kennan's disengagement proposals. They hastily arranged an 'enlarged Bilderberg steering committee meeting' on 25–26 April 1958 in the Netherlands.[30] Their choice of participants was revealing: among the twenty-one men present there were two influential first-time participants, NATO Secretary General Paul-Henri Spaak and *New York Times* columnist Cyrus Sulzberger. Spaak's presence was a clear indication that Bernhard and Retinger were worried about possible negative effects on NATO resulting from the disengagement debate. Moreover, the fact that Sulzberger was invited reflected a desire to influence the debate through one of the most widely read American commentators on international affairs.

Compared to the February 1957 Bilderberg meeting, the discussion at Oosterbeek saw one important change. Though everyone except the British and German socialists as well as Van Zeeland still rejected the various disengagement proposals, the necessity of more positive action by the West was recognized. As the British diplomat John Hope put it in a memorandum for the Foreign Office: 'There was no disposition to underestimate the malevolence of Russia's intentions. There was, however, a fairly widespread tendency to accept the view that the status quo between West [and] East was no longer tolerable.'[31] Public opinion in the West demanded action; Erler, Healey and George Brown, another prominent Labour MP, made clear that their parties would continue to support the calls for a summit conference and disengagement.[32]

In response, Spaak appealed for 'unity and strength' within NATO. Yet, apparently impressed by the repeated assertions that something had to be done, he wrote a memo during the meeting setting out some of the ground rules for any disengagement proposal. 'The conference was surprised [and] pleased by his response', John Hope noted. Spaak said that there were two premises the West ought to agree on: 'the American forces must not leave the continent and Germany must not be neutralized'. American agreement to any scheme to reduce tensions in Europe was necessary in order to prevent a situation in which, after a partial withdrawal, pressures for a complete withdrawal became too strong. 'We must further bear in mind', Spaak continued, 'military views which are that Allied troops are not effectively employed if they are moved out of Germany. There is also a psychological risk for all of the NATO members if Germany refrains from participating in the defence of Europe. This idea might catch on in other countries in Europe and also create the impression in America that Europe is no longer prepared to defend herself.'[33] On the other hand, Spaak did not rule out talking about some of the components of the Polish Rapacki Plan. A European zone of controlled armaments without strategic nuclear weapons, he argued, might be possible as long as such a plan did not discriminate against Germany. He also did not rule out a non-aggression pact with the Soviet Union.

Shortly after the steering committee meeting, Sulzberger published several columns in the *New York Times* based on the Bilderberg discussions. His columns reflected the majority opinion and urged a cautious approach in the disengagement debate. Sulzberger repeated Spaak's warning about a pullback of American forces from Germany: 'It is exceptionally difficult to lodge our divisions and installations in France and the Low Countries. Therefore, if both Russian and American troops started pulling out of Central Europe, there is a serious chance the United States withdrawal would continue right across the Atlantic.' Sulzberger also agreed with Spaak about the danger of a neutralization of Germany. 'Political realities being what they are, it is probable that were this country to become neutral, the rest of the Continent would follow.' Finally, Sulzberger argued that the present balance of conventional forces necessitated the use of tactical nuclear weapons for Europe's defence. Nobody liked the status quo, he concluded, 'but we should not walk into traps in the mere hope of relaxing tension'.[34]

Meanwhile, Dean Acheson had decided to embark on a European tour in order to repair the damage done by Kennan's Reith Lectures. At the September 1958 Bilderberg conference in Buxton, Great Britain, Acheson called for more Western unity – not just by paying lip service to the alliance, but by a real concerted policy. Acheson forcefully stated his conviction that the West should not let itself be guided by public opinion or count upon imminent change in the Soviet Union. Developments in the Soviet Union, Acheson argued, would 'not occur fast enough to affect us in the next decade or more'. In the meantime, the only viable course of action was to strengthen the alliance:

> The [task] of political leadership in the West is to persuade the peoples of the West to develop their power position to the point where intentions hostile to their interests can be frustrated. Without this capacity, and without resolution of purpose, there seems no possibility of achieving two other ends which occupy much of the public discussion in the West: finding some accommodations with the Soviet state; and conducting successfully the cold war, the so-called battle for men's minds. The most colossal mistake is to believe that energetic pursuit of these two ends makes it unnecessary to look to our power position.[35]

Acheson clearly felt that the Eisenhower administration had failed to develop an active policy of leadership, to draw the alliance together after Suez, Sputnik and the disengagement debate.

Ironically, the single most effective challenge to the disengagement movement came from none other than Soviet leader Nikita Khrushchev. His Berlin ultimatum of November 1958 and the ensuing Berlin crisis severely undermined the efforts of Kennan and the British and German socialists to put disengagement on the Western agenda. By March 1959, when Fritz Erler and fellow SPD member Carlo Schmid visited Khrushchev, it was clear that Moscow was not interested in disengagement. Schmid gave a long account of his nine-hour conversation with Khrushchev during a special Bilderberg steering committee meeting on 21–22 March 1959, in Knokke, Belgium. Khrushchev, Schmid said, had left no doubt that he was uninterested in any disengagement or reunification proposals until the question of a peace treaty with East Germany was settled.[36]

Because of Khrushchev's actions, it remains an academic question whether public support for disengagement in Western Europe would have reached levels compelling NATO member states to act along the lines of Healey's and Kennan's proposals. The Bilderberg discussions demonstrate, however, that the transatlantic foreign policy elite took the disengagement debate very seriously. The discussions also show that in Western elite circles, support for disengagement was limited both before and after Kennan's Reith Lectures. Beyond the Labour and the SPD representatives, relatively few Bilderberg members voiced support for disengagement. The Bilderberg meetings therefore acted mainly as a brake on all disengagement schemes. Moreover, the fact that leading SPD members were exposed to pro-Atlanticist and pro-Europeanist thinking in the Bilderberg meetings helped to bring about a fundamental change in the party's attitude towards NATO and European integration in the summer of 1960.[37]

Most Bilderberg participants were convinced that the future of NATO should not be risked by any proposal that might well result in the neutralization of large parts of Europe, the breakdown of NATO solidarity and the withdrawal of American forces from Europe. Instead of drawing the conclusion from NATO's nuclear and political troubles that a disengagement proposal was necessary, they argued that a real solution would be a more equitable and credible defence of Europe based on both a greater contribution of the European non-nuclear powers in nuclear matters and a more flexible strategy involving more conventional forces. The fact that such a policy would in all likelihood delay an end to the Cold War in the short term was judged to be tragic yet unavoidable. They did not feel that the Soviet Union could be trusted to agree to a real, enforceable disengagement settlement. In the final analysis, therefore, they decided that time would simply have to work in favour of the West. An integrated, economically expanding Europe would have to solve, once and for all, the German question, while at the same time creating a powerful force of magnetism for the Eastern European states under Soviet control. And the Atlantic security community would have to keep American power committed in Europe.

Notes

1. On Kennan's thinking see D. Mayers. 1988. *George Kennan and the Dilemmas of US Foreign Policy*, New York: Oxford University Press, 230–239. On Kennan's own version of events see G.F. Kennan. 1972. *Memoirs 1950–1963*, London: Hutchinson, 229–266.

2. The Bilderberg Group had been founded in the early 1950s by a group of Europeans concerned with increasing anti-American sentiment in Europe. The first meeting took place at the Hotel De Bilderberg, in Oosterbeek, the Netherlands, in May 1954. The Bilderberg Group quickly established its reputation as a key meeting place for high-level, off-the-record discussions on foreign policy and economic issues. As such, the group was part of the informal Atlantic alliance – the web of transatlantic networks and organizations that, along with air travel and the telephone, facilitated the enormous increase in contacts among Western foreign policy and business elites in the decades after 1945. On Bilderberg see H. Wilford. 2003. *The CIA, the British Left and the Cold War: Calling the Tune?*, London: Frank Cass; V. Aubourg. 2003. 'Organizing Atlanticism: The Bilderberg Group and the Atlantic Institute, 1952–1963', in G. Scott-Smith and H. Krabbendam (eds.), *The Cultural Cold War in Western Europe, 1945–1960*, London: Frank Cass, 92–105 and V. Aubourg. 2004. 'Le groupe de Bilderberg et l'intégration européenne jusqu'au milieu des années 1960. Une influence complexe', in M. Dumoulin (ed.), *Réseaux économiques et construction européenne. Economic Networks and European Integration*, Brussels: Peter Lang, 411–430; T. W. Gijswijt. 2007. 'Beyond NATO: Transatlantic Elite Networks and the Atlantic Alliance', in A. Wenger, C. Nuenlist and A. Locher (eds.), *Transforming NATO in the Cold War: Challenges Beyond Deterrence in the 1960s*, London: Routledge, 50–63.
3. See the papers Healey prepared for the Bilderberg conference: Denis Healey, 'Diplomacy of Liberation', 3, Box 37, C.D. Jackson Papers, Dwight D. Eisenhower Library, Abilene. See also Denis Healey, 'Nationalism and Neutralism in the Western Community', 8–9, Box 304, Hugh Gaitskell Papers, University College, London.
4. Opposition to nuclear weapons was particularly strong in the Federal Republic, as became clear during the heated public debate in April 1956 over Adenauer's remark that tactical nuclear weapons should be regarded as modernized artillery. See L.S. Wittner. 1997. *Resisting the Bomb: A History of the World Nuclear Disarmament Movement, 1954–1970*, Stanford: Stanford University Press. For the overall importance of the factor of Germany in Western debates over nuclear weapons and strategy see M. Trachtenberg. 1999. *A Constructed Peace: The Making of the European Settlement 1945–1963*, Princeton, NJ: Princeton University Press.
5. C.D. Jackson, 'Memorandum to Luce, Alexander, Donovan etc.', 19 Feb. 1957, Box 37, Jackson Papers.
6. Healey, 'Nationalism and Neutralism in the Western Community', Box 304, Gaitskell Papers, 8.
7. This is how C.D. Jackson put it: Jackson, 'Memorandum to Luce, Alexander, Donovan etc.', 19 Feb. 1957, Box 37, Jackson Papers.
8. Erich Ollenhauer, 'German Reunification'. See the British summary, undated, Foreign Office (hereafter FO) 371 130993, The National Archives, London (UKNA).
9. Paul H. Nitze Handwritten Notes, 15–17 Feb. 1957, Box 60, Folder 1, Paul H. Nitze Papers, Library of Congress, Washington, DC.
10. West German Foreign Minister Heinrich von Brentano had also contributed a paper explaining the official West German position: 'Is the Soviet Union the Only Great Power Which Can Offer Germany Reunification?', Bonn, 25 Oct. 1957, Box 60, Folder 2, Nitze Papers.
11. All quotes are from Kiesinger's handwritten notes , Box 710, Kurt G. Kiesinger Papers, Archiv für Christlich-Demokratische Politik, St. Augustin (ACDP).
12. Ibid. Kiesinger's strong emphasis on creating lasting ties with the United States may have been a calculated effort to offset some of the sharp criticisms Adenauer had made of U.S. policy in the aftermath of the Suez crisis: see H.-P. Schwarz. 1991. *Adenauer. Der Staatsmann*, Stuttgart: Deutsche Verlags-Anstalt, 320ff.

13. Nitze Notes, Box 60, Folder 2, Nitze Papers.
14. As Jackson wrote: 'Interestingly, the most vehement attackers of Healey's position were Pinay and Commin of France, ably but more quietly supported by a Norwegian Socialist, Jens Hauge.' Jackson, 'Memorandum to Luce, Alexander, Donovan etc.', 19 Feb. 1957, Box 37, Jackson Papers.
15. Nitze Notes, Box 60, Folder 2, Nitze Papers.
16. Erler handwritten speech St. Simons Island, Box 13 B, Fritz Erler Papers, Archiv der sozialen Demokratie, Friedrich Ebert Stiftung, Bonn.
17. M.S. Handler, 'West Germans Split on Unification Issue: Kennan Plan Attracting Support In Wake of NATO Meeting', *The New York Times*, 29 Dec. 1957 and W. Lippmann. 1958. 'Mr. Kennan and Reappraisal in Europe'," *Atlantic Monthly*, 201(4), 33–37. On the reactions in Germany see also D. Felken. 1993. *Dulles und Deutschland. Die amerikanische Deutschlandpolitik 1953–1959*, Bonn and Berlin: Bouvier Verlag, 455–456; A. Gallus. 2001. *Die Neutralisten. Verfechter eines vereinten Deutschland zwischen Ost und West, 1945–1990*, Düsseldorf: Droste.
18. Although of course it should be noted that Kennan had opposed NATO and German rearmament – the militarization of containment – from the beginning.
19. Lippmann, "Mr. Kennan and Reappraisal in Europe," 33–37.
20. See Trachtenberg, *A Constructed Peace*, 221.
21. G.F. Kennan. 1958. *Russia, the Atom and the West*, London: Oxford University Press, 36.
22. Ibid., 41. On this point see J. Botts. 2006. 'Nothing to Seek and … Nothing to Defend: George F. Kennan's Core Values and American Foreign Policy, 1938–1993', *Diplomatic History*, 30(5), 839–866. Botts argues that Kennan's motives for developing various plans for disengagement involved his conviction that the United States should not overextend itself abroad because of the many domestic problems the country needed to face.
23. Kennan, *Russia, the Atom and the West*, 64. The proposal for paramilitary forces elicited some of the strongest criticism.
24. Ibid., 56 and 59.
25. For the involvement of Emmett and the American Council on Germany see D. Brinkley. 1992. *Dean Acheson: The Cold War Years 1953–1971*, New Haven and London: Yale University Press, 79–83.
26. 'Text of Acheson's Reply to Kennan', *The New York Times*, 12 Jan. 1958.
27. N. Standford, 'Acheson Rips Administration', *The Christian Science Monitor*, 21 Jan. 1958.
28. Acheson to Harsch, 4 Feb. 1958, Box 20, Joseph Harsch Papers, Wisconsin Historical Society, Madison.
29. Harsch to Acheson, 12 Feb. 1958, Box 20, Harsch Papers.
30. See 'Bilderberg Group. Enlarged Steering Committee Meeting. Oosterbeek', 25–26 Apr. 1958, Box 56-341, Ford Foundation Archives, New York City.
31. Lord John Hope, 'Conference at Bildeberg [sic] 25/26 April, 1958', FO 371 137746, UKNA.
32. Apart from public opinion, Brown listed the following reasons for changing the 'status quo': 'Militarily it is not giving us the assurance of security; politically it leaves us no room for manoeuvre or the extension of our principles of freedom; and humanitarianly [sic.] it leaves millions of our friends who were free before the war under totalitarian domination.' He added that a security system in Europe would mean less spending on defence and more investment in the Third World – the most important battlefield in the Cold War. See George Brown, 'Note', undated, FO 371 137746, UKNA. Brown's note was also attached to the summary of the meeting as 'Appendix D by a British Participant'.

33. 'Note by M. Spaak', undated, FO 371 137746, UKNA.

34. Cyrus Sulzberger, 'Pernicious Abstraction or Panacea?', *The New York Times*, 30 Apr. 1958.

35. Dean Acheson, 'The Western Approach to Soviet Russia', Box 305, Gaitskell Papers.

36. 'Compte rendu d'une conversation récente avec Monsieur N. Krushchev', Box 304, Gaitskell Papers. Around the same time, the SPD announced its *Deutschland Plan*, a final attempt to use disengagement to bring about unification. The plan, however, was more about internal politics within the SPD than a serious proposal. See D. Orlow. 1997. 'Ambivalence and Attraction: The German Social Democrats and the United States, 1945–1974', in R. Pomerin (ed.), *The American Impact on Postwar Germany*, Providence, RI: Berghahn Books, 35–52.

37. This has been recognized in the literature. See H.-J. Grabbe. 1983. *Unionsparteien, Sozialdemokratie und Vereinigten Staaten von Amerika 1945–1966*, Düsseldorf: Droste, 252. In a famous speech in the Bundestag on 30 June 1960, Herbert Wehner announced his party's support for Adenauer's policy of *Westbindung*, i.e., acceptance of the FRG's membership in NATO and acceptance of the priority of European integration over German unification.

Section II

STALIN'S DEATH AND AFTER

A Missed Opportunity?

Chapter 3

Moscow's Campaign against the Cold War, 1948–1955

Geoffrey Roberts

The Soviet Union began to campaign against the Cold War almost as soon as the conflict began. In the late 1940s, the Soviets sponsored a broad-based peace movement, alongside which ran a sustained diplomatic effort to reopen the negotiations on the German question. In March 1952 the two prongs of the Soviet campaign came together in the so-called 'Stalin Note' – a proposal for a peace treaty that would reunify Germany on condition that the country remained disarmed and neutral in the Cold War. In 1954 the Soviet campaign against the Cold War took a new turn with a proposal to establish a pan-European system of collective security that would lead to the dissolution of the Cold War blocs. The Soviet diplomatic campaign was supported by the pro-Moscow peace movement, and by the time of the Geneva summit of July 1955 there was considerable support throughout Europe for the idea that the German question could be resolved and the Cold War ended by the establishment of pan-European collective security structures.

The aim of the Soviet campaign against the Cold War was to end the division of Europe and establish a permanent East-West détente. The Soviet version of how and why the Cold War had begun and how it could be ended was highly ideological and partisan, but Moscow did not view its peace campaign as a zero-sum game. Peace, détente and the containment of a revived Germany were seen as matters of common concern. At the same time, the campaign against the Cold War was also seen as part of the historical process of global transition to socialism. Defeat of the reactionary elements that had instigated the Cold War would, it was believed, promote progressive political advance in different countries and at the international level.

Notes for this chapter begin on page 59.

The Peace Movement

The communist peace movement began to take definite shape at a World Congress of Intellectuals for Peace in Wroclaw in August 1948. This was followed in April 1949 by the First World Congress of Partisans of Peace. Held in Paris and attended by nearly two thousand delegates, the congress claimed to speak for 600 million people in seventy-two countries and passed resolutions condemning NATO, opposing the rearmament of Germany and Japan, and calling for the prohibition of nuclear weapons. The meeting elected a Permanent Committee of the Partisans of Peace (PCPP), which eventually evolved into the World Peace Council (WPC).[1]

While it is not clear to what extent the hand of Moscow was behind the inception of the peace movement, by the time of the Paris congress the Soviets had taken a firm grip on the leadership of the organization. The two main Soviet figures involved in the movement were Alexander Fadeyev, the head of the Soviet Writers' Union, and the writer and journalist Ilya Ehrenburg. From the Russian archives we know that they submitted detailed reports to the Soviet leadership on the activities of the peace movement and were given specific instructions on policies to be pursued by the PCPP and its successor, the WPC.[2]

In March 1950 the WPC met in the Swedish capital and issued the Stockholm Appeal, a petition demanding the prohibition of nuclear weapons. By the end of the year the petition had nearly 500 million signatures. In November 1950 the Second World Peace Congress convened in the Polish capital and launched the Warsaw Appeal, a petition centred on demands for an end to the war in Korea, which secured more than 560 million signatures. At its Berlin meeting in February 1951 the WPC launched the third of the peace movement's international petition campaigns: the demand for a five-power peace pact between Britain, China, France, the Soviet Union and the United States. By December nearly 600 million people had signed this appeal.[3]

The proposal for a five-power peace pact was first put forward by Soviet Foreign Minister Andrei Vyshinsky in a speech at the UN in September 1949,[4] but it did not feature centrally in peace movement campaigning until it was highlighted by Stalin in an interview in February 1951. This was the cue for a sustained mass campaign for a five-power peace pact, and the Politburo's instructions to Fadeyev and Ehrenburg in 1951–52 reflected the high priority attached to this policy demand.[5]

The Struggle for a German Peace Treaty

As far as Soviet diplomacy was concerned, the task was to overcome the Cold War by a revival of postwar negotiations on the German question.

At the Potsdam conference it had been agreed to negotiate a peace treaty for Germany within the framework of the Council of Foreign Ministers (CFM), a forum of the American, British, French and Soviet foreign ministers. However, the first eighteen months of the council's existence were taken up with the discussion of peace treaties for the minor Axis states – Bulgaria, Finland, Hungary, Italy and Romania. Prior to the CFM's Moscow meeting in March–April 1947, the only substantial discussion of the German question concerned a proposal by U.S. Secretary of State James F. Byrnes for a 'Twenty-Five-Year Treaty for the Disarmament and Demilitarization of Germany'. Byrnes broached the idea at the first meeting of the CFM in London in September 1945. Vyacheslav Molotov, the Soviet foreign minister, was interested in further negotiations but was overruled by Stalin.[6] At the Paris CFM meeting in April 1946 Byrnes formally tabled his proposal, prompting the Soviets to conduct an extensive internal consultation about their response to Byrnes's draft treaty.[7] The consensus that emerged from this exercise was that the Byrnes proposal was dangerous because it could lead to a premature end to the Allied occupation of Germany – before the country had been thoroughly demilitarized, denazified and democratized and before the Soviets had extracted their reparations payments. This was the substance of Molotov's response to the Byrnes proposal at the July 1946 CFM, but he did not completely close the door on the draft treaty, saying only that it required radical revision.[8]

At the Moscow CFM in 1947, the Soviets tabled their own draft treaty 'On the Demilitarisation of Germany and the Prevention of German Aggression', which formally stated their view that the country should remain occupied for the foreseeable future. Molotov also proposed that the Allies draft a constitutional document providing for the election of a provisional German government. This provisional government would be charged with drawing up a permanent constitution for the country and with the continuing implementation of the Potsdam agreement on the disarmament, democratization and denazification of Germany. In due course the new German government would also negotiate the terms of a peace treaty.[9]

After six weeks of negotiations the Moscow CFM closed without agreement, but the discussion resumed at the London meeting of the council in November 1947. Again, Molotov pushed hard for an agreement on the negotiation of a German peace treaty.[10] However, by this time the Western powers had embarked on the path leading to the postwar division of Germany and to the establishment in May 1949 of an independent West German state. The London CFM ended in complete failure, and the next meeting of the council did not take place until after the Berlin airlift crisis of 1948–1949. While this crisis was provoked by a Soviet blockade of land access routes to West Berlin, Moscow's aim was not to force the Western powers to withdraw from the German capital but to secure their return to the negotiating table. When the Western powers agreed to a further discussion of the German question at a session of the CFM in Paris in June 1949, the blockade was lifted.

The Soviet representative at the Paris CFM was Vyshinsky, who had replaced Molotov as foreign minister in March 1949. His instructions were to seek the restoration of four-power control of Germany. A secondary goal was an agreement to negotiate the draft of a German peace treaty. There were two new wrinkles in Soviet policy: first, the negotiation of a draft peace treaty was no longer tied to the prior formation of a united German government; second, Allied occupation forces were to be withdrawn a year after the conclusion of such a treaty.[11] These changes represented a substantial policy shift. The Soviets had previously favoured a prolonged occupation of Germany and a piecemeal process of negotiation leading to an all-German government and the signature of a peace treaty. Now they sought a rapid Allied withdrawal as a means of averting the further integration of West Germany into the Western bloc.

Like its predecessors in Moscow and London, the Paris CFM failed, and in the months that followed the division of Germany deepened, as did the process of Cold War polarization. In September 1949, parliamentary elections were held to complete the formation of the new Federal Republic of Germany (FRG). Stalin retaliated by founding the German Democratic Republic (GDR) in October 1949. In May 1950 the American, British and French foreign ministers issued a statement urging the speedy integration of the FRG into the Western European defence sphere. June 1950 saw the outbreak of the Korean War and the ensuing acceleration of Western plans for rearmament. In August Winston Churchill called for the creation of a European army, and in September the Western powers paved the way for German participation in such an army when they formally terminated the state of war with Germany. In October the French government proposed the Pleven Plan for a European army with German contingents. Meeting in Brussels in December, the three Western foreign ministers agreed in principle to a West German military contribution to the defence of Western Europe.

The Soviets responded to these developments with a conference of Eastern European foreign ministers that issued a declaration opposing the remilitarization of West Germany. The meeting, held in Prague in October 1950, called also for the negotiation of a peace treaty for Germany and the establishment of an all-German council of representatives of the FRG and the GDR that would prepare the way for the formation of an all-German government.[12] When the Western powers ignored the Prague declaration, the Soviets proposed another CFM meeting to discuss the German question. The Western powers agreed, as long as the CFM could also discuss the basic causes of tension with the Soviet Union (in their view, communist aggression). This diplomatic exchange led in March 1951 to a meeting in Paris of deputy foreign ministers charged with preparing the agenda for a future CFM meeting. The Soviet representative was Deputy Foreign Minister Andrei Gromyko, and his brief was to secure a CFM agenda with three main points: (1) the implementation of the Potsdam agreements on the demilitarization of Germany; (2) the rapid conclusion of a peace treaty with Germany and the withdrawal of occupation forces; and (3) the improvement of the political atmosphere in Europe and steps towards the reduction of armaments.[13] Judging by Gromyko's directives, the Soviet intent was serious, constructive negotiations on the German question, but only if the Western powers were prepared to step away from their plans for German remilitarization. The Paris discussions dragged on until June 1951, but no agreement was reached on reconvening the CFM, let alone an agenda for such a meeting.

In September 1951 the Soviets decided to adopt a new strategy that entailed the GDR government and the German communists campaigning for a peace treaty and calling for the formation of an all-Germany council to discuss the issue. If the Bonn government refused to play ball, the GDR would then call on the four occupying powers to negotiate a peace treaty. The USSR would respond positively to this proposal and would issue its own draft of a peace treaty with the aim of strengthening the political campaign within Germany for reunification and adding to public pressure on the Western powers to return to the negotiating table. Broadly speaking, this sequence of events unfolded as planned in late 1951 and early 1952, and on 10 March the Soviets issued the so-called Stalin Note, which contained a draft of the principles of a German peace treaty. According to the Soviet proposal there would be a united Germany; Allied occupation forces would be withdrawn within a year of the signing of a peace treaty; Germany's armed forces would be limited to levels necessary for national defence; and, crucially, Germany would pledge not to enter into any coalition or military alliance directed against states it had fought during the last war – i.e., the country would not be allowed to participate either in NATO or in the planned European Defence Community (EDC) then under negotiation.

The Western powers' response on 25 March was a proposal for free all-German elections to elect a government – a government that would be free to enter any defensive associations it liked – to negotiate the peace treaty. This was unacceptable to the Soviets, but on 9 April they did agree there could be discussions of free all-German elections. However, the real stumbling block in the negotiations was not elections but the Soviet de-

mand for advance guarantees that a united Germany would not participate in the Western bloc. While the West wanted a united Germany that
would be free to decide its own (pro-Western) foreign policy, the Soviets
wanted an agreement that would preclude a revival of German aggression, irrespective of the outcome of any elections. The Soviet-Western exchange of diplomatic notes continued for another few months, but the
gulf between the two sides could not be bridged. By the end of the year
the Soviets had lost interest and did not even bother to reply to the final
Western note of September 1952. The last Soviet note in the sequence was
issued on 23 August. That same day Vyshinsky met with Walter Ulbricht,
the East German communist leader. Ulbricht welcomed the note, saying it
would strengthen the GDR's struggle for a united Germany. Some people,
said Ulbricht, thought that since the GDR had embarked on the course
of building socialism there would be no more talk of German unity, but
the Soviet note made it clear that the aim remained a united, democratic
Germany.[14] If, as some historians say, the March note was purely a propaganda exercise designed to disrupt or delay West German rearmament
and the formation of the EDC, Ulbricht was not privy to this information.
To all intents and purposes the Soviet aim of a peaceful and democratic
Germany was a real one. Of course, the Soviets intended to do all they
could to buttress the position of their supporters in a future united Germany, but that did not preclude a serious political compromise with the
West, including giving up communist control of the GDR.

Moscow's diplomatic campaign for a German peace treaty was supported by the communist peace movement. Particularly important were
the campaigns in France against the EDC and in Britain against German
rearmament. In West Germany the activities of the communist peace
movement linked up with social democratic opposition to rearmament
and with the development of a movement in favour of a neutral Germany.
Stalin, however, was sceptical that the campaign would succeed. In his
last known comments on the German question, Stalin told a delegation of
GDR leaders in April 1952:

> Whatever proposals we make on the German question the western powers
> won't agree with them and they won't withdraw from West Germany. To think
> that the Americans will compromise or accept the draft peace treaty would
> be a mistake. The Americans need an army in West Germany in order to keep
> control of Western Europe … The Americans are drawing West Germany into
> the [NATO] pact. They will form West German forces … In West Germany an
> independent state is being formed. And you must organise your own state. The
> demarcation line between West Germany and East Germany should be consid-
> ered a frontier, and not just any frontier but a dangerous frontier.[15]

The Post-Stalin Peace Offensive

Stalin had lost interest in a German peace treaty by the end of 1952, but after his death in March 1953 the new Soviet leadership took the opportunity to relaunch their proposal for a united but neutral Germany. Molotov was reappointed foreign minister, and he and his officials devised a proposal to bridge the gap between the Western demand for free all-German elections and the Soviet desire for guarantees against future German aggression. What they proposed was the formation of an all-German provisional government whose primary task would be the preparation of national elections. By early May the new policy had been formulated and submitted to the Soviet leadership, but its implementation was delayed by the growing crisis in the GDR that culminated in the East German uprising of June 1953. This was followed by the arrest of the Soviet security chief Lavrentii Beria and his denunciation as an imperialist agent seeking to hand the GDR over to the capitalists. In mid-July, however, the Soviets faced a Western note proposing a foreign ministers' conference on the German question. This spurred the Soviet leadership to approve the Foreign Ministry's earlier proposals. On 4 August Moscow replied to the Western note, agreeing to a foreign ministers' conference on the German question. On 15 August the Soviets issued a separate note on the German question, including the proposal for a provisional government. This initial exchange led to a further series of Soviet and Western notes, much like those of the 1952 round, though this time agreement was reached on holding a foreign ministers' conference in Berlin in January 1954.

For the communist peace movement, the period immediately after Stalin's death saw the continuation of the campaign for a five-power peace pact.[16] At the WPC's meeting in Budapest in June 1953, however, an appeal was launched for negotiations between the five great powers. This became part of a general campaign for 'the peaceful settlement of international problems'. The rationale for the new campaign was that unlike the Stockholm and Warsaw Appeals and the peace pact petition, the concrete demands of the peace movement would differ from county to country, depending on local circumstances.[17] These concrete demands would, however, be shaped by Moscow's foreign policy priorities. In effect, the new strategy meant that the peace movement had been transformed from a relatively independent campaigning body into an auxiliary of Soviet diplomacy. That new role did not lessen its importance to Soviet foreign strategy, since public opinion in the West was still seen by Moscow as the force that would tip the balance in the USSR's favour, not least in relation to the campaign for European collective security.

In strategic terms the most important function of the peace movement was to contribute to the reduction of international tensions. This new strategy was connected to changes in Soviet discourse on international relations after Stalin's death. Of particular importance was the introduction into Soviet discourse of the concept of 'world society' and the importance that was ascribed to 'international public opinion'. Within this discourse the peace movement began to be seen as a component of world public opinion and as part of an emergent infrastructure of international civil society.[18] This new discourse entailed a further broadening of the peace movement's political character, and the gatherings organized by the WPC were much more diverse than their equivalents during the Stalin era.

The Campaign for European Collective Security

The Soviet campaign for European collective security began on 10 February 1954, when Molotov unveiled Soviet proposals at the Berlin foreign ministers' conference: instead of a Western EDC there should be a pan-European collective security agreement.[19] Under the terms of this agreement all European states would sign a treaty pledging to aid each other if attacked. Both German states would be signatories, and the treaty would provide the context for their future reunification – which, said Molotov, would be facilitated rather than delayed by the establishment of a system of European collective security.

Throughout the Berlin conference the Soviets monitored the press and public response to their proposals and took particular note of the great interest in the proposal for European collective security.[20] After his return to Moscow, Molotov's officials assessed how to further the collective security campaign, especially in the face of Western objections that Soviet proposals would mean the collapse of NATO and the withdrawal of the United States from European affairs. The result of their deliberations was a radical new proposal: the U.S. could join the European collective security organization, and the USSR could join NATO. On 26 March Molotov sent a long note to the Soviet leadership explaining the rationale for such a policy. He began by emphasizing the positive response of Western public opinion to the Soviet proposal for European collective security, especially in France. However, Western opponents of the Soviet proposal were saying it was a negative policy that was directed at undermining NATO and dislodging the United States from Europe. The USSR should, therefore, simultaneously propose the United States' participation in a system of European collective security and the possibility of Soviet membership of NATO. Molotov assessed the probable outcome of this dual proposal as follows:

Most likely the organisers of the North Atlantic bloc will react negatively to this step of the Soviet government and will advance many different objections. In that event the governments of the three powers will have exposed themselves once again as the organisers of a military bloc against other states and it would strengthen the position of social forces conducting a struggle against the formation of the European Defence Community.

...

Of course, if the statement of the Soviet government meets with a positive attitude on the part of the three western powers this would signify a great success for the Soviet Union since the USSR joining the North Atlantic Pact under certain conditions would radically change the character of the pact. The USSR joining the North Atlantic Pact simultaneously with the conclusion of a General European Agreement on Collective Security in Europe would undermine plans for the creation of the European Defence Community and the remilitarisation of West Germany.

The Foreign Ministry considers that raising the question of the USSR joining NATO requires even now an examination of the consequences that might arise. Bearing in mind that the North Atlantic Pact is directed against the democratic movement in the capitalist countries, if the question of the USSR joining it became practical it would be necessary to raise the issue of all participants in the agreement undertaking a commitment (in the form of a joint declaration, for example) on the inadmissibility of interference in the internal affairs of states and respect for the principles of state independence and sovereignty.

In addition the Soviet Union would, in an appropriate form, have to raise the question of American military bases in Europe and the necessity for states to agree to the reduction of military forces, in accordance with the position that would be created after the USSR's entry into the North Atlantic Pact.[21]

It is evident from these remarks that while Molotov did not expect the Soviet initiative to succeed, he did not rule out the possibility that it might. In that event the USSR would be prepared to join NATO, if the terms were right. In line with this new approach, the Soviets issued a note at the end of March 1954 that announced two amendments to their draft treaty on European collective security. First, the U.S. would not be excluded from formal participation in a system of European collective security. Second, if NATO relinquished its aggressive character, the USSR would consider participation in that organization.[22] The Western states rejected the note on grounds that the USSR's participation in NATO would be incompatible with the aims of the organization, but Soviet analysts noted its positive impact on Western public opinion.[23]

While the Soviet campaign for European collective security was at a diplomatic impasse by mid-1954, hopes ran high in Moscow that it could still succeed through political pressure. Soviet attention focused on France, where there was strong communist and Gaullist opposition to the ratification of the EDC treaty. A campaign to persuade French public opinion to eschew the EDC in favour of European collective security was soon underway in the Soviet and communist press. At the end of August, the Soviet campaign against the EDC was crowned with success when the French National Assembly rejected ratification by a large majority. On 10 September the Soviets issued a statement welcoming the collapse of the EDC project and reiterating their proposal for European collective security. On 23 October the Soviets proposed the convening of a conference on collective security. By this time, however, the West had adopted a different plan – the direct admission of West Germany into NATO. The Soviets saw this as a setback but far from an end to the struggle against German rearmament. In the absence of Western agreement to participate in a conference on collective security, the Soviets pressed on alone and at the end of November convened a conference in Moscow attended by themselves and their Eastern European allies. The Soviets also began to map out contingency plans for a defensive alliance to counter a rearmed FRG integrated into NATO. In May 1955 West Germany joined NATO, and the Soviets countered by convening another conference on collective security, this time in Warsaw, where a Treaty of Friendship, Co-operation, and Mutual Assistance was signed by the USSR and its Eastern European allies. Even so, the door to collective security remained open, and the terms of the Warsaw Pact provided for its dissolution in the event of a pan-European treaty.

The Soviet campaign had not been entirely unsuccessful. It had forced the West to propose a leadership summit – the first such gathering since the end of the Second World War. This took place at Geneva in July 1955. The directive for the Soviet delegation to the summit[24] defined the USSR's overriding aim as the reduction of international tensions and the development of trust between states. Western objections to previous Soviet proposals on collective security were to be dealt with by the introduction of new arrangements in two stages: during the first stage (2–3 years) NATO and the Warsaw Pact would remain intact and the two sides would pledge non-aggression and political cooperation; only then, in the second stage, would the two organizations be replaced by a new system of pan-European collective security.

From the public relations point of view the summit was a great success and was surrounded by much talk about 'the spirit of Geneva' – the idea that there was a new atmosphere in world politics that would facilitate the speedy resolution of international problems and the establishment of a permanent détente. However, the only decision taken was to convene a foreign ministers' conference in Geneva to discuss European security and the German question. Just before the Geneva summit, the WPC convened a World Peace Assembly in Helsinki. Ehrenburg's report to the Soviet leadership on the assembly noted that in political terms it was a much more diverse meeting than previous peace congresses, but he emphasized, too, the delegates' support for Moscow's foreign policy and concluded that 'the World Peace Assembly is evidence of the great turn among broad sections of international public opinion in favour of negotiations and the reduction of international tensions'.[25]

Ehrenburg's optimism is supported by polling data collected by the U.S. Information Agency and the Department of State. In the aftermath of the Geneva summit, a sizeable plurality of people in Britain, France, Italy and West Germany favoured replacing NATO with a pan-European collective security system. As the American analysts commented: 'Putting it conservatively, the foregoing data tend to show that attitudes favorable to NATO's future are by no means firmly structured in the minds of either the general public or the upper groups of Western Europe. NATO, in fact, appears highly vulnerable from the opinion point of view. At the least, it appears that the people of Western Europe are now willing to consider security arrangements alternative to NATO and defense measures alternative to present NATO dispositions.'[26]

Partly as a response to the disturbing drift of Western public opinion, London, Paris and Washington began to formulate their own proposals for European collective security. These proposals were remarkably similar to those of the Soviets, including a European security pact under which the signatories would renounce the use of force, limit the size of their armed forces and pledge collective defence against aggression, irrespective of whether the attackers or the victims were NATO members. Aware that such a proposal was in the pipeline, the Soviets reworked their own collective security proposals. Their new plan was to reintroduce the proposal for a phased introduction of pan-European collective security, but if the West rejected an all-embracing pact, Molotov would then propose a security treaty embracing a smaller group of countries, perhaps only the four great powers and the two German states. Under this latter proposal there would be no time limit on the liquidation of existing groupings such as NATO and the Warsaw Pact. If this proposal was rejected the Soviets would next propose a four-power non-aggression treaty, and if that was unacceptable there could be a simple non-aggression agreement between NATO and the Warsaw Pact. The Soviets were also prepared to contemplate the establishment of a controlled military zone in Central Europe in which armed forces would be limited in size and subject to inspection.[27]

In arriving at this more flexible position on European collective security, the Soviets had placed themselves on a path of convergence with the Western powers, and the foreign ministers' conference got off to a good start when it opened at the end of October. As John Foster Dulles, the U.S. secretary of state, said on 2 November: 'I have examined in parallel columns the proposals put forward by the Western powers ... and compared them with the proposals and positions advanced by Mr. Molotov ... I found that there was a very considerable parallelism in our thinking ... we have, I think, achieved a quite remarkable degree of parallel thinking with respect to the concept of European security ... It seems to me that we have reached a point where as a result of constructive thinking on both sides we can see a realizable vision of security in Europe.'[28] There was a catch, however. The West wanted something in return for a European security pact: all-German elections leading to a united Germany that would be free to join NATO. Halfway through the conference, Molotov returned to Moscow for consultations and tried to persuade the Soviet leadership to negotiate a deal with the West that would concede all-German elections in exchange for European collective security. But he was overruled by party leader Nikita Khrushchev – by now the dominant voice among Soviet leaders – and returned to Geneva with instructions to veto any further discussion of all-German elections.[29] The conference collapsed soon after.

The Soviet campaign for European collective security did not end in 1955. At the twentieth party congress in February 1956 Khrushchev reiterated the Soviet programme for collective security in Europe, including the gradual reunification of Germany on the basis of a rapprochement between the two German states. But, as the Russian historian Natalia Yegorova has noted, while 'the proposal to create a system of collective security remained in the arsenal of Soviet diplomatic tactics and strategy for a long time and was put forward by Soviet representatives at various international meetings and negotiations with the western powers ... these proposals had a rather propagandistic character'.[30] The Soviet campaign for European collective security continued, indeed, for another twenty years and culminated with the Conference on Security and Co-operation in Europe in 1975. Under the terms of the 1975 Helsinki Final Act, Europe's borders were frozen and peace, cooperation and consultation were pledged across the Cold War divide. When it was put to Molotov that the pan-European conference was an old idea of his, he readily agreed.[31] But freezing and stabilizing Europe's Cold War divisions in the 1970s was a far cry from the Soviet ambition in the 1950s to dissolve the Cold War blocs and replace them with all-embracing pan-European collective security structures.

Conclusion

The Soviet campaign to end the Cold War of the 1940s and 1950s was motivated mainly by the fear that the FRG's integration into the Western bloc would lead to a German resurgence and the threat of a new world war. Moscow's initial response to this danger was to try to negotiate a

German peace treaty that would signal a return to the tripartism of the Potsdam conference. Simultaneously, the Soviets waged a massive political campaign to pressure Western governments into seeking a renewed détente. That Soviet peace offensive continued after Stalin's death and in 1954 took the form of a campaign for a European collective security system that would result in the dissolution of the Cold War blocs.

At the time, Western political leaders dismissed the Soviet campaign for European collective security as a propaganda exercise, and many historians have been content to accept this characterization of Moscow's policy. This essay has attempted to show that, on the contrary, the Soviet campaign to end the Cold War was authentic and seriously intended. Certainly, that was how the Soviet leadership saw the campaign, and that was what their officials schemed to achieve in negotiations with the Western powers. However, not everyone in the Soviet leadership was prepared to pay the necessary price for European collective security: free all-German elections leading to Germany's reunification and the inevitable loss of communist control in the GDR. The main proponent of a compromise with the West along these lines was Molotov, and its main opponent was Khrushchev, who prioritized holding on to the GDR. After Khrushchev's fall in 1964, the Soviet leadership revived the idea of European collective security but with the aim of seeking a Cold War détente rather than the dissolution of the Cold War system. Not until the Gorbachev era did the Soviets return to the more radical perspective of ending the Cold War and creating an all-embracing system of European collective security.

Notes

1. On the communist peace movement see M.D. Shulman. 1963. *Stalin's Foreign Policy Reappraised*, Cambridge, MA: Harvard University Press. Also L.S. Wittner. 1993. *One World or None: A History of the World Nuclear Disarmament Movement Through 1953*, Stanford, CA: Stanford University Press, 175–180; G. Wernicke. 1998. 'The Communist-Led World Peace Council and the Western Peace Movements', *Peace & Change*, 23(3), 265–311; and T. Johnston. 2008. 'Peace or Pacifism? The Soviet "Struggle for Peace in All the World", 1948–1954', *Soviet and East European Review*, 86(7), 259–282.
2. See the files on the peace movement in the Molotov fond in Rossiiskii Gosudarstvennyi Arkhiv Sotsial'no-Politicheskoi Istorii (hereafter: RGASPI) F.82, Op.2, Dd.1396–1403.
3. Detailed statistics on the three signature campaigns may be found in RGASPI, F.82, Op.2, D.1402.
4. *Vneshnaya Politika Sovetskogo Souza: 1949 god*, Moscow: Gospolitizdat, 1953, 441ff.
5. RGASPI, F.82, Op.2, D.1397, Ll.27–29, 51–52, 72–74, 115–116, 147–148, 158–159, 190–192.
6. V. Pechatnov. 1999. 'The Allies Are Pressing on You to Break Your Will...', Cold War International History Project, Working Paper 26.
7. Ibid., 18.

8. V.M. Molotov. 1949. *Problems of Foreign Policy: Speeches and Statements, 1945–1948*, Moscow: Foreign Languages Publishing House, 55–69.
9. The Soviet documents on the Moscow CFM may be found in G.P. Kynin and J. Laufer (eds). 2003. *SSSR i Germanskii Vopros*, vol.3, Moscow: Mezhdunarodnye Otnosheniya.
10. Molotov, *Problems of Foreign Policy*, 343–456, 503–555.
11. RGASPI, F.82, Op.2, D.1164, Ll.15–86; *Sovetsko-Amerikanskie Otnosheniya, 1949–1952*, Moscow: Materik 2006, doc.14.
12. The stenograms of the Prague conference may be found in RGASPI, F.82, Op.2, D.1335, Ll.57–96.
13. *Sovetsko-Amerikanskie Otnosheniya, 1949–1952*, doc.109.
14. RGASPI, F.82, Op.2, D.1171, Ll.104–106.
15. *Istochnik*, no. 3, 2003, 122, 125.
16. RGASPI, F.82, Op.2, D.1398, Ll.78–79; D.1403, Ll.62–63, 66–67.
17. Rossiiskii Gosudarstvennyi Arkhiv Noveishei Istorii (hereafter: RGANI), F.5, Op.30, D.33, Ll.64–71.
18. For some examples of the new discourse dating from early 1954, see the following *Izvestiya* articles: 'Za Edinuu, Mirolubivuu Germaniu za Mir v Evrope', 12 Feb. 1954; 'Berlinskoe Soveshchanie Chetyrekh Derzhav', 20 Feb. 1954; 'Zarubezhnye Otkliki na Notu Sovetskogo Pravitel'stva Pravitel'stvam Frantsii, Veliokobritanii, i SShA ot 31 Marta', 7 Apr. 1954; 'Angliiskaya Obshchestvennoct' Vystupaet za Dal'neishuu Razryadu Mezhdunarodnoi Napryazhennosti', 25 Apr. 1954.
19. A more detailed review of the Soviet campaign for European collective security may be found in G. Roberts. 2008. 'A Chance for Peace? The Soviet Campaign to End the Cold War, 1953–1955', Cold War International History Project, Working Paper 57.
20. Arkhiv Vneshnei Politiki Rossiiskoi Federatsii (hereafter: AVPRF) F.082, Op.42, Pap.287, D.35, Ll.34–47.
21. Ibid., Ll.56–59.
22. 'Note of the Soviet Government … 31 March 1954' Supplement to *New Times*, no. 14, 3 Apr. 1954.
23. See, for example, I. Koblyakov, 'Otnoshenie v Zapadnoi Germanii k Itogam Berlinskogo Soveshchaniya' (report dated 16 June 1954), AVPRF, F.082, Op.42, Pap.287, D.35, Ll.172–193 and B. Vronsky, 'Zhiznnost' Idei Sozdaniya Kollektivnoi Bezopasnosti v Evrope', *Izvestiya*, 25 May 1954.
24. 'Direktivy dlya Delegatsii SSSR na Soveshchanii Glav Pravitel'stv Chetyrekh Derzhav v Zheneve', AVPRF F.06, Op.14, Pap.3, D.43, Ll.120–156.
25. 'Ob Itogakh Vsemirnoi Assamblei Mira (22–29 Iunya 1955g. Khel'sinki)', RGANI, F.5, Op.20, D.356, Ll.146–153.
26. Eisenhower Papers, A. Whitman File, International Meeting Series, Box 2, Geneva Conference 1955 File (3) & (4).
27. 'Direktivy Dlya Delegatsii SSSR na Soveshchanii Ministrov Inostrannykh Del Chetyrekh Derzhav v Zheneve', AVPRF, F.06, Op.14, Pap.3, D.46, Ll..73–108.
28. *Department of State Bulletin*, 14 Nov. 1955, 780–781.
29. A.A. Fursenko (ed). 2004. *Prezidium TsK KPSS, 1954–1964: Chernovye Protokol'nye Zapisi Zasedanii Stenogrammy*, Moscow: Rosspen, 58–60 and A.A. Fursenko (ed). 2004a. *Prezidium TsK KPSS, 1954–1964: Postanovleniya, 1954–1958*, Moscow: Rosspen, 104–107.
30. N.I. Yegorova. 2003. 'Evropeiskaya Bezopasnost', 1954–1955gg: Poiski Novykh Podkhodov', in N.I. Yegorova and A.O. Chubar'yan (eds), *Kholodnaya Voina, 1945–1963gg: Istoricheskaya Retrospectiva*, Moscow: Olma-Press, 480.
31. V. Molotov. 1993. *Molotov Remembers: Inside Kremlin Politics*, Chicago: Ivan R. Dee, 75.

Chapter 4

STALIN'S DEATH AND ANGLO-AMERICAN VISIONS OF ENDING THE COLD WAR, 1953

Jaclyn Stanke

Now that the Cold War is over, historians have questioned whether there were missed opportunities to bring it to an earlier conclusion, Joseph Stalin's death in 1953 being one such moment. At the time several American and British government officials believed his passing provided an opening to either end the Cold War or bring about some kind of reversal in its course. In fact, three visions were articulated to this effect in 1953. All depicted *what* an end to the Cold War would look like as well as *when* and *how* it could be brought about, but they diverged, sometimes drastically, on means and timing. The first envisaged a complete destruction of the Soviet system. The second saw some kind of transformation as possible within it. And the last pictured a possible East-West détente. An examination of these visions may not produce a definitive answer as to whether there was a missed opportunity in 1953 – indeed, so many variables, including strong and stable Western institutions like NATO and the European Community, which helped make the 1970s era of détente possible, were either not yet present or still in their formative stages – but does raise questions as to whether anyone at the time was perceptive in forecasting the eventual character and pace of the Cold War's conclusion nearly forty years later.

The Psychological Warriors: Dissolution of the Soviet Union

Following Stalin's death, the first vision to emerge was that of the psychological warriors within the new Eisenhower administration, most notably C.D. Jackson, the special assistant for psychological warfare, Walt Rostow, head of the Soviet Vulnerabilities Project at the Massachusetts Institute for Technology (MIT), and the members of the Psychological Strategy Board (PSB). Collectively, their vision of an end to the Cold War meant the dissolution of the Soviet Union and its control over Eastern Europe. They argued that Stalin's death presented a unique opportunity to subvert the Soviet system by unleashing a power struggle amongst his successors (or enhancing the power struggle they believed was already going on). Unless the administration immediately executed a comprehensive psychological warfare programme to sow seeds of disorder within the Soviet Union and bring the Soviet system down, the moment to achieve complete victory in the Cold War would be lost.

Prior to the event, the PSB had been developing a psychological warfare strategy to exploit Stalin's passing in the Soviet Union and Eastern bloc countries.[1] Likewise, Rostow's Vulnerabilities group was studying ways to weaken the Soviet system.[2] Working independently, both came to the same conclusion: Stalin's death could cause a split among the inner circle as well as ignite dissatisfactions among various groups in the Soviet system, providing a prime moment to destabilize the system.

When Stalin died, the moment to initiate such measures came. Perceiving dismay, confusion and fear emanating from the Kremlin, Jackson argued, 'Our task ... is to perpetuate the confusion as long as possible, and to stave off as long as possible any new crystallization' of Soviet power. If done properly, the first steps would lead to further opportunities to advance the eventual disintegration of the Soviet empire.[3] He worked with Rostow on what became the opening gun of their psychological warfare campaign: a presidential speech offering four-power talks. Real negotiations were not the point. Rather they hoped to provide Stalin's successors with issues upon which they might divide, revealing the conflicts believed existent among them. An offer of talks made it seem as if the intended audience was Stalin's successors, but in fact it was the peoples of the Soviet Union and Eastern bloc nations.[4]

Jackson directed George Morgan, acting director of the PSB, to develop the follow-up, especially the psychological component 'for the exploitation of Stalin's death and the transfer of power to new hands' to help make 'real progress toward our national objectives', which included a retrenchment of Soviet power and influence in the bloc countries, Communist China and world affairs and a fundamental change in the Soviet system, as reflected in the Soviet Union's conduct on the international scene. The draft presumed a presidential address as the initial major move in the campaign. Despite pronouncements to seek negotiations, make adjustments and settle outstanding issues, the PSB then based the remainder of the plan upon a power struggle erupting in the Soviet Union. Thus, now was the time to promote and exacerbate fissures within the new Soviet leadership and between different interest groups and nationalities in the Soviet Union. Attempts to divide the Soviet Union from Communist China and the Eastern European satellites should also be made. For nearly fifteen pages the plan outlined ways to disrupt the Soviet system through both covert and overt means. It was hoped the campaign would culminate with the communist system breaking out in internal conflict, resulting in the demise of the Soviet system.[5]

Jackson presented his idea to Eisenhower a week after Stalin's passing. He said the presidential address 'was to be considered both as a dramatic psychological move and also as a serious policy proposal not to be dismissed as merely a propaganda effort'. Though he spoke of inducing liberalizing changes in the Soviet Union, he also stated the United States could achieve a propaganda victory leading to an end of the Soviet system if properly carried out. Regardless of whether the Soviet Union accepted or rejected the offer of talks, the United States would win. If the Soviets accepted, which he doubted, the United States could press its case on issues while the Soviets were unprepared. If they rejected it, the blame for the continuation of the Cold War would rest with the Soviets. He stressed that the speech must be made soon, before a major meeting of Soviet and satellite leaders took place, and added, 'The follow-up would have to be swift, sure and coordinated.'[6]

Eisenhower supported the idea of a presidential address (but rejected Jackson's proposal to offer four-power talks). Over the next month, work took place on what eventually became his 'Chance for Peace' address.[7] Because Eisenhower went ahead with it, some have argued he sided with the psychological warriors in his administration, viewing Stalin's death as a moment to be exploited for Cold War purposes. There is some merit to viewing the speech in this light; however, as will be seen, Eisenhower's response to Stalin's death was riddled with conflicting impulses, and he did not go through with his speech solely for propaganda purposes. More importantly, it was not the speech Jackson had envisaged.

Given the change in content, audience and most importantly timing, the speech was not the opening gun in a concerted psychological campaign to end the Cold War. Jackson complained about the tone the speech had taken on and remained unconvinced the Soviets would be compelled to give up their global ambitions by 'genial, bourgeois talk about schools and hospitals for the ignorant and sick'.[8] He was most upset by his inability to convince the president to go forward in the immediate aftermath of Stalin's death. By the time the speech was given, over a month had passed and Stalin's successors had completed a rather smooth transition and launched their own peace offensive. In his view, an opportunity to end the Cold War by sowing the seeds of the Soviet Union's destruction had been missed.[9]

Churchill and Eisenhower: Transforming the Soviet Union

The second vision following Stalin's death bore some similarity to the first in that it also foresaw major change in the Soviet system. In particular, the Soviet Union and its satellites could somehow be reformed, becoming 'normal states' in a liberal world order. This vision foresaw an end to the Cold War and a divided world, but over a longer period of time. British Prime Minister Winston Churchill and Eisenhower subscribed to this outlook but differed on how to achieve it.

Eisenhower's previously mentioned speech was neither a bid for peace nor a simple propaganda ploy, but rather a bit of both as he sought to transform the Soviet system. Eisenhower's world view did not preclude Soviet entrance into the liberal internationalist order. According to Ira Chernus, Eisenhower held an Augustinian conception of the world in which the City of Man was obligated to try to create the perfect community and work towards the ultimate peace to come in the City of God. Hence, Eisenhower drew on Wilsonian thought to work towards the alleviation of the eternal problems of chaos and instability that nonetheless precluded the permanent achievement of peace on this earth.[10]

With respect to overcoming the Cold War, Eisenhower's blending of Wilsonian ideals within an Augustinian framework meant, to some extent, the conversion of souls such that the Soviet system and those living under it could and should undergo a transformation, allowing entrance into the international system. As for the possibility of it happening, Eisenhower once said of communism that 'the tyranny and threat represented in the announced and implacable antagonism to our form of government and society *will not always be with us*'.[11] Furthermore, he equated communism with slavery. Freeing those enslaved and uplifting them was necessary, a correlation in line with Chernus's contention that for Eisenhower the attainment of a just and lasting peace rested on the moral condition of people. Despite the current 'enslaved' status of those behind the Iron Curtain, Eisenhower hoped for a change in their social condition, remarking: 'the history of mankind proves that all systems of slavery sooner or later are destroyed, usually from internal convulsion'.[12] Changing their social condition, then, would transform their moral condition. Eisenhower believed this because he viewed the Russian people as separate from the Soviet government – a significant conceptual legacy of the Wilson era, according to David Foglesong.[13]

Eisenhower's perception of an affinity between Americans and Russians was neither unique to him nor to the era in which he lived. Foglesong documents a tradition of Americans believing that Russians shared their yearning for freedom, but oppressive systems held back their true and natural character. Given that, nineteenth-century missionaries wished to rescue Russians from Orthodoxy and tsarist despotism, while twentieth-century Americans wanted to free them from godless communism. The desire to transform the Russian people was not just a function of the Cold War, but rather 'part of a century-long American drive to penetrate, open and reshape Russia'.[14] Eisenhower, then, fitted this mould.

Foglesong further notes that many Cold Warriors had 'the confidence that American material abundance would prove irresistibly attractive to any Russian exposed to its charms'.[15] Indeed, the economic approach seemed to motivate Eisenhower in 1953. In his inaugural address, he wanted to include something to the effect that 'everybody can help in productivity'. Recognizing it was 'one of the factors of peace because it relieves pressures in the world that are favorable to Communism', he continued, 'We must point out something that is very important and where every man feels he can do a part. That is the reason for the preacher and the teacher and the mother in the home, but workmen can help produce something more to allay this starvation and distress in the world'. Additionally, productivity did not mean 'sweating the boys more', but rather, 'when a fellow is working at his maximum capacity and efficiency he is doing something not just for his pocketbook or the profit of the country, but the world'. Overall, Eisenhower felt 'everybody who is contributing something to satisfy the basic human needs in this great world is doing something to promote peace'.[16] Therefore, he tended to advocate the improvement of people's lives by way of economic betterment from the savings currently devoted to defence.

It was this impulse that lay behind his 'Chance for Peace' address, with its emphasis on the costs of the Cold War, the potential improvement to lives and standards of living worldwide, and his proposal for a World Aid Fund. The problem was he did not follow the speech up with any measures to obtain these ends. Moreover, while he expressed his desire for peace with this speech, he also waged Cold War in his eventual endorsement of the PSB plan. Worse yet, by doing both (and rather half-heartedly at that) instead of one or the other, he failed to bring about an end to the Cold War.[17]

Churchill also believed the Soviet Union could be transformed, and he shared Eisenhower's view that an overall betterment in people's lives and standards of living were the marks of a lasting peace. He once said, 'We have had a leisured class. It has vanished. Now we must think of the leisured masses. Why not? It isn't impossible. When there is no longer a risk of war a lot of money will be set free, it will be available to provide leisure for the people'.[18] Indeed, he believed science 'could use its marvels for improving the lot of man' so 'the leisured classes of his youth might give way to the leisured masses of tomorrow'.[19] This vision included the Soviet bloc, recognizing that winding down the arms race would allow the money 'now spent on armaments to provide better conditions for the Russian people'.[20] Moreover, trade and personal contacts could open up the Soviet system. He once commented, 'Russia fears our friendship more than our enmity', meaning the Soviets were well aware that exposure to Western products, people, and values could undermine the system or force a fundamental change to accommodate people's desires.[21] Churchill also believed tyrannies could not last. The human impulse for freedom would eventually assert itself, bringing liberty for those behind the Iron Curtain. As he told his private secretary, 'if I lived my normal span I should assuredly see Eastern Europe free of Communism'.[22]

Churchill's conception of peace and ending the Cold War was grounded in European liberalism and a somewhat Whiggish view of history in which liberty's advance was inevitable. He relied on realpolitik to achieve these ends and was willing to engage in old-school diplomacy where bargaining, compromise, spheres of influence and a balance of power were acceptable. This does not mean Churchill practiced amoral diplomacy. Rather, Robert Kaufman suggests, he based his diplomacy on principled internationalism, blending ideals with national self-interest. Churchill found totalitarian regimes, whether fascist or communist, inherently evil for they deprived people of freedom. Yet, as John Young notes, he was willing to tolerate spheres of influence by authoritarian regimes in the short term. The key to understanding this seemingly contradictory position, Kaufman suggests, is that Churchill 'recognized ... that absolute morality was the standard against which to measure the often significant degrees of difference among relative moral and geopolitical evils' and 'evaluated moral choice in international politics not just by its intentions, but by its consequences'.[23] Thus, it was better to achieve an imperfect détente than continue a spiralling arms race and life lived in perpetual fear.

Churchill expected the Cold War would end over time, but simply waiting for the tyrannical rule of communism to disintegrate was unacceptable when one could advance the process. Young notes that Churchill believed the way to do this was to reduce Cold War tensions and establish some kind of modus vivendi with the Soviets. Then the West could open up the Soviet system and bring about a transformative change by trade, personal contacts and the achievements of science.[24] First, securing some kind of Cold War détente was required, and that is what Churchill sought after Stalin's death. Because his views were less conflicted than Eisenhower's, the prime minister was able to act on them more consistently and coherently than the American president.

Churchill and the State Department: The Détente Option

The final vision engendered by Stalin's death entailed a lessening of international tensions through some kind of détente, a position put forth by senior members of the U.S. State Department and Churchill. While détente was the means to a larger end for the prime minister, for Charles Bohlen, ambassador-designate to the USSR, and Paul Nitze, the outgoing director of the Policy Planning Staff, it seemed a way to resolve outstanding issues in the Cold War and mitigate its worst features, but not necessarily end it.

Following Stalin's death, Churchill said he was not looking for 'world peace but world easement'.[25] In his opinion, the best way to start was a summit meeting in order to make contact, establish relations and build trust and understanding for later negotiations. The complications Churchill's summit proposal caused for Western plans for German rearmament, and therefore the near-unanimous Foreign Office and Allied opposition it encountered, are well documented. For brevity's sake, this essay argues he did not immediately seek a summit after Stalin's death. Rather the smooth transition and peace offensive of Stalin's successors influenced his decision to probe the changes he saw taking place. Dissatisfied with Eisenhower's 'Chance for Peace' address and worried that the French sought four-power talks that would fail in order to make the case for German rearmament, Churchill publically called for a summit in May 1953, ten weeks after the Soviet leader's passing. He thought détente now possible, but also wished to steer Western policy onto a path more likely to achieve it.[26]

Because Churchill never obtained a summit with the Soviet Union, what he proposed to offer is unclear. It seems, though, that the key was taking Soviet security interests into account without sacrificing the West's.[27] Germany was the problem. The Atlantic Alliance needed a rearmed Federal Republic while the Soviets feared a revived and militarized Germany, especially if united. Thus, in May Churchill considered a united and neutralized Germany as part of a settlement with the Soviet Union but quickly set this possibility aside.[28] He then turned his attention to a possible mutual security arrangement, similar to the Locarno Treaty of 1925 (which he first suggested publicly in his speech calling for a summit). The idea contained problems, as his Foreign Office pointed out. Klaus Larres, moreover, finds Churchill's plan unrealistic as the British did not have the power to back any security treaty between the Soviet Union and a reunified Germany. Larres, however, assumes Britain would have been the sole guarantor of any treaty.[29] Churchill recognized that British power alone was not enough to prevent German aggression against the Soviet Union. It required the whole Western alliance, especially the nuclear strength of the United States, noting, as his thoughts on the matter developed, '[l]arger combinations might alter the proportions'. But because Western Europe, including Germany, also had to be protected from Soviet aggression, Churchill believed it vital to move forward on German rearmament. For Churchill, then, the best arrangement seemed to be a unified Germany aligned with the West, followed by some type of Locarno agreement backed up by NATO forces and the nuclear arsenal of the United States.[30]

Had Churchill been able to meet with Eisenhower in mid-1953, it looks likely he could have secured agreement on a summit with the Soviets.[31] However, French delay in arranging a tripartite allied summit and his own stroke in June prevented him from meeting with the president, and perhaps the best opportunity for paving a path towards an early end to the Cold War was lost. His ideas may have proved troublesome and difficult to implement, but at least Churchill had the willingness, the courage and the imagination to devise novel solutions to break the Cold War stalemate.

For members of the U.S. State Department, the death of Stalin, the smooth transition of his successors, and their peace offensive signalled the possibility of détente. However, since the psychological warriors within the Eisenhower administration had already set the tone and terms of the debate, much of what State had to say was but a reaction, and they disagreed with most of the PSB plan. They did not believe a power struggle was taking place behind the Kremlin walls, or that any intrigues would culminate in the fall of the Soviet Union. The department thought the PSB's plan dangerous and counselled against any provocation. Incorporating Bohlen's views into the official departmental position, Walter Bedell Smith warned that 'an aggressive heightening of Cold War pressures, especially in the field of covert propaganda' would only assist the consolidation of the new regime's power. If the new leaders felt under attack, they would most likely harden their position and any future negotiation would be more difficult. Subsequently, the State Department consistently opposed any presidential speech at this time, especially one proposing talks, fearing that the Soviets could use it to play up divisive tendencies within the Atlantic Alliance. Like Churchill, the State Department thus thought it best to wait and see what developed, especially after the peace offensive got into full swing. Any speech could hinder further changes and the settlement of outstanding issues.[32]

Within the American diplomatic community, Bohlen demonstrated perhaps the most imagination. He opposed any presidential address but thought it might later be 'profitable to meet with the Russians on some of the subjects on which we have made no progress in the past – to test out the attitude of the new Soviet rulers if for no other reason'. The United States might want to consider 'some suggestion or proposal of the Western Powers which would present the new leadership with a new diplomatic or political situation not before the Soviet Government during the latter phases of Stalin's life and therefore on which his views would not be known'. He briefly considered the possibility of a four-power foreign ministers' meeting 'for a general discussion without agenda and for a strictly limited period of time to exchange views',[33] to discern whether or not a positive change in Soviet foreign policy existed.

A conversation with the British Foreign Office's Frank Roberts perhaps illuminates why Bohlen advocated a wait-and-see approach. In lessening internal tensions, he believed, the new Soviet leaders had gone much further than was immediately required with the change in government. If such moves continued, the new men in power could possibly impart foreign policy change with a momentum that would be difficult to stop or turn back, even if they later wished to do so. Regarding external matters and the Soviet peace offensive, Bohlen felt everything was building up to a new offer on Germany. He did not exclude a possible Soviet withdrawal from Eastern Germany. He said the satellites posed a particular problem for the new leaders and the West should be prepared to exploit it carefully, but not along the lines wanted by the 'inexperienced psychological warriors in Washington'.[34] Thus to Bohlen, rather than heightening Cold War tensions, it was more beneficial to either improve things or let them be momentarily. In that way, dramatic changes within the Soviet system might take place on their own, drastically altering the Cold War.

Nitze argued that a presidential address could derail the recently resumed talks on the Korean War as well as ruining the chance of a possible détente after a Korean settlement. His Policy Planning Staff found it conceivable that the peace offensive was designed to test the feasibility of dealing with some outstanding issues in the Cold War, but without serious risk to Soviet objectives. A presidential speech might send the wrong signals. The Soviets might conclude that the United States was intransigent and that there was no point in bringing an end to the Korean War or taking measures for the resolution of any other issues either. Like Bohlen, the Policy Planning Staff suggested waiting out the peace offensive in order to determine its true character and significance. A premature speech could put an abrupt end to further Soviet developments and thus any chance for détente.[35]

In the end, State Department officials, like Churchill, were dissatisfied with Eisenhower's decision to go ahead with his speech. In their minds, an opportunity had been lost to see how the changes in the Soviet Union might unfold and whether any chance for détente, or something more, was possible.

Conclusion

Following Stalin's death, competing visions appeared concerning how the Cold War could be brought to a conclusion and what such an end would be like. Despite their emergence, very little was done to secure the ends envisaged for one reason or another (too dangerous, complications for the Western alliance, difficulty in ascertaining the sincerity of the Soviet peace offensive). To some extent, it was easier to stay the course than try to change things. Nevertheless, an examination of the visions put forth allow us to ask if individuals who imagined a possible end to the Cold War in 1953 were on the mark, or at least on track, in their assessments, especially with respect to what it would look like, not to mention when and how it would take place.

The Cold War concluded peaceably, perhaps as a result of a negotiated détente in the late 1980s (and also because the East had been opened up earlier to increased trade and contact with the West). Also, looking at the revolutions of 1989 and the demise of the Soviet Union in 1991, the end of the Cold War did in fact come to mean the end of the Soviet system and the Iron Curtain. Thus, many of the individuals discussed were correct in terms of what the Cold War's conclusion might look like. However, it seems those who pictured it happening over the long term, especially *after* an easing of tensions and an opening of the East to Western trade, loans, peoples and ideas, were better at predicting when the end might come as well as how. Thus, it could be that an opportunity to begin this process and bring an earlier, though not immediate, end to the Cold War was truly lost when Winston Churchill and Charles Bohlen were unable to gain acceptance of their ideas in 1953.

Notes

1. PSB D-24: Program of Psychological Preparation for Stalin's Passing From Power (approved by the Psychological Strategy Board), 1 Nov. 1952, *Foreign Relations of the United States, 1952–1954,* vol. VIII, Washington, DC: Government Printing Office, 1059–60 (hereafter *FRUS* with year and volume).

2. The MIT group submitted its government-commissioned Vulnerability Study to the Truman administration, but for the general public it was published as *The Dynamics of Soviet Society in 1953*, with editions in 1954 and 1967. Version consulted: W. Rostow et al. 1954. *The Dynamics of Soviet Society*, New York: Mentor Books, esp. 168–182 and 239–246. Also see Condensation of CENIS Study, The Problem of Succession, 11 Feb. 1953, White House Office, National Security Council Staff Papers, 1953–1961, Psychological Strategy Board (PSB) Central Files, box 8, folder 'PSB 000.1 USSR (File #1) (2)' (hereafter WHO/NSC/PSB with box and folder), Dwight D. Eisenhower Library, Abilene, Kansas (hereafter DDEL), which was submitted to the PSB.

3. Jackson to Cutler, 4 Mar. 1953, C.D. Jackson Papers, box 37, folder 'Time Inc. File—General Robert Cutler' (hereafter CDJP with box and folder), DDEL.

4. For information and early development of the speech: Rostow to Jackson, 4 Mar. 1953, and 'Annex 4' of Notes on the Origin of the President's Speech of 16 Apr. 1953, both from CDJP, box 85, 'Time Inc. Files—State of Union—Jan. 1953 (Evolution) (2)'; Appendix A: The March 6, 1953, Draft of the Proposed 'Message' and Related Documents in W. Rostow. 1982. *Europe After Stalin: Eisenhower's Three Decisions of March 11, 1953*, Austin: University of Texas Press, 84–94; and Notes on the Origin of the President's Speech of April 16, 1953 (Rostow paper), 11 May 1953, *FRUS, 1952–1954*, VIII: 1176–1179. Also see two similar drafts by Rostow of 'A Message to the Soviet Government and the Russian Peoples' undated [6 Mar. 1953], CDJP, box 85, 'Time Inc. File—Stalin's Death Speech Text Comments—Full Evolution)'; 'Supporting Thinking for Message to Soviet Government and Russian Peoples', undated [6 Mar. 1953], WHO/NSC/PSB, box 9, 'PSB 000.1 USSR (File #3) (2)'; Memorandum of Conversation between Jackson, Hughes, Nitze, Bohlen and Ferguson, 7 Mar. 1953, Record Group 59: Records of the State Department, Papers of the Policy Planning Staff, 1947–1953, box 72, folder 'Eisenhower 1953' (hereafter PPS with box and folder), National Archives, College Park, Maryland (hereafter NA); and Jackson to Dulles, 10 Mar. 1953, CDJP, box 85, 'Time Inc. File—Stalin's Death Speech Text and Comments—Full Evolution'.

5. 'Draft Outline: Plan for Psychological Exploitation of Stalin's Death', 9 Mar. 1953, WHO/NSC/PSB, box 8, 'PSB 000.1 USSR (File #2) (1)' and 'PSB 000.1 USSR (File #2) (2)'.

6. Memorandum of Discussion at the 136th Meeting of the National Security Council, 11 Mar. 1953, *FRUS 1952–1954*, VIII, 1117–1125; also see the memorandum Jackson submitted to the NSC: Draft Plan for NSC: Proposed Plan for a Psychological Warfare Offensive, undated, CDJP, box 85, 'Time Inc. File—Stalin's Death Speech Text and Comments—Full Evolution'.

7. The speech is reprinted in *FRUS, 1952–1954*, VIII, 1147–1156.

8. Quoted in E.J. Hughes. 1963. *The Ordeal of Power: A Political Memoir of the Eisenhower Years*, New York: Atheneum, 106–107.

9. Jackson to Eisenhower, 2 Apr. 1953, CDJP, box 41, 'Time Inc. File—Eisenhower, Dwight D. Corr. Through 1956 (2)'.

10. I. Chernus. 1999. 'Eisenhower: Turning Himself Toward Peace', *Peace & Change* 24(1), 62–74.

11. Eisenhower to Stilian, 23 Aug. 1953 in L. Galambos (ed.). 1978. *The Papers of Dwight D. Eisenhower*, vol. XII, Baltimore: Johns Hopkins University Press, 488–489, (hereafter *EP* with volume) (emphasis in the original).

12. Eisenhower to Clement, 9 Jan. 1952, *EP*, XIII, 868.

13. D.S. Foglesong. 1999. 'Roots of "Liberation": American Images of the Future of Russia in the Early Cold War, 1948–1953', *International History Review* 21(1), 61–62. For examples of Eisenhower seeing Russians as the same: D.D. Eisenhower. 1948. *Crusade in Europe*, Garden City, NY: Doubleday, 470–474; Eisenhower to Thompson, 8 Aug. 1945, *EP*, VI,

257; Eisenhower to Clay, 11 Dec. 1945, *EP*, VII, 619; and Eisenhower to his wife, 24 Nov. 1942 in J.S.D. Eisenhower (ed.). 1978. *Letters to Mamie*, Garden City, NY: Doubleday, 65.

14. Foglesong, 'Roots of "Liberation"', 59 and 63–69.

15. Foglesong, 'Roots of "Liberation"', 71.

16. All quotes from R.J. Donovan. 1956. *Eisenhower: The Inside Story*, New York: Harper and Brothers, 3–5.

17. Melvin Leffler has recently argued that Eisenhower was interested in peace but could not overcome his fears; communism posed too many dangers to the American way of life. With so much at stake, he was not willing to take big chances for peace and instead pursued objectives to strengthen the West. See M. Leffler. 2007. *For the Soul of Mankind: The United States, the Soviet Union, and the Cold War*, New York: Hill and Wang, chap. 2.

18. For quote see Lord Moran. 1968. *Winston Churchill, The Struggle for Survival, 1940–1955*, London: Sphere Books, 470–471; also see J.W. Young. 1996. *Winston Churchill's Last Campaign: Britain and the Cold War, 1951–5*, Oxford: Clarendon Press, vi–vii, 9–10, and 21.

19. J. Colville. 1987. *Fringes of Power: Downing Street Diaries, 1939–1955, volume II: October 1941–1955*, London: Sceptre, 344.

20. Moran, *Struggle for Survival*, 451–452.

21. C.L. Sulzberger. 1969. *A Long Row of Candles: Memoirs and Diaries (1934–1954)*, New York: Macmillan, 661.

22. Colville, *Fringes of Power*, 316.

23. R.G. Kaufman. 1992. 'Winston S. Churchill and the Art of Statecraft: The Legacy of Principled Internationalism', *Diplomacy and Statecraft* 3(2), esp. 160–161, 179 and 181; Young, *Churchill's Last Campaign*, esp. 8–10 and 40.

24. Young, *Churchill's Last Campaign*, passim.

25. Moran, *Struggle for Survival*, 432–433.

26. For further explication of this argument, see J. Stanke. 2001. 'Danger and Opportunity: Eisenhower, Churchill, and the Soviet Union after Stalin, 1953', Ph.D. dissertation, Emory University, chap. 4.

27. Churchill's remark that the Soviet Union was 'a riddle wrapped in a mystery inside an enigma' is oft-quoted. Taken alone it suggests the impossibility of understanding Soviet designs, making negotiations and settlements with them futile and naïve. Anders Stephenson reminds us that what Churchill said next is more important. Despite the mysteries of Soviet policy, he asserted: 'But perhaps there is a key. That key is Russian national interests.' See Stephenson's review of G. Gorodetsky's *Grand Delusion* in *Diplomatic History* 25(1), 139ff. (note 5).

28. Strang to Churchill, 30 May 1953, Foreign Office Papers (Foreign Secretary's Papers), file 794 attaching 'A unified, neutralised Germany' (hereafter FO 800 with file), National Archives, Kew, England (hereafter UKNA); Churchill to Strang, 31 May 1953, FO 800/794.

29. Cabinet Conclusions ([19]53), file 26, 29th conclusions, minute 1, 28 Apr. 1953, UKNA. For Foreign Office views, see Strang Memorandum, 27 Apr. 1953, FO 800/699; Dixon Memorandum, 3 May 1953, FO 800/821; Roberts to Reilly, 20 July 1953, Foreign Office Papers (General Files), file 103666 (hereafter FO 371 with file), UKNA; and Roberts's minute, 28 July 1953, FO 371/106526. For Larres's argument: K. Larres. 1995. 'Eisenhower and the First Forty Days after Stalin's Death: The Incompatibility of *Détente* and Political Warfare', *Diplomacy and Statecraft* 6(2), 435 and Larres. 1994. 'Preserving Law and Order: Britain, the United States, and the East German Uprising of 1953', *Twentieth Century British History* 5(3), 336–337.

30. Churchill to Strang, 31 May 1953, FO 800/794; Churchill to Minister of State, 13 June 1953, Premier Papers, file 449, UKNA; Luce/Rome to Dulles no. 84, 7 July 1953, Record

Group 59: Records of the State Department, Decimal Files Series, 641.65/7-753 (hereafter RG 59 with filing information), NA, which reports Dixon clarifying Churchill's Locarno idea for the Italian president. Also see Visit of the German Chancellor to the United Kingdom, May 14–15, 1953: Conversation at No. 10 Downing Street at 12 noon, 15 May 1953, FO 800/794.

31. Points Developed at Conferences at J.F. Dulles' House, 7 June 1953, Papers of John Foster Dulles (hereafter JFDP), Subject Series, box 1, folder 'Bermuda Conference—FMs Meeting', DDEL; Bermuda Conference: Four Power Meeting, 18 June 1953, C.D. Jackson Records, box 2, folder 'Bermuda Conference Briefing Book (2)', DDEL; and Memorandum of Discussion at the 150th Meeting of the NSC, 18 June 1953, *FRUS, 1952–1954*, VII, 1586–1590.

32. Expressed opposition to the speech and the PSB plan are found in numerous documents. For Bohlen's views: Department of State Intelligence Estimate No. 50, Implications of Stalin's Collapse, 4 Mar. 1953, *FRUS, 1952–1954*, VIII, 1086–1090; Policy Implications of Stalin's Death, 10 Mar. 1953, *FRUS, 1952–1954*, VIII, 1111; Bohlen Memorandum, 7 Mar. 1953, *FRUS, 1952–1954*, VIII, 1100–1102; Schwartz to MacArthur, 6 Mar. 1953, RG 59, 761.00/3-653, Memorandum of Conversation between Jackson, Hughes, Nitze, Bohlen, and Ferguson, 7 Mar. 1953, PPS, box 72, 'Eisenhower 1953'; and Memorandum by Bohlen, 1 Apr. 1953, JFDP, Draft Presidential Correspondence and Speech Series (hereafter DPCSS), box 1, folder 'Pres. Speech April 1953 (1)'. For Nitze's views: Memorandum of Conversation between Jackson, Hughes, Nitze, Bohlen, and Ferguson, 7 Mar. 1953, PPS, box 72, 'Eisenhower'; Policy Planning Staff Meeting Notes, 9 Mar. 1953, PPS, box 78, 'S/P Mtg. Notes 1953'; Nitze Memorandum to the Secretary of State, 10 Mar. 1953, *FRUS, 1952–1954*, VIII, 1107–1108. Also see P. Nitze. 1989. *From Hiroshima to Glasnost: At the Center of Decision*, New York: Grove Weidenfeld, 101–116.

33. Bohlen Memorandum, 7 Mar. 1953, *FRUS, 1952–1954*, VIII, 1101–1102. Bohlen soon reconsidered this position, and in the policy estimate written for the NSC he simply stated the department was urgently examining possibilities for the West to confront the Soviets with a new situation. He said nothing about a four-power meeting, something he later regretted. See Policy Implications of Stalin's Death, 10 Mar. 1953, *FRUS, 1952–1954*, VIII, 1111 and his memoirs: C. Bohlen. 1973. *Witness to History, 1929–1969*, New York: Norton, 371.

34. Roberts to Strang, 9 Apr. 1953, FO 371/106532.

35. Memorandum of Conversation between Jackson, Hughes, Nitze, Bohlen, and Ferguson, 7 Mar. 1953, PPS, box 72, 'Eisenhower'; Policy Planning Staff Meeting Notes, 9 Mar. 1953, PPS, box 78, 'S/P Mtg. Notes 1953'; Nitze Memorandum to the Secretary of State, 10 Mar. 1953, *FRUS, 1952–1954*, VIII, 1107–1108; Policy Planning Staff Special Meeting notes, 2 Apr. 1953, PPS, box 78, 'S/P Mtg. Notes 1953'; and Nitze to Dulles, 2 Apr. 1953, JFDP, DPCSS, box 1, 'Pres. Speech April 1953 (1)'.

Chapter 5

Soviet Intellectuals after Stalin's Death and Their Visions of the Cold War's End

Vladislav Zubok

There was no public discussion in Soviet society in the 1950s and 1960s on the strategies and possible outcomes of the Cold War. Such a discussion was precluded by the nature of the Soviet regime, and also by its ideology, which 'scientifically' predicted the inevitability of the triumph of social-ism (and the Soviet Union) over capitalism. The Soviet leadership banned discussion of nuclear war. Nikita Khrushchev boasted about an inevitable triumph of the Soviet way of life over American capitalism while threaten-ing the West with Soviet nuclear missiles.[1] Surprisingly, beneath the col-lective denial of nuclear threat, some Soviet intellectuals became engaged rather early in a new and profound inquiry. How could the 'inevitable' transition from capitalism to communism be achieved without a suicidal nuclear war? Could Khrushchev's policies trigger a catastrophe? If so, what could be done to prevent it? From these new questions emerged fresh visions on international security and possible outcomes of the East-West conflict.

Botvinnik: A Peaceful Socialist Revolution as a Solution

The first years after Stalin's death became the time of the most danger-ous escalation of nuclear programmes in the United States and the Soviet Union, culminating in the detonation of the Soviet hydrogen bomb in Au-gust 1953 and especially in American thermonuclear tests in February–March 1954. In the United States nuclear physicists debated the dire con-

---

sequences of the invention of thermonuclear weapons. The British and French leaders, and President Dwight Eisenhower and his Secretary of State John Foster Dulles, privately realized that a thermonuclear war was unacceptable, as it would lead to the elimination of human civilization. To quell public disquiet, Eisenhower in December 1953 came up with the 'Atoms for Peace' programme. After the crew of the Japanese fishing boat *Lucky Dragon* fell victim to radioactive fallout from a U.S. test, American authorities had to give a public explanation. At a press conference on 10 March 1954, Eisenhower and Lewis Strauss, head of the Atomic Energy Commission, admitted that a thermonuclear war could endanger civilization. Still, the U.S. leadership saw no substitute for nuclear deterrence of the communist bloc and even encouraged the nuclearization of NATO.

On 1 April 1954, a group of Soviet nuclear physicists sent a draft article, 'The Dangers of Atomic War and President Eisenhower's Proposal', to three Soviet leaders: Malenkov, Khrushchev, and Molotov. Among the authors were Igor Kurchatov, scientific leader of the Soviet nuclear project, and Vyacheslav Malyshev, the head of the Soviet atomic ministry.[2] 'Modern atomic practice, based on the utilization of thermonuclear reaction', they wrote, 'allows increasing the explosive energy contained in a bomb practically to an unlimited extent. Defence against such a weapon is practically impossible [so] it is clear that the use of atomic weapons on a mass scale will lead to the devastation of the warring countries. One cannot help admitting that a huge threat, which could obliterate all life on Earth, hangs over mankind.' The authors suggested exposing the duplicity of Eisenhower's Atoms for Peace programme and publicizing the dangers of thermonuclear war.[3]

The Soviet ideological dogma about war and peace had no room for these revelations. The cornerstone of this dogma was Lenin's theory of imperialism, predicting the inevitability of wars produced by the struggle between capitalist great powers. Lenin posited in 1916 that contemporary imperialism was the product of global capitalism in its monopolistic phase. A small group of monopolists, industrialists, bankers and their political agents at the head of modern states exploited the resources of colonies and the non-Western world while using their extraordinary profits to bribe petty bourgeoisie and parts of the working class in Western countries. Lenin's 'scientific' prediction became a foundation for Stalin's propaganda of permanent militarization and war preparedness. While imperialism existed, the theory went, world wars were inevitable. The only solution was the world's revolutionary transition from capitalism to socialism.

In 1953–55 the Kremlin leaders disagreed on how adapt the Leninist theory to the nuclear age. Georgy Malenkov apparently perceived an opportunity to score a propaganda victory over the United States and appeal to the anti-nuclear movement in the West. On 12 March 1954, he said in a public speech that the continuation of the Cold War between the USSR and the United States would lead to hostilities, 'which with modern weapons would mean the end of world civilization'.[4] Molotov and Khrushchev came to an opposite conclusion: admitting the power of thermonuclear weapons at the time, when the USSR still did not have them, would indicate weakness. They claimed that Malenkov's thesis would send the wrong signal to the enemy and would demoralize the Soviet people. For Molotov, another war would bring a 'final victory' over 'the aggressive forces of imperialism'. Malenkov recanted and began to speak according to the dogma.[5] Only in February 1956, at the twentieth Party Congress, did the Kremlin carefully adopt some revisions to the Leninist doctrine of war and peace. The updated dogma now said that the growth of the socialist camp and the new strength of progressive forces around the world created a new situation in which a world war was no longer inevitable. The party avoided addressing the apocalyptic scenario of nuclear war, and Soviet military doctrine remained firmly based on the idea of 'final victory'.

On 29 May 1954, the world chess champion Mikhail Botvinnik sent a private memorandum to Party Secretary P.N. Pospelov with the title 'Is Socialist Revolution in the West Possible without a Third World War?' Botvinnik (1911–95) was born into a Russian-Jewish family in Finland, then part of the Russian empire. His family welcomed the Russian Revolution as an emancipation from oppression and discrimination for all people, including Jews. Botvinnik once said: 'My situation is "complicated": I am Jewish by blood, Russian by culture, and Soviet by upbringing.'[6] He combined prodigious achievements in chess with genuine communist idealism. Soviet Ambassador to Great Britain Ivan Maisky, after talking with Botvinnik before a world championship in London in January 1935, wrote in his diary: 'He is modest, profound, and with a gift of observation. During two days in London he noticed more than some of our comrades at the embassy. He is a member of the Komsomol [the League of Communist Youth].'[7] Later Botvinnik joined the Communist Party, not for his career's sake but out of deep conviction. He belonged to the ranks of intellectuals who believed in Lenin's genius and adhered to a concept of world revolution, even when Stalin quietly abandoned it.

Botvinnik began his memo with quotations from Lenin and Stalin. 'Up to now socialist revolutions followed every world war. After World War One the Great October socialist revolution occurred in Russia', he wrote, adding, 'The same occurred after the Second World War in 1945–49, in China, Poland, Rumania, Bulgaria, Czechoslovakia, Albania, East Germany.' He concluded, 'The Third World War cannot help leading to the complete crash of imperialism, i.e. socialist revolution in the West.' Then he tackled the main paradox: there was no doubt, wrote Botvinnik in his memo, that the masters of monopoly-state capitalism would not hesitate 'to make use of the atomic bomb' to unleash a nuclear war if their way of life and profits were endangered by the socialist revolution. How, then, could the socialist transformation of the world be carried out without triggering a war of annihilation?[8]

Botvinnik offered a solution. The Soviet leadership and Western communists, he wrote, should isolate the monopolist bourgeoisie in Western countries by appealing to the masses of petty owners, specifically by guaranteeing to them their material immunity in case of a socialist transformation. This concession to the small property-owners would bring them into a broader popular coalition supporting socialist transformation. But this was not enough, Botvinnik continued, to prevent a danger of nuclear war. The communist must offer a concession to the top monopolist bourgeoisie as well, guaranteeing them between a quarter and an eighth of their wealth. As a convinced revolutionary, Botvinnik understood that his suggestion was heretical. Still, he concluded: 'If such a compromise can liberate humanity from an atomic war and bring the victory of socialism (without war), it should not be rejected.'[9] Botvinnik suggested that this compromise should be included into the Party Programme of the CPSU and the programmes of Western communist parties.[10]

Pospelov, the recipient of the letter, was a graduate of the University of Red Professors in 1930 and, in contrast to many classmates who were victims of the great terror, he had made his career by 'unmasking' ideological deviations. In his letter to the Politburo and Secretariat, he claimed that Botvinnik 'develops liberal-pacifist, anti-Marxist conception of a "compromise" with imperialists with the objective of avoiding a third world war.' He suggested a personal interview to warn Botvinnik of the 'anti-Marxist' character of his memo. If the chess player refused to recant, he should be expelled from the party.[11] Yet the party leaders disagreed among themselves at this point over the security doctrine. Botvinnik, looking for support, sent another copy of his memo to Malenkov. As a result, Botvinnik stayed in the party and even had the cheek in December 1954 to write to Pospelov again, stubbornly defending his viewpoint. Botvinnik wrote that he could not hide his doubts from the party. 'I prefer to be wrong again rather than be guilty of insincerity.' He was offended by Pospelov comparing his views to those of the anti-nuclear British Labourist left: 'I stand for revolution, for the destruction of state machinery, and the Labourists are for reforms. I stand for taking economic and political power from the monopolists, and the Labourists let them keep this power.'

Also, Botvinnik insisted that the communists should develop new ideas to undermine the mass social base of monopoly capitalism. 'If this base grows weaker, the probability of atomic war diminishes.' He then commented that 'in the West the majority of people are sufficiently fed and clothed, educated, and housed, so they do not feel urgent need of socialist revolution.' He then argued that the danger of war, and not oppression, destitution, or overexploitation, had now become the central issue for Western societies, creating 'a national (if not all-human) crisis'. 'It seems to me that today the genuine interests of the mass of people and of the working class point to such a socialist revolution that would occur without an atomic catastrophe.' Botvinnik's memo boiled down to a novel idea: in the nuclear age, all-human (*obschechelovecheskie*) interests should be placed above working-class, proletarian interests. This idea turned the Soviet ideological world view upside down. In his logical (as well as ideological) scheme, a historical compromise to prevent a nuclear war and save humanity became an essential precondition for a global social transformation.

Landau: The Peaceful Liquidation of Soviet System

Soviet nuclear physicist Lev Landau also sent a memo to the party leadership: a request to travel abroad. Landau wanted to defect to the West. Unfortunately for him (and fortunately for historians), his frank views on Soviet realities, shared with a few trusted friends, reached the KGB. Landau (1908–68) was born into a Russian-Jewish family of professionals in the cosmopolitan milieu of Baku. He studied physics in Europe and was a favourite student of Niels Bohr. Like Botvinnik, he became a passionate believer in the Bolshevik vision of a world socialist revolution, but his belief came to an abrupt end in 1938, when he was arrested and imprisoned. With a colleague, Landau had made leaflets that blamed Stalinists for betraying revolutionary principles. Only the appeal of another famous physicist, Peter Kapitsa, to Stalin and Molotov saved Landau's life. He returned to theoretical physics and in 1946 was dragooned into the Soviet atomic project. Soviet militarism and the anti-Semitic campaign of 1949–53 further eroded Landau's communist illusions, and he developed strong doubts about making nuclear weapons for Stalin's regime. But Stalin's death revived Landau's optimism and socialist illusions. He believed that the 'true Leninist' socialist principles would be 'restored'. Typically for Soviet intellectuals of his generation, he drew a distinction between Stalinism and Bolshevism. In 1953–56 he liked to quote from Anton Chekhov: 'Time will come when we shall see diamonds in the sky!' Finally, the Soviet suppression of the Hungarian revolution in November 1956 killed Landau's last hope in the future of the Soviet project, and he escaped from politics to the world of theoretical physics. His lectures and seminars not only were brilliant but also flouted Soviet academic rules and regulations.

He regularly listened to foreign broadcasts and shared what the 'enemy voices' reported with his friends.[12]

The KGB had a thick file on Landau. In a memorandum to the party authorities on 20 December 1957, the secret police concluded that 'during many years he [Landau] had been a person with definitely anti-Soviet views, hostile to all Soviet realities'. According to reports by KGB agents, in 1947 the physicist had complained that he was reduced to the state of a 'scientific slave', and that there was no freedom for scientific creativity in the Soviet Union. The KGB described Landau's students as a group of 'anti-Soviet nationalist scientists of Jewish nationality'. In fact, the KGB materials, if they are taken verbatim, represent Landau as a principled cosmopolitan intellectual, not a Zionist. In 1956 he condemned Israel, along with France and Britain, for the war against Nasser's Egypt. When another Russian-Jewish physicist supported Israel, Landau replied: 'You are supporting imperialism – what awful company you are in! Are you so blinded by nationalism?' Landau's top priority was intellectual and scientific freedom. For him there could be neither 'national' science nor 'nationalist' scientists. In March and October 1956, in a private conversation with his co-author M. Lifshits that was secretly recorded by the KGB, Landau discussed the pros and cons of defecting during a trip abroad. He believed that he could do more for theoretical physics if he worked in the United States.[13]

Landau's views on revolution and social transformation bore the traces of his earlier beliefs but were unmistakably anti-regime. According to agents, he admired the Hungarian revolution. 'Practically the entire Hungarian people rebelled against their oppressors, against the small Hungarian clique and, above all, against our [Soviet] clique.' His admiration for the Hungarian revolution bore traces of his earlier worship of the Russian revolution, a popular rebellion as a tool of historical transformation. At the same time, on 12 November 1956 after the Soviet suppression of the Hungarian revolution, he said, according to the KGB informer, 'Our leaders decided to cover themselves with blood. They are criminals ruling our country.' When a friend of Landau said that this would have been inconceivable under Lenin's rule, Landau responded: 'Lenin was not innocent at all. Remember the suppression of the Kronstadt rebellion [of the anti-Bolshevik sailors in 1921]? It was a dirty story. The [sailors] advanced a democratic agenda and got bullets in return.' Landau abandoned his earlier illusions of 'genuine' Bolshevism. The bureaucratic terrorist regime, he concluded, 'was not an error', but the logical consequence of Leninism. 'This was what [Bolshevik] revolution was about.' He compared the Soviet regime to 'a fascist system'. Still, his earlier socialist ideals did not vanish completely. In another wiretapped conversation he spoke approvingly of the revolution of 1917 'to get rid of the bourgeoisie, to construct socialism'.

In a word, Landau wanted still to believe in socialism yet make this belief compatible with scientific freedom.[14] In the aftermath of the Soviet invasion of Hungary, Landau concluded that the Soviet system could not be reformed: 'it simply cannot change'. The regime was the 'dictatorship of a bureaucratic class. It is not a socialist system, because the means of production are in the possession of bureaucrats, not in the people's possession.' This view was not a break with socialist ideals. In fact, it was similar to the Trotskyite thesis that Stalinism was the rule of a bureaucratic class that degraded and deformed 'socialism' in the Soviet Union. This view became widespread among Soviet writers, scientists and students after Khrushchev's denunciation of Stalin at the twentieth Party Congress and even generated a rare public discussion amongst educated Soviet citizens, triggered by the publication of an anti-bureaucratic novel in the literary journal *Novy Mir*. Yet Landau was one of the few Soviet intellectuals who had the intellectual boldness to follow the thesis about 'bureaucratic degeneration' of socialism to its logical conclusion.

The Hungarian revolution opened Landau's eyes to the possibility of a similar people's rebellion in the Soviet Union. 'This proposition was ridiculous even a year earlier', he acknowledged in January 1957, according to the KGB informant's report. Also, Landau began to dream about a military coup that would topple the party bureaucracy. He said to another scientist on 4 December 1956, 'This is what I believe in: if our system can be liquidated without a war – by revolution or evolution, does not matter – then there will be no war at all. Without fascism, no war can occur.'[15] But could the communist bureaucracy loosen its grip on power without a fight? And could it make use of the nuclear weapons at its disposal? How could such a system exist without provoking, sooner or later, a world war that would become nuclear? 'If our system cannot collapse peacefully', he reflected in a conversation with a colleague (who was apparently a KGB informant), 'then a third world war with all its horrors becomes inevitable'. And he concluded, 'Therefore, the issue of a peaceful liquidation of our system is the vital issue for the future of the entire humanity.'[16] It is quite apparent that in his reflections, Landau, like Botvinnik, remained influenced by Lenin's theory of war and imperialism. He just switched the plus and the minus in Leninist theory: instead of 'monopoly-capitalist' countries of the West, it was the 'fascist' Soviet Union that constituted the source of inevitable world confrontation.

Sakharov: Global Intelligentsia and the 'Escalation of Peace'

In 1962–67, Andrei Sakharov, another Soviet nuclear physicist, began to reflect on the conditions under which a nuclear war could be prevented. His participation in nuclear tests in the atmosphere, his conversations with his colleagues in a secret nuclear design bureau and his growing awareness of the insensitive, flywheel nature of the Soviet military-industrial complex – in particular his confrontations with Khrushchev and the Soviet military over nuclear testing – brought Sakharov to a world view that diverged radically from the Soviet one. In similar fashion to Botvinnik, Sakharov came to regard the Cold War nuclear build-up as a cause of great concern, but also as a stimulus for innovative thinking.

Sakharov (1921–89) had never been either a party loyalist like Botvinnik or a disillusioned idealist like Landau. He was born in Moscow into a family that belonged to the milieu of the old Russian intelligentsia. As a child he was baptized in the Orthodox Church; his godfather, musician Alexander Goldenveizer, was a friend of Leo Tolstoy. Tolstoyan ethical views formed the family's ethos. Sakharov's grandfather came from a family of Orthodox priests and became involved in public campaigns, inspired by Tolstoy and other Russian writers, to abolish capital punishment. A passion for science and his work in scientific labs insulated Sakharov from Soviet ideological storms and reeducation campaigns. He grew up in a Stalinist cultural environment and became Soviet in habits and world view, yet managed to preserve his family's ethical outlook. After 1966, beginning with the trial of the writers Sinyavsky and Daniel, who had been arrested by the KGB for their publications abroad, Sakharov became involved in the budding human rights movement. In contrast to Landau, Sakharov continued to hope for the gradual transformation of the Soviet regime towards social democracy. Until the end of the 1960s he remained 'optimistic and positive regarding Soviet realities and the prospects' and recognized that 'socialism had much to its credit' over capitalism. He used his special connections to Khrushchev, and then Brezhnev, to try to appeal to the Kremlin leaders' common sense and pragmatism. Even in the early 1970s, he commented in his diaries that he still believed in the value of 'some elements of socialism' more than his opponents in the party, the military and the KGB. 'In this sense', Sakharov wrote with a touch of irony about his cynical KGB persecutors, 'I am more a Homo Sovieticus than them.'[17]

Sakharov's search for a vision to overcome the dangerous East-West conflict was inspired by first-hand knowledge of the dreadful nature of nuclear weapons. Yet in search of solutions he reached back not to Leninism but rather to the humanist ideals of the Russian intelligentsia, and blended these ideals with modern technocratic dreams. Sakharov believed in human progress, and for him the only correct path for this progress was through 'scientific-democratic' reforms and gradual changes in politics, economics and culture. Sakharov concluded that the only chance for humanity to avoid a thermonuclear catastrophe was dialogue between the Soviet Union and the West, mutual compromises and change. Like Landau and many others, he believed that the main obstacle to progress in the USSR was 'a special class, a new bureaucratic elite that had seized power, and substituted its own interests for the interests of the people and socialist transformation'.

Sakharov also found a historical force, alternative both to the ruling bureaucracy and violent revolution. He came to believe that the global intelligentsia, scientists and artists of the East and the West could and should play a crucial role in an evolution of the two rival systems, Soviet communism and Western capitalism. The intelligentsia, in the position of advisers to the political leadership and exercising growing influence in the military-industrial complexes, could 'help bring about the escalation of peace'. This intelligentsia, according to Sakharov, would gradually help to transform the existing bureaucratic and military elites, and even eclipse them in influence. In an interview with the journalist Ernst Henri for the influential Soviet weekly *Literaturnaia Gazeta* in 1967, Sakharov expressed approval of the rise of anti-Vietnam protest in the United States. He said, 'When the intelligentsia denies the existing war machinery its active and passive support, when this intelligentsia helps American people understand that the cause of peace is more important than domestic issues, then the war machinery would begin to wane and would eventually come to the grinding halt. The escalation of war would be replaced by the escalation of peace, on the basis of universal exploitation of scientific discoveries.'[18] In other words, the transnational alliance of intellectuals, above all scientists, could bring the Cold War to a gradual termination through détente and reform.

Sakharov's thesis was not his personal discovery. He belonged to the growing transnational movement linking Soviet scientists, above all nuclear physicists, and their Western colleagues. In 1955, Sakharov and many of his colleagues had been very impressed with the Russel-Einstein Manifesto: its signatories spoke not as citizens of nations or adepts of ideologies, but as human beings, concerned about the prospect of the extinction of life on Earth. Sakharov, along with the Soviet physicists' community, read and discussed publications in the journal *Bulletin of the Atomic Scientists* that raised the issue of scientists' public responsibility for the consequences of their discoveries, and propagated the universal interests of humanity in the nuclear age. Evgeny Rabinovich (known in the US as Eugene Rabinowitsch), one of the founding editors of this journal, was a Russian-Jewish émigré from Saint Petersburg who had many friends among Soviet physicists. Also, starting in 1957 a group of Soviet physicists participated in regular meetings with their Western colleagues in the Canadian town of Pugwash, Nova Scotia. Although Sakharov and other 'secret' physicists could not go abroad to participate directly in the Pugwash and other international meetings, these transnational discussions served as a live link connecting them, along with other Soviet scientists, with the intellectual world beyond the Iron Curtain. In their respective positions of influence across the political divide, Sakharov and his colleagues acted as part of the transnational lobby of scientists that helped to bring about the partial test ban treaty of 1963, the anti-ballistic missile treaty of 1972 and other important East-West agreements on the regulation of the nuclear arms race.[19]

In February 1968, Sakharov sat down to summarize and articulate his world view. In April, he finished his essay 'Reflections on Progress, Peaceful Coexistence, and Intellectual Freedom'. He later admitted that he had written it under the direct influence of the Prague Spring, the time of peaceful reforms in Czechoslovakia initiated by the leadership of the Czechoslovak communist party. At that time events in Czechoslovakia seemed to prove Landau wrong: the communist system could, after all, be peacefully reformed, without a revolution, a military coup or the threat of war! The Prague Spring appealed to Sakharov's aversion to violence, especially revolutionary violence. He had already concluded that any political coup or other revolution in the Soviet Union would only throw the society back into violent chaos. The Czech reforms gave him a missing link in his understanding of human evolution, an alternative to the revolutionary violence as the only available 'vehicle' of social transformation. During the 1980s, by now exiled from Moscow because of his opposition to the Soviet invasion of Afghanistan, Sakharov admitted that he had been naïve and overly optimistic in his 1968 pamphlet.[20] In fact, this 'naïveté' and 'optimism' was an important historical and ideological phenomenon: it became the only way of breaking the deadly spell that the Leninist-Stalinist logic of revolution and war had exercised on Soviet intellectuals and the political leadership for many decades.

Soviet Intellectuals and the Cold War's End

How much impact did the reflections of the Soviet intellectuals Botvinnik, Landau and then Sakharov have on the actual outcome of the Cold War on the Soviet side? Aside from the physicists' impact on the East-West talks on nuclear tests and the deployment of new strategic systems, there are no traces of the intellectual visionaries having any direct influence on the decision-making process in the Kremlin. Soviet leaders from Khrushchev to Brezhnev did not seek advice from intellectuals. Sakharov recalls in his memoirs how shocked he was when Marshal Mitrofan Nedelin, the commander of the Soviet missile forces, and then Nikita Khrushchev reminded him crudely that nuclear scientists had no say whatsoever in political matters. Even Mikhail Gorbachev, on the basis of existing evidence, did not think too much of Andrei Sakharov as a political thinker. In 1985–89, he could speak about him in the presence of his Politburo colleagues and advisers with a tinge of dismissal, even contempt.[21]

Yet the historical significance of the 'naïve' visions articulated by Soviet intellectuals and analysed here must not be assessed according to their *direct* impact. Much more important, although more difficult to assess, was their indirect role as the avatars of the erosion of the Soviet black-and-white security thinking. The reflections of the three intellectuals may appear to be naïve, yet they set in motion the train of intellectual imagination among party intellectuals and those who had grown up as true believers in socialist and communist utopia. The threat of nuclear war remained in their focus. A group of 'enlightened' party apparatchiks – party intellectuals who worked as speechwriters and advisers to Leonid Brezhnev and Yuri Andropov – may have held Sakharov's views in contempt, yet they were constantly subjected to the polemics that these views provoked in international media. The rising tension between 'old thinking' based on Leninist-Stalinist tenets and 'new thinking' informed by the realities of nuclear age, the realization that no 'realist' recipes could break the vicious circle of the East-West confrontation sank into these people's minds. Most of them, like Botvinnik, continued to believe in a Soviet, Marxist-Leninist framework, yet this framework no longer prevented them from producing novel, far-reaching scenarios, and they could no longer dismiss their own doubts as Western 'influence' and 'liberal-pacifist views', as Pospelov had tried to do.[22]

During the years of détente, and even more after its collapse in the early 1980s, the 'enlightened' apparatchiks and *institutchiks*, established party advisers, political pundits and ideologists began to work increasingly closely with established scientists, such as the physicists Yevgeny Velikhov, Roald Sagdeev, and others, who had been part of the transnational community of scientists. The leading Kremlin doctor Yevgeny Chazov and other Soviet physicians joined another influential transnational network, International Physicists for the Prevention of Nuclear War (IPPNW). Anti-nuclear pacifism, once castigated by Soviet propaganda, became an 'insider' belief within Kremlin circles. These circles included Anatoly Gromyko, the son of the Soviet foreign minister. Discussions within these networks became an indispensible preparation for the radical revision of Soviet thinking about security.

This revision emerged into the open when Mikhail Gorbachev came to power in 1985. Although Gorbachev and his advisers (perhaps with the exception of Alexander Yakovlev) were not fond of Sakharov's dissident activities, the new general secretary shared Sakharov's concerns about the danger of nuclear war. As a nuclear neophyte, Gorbachev abhorred his new responsibility as commander-in-chief to press the 'nuclear button' in the case of conflict with the United States and NATO. His initial moral repugnance towards nuclear weapons was enhanced by Ronald Reagan's Strategic Defense Initiative and especially by the catastrophe at the Chernobyl nuclear plant in April 1986. Of crucial importance was that Gorbachev, in contrast to his predecessors, was very fond of intellectuals, liked to discuss his views with them and expressed his own thoughts in philosophical-political tracts. As a Soviet communist leader, Gorbachev was the first since Lenin to take ideas with utmost seriousness. During the spring and summer of 1986, Gorbachev's 'new thinking' on nuclear issues rapidly reached some of the same conclusions that Botvinnik and then Sakharov had reached decades earlier.[23]

Especially important in Gorbachev's 'new thinking' was the concept, enunciated by Botvinnik in 1954, of an 'all-human crisis' and the prevalence of the interests of humanity's survival over ideological schemes. Gorbachev's intellectual evolution, when compared to the views of the intellectuals we have explored, followed a similar pattern. Starting from communist idealism, it was nourished by the experience of the Second World War and the resulting abhorrence of war and violence, and adhered to a framework of Leninist theory about war and imperialism. Similar to Botvinnik and Landau, and later Sakharov, Gorbachev and his 'enlightened' advisers came to the conclusion that the nuclear revolution had created a global crisis and 'all-human' interests demanded the end of the political-ideological confrontation.[24] They began to think about the end of the Cold War not as an inevitable replacement of the capitalist 'formation' by the socialist one, but rather as a global reformist project, where the West and the Soviets would cooperate to salvage each other and the rest of humanity from the abyss of nuclear war. In a sense, Gorbachev's ideas of a 'common European home' from 1988–89 were, to an extent, plagiarism of Sakharov's earlier schemes. Of course, Gorbachev was not in a position to offer a historic compromise to Western capitalism such as Botvinnik had suggested earlier. On the contrary, he knew that the Soviet Union desperately needed the products and advice of Western capitalists. And in fact, it was Gorbachev who made virtually all the concessions to Western partners to end the Cold War, facilitating and tolerating the peaceful anti-communist revolutions in Eastern Europe, the collapse of the Berlin Wall, and finally the financial crisis and disintegration of the Soviet Union.

There were, of course, numerous other reasons – domestic and international, economic and political – for the peaceful collapse of communism in Eastern Europe and the end of the Cold War. At the same time, Gorbachev's remarkable acquiescence to these events as historically inevitable is impossible to explain without taking account of his ideological imagination. And the logic of this imagination was in its basic features similar to that which had stimulated the reflections of one chess master and two nuclear physicists years earlier. Marxism-Leninism taught that 'ideas become a material force when they conquer the masses'. The ideas expressed by three extraordinary thinkers in the Soviet Union in 1954–68 never became a mass ideology. On the contrary, those thinkers spotted, each in a different way, a universal and existential problem that did not fit the deterministic logic of Marxist-Leninist ideology and Soviet official views about war and peace. The destruction of civilization as an imagined end of the Cold War clashed with the existing Soviet world view, was a painful reminder of the recent tragedy of the Second World War and stimulated thinking about unorthodox, counterintuitive scenarios. In Botvinnik's example this cognitive discovery led him to conclusions that clashed with his revolutionary convictions and undermined his narrow party loyalties. In the case of Landau, his thinking about the nuclear threat helped him reconcile his repugnance for the Soviet regime with his libertarian and socialist ideals. As for Sakharov, his first-hand experience of nuclear horror led him to the vision of convergence between the two systems on the basis of common efforts by the world intelligentsia.

In the end, the recognition of the universality of nuclear destruction contributed powerfully to the emancipation of Soviet intellectuals, and ultimately of the Kremlin's policymakers, from the lethal spell of Leninism, one of the most powerful and potentially suicidal ideological obsessions of the last century. At the same time, neither Botvinnik nor Sakharov could imagine that the end of the East-West confrontation would involve a Soviet collapse. Even Landau, who had imagined such a scenario, could not conceive that it would occur as an unwitting by-product of the Kremlin leadership's policies. As on countless previous occasions, historical events exceeded even the most daring visions of intellectuals.

Notes

1. See A. Fursenko and T. Naftali. 2006. *Khrushchev's Cold War*. New York: Norton.
2. 'The Danger of Atomic War and President Eisenhower's Proposal', memorandum from Malyshev to Khrushchev, 1 Apr. 1954, Rossiiskii gosudarstvennyi arkhiv noveishei istorii [Russian state archive of contemporary history] (RGANI), Moscow, fond [collection]. 5, opis [series]. 30, delo [file]. 16, list [page]. 38–44.
3. 'The Danger of Atomic War', list 39, 40, 41; also Y. Smirnov and V. Zubok. 1994, 'Moscow and Nuclear Weapons After Stalin's Death', *Cold War International History Project Bulletin*, 4(Fall), 14–15.

4. For Malenkov's speech, see *Pravda*, 13 Mar. 1954.
5. *Pravda*, 27 Apr. 1954.
6. Reference to Botvinnik's memoirs in Elektronnaia evreiskaia biblioteka, http://www.eleven.co.il/article/10719, accessed on 22 Sept. 2009.
7. L.V. Pozdeeva, O.A. Rzheshevsky and Yu. A. Nikiforov (eds). 2006. *Nauchnoie Nasledstvo. Tom 33. Ivan Mikhailovich Maisky. Dnevnik Diplomata. London 1934–1943*, vol. 1, Moscow: Nauka, 69.
8. 'Turnir dlinoi v tri desiatiletiia. TsK KPSS – M.M. Botvinnik', *Istoricheskii arkhiv*, 2(1993), 59.
9. Ibid., 60–62.
10. Ibid., 62–63.
11. Pospelov to the CC CPSU, 19 June 1954, ibid., 64.
12. K. Drobantseva-Landau. 1999. *Akademik Landau. Kak My Zhili*. Moscow: Zakharov; 'Genii Landau. K 100-letiiu so dnia rozhdenia', 2008. *Priroda* 1, especially recollections by S.S. Gershtein, 22–25.
13. 'Spravka KGB SSSR na akademika L.D.Landau', *Istoricheskii arkhiv*, 3 (1993), 153, 154, 155, 156–157.
14. *Istoricheskii arkhiv*, 3(1993), 155, 156–157, 158.
15. Ibid., 159.
16. *Istoricheskii arkhiv*, 3(1993), 159.
17. Houghton Library, Harvard University, Andrei Sakharov Papers (hereafter Sakharov papers), MS Russ 79, box 50, folder S.II.2.5.172.
18. Sakharov papers, MS Russ 79, box 51, folder S.IV.2.1.01.
19. M. Evangelista. 2002. *Unarmed Forces: The Transnational Movement to End the Cold War*, Ithaca, NY: Cornell University Press; M. Spencer. 1995; '"Political" Scientists', *Pugwash Online*, http://www.pugwash.org/reports/pim/pim1.htm (last accessed 15 Feb. 2009); A.E. Rabinovich. 2004; 'Evgeny Rabinovich: "Golos Sovesti Atomnogo Veka"', *Nestor* 4, 306–324.
20. A. Sakharov. 1968. *Reflections on Progress, Peaceful Coexistence, and Intellectual Freedom*, New York: Norton; also A. Sakharov. 1998. *Materialy konferentsii k 30-letiiu raboty A.D. Sakharova "Razmyshleniia o progresse, mirnom sosuschestvovanii i intellektualnoi svobode"*, Moscow: Prava Cheloveka, 15–21, 41–43. See also Sakharov's recollections in the handwritten versions of his memoirs in Sakharov papers, MS Russ 79, box 50, folder S.II. 2.5. 172.
21. A. Sakharov. 1992. *Memoirs*, New York: Vintage; A. Chernyaev, V. Veber and V. Medvedev (eds). 2006. *V Politbiuro TsK KPSS … Po zapisiam Anatolia Cherniaeva, Vadima Medvedeva, Georgiia Shakhnazarova (1985–1991)*, Moscow: Alpina Business Books.
22. See R. English. 2000. *Russia and the Idea of the West: Gorbachev, Intellectuals, and the End of the Cold War*, New York: Columbia University Press; A. Chernyaev. 1995. *Moia zhizn i moe vremia*, Moscow: Mezhdunarodnye Otnosheniia; G. Shakhnazarov. 2001. *S vozhdiami i bez nikh*, Moscow: Vagrius.
23. V. Zubok. 2007. *A Failed Empire: The Soviet Union from Stalin to Gorbachev*, Chapel Hill: University of North Carolina Press, chap. 9; also V. Zubok. 2000. 'Gorbachev's Nuclear Learning', *Boston Book Review*, (April–May) .
24. Zubok, *A Failed Empire*, chaps. 9 and 10.

Section III

ALTERNATIVE VISIONS
OF THE 1960S

Chapter 6

Towards a New Concert of Europe
De Gaulle's Vision of a Post–Cold War Europe

Garret Martin

Forty years after his death, former French President General Charles de Gaulle remains a towering and divisive figure in the history of the Cold War. During his time as French leader between 1958 and 1969, his bold and fiercely independent policies often won him praise throughout the world, but also strong criticism from France's Western allies. Moreover, what he meant by the expressions 'European Europe', or a 'Europe from the Atlantic to the Urals', was never clearly spelt out. Vagueness and a certain blurring of categories might have suited de Gaulle's purposes, but his allies greatly resented his resort to deliberate ambiguity.[1]

Thus, the ultimate aims of de Gaulle's foreign policy still remain subject to debate, but we can refer to two main different interpretations when it came to his vision of the end of the Cold War: certain scholars suggest that he pursued clear aims and possessed a clear method to overcome the Cold War, while others view his détente policies as an attempt to create a unique position for France in a world divided into blocs.[2] This chapter will argue that de Gaulle did pursue a clear agenda to overcome the Cold War, with the ultimate objective of establishing a new Concert of Europe. It will focus on his long-term political philosophy, the context of the mid-1960s, which appeared more favourable for change in Europe, and the strategies that he adopted to fulfil his overarching vision.

De Gaulle's Political Philosophy

When de Gaulle came back to power in June 1958, he could already boast an illustrious and long career that had included leading the French resistance against the Nazi occupation during the Second World War. The Cold War dominated international affairs by the time he returned to office, but he had developed the main tenets of his political philosophy well before the emergence of the East-West conflict. These same principles would continue to shape his approach to the world stage during his presidency.

De Gaulle naturally placed France at the heart of his action. He believed France could only be at its rightful rank as a great power, which in turn depended on establishing a strong leadership that could fiercely protect the state's independence of action. This complete commitment to France fitted with a central aspect of his understanding of international affairs, as described by U.S. Ambassador to France Charles Bohlen: '[the] fundamental and basic element in de Gaulle's foreign policy is his strongly held and unchangeable conviction that the nation (the state and not the people) represents the permanent unit in international affairs'.[3] The centrality de Gaulle attached to the nation-state derived from his understanding of history, which deeply influenced his overall thinking. He interpreted history as an essentially tragic development, with violence and war as forces continually shaping the world. Amidst such a tough environment, where only power counted, nations remained the main players of history, and international life reflected the struggle between competing national interests, their opposition or their temporary agreement.[4]

Conversely, de Gaulle's emphasis on historical *longue durée* led him to downplay the importance of ideology, which he defined as 'temporary and mortal';[5] and nowhere did this appear more obvious than in de Gaulle's pragmatic attitude towards the Soviet Union and communism. His philosophy of history pushed him to believe in 'Russia' and to call for dialogue many times during his career, despite his opposition to communism.[6] As he told his mother in 1936 when the German threat reemerged, regardless of what one thought of Soviet Russia, it still provided the best fallback alliance for France. Thirty years later, he could again refer to a 'political and affectionate reality as old as our two countries [France and Russia], which is linked to their history and geography'.[7] Ideological differences, for de Gaulle, did not need to impede cooperation if that suited the national interests of both parties, nor could ideological solidarity forever mask conflicting national policies.[8]

Struggle played an intrinsic part in de Gaulle's vision of history, a Bergsonian competition where nations – rather than ideologies – strove to flourish and realize their potential, and where they required visionary leadership exercised by a strong state in order to succeed. But alongside competition and leadership, balance also played a vital role in de Gaulle's philosophy. National policies had to be governed by measure and self-restraint in what was an inextricably interdependent world system.[9]

De Gaulle looked to historical precedents to support his belief in balance: There was, though, a notion that was mentioned in no treaty and that is called equilibrium, which was then the European equilibrium. All nations agreed tacitly to prevent anyone from acquiring excessive power at the expense of others. It is in the name of European equilibrium that Europe made war: first to Louis XIV, then to the French Revolution, then to Napoleon ... Thanks to this notion, smaller states like the Netherlands and Belgium had their existence guaranteed.[10]

The quest for balance was intended as a means, not an end, and de Gaulle could express it in different ways: a moderation of power, a refusal of hegemony and alignments, and the sharing of a community of values. All of these principles aimed towards the end goal of peace, which depended on a continuous commitment to the idea of balance.[11] And from de Gaulle's perspective, balancing German power and solving the 'German problem' appeared as a vital precondition for peace and stability in Europe.

Thus, the fundamental pillars of de Gaulle's political philosophy – struggle, the deep influence of history, the notion of balance and the centrality of states in international affairs – predated the Cold War. This is not to say, however, that his ideas were not influenced in any way by, or ignored, the East-West conflict. In the tense context of 1947, for example, he warned about the danger posed by the Soviet Union extending its control over two-thirds of the European continent, and the fact that it controlled a bloc less than five hundred kilometres away from France's borders.[12] Years later, when the threat seemed to fade away, he remained wary of the Soviet Union. Nonetheless, the profound influence of history on his political philosophy made him less likely to view the Cold War as a permanent state of affairs, or even a real break in history. As the risks of Russian aggression diminished, de Gaulle increasingly came to view the Cold War as an abnormal phenomenon resulting from the particular circumstances of the Second World War.[13] He saw it as unacceptable because he believed Yalta had completely undermined the interests of France and Europe. Besides deciding the fate of Europe without involving European powers, the wartime deal between the United States and the Soviet Union had also proceeded to divide the continent into two blocs, thereby undermining the old European balance system.[14]

Moreover, de Gaulle also rejected the Cold War because the bipolar order did not fit with historical precedents: 'It has never happened in modern times that one or two nations hold all the power. The U.S. and the Soviet Union have all the means of power. All my life, I saw the power of Britain, France, Germany, Russia, a bit Italy, Japan before. It created equilibrium. Today all has changed. Yet France cannot accept that all the power of the world is shared between two countries. Deep down, all countries agree with us.'[15] Influenced by views deeply rooted in history, de

Gaulle perceived the Cold War as a transient phenomenon that could be and should be overcome in Europe.

The 1960s: A Favourable Context

De Gaulle's opposition to the Cold War and the bipolar order became more pronounced in the years before his return to power. Despite initially welcoming the signing of the Atlantic Pact in 1949, de Gaulle shifted to a more lukewarm stance during the 1950s, especially after the crisis surrounding the European Defence Community and the Suez War. He resented the objective deterioration of France's position within the Atlantic Alliance and the 'subordination' of French leaders to their American counterparts.[16] At the same time, de Gaulle spoke more openly about reaching out to the other side of the Iron Curtain. Following his first reference in March 1950 to a Europe from the Atlantic to the Urals, he called on France to take a more active role in East-West affairs, claiming a status as 'the most qualified historically, geographically and politically to create a bridge with the East'.[17] Both his uneasiness towards an American protectorate and his desire to start a dialogue with the Eastern bloc stemmed from his belief that the world was undergoing dramatic change. If neither of the superpowers was willing to resort to war in the nuclear age, then this would make the blocs obsolete in the long-run. NATO could no longer guarantee the survival of Western Europe, while the Soviet Union could not indefinitely maintain the populations of Eastern Europe in a state of war–like tension. De Gaulle firmly believed that the East could not forever resist the appeal of détente.[18]

Thus, the French leader came back to office with a real optimism about the prospects of overcoming the Cold War order in Europe and transforming relations with the Soviet Union. He wasted no time in sending a number of signals to the Soviet leaders during his first years in power. In 1959, he recognized the Oder-Neisse line and referred once more to a 'Europe from the Atlantic to the Urals'. In 1962, he publicly claimed that close Franco-German cooperation would make possible the establishment of a new European equilibrium between East and West. Convinced that Russia would eventually discard communism, he believed it would agree to play a role in a new post–Cold War European security system.[19] De Gaulle's optimism regarding the likely evolution of Europe was closely tied to his predictions about the future of the communist world, as he explained in detail during his press conference in March 1959: the Soviet leaders understood the dangers created by nuclear weapons and the need for peace, the Russian people aspired to a better life and freedom, and

Moscow could see the desire for independence of the peoples of Eastern Europe, who, without necessarily wanting to give up their social regime, craved emancipation. Moreover, de Gaulle believed that the communist camp would fragment because of the likely rivalry between Russia and communist China. Considering all these factors, he reached the conclusion that the communist world could not escape fundamental change.[20]

De Gaulle's confidence in his outlook remained firm despite the difficult period between 1958 and 1962, when a number of domestic and international obstacles undermined his chances to pursue his ambitious agenda for Europe. Aside from the fact that he had to assign priority to economic recovery and the divisive Algerian War, the renewed context of East-West tension over Berlin and Cuba removed any opportunity for a meaningful dialogue between the two sides of the Iron Curtain. But as these challenges faded away after 1962, international developments appeared to move in a direction that confirmed the validity of de Gaulle's forecasts. Buoyed by these changes, he increasingly perceived Europe as ready to overcome its division inherited from the Cold War.

De Gaulle could first point to the lessons of the Cuban Missile Crisis. While he fully supported the U.S. during the crisis, he also felt that the whole episode vindicated his beliefs about the improbability of a superpower confrontation in the nuclear age. The Cuban Missile Crisis proved a turning point because it demonstrated that neither the U.S. nor the Soviet Union wanted war, especially the latter.[21] 'Russia would never dare' became a leitmotif for de Gaulle, opening up the prospect that Moscow might be willing to consider peace. At the same time, since the Americans seemed hesitant to risk a nuclear war to defend Europe, this provided, in his view, the best justification for his policy of independence and the establishment of a national deterrent.[22] Secondly, the superpowers' unwillingness to risk nuclear war undermined their ability to control their allies, especially in regards to the Sino-Soviet relations. Soon after the Cuban Missile crisis and the Sino-Indian war, de Gaulle could claim:

> We are witnessing the clash between two massive land masses, Russia and China, which are going to move further and further apart. The Russians will be in an increasingly difficult position. Either they stay allied with China, but China will chew them up when it becomes stronger. Or the Russians will fight China, but this will mean the end of the 'Reds' and the communist camp will crumble. Maybe it has already happened.[23]

The Sino-Soviet split offered an opportunity to change the global balance and the balance in Europe. Not only could he hope to strengthen France vis-à-vis the Soviet Union by establishing diplomatic relations with communist China in January 1964, but he anticipated that the growing hostility between the two communist giants would push Russia to seek peace with the West.[24]

Additionally, Russia had to contend with the fact that its Eastern European allies, especially Romania, were using the Sino-Soviet split to act more independently.[25] By doing so, not only did they mirror de Gaulle's own ambitions for Western Europe, but they also signalled the reemergence of a certain national identity in Eastern Europe. This struck de Gaulle as a vital development, one clearly underlined by the visit of Romanian Premier Ion Maurer in the summer of 1964 – a visit instigated by Bucharest.[26] As Hervé Alphand, at the time the French ambassador to Washington, noted in his diary a few days after Maurer's visit: 'De Gaulle can feel change is occurring in the world. As proof of this, the conversations he just had with the Romanian representative. The Romanian representative was in Moscow before his visit to France. [Nikita] Khrushchev was incapable of imposing his will as he is weakened by internal problems and his conflict with Mao [Ze Dong]. So the Eastern European satellites seem to be taking their distances from Moscow'.[27]

The Soviet Union naturally appeared less threatening, considering its difficulties with China and its Eastern European allies. As de Gaulle instructed his new ambassador to Moscow, Philippe Baudet, in spring 1964, his general posture should be to show the Russians that 'we are not afraid of them any more'.[28] But more fundamentally, de Gaulle believed that Soviet weaknesses suggested a more profound failure of the communist bloc. This reflected a number of central communist predictions that had not come to pass:

> 1. The demise of nations under a common ideology. But that has not happened. Some nations are under the rule of the communist system. They remain and are even powerful. We can see those two opposing each other; 2. The growth and victory of communism in other industrialised countries besides Russia. There are occupations (Eastern Europe and Central Europe). Nowhere have we seen a modern country spontaneously giving in to communism; 3. The establishment of communism in countries of the third world and straight obedience. China did receive communist rule. But it rejected obedience ... 4. The economic and social success of the system as opposed to others. Despite some successes and great efforts, the system has failed.[29]

Not only did the external challenges faced by the Soviet Union push it towards peace with the West, but it could not ignore the pressure of its population for a better life. Indeed, de Gaulle attributed a high importance to this sociology of development in his vision of the political future of communist states. He was convinced that the industrial growth of the Soviet Union – and its satellites – would create a larger demand from its population for consumer goods, as well as for more peaceful, freer and quieter living conditions.[30] This raised the possibility that the communist regimes in the East might one day evolve in a way compatible with changes in the West. After all, de Gaulle claimed that the free world and the communist bloc were moving in the same direction, as he told Harold Wilson: 'There are fewer differences than before with Eastern Europe in the economic and social spheres'.[31]

The supposed economic and social convergences between both sides of the Iron Curtain, combined with the growing plurality within both blocs, helped convince the French president by early 1965 that Europe was undergoing a fundamental transformation: 'There is a change lately. We can feel it everywhere. The Cold War is out of date ... The Soviet bloc is crumbling ... As to the Western bloc, it is also crumbling. France has recovered its freedom.'[32] With power no longer concentrated in the hands of the superpowers, de Gaulle saw a real opportunity to overcome the Cold War order and establish a new security balance in Europe. The press conference of 4 February 1965 gave him a chance to outline in detail how he envisaged the reunification of the continent. The press conference proposed a European solution to the central problem of Germany's division.[33] Arguing that the German problem could not 'be solved by the confrontation of the ideologies and the forces of the two camps opposed to each other', he suggested instead that it needed to be considered from a different perspective: 'the entente and conjugated action of the peoples that are and will remain most interested in the fate of Germany, the European nations'.[34] But, he carefully added that such a solution could only occur in the long term and depended on many conditions. The Eastern bloc would have to evolve so as to allow Russia to move away from totalitarianism and let the satellite states play a more significant role in Europe. The states of Western Europe would have to extend their organization to cover political and defence matters. West Germany would have to accept that any reunification would involve a settlement on its borders and weapons that was accepted by all its neighbours. Finally, a solution to the German question would only become possible once a general 'détente, entente and cooperation' had developed between all the European states.[35]

A Strategy for Change: Towards a new Concert of Europe

De Gaulle's long-standing political philosophy, along with his belief that Europe was becoming ripe for fundamental change, shaped his decision to outline his vision of how the continent could overcome its division inherited from the Cold War. Through the tryptich 'détente, entente and cooperation', he emphasized that the end of the Cold War would result from an incremental process of détente, thereby reversing the previous orthodoxy that détente would follow German reunification. This press conference marked a definite turning point in the evolution of French foreign policy.[36] Yet while his vision appeared optimistic and detailed in some respects, the French president remained vague when it came to explaining how he hoped to achieve this objective, and what kind of order would succeed the Cold War in Europe.

Nonetheless, despite the ambiguity of his words, de Gaulle's actions after the press conference of February 1965 do provide some helpful clues about his multi-pronged strategy. Firstly, he still regarded the establishment of a Western European political union, centred on the Franco-German partnership, as a precondition for creating a new equilibrium in Europe. But de Gaulle had shifted away from his previous idea that a Western European political union would need to precede dialogue with the East, preferring instead to subordinate his Western European aims to the larger objective of achieving overall European reconciliation.[37] The relative failures of the Fouchet Plan and the Franco-German Treaty had dampened de Gaulle's hopes for immediate progress on the Western European front. Instead he anticipated that progress in East-West détente could help achieve Western European political unity.[38]

Secondly, de Gaulle rejected the notion that détente should be the competence of either the Atlantic Alliance or the Warsaw Pact, as it contradicted his view that European reunification would eventually lead to the dissolution of the military alliances.[39] He naturally closely connected his policy towards NATO with his attempt to foster an East-West rapprochement. On the one hand, he justified the withdrawal from NATO's integrated military structure as the consequence of changes in East-West relations since 1949 – although France remained a member of the Atlantic Alliance as a fallback guarantee in case the Soviet threat reemerged.[40] On the other hand, he hoped disengagement from NATO would become the motor for new East-West relations in Europe.[41] France's policy towards the Atlantic Alliance could only be understood by referring to de Gaulle's press conference of 4 February 1965. Ending military integration became a precondition for any East-West rapprochement, since the former prevented European states from reclaiming their independence. Moreover, if French moves proved contagious within the Western bloc, they were equally likely to do so in the Eastern bloc. Romania, which relied on French policy to resist the Soviet integration efforts through the Warsaw Pact, seemed a particularly good example of this.[42]

Thirdly, French leaders did not hesitate to use the withdrawal from NATO as a bargaining card when dealing with their Eastern-bloc counterparts. This strategy featured very prominently during French Foreign

Minister Maurice Couve de Murville's various trips behind the Iron Curtain in the spring and summer of 1966. Whenever he talked with communist officials, he reiterated the argument that France's policy towards the Atlantic Alliance could serve the cause of détente in Europe: 'That is why we left NATO. This policy is part of our plan for the whole of Europe, which aims to have Western European and Eastern European states living in normal conditions.'[43] At the same time, France sought to find a balance between favouring the reemergence of Eastern European states while seemingly not trying to drive a wedge between them and their powerful Soviet protector. In the long run, de Gaulle expected them to become more independent from Moscow and pushed them to act in line with their national personality. As he confided to Zenon Kliszko, the vice-marshal of the Polish parliament, 'an ideology does not prevent a state from being a state, with its own ambitions and policies'.[44] He underscored the importance of this during his trips to Poland and Romania, since he felt that a firm Soviet grip on Eastern Europe would favour the maintenance of U.S. influence on Western Europe.[45] But, equally, de Gaulle did not condemn the ties linking the communist states to their Soviet patron. While the French president opposed blocs, he viewed spheres of influence in a more nuanced way, even accepting them to a certain extent when they resulted from historical roots or affinities, and he could hardly afford to antagonize the Soviet Union, since he needed its cooperation for his overall goal of establishing a post–Cold War order in Europe. [46]

Indeed, the fourth part of de Gaulle's strategy – and the most important one – involved mediating between West Germany and the Soviet Union so as to create a positive Paris-Moscow-Bonn triangle: 'It is essential to push [West] Germany towards a rapprochement with Russia. We have to disarm their reciprocal aggression. It is our game, it is the only one.'[47] If France could change the reciprocal perceptions of the German and Soviet threat, this could effectively begin the process of dissolving the military blocs. If the Soviet and German threats were relative illusions to each other, there would be no justification for keeping both NATO and the Warsaw Pact. The regimes in Eastern Europe would no longer be able to use the threat of Germany as they had in the past to justify the Cold War against the free world.[48] French leaders needed to convince both states that such a rapprochement was in their interests. They wooed their Soviet counterparts because they felt that France and the Soviet Union could act as role models by encouraging their respective allies to follow their détente path. Additionally, reverting to the historic alliance with Russia offered a way of containing any resurgence of German ambitions in the future.[49] De Gaulle, in particular, argued in Moscow that the division of Germany was not normal, that it created an element of instability and could not last forever. At the same time, however, he added that he was in no hurry to see reunification happen, and that when it did, it would have to be as part of a controlled process.[50] In regards to the West Germans, the French president wanted them to understand that Russia, not the U.S., held the key to reunification.[51] By offering the prospect of German unity, albeit with some limits on borders and access to nuclear weapons, de Gaulle hoped he could entice Bonn to gravitate away from Washington and towards Paris.

Thus, de Gaulle pursued a multi-pronged strategy with the overarching aim of overcoming the Cold War order in Europe and replacing it with a new pan-continental security system.[52] He hoped that a German-Soviet détente, mediated by France, could eventually convince Moscow to abandon East Germany and allow reunification. Reunification would of course also depend on meeting conditions on borders and nuclear weapons, but de Gaulle did not outline a clear idea as to how the two Germanys actually should proceed, aside from the establishment of some sort of confederation.[53] The French president expected that the eventual departure of the U.S. from Europe could be bought in exchange for Russia making these concessions on Germany.[54] De Gaulle rarely expressed his views on the future role of the U.S. in Europe. On the one hand, he certainly welcomed a continued U.S. security guarantee as long as a possible Soviet threat remained. Yet he hoped and expected that the U.S. would not maintain a direct role in Europe once the Cold War had faded away, reverting instead to its traditional role of underwriter of the European security system.[55]

The end result would resemble a modernized version of the Concert of Europe of the nineteenth century. The two main pillars of the system would be France and the Soviet Union, as nuclear powers, but the system would be guaranteed by an interlocking set of checks and balances. Paris and Moscow would contain Bonn, while a closer union between the states of Western Europe – including a reunified Germany tied to France – would be theoretically strong enough to contain a declining Soviet power.[56] Finally, the nuclear balance of terror between both superpowers would provide an additional element of equilibrium, allowing Western Europe to act as the arbiter between the Soviet Union and the Anglo-Saxon powers, as de Gaulle indicated in his memoirs.[57]

Conclusion

Despite de Gaulle's grand hopes, this modernized Concert of Europe would never come to be. Though the Soviets may at first have welcomed the idea of a greater Europe from the Atlantic to the Urals, they became increasingly disturbed by its implications in 1967–68, when the French president promoted the idea during trips in Eastern Europe. His calls in Gdansk in September 1967 for the Polish people to be less subordinate to their powerful neighbour drew sharp objections from Polish leader Wladislaw Gomulka.[58] The decision by the Warsaw Pact troops to enter Czechoslovakia on the night of 20–21 August 1968 and put an end to the Prague Spring proved even more significant. This invasion – more than simply an '*incident de parcours*' (a hitch) – caused serious repercussions.[59] De Gaulle was forced to say goodbye to his grand design to overcome the Cold War order. East and West were not converging, despite his best hopes, nor were the Soviets prepared to abandon their grip on Eastern Europe. As Alphand, by then the secretary general of the Quai d'Orsay, summed up a few days later in his diary: 'It is maybe indeed the end of a grand effort to reunite two worlds beyond ideology'.[60]

Ultimately, de Gaulle's grand design and vision of a post–Cold War Europe suffered from a series of flaws and contradictions.[61] He underestimated the role of ideology, in particular when it came to the communist bloc.[62] His plan for a new European security order effectively depended on the Soviet Union giving up its global ambitions and accepting a more traditional balancing role on the continent. Yet the Kremlin leaders were simply not prepared to follow that path. More generally, de Gaulle's blueprint for overcoming of the Cold War order was in many ways too complex. It could only succeed through an extraordinary concordance of events and changes, whereby all states would realize that it was in their interest to follow the Gaullist vision.[63]

Notwithstanding these failures, de Gaulle left a lasting impression on the history of the Cold War. Although the conflict did not end in the way he had imagined, he still played an important role because of the fact that he outlined an alternative to the bipolar order. Through his trips to the Soviet Union, Poland and Romania, he helped the cause of the rapprochement between the two divided blocs in Europe and imposed the principle that East-West détente should precede the reunification of Germany. De Gaulle's bold and pioneering policies inspired subsequent statesmen, even if they did not necessarily share the same objectives. This was the case, for example, for the Ostpolitik of West German Chancellor Willy Brandt, or for U.S. President Richard Nixon's attempts to normalize relations with Communist China. Furthermore, de Gaulle acted as a symbolic role model for the rest of the world by thumbing his nose at the superpowers. Both China and France were in part able to do that because of the disappearance of fear: by the 1960s, they had become sufficiently strong within the framework of their respective alliances that they no longer suffered from the insecurities that had led them to seek alliances in the first place.[64] De

Gaulle did, therefore, contribute to an important transformation in the nature of the Cold War and even, to an extent, to hastening its demise. It did
not end in exactly the manner in which he had predicted. Yet after 1989
his vision of a world without blocs and of a Europe stretching from the
Atlantic to the Urals suddenly looked much less quixotic than it had done
two decades earlier.

Notes

1. F. Logevall. 1999. *Choosing War: The Lost Chance for Peace and the Escalation of War in Vietnam,* Berkeley: University of California Press, 104; E. Mahan. 2002. *Kennedy, De Gaulle,
   and Western Europe,* New York: Palgrave Macmillan, 27.
2. T. Schwartz. 2003. *Lyndon Johnson and Europe: In the Shadow of Vietnam,* Cambridge:
   Harvard University Press, 100; S. Romano. 1992. 'L'Europe de l'Atlantique à l'Oural:
   concepts et réalités', in Institut Charles de Gaulle (ed.), *De Gaulle en son siècle,* vol. 5,
   Paris: La Documentation française, 507.
3. See Bohlen paper, undated, document 27, *Foreign Relations of the United States* (hereafter
   FRUS), 1964–1968, vol. XII.
4. See M. Vaïsse. 1998. *La grandeur: politique étrangère du Général de Gaulle 1958–1969,* Paris:
   Fayard, 23–24.
5. As de Gaulle claimed in February 1951, cited by P.-M. de la Gorce. 1969. *La France contre
   les Empires,* Paris: Editions Bernard Grasset, 210.
6. M.-P. Rey. 1991. *La tentation du rapprochement: France et URSS à l'heure de la détente (1964–
   1974),* Paris: Publications de la Sorbonne, 18.
7. 1936 letter quoted by M. Vaïsse. 2006. 'Avant-propos', in M. Vaïsse (ed.), *De Gaulle et la
   Russie,* Paris: CNRS Éditions, 9; C. de Gaulle. 1970. *Discours et Messages,* vol. 5, Paris:
   Plon, 41–43, Reply to toast given by Nikolai Podgorny, 20 June 1966. The author is responsible for all translations from French to English.
8. C. de Gaulle. 1970. *Discours et Messages,* vol. 4, Paris: Plon, 179, press conference, 31 Jan.
   1964.
9. D. Calleo. 1994. 'De Gaulle and the Monetary System: The Golden Rule', in N. Wahl
   and R. Paxton (eds), *De Gaulle and the United States, 1930–1970: A Centennial Reappraisal,*
   Oxford: Berg, 239.
10. C. Mauriac. 1970. *Un autre de Gaulle: journal 1944–1954,* Paris: Hachette, 342, 22 Mar.
    1949.
11. Vaïsse, *La grandeur,* 39–40.
12. C. de Gaulle. 1970. *Discours et Messages,* vol. 2, Paris: Plon, 102, speech in Rennes, 27 July
    1947. For views that would have put de Gaulle at odds at the time with George Kennan,
    a Gaullist *avant l'heure,* see John Harper's contribution in this volume.
13. Bohlen to Bundy, 2 Mar. 1963, document 270, *FRUS, 1961–1963,* Vol. XIII.
14. See De Gaulle, *Discours et Messages,* vol. 2, 102, speech in Rennes, 27 July 1947; De Gaulle-
    Wilson meeting, 3 Apr. 1965, Ministère des Affaires Étrangères Français (hereafter
    MAEF), Cabinet du Ministre (CM), Couve de Murville (CDM), vol. 379. The opposition
    to the Cold War stalemate was shared by de Gaulle's successors, including long-time
    opponent François Mitterrand; see Frédéric Bozo's contribution in this volume.

15. De Gaulle-Rockefeller meeting, 3 Oct. 1963, MAEF, CM, CDM, vol. 376.
16. F. Bozo. 1996. *Deux Stratégies pour l'Europe: De Gaulle, les États-unis et l'Alliance Atlantique 1958–69*, Paris: Plon, 29–30.
17. Rey, *La tentation*, 17; claimed by de Gaulle in Dec. 1954, cited by Gorce, *France contre les Empires*, 173.
18. C. de Gaulle. 1971. *Memoirs of Hope: Renewal and Endeavor*, New York: Simon and Schuster, 201.
19. G.-H. Soutou. 2003. 'De Gaulle's France and the Soviet Union from Conflict to Détente', in W. Loth (ed.). *Europe, Cold War and Coexistence, 1953–1965*, London: Frank Cass, 173–175.
20. Gorce, *France contre les Empires*, 209.
21. See de Gaulle-Margerie meeting, 4 June 1963, MAEF, CM, CDM, vol. 375; Couve de Murville-Schroeder meeting, 12 Nov. 1965, MAEF, CM, CDM, vol. 381.
22. J. Lacouture. 1986. *De Gaulle: vol. 3 Le Souverain*, Paris: Seuil, 387; M. Vaïsse. 1993. '"Une hirondelle ne fait pas le printemps"': La France et la crise de Cuba', in M. Vaïsse (ed.), *L'Europe et la Crise de Cuba*, Paris: A. Colin, 104–105.
23. A. Peyrefitte. 1994. *C'était de Gaulle*, vol. 1, Paris: Fayard, 315–316, Council of Ministers, 7 Nov. 1962.
24. De Gaulle-Erhard meeting 1, 19 Jan. 1965, MAEF, CM, CDM, vol. 379; Peyrefitte, *C'était de Gaulle*, vol. 1, 320, Meeting 13 Mar. 1963.
25. Speech to l'Assemblée Nationale, 28 Apr. 1964, Fondation Nationale des Sciences Politiques (hereafter FNSP), Fonds Maurice Couve de Murville (CDM), carton 1.
26. De Gaulle-Maurer meeting, 28 July 1964, MAEF, CM, CDM, vol. 378; Bucharest to Foreign Office (hereafter FO), Telegram 1, 2 July 1964, United Kingdom National Archives (hereafter UKNA), FO 371/177619.
27. H. Alphand. 1977. *L'étonnement d'être: journal, 1939–1973*, Paris: Fayard, 435, diary entry 30 July 1964.
28. Paris to FO, 14 Mar. 1964, UKNA, FO 371/177870.
29. C. de Gaulle. 1987. *Lettres, Notes et Carnets*, vol. 10, Paris: Plon, 75, Reflections on the subject of the adapted political and social choice for France, undated.
30. Gorce, *France contre les Empires*, 219.
31. See de Gaulle, *Discours et Messages*, vol. 4, 155, televised speech, 31 Dec. 1963; De Gaulle-Wilson meeting, 3 Apr. 1965, MAEF, CM, CDM, vol. 379. The vision of a smooth socio-economic rapprochement between East and West was one later shared by Mitterrand; see Bozo's contribution in this volume.
32. A. Peyrefitte. 1997. *C'était de Gaulle*, vol. 2, Paris: Fayard, 313, meeting 4 Jan. 1965.
33. Soutou, 'De Gaulle's France', 180.
34. De Gaulle, *Discours et Messages*, vol. 4, 341, press conference, 4 Feb. 1965.
35. Ibid.
36. Bohlen to Rusk, telegram 4451, 5 Feb. 1965, National Archives Record Administration (hereafter NARA), Record Group 59 (RG 59), Central Foreign Policy Files (CFPF), 1964–1966, box 2178.
37. Compare speech to l'Assemblée Nationale, 12 June 1963, FNSP, CDM, Carton 1, to De Gaulle, *Discours et Messages*, vol. 5, 101–104, Press conference, 28 Oct. 1966. In this respect, de Gaulle differed from Mitterrand's vision in 1989, which made the Western European dimension dominant; see Bozo's contribution in this volume.
38. A. Peyrefitte. 2000. *C'était de Gaulle*, vol. 3, Paris: Fayard, 263, Council of Ministers, 9 Aug. 1967.
39. Crouy-Chanel to Couve de Murville, telegram 568-576, 8 June 1966, MAEF, Service des Pactes 1961–1970, Vol. 272.

40. De Gaulle, *Lettres, Notes et Carnets*, vol. 10, 261–262, De Gaulle to Johnson, 7 Mar. 1966.

41. Bozo, *Deux Stratégies*, 163.

42. Draft Circular, undated, MAEF, Service des Pactes 1961–1970, Vol. 261.

43. Couve de Murville-Gomulka meeting, 20 May 1966, MAEF, CM, CDM, Vol. 383.

44. De Gaulle-Kliszko meeting, 13 May 1966, MAEF, CM, CDM, Vol. 383.

45. De Gaulle-Ceausescu meeting, 14 May 1968, MAEF, Secrétariat Général (SG), Entretiens et Messages (EM), Vol. 34.

46. For his acceptance of spheres of influence, see de Gaulle-Cyrankiewicz meeting, 10 Sept. 1965, FNSP, CDM, Carton 9; E. Burin des Roziers. 1985. 'Le non-alignement', in E. Barnavi and S. Friedlander, *La politique étrangère du Général de Gaulle*, Paris: Presses Universitaires de France, 72.

47. See Peyrefitte, *C'était de Gaulle*, vol. 3, 206, meeting 5 Dec. 1966, 206

48. E. Kolodziej. 1974. *French International Policy under De Gaulle and Pompidou: The Politics of Grandeur*, Ithaca, NY: Cornell University Press, 350–351.

49. Bohlen to Rusk, airgram 2425, 24 June 1966, NARA, RG 59, CFPF, 1964–66, Box 2180; CIA Intelligence Info Cable, 25 Aug. 1965, Lyndon Baines Johnson Library, Presidential Papers, National Security Files, Country Files, Box 172. German politician Franz Josef Strauß shared de Gaulle's assumption that Europe had a unique role to play in the world, but he was highly sceptical of the claim that Moscow would be ready to recognize any European state as an equal partner: 'One cannot ignore the law of mathematics'. See Ronald Granieri's contribution on Strauß in this volume.

50. De Gaulle-Brezhnev-Kosygin meeting, 21 June 1966, MAEF, SG, EM, Vol. 27.

51. De Gaulle-Kiesinger meeting, 14 Jan. 1967, MAEF, SG, EM, Vol. 29.

52. See G.-H. Soutou. 2000. 'La décision française de quitter le commandement intégré de l'OTAN (1966)', in H.-J. Harder (ed.), *Von Truman bis Harmel: Die Bundesrepublik Deutschland im Spannungsfeld von NATO und europäischer Integration*, Munich: Oldenbourg, 194–196.

53. De Gaulle-Brezhnev-Kosygin meeting, 21 June 1966, MAEF, SG, EM, Vol. 27.

54. P. Maillard. 2001. *De Gaulle et le Problème Allemand: Les leçons d'un grand dessein*, Paris: Guibert, 226.

55. The reference to the U.S. as the underwriter of Europe featured in the briefing for de Gaulle's trip to Moscow, according to a Quai source, see Jean de la Grandville-Richard Funkhouse meeting, 9 July 1966, NARA, RG 59, Records of the Ambassador Charles Bohlen, Box 33; see also Alphand, *L'étonnement d'être*, 445, diary entry, 3 Jan. 1965.

56. Soutou, 'La décision française', 194–196. The vision of a Concert of Europe was also shared by de Gaulle's successor Valéry Giscard d'Estaing; see Georges-Henri Soutou's contribution in this volume.

57. See T. Schreiber. 2000. *Les Actions de la France à l'Est, ou les Absences de Marianne*, Paris: Harmattan, 75.

58. M.-P. Rey. 2010. 'De Gaulle, French Diplomacy, and Franco-Soviet Relations as Seen from Moscow', in C. Nuenlist, A. Locher and G. Martin (eds), *Globalizing de Gaulle: International Perspectives on French Foreign Policies, 1958–1969*, Lanham, MD: Lexington Books, 36.

59. M. Debré. 1993. *Trois Républiques pour une France: mémoires tome IV*, Paris: Albin Michel, 259.

60. Alphand, *L'étonnement d'être*, 513, diary entry, 25 Aug. 1968.

61. See for example Vaïsse, *La grandeur*, 679 for a detailed listing of these contradictions.

62. Lacouture, *De Gaulle: vol. 3*, 556.

63. S. Hoffmann. 1974. *Éssais sur la France: Déclin ou Renouveau?*, Paris: Éditions du Seuil, 375.

64. J.L. Gaddis. 2006. *The Cold War: A New History*, London: Penguin, 143.

Chapter 7

FRANZ JOSEF STRAUß AND THE END OF THE COLD WAR

Ronald J. Granieri

It may appear paradoxical to discuss the end of Cold War in relation to someone who died before the Cold War ended, having last occupied a cabinet-level position forty years ago. Franz Josef Strauß, however, was a paradoxical personality. He was at the same time populist and intellectual, traditionalist and modernizer, regional politician and European statesman. He enjoyed great success but ultimately failed to reach the highest office he sought. Perhaps most paradoxical of all, his vision for Europe's global role, a political non-starter when he first developed it, remains important both for our understanding of his era and for the current international situation.

The mid-1960s saw increasing stability in Europe and decreasing fear of immediate conflict, which led to proclamations such as that from Ludwig Erhard in 1965 that 'the postwar era is over'.[1] Many believed that the Cold War was about to enter a new phase, and most scholars since have linked this general sentiment to the movement in favour of East-West détente. That was not the only possible vision, however. Strauß offered an alternative vision for a post–Cold War future, in which a more independent Europe, built on but transcending Franco-German cooperation, would assert itself vis-à-vis both the United States and the USSR. This vision required giving initial priority to Western European integration over East-West détente in the hope that a stronger Western Europe would be better able to manage the process of opening to the East than individual national efforts. The resulting international system would be both modern (in part because of the influence of new technologies) and more traditional, returning to the competitive polycentrism of earlier eras. Contrary to those who hoped détente would lead to generalized peace, Strauß assumed continued ideo-

Notes for this chapter begin on page 116.

logical and geopolitical tensions as world powers sought to advance their interests, acting on a global rather than European stage. Although his vision foundered on the shoals of domestic and international politics, his attempts to imagine a world order beyond Soviet-American bipolarity were provocative, and they deserve mention in any discussion of the policy alternatives of the 1960s. Since even advocates of détente had difficulties imagining how a post–Cold War international system could, should or would function after what the advocates of détente called the recognition of international realities, it is important for scholars to examine the full variety of visions for that future.

Strauß's period of greatest intellectual creativity, from 1963 to 1969, was a transitional era both personally, as he sought a channel for his thwarted political ambitions after his resignation as defence minister in the aftermath of the *Spiegel* affair, and for the Federal Republic as a whole. As the aged Konrad Adenauer retired in October 1963, he turned power over to Erhard, who, despite his personal popularity, enjoyed much less authority. Erhard's weakness created a political vacuum in which different individuals and groups stepped forward to attack problems they felt had been allowed to drift in the latter Adenauer years. New ideas, however, brought new conflicts that Erhard was unable to manage, which would doom his chancellorship. Within the CDU/CSU, this was the era of conflict between 'Atlanticists' and 'Gaullists' over the direction of European and Atlantic relations.[2] Strauß was considered a leader of the 'Gaullist' faction, and he did express great admiration for the French president as he criticized Erhard and Foreign Minister Gerhard Schröder for their excessive reliance on the Americans. As we will see, however, his vision went beyond echoing French policy.

Polarizing during his lifetime, Strauß remains a controversial figure in German historiography, and objective studies of his political legacy are rare. This is unfortunate, not because of any partisan desire to 're-habilitate' Strauß, but because such polarization threatens to obscure his significance in postwar German history. For all his irresponsibility and excesses, Strauß played a crucial role in the political development both of Bavaria and of the Federal Republic, as well as in the development of the Atlantic community and Germany's place in it. Of special significance for this study is Strauß's role as a political intellectual. Strauß attempted to develop and defend new ideas to a degree unusual among professional politicians. Famous as the possessor of the highest grade on the *Abitur* (the German school-leaving exam) in the history of Bavaria, he had risen from relatively humble origins as the son of a Munich butcher and planned to pursue an academic career until the war intervened (quite literally – the Allied bombing of Munich destroyed his unfinished dissertation on ideas of world empire in Roman historiography.) Even as he rose within the ranks of the CSU he cultivated his intellectual image, whether in his weakness for Latin phrases or in a dangerous tendency to insist on his own infallibility.

His relationship with the West German intellectual scene was ambivalent, to say the least. Despite frequent outbursts of populist demagogy, Strauß wanted very much to be accepted as a theorist and a creative mind. He often presented himself as the defender of common people against the intellectual elite, denouncing the 'spirits of disorder and destruction, the forces of a value neutral, pseudo-democratic and commercially profitable nihilism ... at work all around us'.[3] Nevertheless, when Günther Gaus wanted to discuss Strauß's problems with intellectuals in a 1964 interview, the Bavarian responded: 'You do me an injustice, Herr Gaus. After all, I am an intellectual too ... Unless you know of a licensing office that officially marks people intellectuals.'[4] As he moved within German, European, and transatlantic elite networks, Strauß also profited from the institutional advantages of German politics. His position as CSU chair guaranteed him an audience, allowing him to play kingmaker within the CDU/CSU, and also to travel and speak on current events without being bound either by ministerial responsibility or the limits of a particular portfolio.[5]

The tension between the politician and the intellectual spurred Strauß to seek ever-larger audiences for his ideas. After a series of speeches and interviews prepared the ground in 1963–64, he made a splash with his first book on German and European politics, published in Britain in 1965 as *The Grand Design* and then in German translation as *Entwurf für Europa*.[6] Strauß combined a call for Western Europe to develop its own military forces and a central political union built around Franco-German cooperation with increasing criticism of an emerging U.S.-Soviet 'condominium' in Europe. He did not reject the idea of Atlantic partnership but attempted to place it within a broader historical and geopolitical context, reflecting his assumption that Europe had a unique role to play in the world. His arguments drew on conservative resentments at German division, as well as de Gaulle's critique of American dominance. At the same time, his positions departed from both traditional German nationalism and Gaullism in challenging ways. Strauß tried to develop a conservative counter-policy to the dominant Atlanticist consensus. In his vision, the superpowers would share global influence with other power centres, such as a united Europe.

Strauß saw transatlantic tensions as signs of a maturing relationship. Rejecting extreme versions of the Atlanticist/Gaullist dichotomy, he denied the need to choose between Washington and Paris. Instead he argued that anyone who worked towards building a stronger Europe 'is not only a good patriot, but also a good European and Atlanticist'.[7] The goal, he felt, should be to overcome national divisions within Europe and American dominance of the Atlantic Alliance at the same time, because both had become obsolete. As he concluded in a 1964 speech in Milwaukee: 'A Europe that relies on America for everything is more of a burden than an actual help. An independent Europe that freely accepts its duties ... is the best guarantee for the future of the free world'.[8] The Americans needed Europe 'as a second independent power on their side', and Europeans had 'no right to lay the burden of their defence permanently on the shoulders of their American friends'.[9]

For Strauß, Atlantic partnership centred on the traditional elements of national sovereignty: diplomacy and defence. This meant replacing the Atlantic Alliance, which left important strategic decisions in American hands, with one resting on 'two pillars'. He proposed a European nuclear force built on the French *force de frappe,* with German (while denying any interest in specifically German national nuclear forces) as well as British participation.[10] The transformation of NATO 'from an American protective alliance to a European-American alliance of partners' was 'the necessary condition for the emergence of a European union'.[11] A unified Europe could only emerge, however, if Europeans were determined to be a partner of the United States, 'and not a mere glacis that trembles before Moscow, the capital of a euro-Asiatic colossus'. Europe should not become 'a third force, that wanders in some value neutral area' trying to play the superpowers against each other, but rather 'the second power of the free world next to the USA in the Atlantic region'.[12] European policy should no longer remain 'a function of American security policy, which proceeds from different interests than our own'.[13]

The creation of the new Atlantic community with a strong Europe had both geopolitical and historical significance for Strauß. European integration would mean a triumph over 'Yalta', a term he used, as de Gaulle did, to symbolize the superpower division of, and dominance over, Europe.[14] Strauß attacked this status quo and rejected any suggestion that it should be made permanent, declaring in one television interview: 'Should the demarcation line of Yalta, an agreement between Russians and Americans, determine the rest of our earthly existence as Europeans? That is completely unnatural!'[15]

In response to criticisms that his European focus was old-fashioned, Strauß argued European integration was a necessity in the modern world. 'As long as the states of Europe cannot bring themselves to develop a common policy', he told an audience in Madrid, 'they will be helpless in the face of developments in world affairs'. World politics were forcing Europeans 'to give up the role of a mere object in politics, in order to make Europe a subject'. That meant opposing 'a developing Soviet-American global arrangement along the lines of Yalta … because the status quo in Europe threatens the peaceful and sensible development of our own continent'. The 'political consequences' of this realization 'begin with Franco-German partnership, continuing into a further deepening and widening of the European Communities and should culminate first in a coordinated, and then in an integrated foreign and security policy'.[16]

Strauß's vision focused on Western Europe and the EEC, building on Franco-German cooperation. At the same time he could be critical of de Gaulle. Close relations with France were just the first step on a long road: 'Europe cannot be replaced by France, and can also not be replaced by a Franco-German Union', he wrote, but no Europe was possible against France and Germany either.[17] Warning against European arguments that were 'too abstract', Strauß argued that European integration should develop out of cooperation between those states ready to do so, with the ultimate goal being integrated political institutions.[18] The resulting political union should be open to other states but 'will not be built as long as the participating states do not come to a basic understanding about the foreign and security policy of a unified Europe'. Rejecting earlier hopes that economic cooperation would lead automatically to political integration, Strauß argued that Europeans 'must give up our earlier illusions' and move from economics to politics.[19]

Strauß agreed with basic elements of de Gaulle's vision: 'namely, the need to create an independent Europe: a Europe that does not simply cling to the skirts of the Americans, a Europe that fulfils its historic function instead of simply acting as the geographic arena for a demarcation line that was created without European influence in 1945 between the Americans and Russians at Yalta'. At the same time, he believed some elements of de Gaulle's vision 'simply no longer [made] sense, such as the idea that any European state – no matter its name, no matter how glorious its history, no matter how impressive its traditions – will be recognized in Moscow as an equal partner. One cannot ignore the laws of mathematics'.[20] Although de Gaulle had opened the discussion of greater European autonomy, a Europe of the fatherlands could only be 'an intermediate stage' on the way to a supranational community.[21]

This integrated and independent Europe could then conduct an independent foreign policy. Criticizing the détente policies of his domestic rivals and, by extension, the Americans, which focused on bilateral contacts between the Federal Republic and individual Eastern European states, and which placed improvement in the East-West climate ahead of Western European integration, Strauß complained that a 'policy of movement' too often meant a policy of concessions to the East. What he advocated was a 'game with divided roles' (*Spiel mit verteilten Rollen*), with each ally playing a role on behalf of the community as a whole, tailored to his particular strengths. Thus he argued that de Gaulle had a special role to play as Europe's representative to Eastern Europe and other parts of the world.[22] This game was temporary, until the emergence of an integrated Western Europe that could negotiate with the Soviets and the Americans over the future of Eastern Europe on a level of true equality.[23]

Strauß's arguments for greater Western European integration eventually led him to break with de Gaulle on the decisive question of British EEC membership, especially after de Gaulle's veto of the second British application in 1967. Strauß's enthusiasm for British membership, however, did not signal an embrace of Atlanticism but a desire for the British to join a more independent Europe and to push the French to reconsider their self-isolation.[24] The EEC was not a 'corporation, in which one can buy stock'. Membership candidates needed to accept the Community's larger political goals[25] – a stance not so different from that of de Gaulle. Unlike de Gaulle, however, Strauß thought Britain was close to accepting those conditions, and he welcomed further negotiations.[26] Thus, while Strauß had begun his search for an alternative to the growing Atlanticist consensus by identifying himself closely with the Gaullist vision of a stronger Europe, his conception of Europe's future was both more flexible and more expansive than de Gaulle's. Strauß embraced a deeper level of integration and a wider membership in this Europe, which would remain one of the pillars of the new Atlantic community.

Their different visions for the future of Europe highlighted one of the central points of difference between Strauß and de Gaulle, the issue of nationalism. Strauß certainly believed that the Federal Republic should become more assertive. Although he admitted that its original parentage was unclear, he was one of the popularizers of the phrase that the Federal Republic 'should not claim to be an economic giant but allow itself to be treated like a political dwarf'.[27] Such arguments resonated with conservative audiences and served immediate political purposes. Strauß often argued that the CDU/CSU needed to address national issues, lest national-minded voters drift to fringe parties such as the emerging National Democratic Party (NPD). As the differences between the larger parties appeared to shrink, those national-minded voters could supply a crucial margin of victory in a national election.[28]

Nevertheless, Strauß recognized the realities of Germany's position in a divided Europe. No responsible German politician could speak, as de Gaulle did, of national *grandeur*. Thus Strauß spoke of sovereignty but increasingly rejected the idea that sovereignty should rest primarily in the nation-state. No single European state could hope to match continental powers such as the U.S. or USSR (or eventually China), he declared on several occasions.[29] Thus Strauß wanted to 'embed the German question within a larger European context, and to work for the reunification of Europe, of which the reunification of Germany is just a part'. He called this the 'Europeanization of the German question'.[30] In a widely distributed interview with *Die Zeit* on 8 April 1966, he declared: 'I do not believe in the re-creation of a German national state, not even within the borders of the four occupation zones.' Rather, he embraced the idea of the two German states coming together within a European political union. Although it was possible that a 'miracle might happen', he could not 'imagine that a pan-German national state could reemerge'.[31] That July, in a speech to the Royal Institute for International Affairs in London, he went further, arguing the Germans should accept a European confederation that included both German states as separate members, as long as there was complete freedom of choice in the GDR.[32]

Responding to criticisms that his European ideas would delay détente, Strauß claimed that the East Germans and the Soviets wanted to encourage the Germans to think in purely national terms, since that would hinder the development of Europe and encourage the Germans to compromise their ties to the West.[33] The Germans should resist that temptation, and not 'waste [their] energy on a nation-state restoration', since nation states were 'anachronistic structures that can no longer fulfil their function' thanks to the 'technical revolution' in the world. They should instead work on 'the creation of a continental system which would naturally make the coming together of their nation possible again.'[34]

Europeanization of the German question was thus for Strauß not primarily an idealistic position as much as a logical result of the 'laws of mathematics' of the international system that he encouraged de Gaulle to recognize. Western Europeans, based on their size and especially on their population and their industrial capacity, could only play an appropriate role in the Concert of the Great Powers 'if they can give up their little nation-state organization, their back garden existence [*Schrebergärtner-Dasein*], their little niche idyll' and embrace political integration.[35] He believed, based on 'historical experience', that the 'reunification of Germany is not possible without the prior creation of a European architecture'.[36] Since chances for freedom and unity were so small, the Germans 'should guard against dealing in excessively idealistic conceptions of the historical possibilities of the present and future, and especially free ourselves from the superstition [*Aberglauben*] that the rest of the world feels responsible for carrying out the charge of the German Basic Law'.[37]

With his arguments about Western European and German integration, Strauß tried to find a position that was linked to the mainstream but also pointed in new directions. Strategic and political considerations did not stand alone, however. Economic arguments provided another important aspect of his vision. As the finance and economic spokesman for the CDU/CSU after 1964, and later as finance minister in the grand coalition from 1966 to 1969, he challenged the more market-oriented positions identified with Ludwig Erhard. Strauß advocated more Keynesian management of the economy and social policies focused on controlling budgets and maintaining a strong currency. Germans and Western Europeans needed to embrace automation and continental cooperation to maximize investment in the 'technologies of the future', even if it meant restricting consumption in the short term.[38]

This combination of managerial authoritarianism and conservative *dirigisme* linked Strauß with both powerful economic interests and more progressive voices. He became an enthusiastic booster of Jean-Jacques Servan-Schreiber's 1967 bestseller, *The American Challenge*, in which the liberal French journalist called for greater European cooperation to compete with American economic power.[39] Strauß and Servan-Schreiber were the most prominent voices in a larger wave of publications in the mid to late 1960s that emphasized the need to overcome national thinking through technocratic management in a 'planetary age'.[40]

Servan-Schreiber focused on the American technological lead over Europe, the dominance of American multinational corporations in global commerce, and the need for Europeans to adopt some forms of American managed capitalism in order to preserve European independence in the world. Simple Atlanticism was not enough, since it would consign Europe to permanent dependence on American capital. Thus the answer had to be an effective European federation, even if that meant sacrificing national sovereignty. Even though the book suggested a clash between European and American interests, Servan-Schreiber was anything but anti-American. His main target was European provincialism. Declaring that 'our problems are rooted in the need to change the hopelessly ossified European societies which find it so difficult to become more flexible', Servan-Schreiber envisaged a future in the hands of a revitalized European left that could embrace managerial technocratic values and 'recapture its identity and its competence to once again become an indispensable progressive force'.[41]

The pairing of the conservative Strauß and the liberal Servan-Schreiber was at first blush unusual.[42] It has also been ignored by the relevant scholarship on *The American Challenge*.[43] Europeans have proven uninterested in exploring these connections, and American attitudes, then as now, ranged from condescending praise for European desire to emulate American methods[44] to criticizing the Europeans for their failure to submit to American leadership with better grace.[45] Strauß, however, saw in Servan-Schreiber a kindred spirit. His embrace of Servan-Schreiber's ideas separated him not only from de Gaulle but also from many fellow Christian Democrats who still yearned for a return to pastoral virtues. Strauß wrote the foreword to the German edition of *The American Challenge*. Calling it 'a book for a France on a better path to Europe' that would be free of all 'taboos', Strauß saw it as a 'cry against a mentality that inclines toward assigning the Europeans in their relations with the USA the role of the Greeks opposite the Roman Empire'.[46]

For Strauß, technocratic ideas complemented his geopolitical arguments for greater Western European global autonomy. Since no European state could guarantee its security individually, a political union should do it; and since no individual European state could dream of competing directly with the United States economically, the only answer was greater European cooperation in research, development and economic planning. Strauß put these ideas to work both in his industrial policies in Bavaria, and on a European scale with the Airbus consortium, where a combination of subsidies and government contracts supported the development of industries such as aerospace, computers, automobiles, oil and chemicals.[47] Such industrial policy secured further contracts, funding and influence for German firms, while also creating the kind of European-wide economies of scale that would allow the Europeans to meet the American challenge. Even before Servan-Schreiber's book appeared, Strauß wrote to Erhard in 1966 warning of American economic dominance and calling for 'stronger European cooperation and coordination' that 'could secure for Europe a better chance to stand up to the Americans'. Without such European action, dependence on American technology would make Europe 'politically and militarily ... a complete satellite of the United States of America'.[48] Strauß urged the government to 'give German industry the encouragement to unite on the European level ... Only in this way can we create a European industrial potential that has a chance to compete.' Otherwise, Europe 'will have nothing more to offer. We will become industrial licensees of the USA.'[49]

Strauß hoped that his identification with Servan-Schreiber would allow him to cultivate a new image as the leader of a modern conservative pro-European movement. As the 1969 West German elections approached, he attempted to take advantage of his high profile, preparing for the future by releasing a new edition of *The Grand Design*. Expanded and revised under the title *Challenge and Response*, with a foreword by Servan-Schreiber, the book offered a more detailed discussion of the future of Germany and Europe, including both more detailed economic discussions and stronger rhetoric about overcoming the nation-state. The German edition appeared in 1968, with English, French, Italian and Spanish editions, including a new postscript, in early 1969.[50]

Such grandiose plans were, however, overtaken by events. By early 1969, Strauß's European vision appeared passé, if not dangerous. A new age had dawned, with its emphasis on détente and Ostpolitik, and plans for the political and military integration of Western Europe were considered irrelevant at best, if not retrograde and dangerous.[51] The end of the Prague Spring guaranteed that progress on détente depended on accepting the status quo of a divided Europe and would also have to proceed at a speed that was at least accepted, if not determined, by the superpowers. Social democratic advocates of détente had already made their peace with accepting the status quo as a means to overcome it, most famously in Egon Bahr's vision of 'Change through Rapprochement'.[52] Strauß's vision, based on challenging the status quo directly, was increasingly out of step with the times. The irony here is that the conservative politician came under attack for being too radical, while progressives argued that the best policy involved accepting international realities. Strauß was frustrated by the contradictory objections to his vision: 'The current situation is unsatisfactory; the reestablishment of the German Reich is impossible in the conceivable future, and our assumption into Europe is not wanted, because our neighbours think we will be too strong a part of it.'[53]

Strauß continued to make variations of his European arguments into the 1970s, but changes in the domestic and international environment pushed European political integration down on the agenda. In opposition after 1969, the CDU/CSU adopted a critical attitude towards Willy Brandt's Ostpolitik, and Strauß adopted more nationalist and anti-communist tones, rejecting compromises with the East. He also increasingly emphasized Atlanticism, defending NATO against an allegedly resurgent neutralism represented by both the SPD and the Greens and downplaying his earlier Gaullist enthusiasms. Those positions were consistent with the anti-communist and nationalist positions he had adopted in the 1950s, but nonetheless they represented a retreat from the more creative positions he had advanced in the mid-1960s. By the 1980s, when the CDU/CSU returned to government, Strauß, who remarked after the ratification of the major Ostpolitik treaties that 'pacta sunt servanda', presented himself as a realist. He worked within the new international system, negotiating credits for the GDR and even, spectacularly, flying his own plane to Moscow in 1987 to meet with Mikhail Gorbachev.[54] As Bavarian minister president after 1978, he hosted all major international visitors to the Federal Republic, from Ronald Reagan to Erich Honecker. Each action represented his efforts to play the role of statesman, though his vision for Europe faded as circumstances offered little chance for its realization. Whether Strauß would have been willing or able to work more practically towards his European vision under different circumstances, or if the nationalism he also encouraged would have undermined it anyway, is an intriguing if ultimately unanswerable question. By the time of his death in October 1988, his public reputation centred less on any grand European ideas than on his role as Bavaria's 'uncrowned king'.

From a post–Cold War perspective, Strauß's vision for Europe appears less incorrect than ill-timed. Despite the initial atmosphere of experimentation, the mid-1960s were not the right time to speculate on the creation of an independent Western Europe. The Americans had become worried that an integrated Europe would be a Gaullist Europe and did not want to see such a thing, especially as long as the French government appeared interested in thwarting American policy at every turn. If anything, it was more in the logic of a superpower to seek dialogue with their chief rival than to help build a new potential competitor. Thus successive American administrations from Kennedy through Nixon accelerated their search for détente with the Soviets to stabilize the international status quo.

Even if the Americans had been more amenable, the state of European politics offered another roadblock: no matter how attractive Strauß tried to make the idea of a Franco-German alliance at the core of Europe, actual French policy was a barrier to progress. Strauß recognized this, and after 1966 he hoped to win the British over to Europe as a way to encourage French reconsideration, but the British were themselves too ambivalent about their place in Europe to support major initiatives. Although German policy priorities remained centred on encouraging political integration in Europe, the realization of such priorities was pushed further into the future. Just as détente reinforced the role of the superpowers, it also encouraged Atlanticism, since efforts at Western European integration appeared as old-fashioned Cold War thinking, compared to the need to reduce tension between East and West. The possibility that a day might come when there would be no division of Europe at all was not on anyone's radar.

This leads us back to the paradox of Franz Josef Strauß. Although his critics claimed he was an incorrigible 'Cold Warrior', his vision of an integrated Western Europe operating on a global scale as the equal to the continental superpowers offered a glimpse into the possibilities of the post–Cold War world. As he wrote to a colleague in 1966: 'I am neither a Pan-German dreamer nor an emotional nationalist; rather, I am trying ... to help create the historical basis from which a free and independent Europe could emerge'.[55] Unlike many progressive visionaries of his era who aimed at accepting and managing the Cold War status quo, Strauß aimed at transcending both the Cold War and the nation-state. Provocative and ultimately rejected in his own era, his ideas have great significance for our own. The postscript to *Challenge and Response*, written in early 1969, could have been written last week. 'Europe needs power resources of its own to safeguard its freedom', Strauß declared, dismissing those who expected Europe to renounce an international role as 'daydreaming about the world they would like to see and [failing] to see the world as it is."[56] Although he failed to translate his vision into concrete politics, his ideas still have value in any discussion of Europe's future. A politician would read that sentence as criticism; an intellectual would see it as high praise. Franz Josef Strauß earned both.

Notes

1. K. Hildebrand. 1984. *Von Erhard zur grossen Koalition,* Stuttgart: Deutsche Verlags-Anstalt, 160
2. T. Geiger. 2008. *Atlantiker gegen Gaullisten: aussenpolitischer Konflikt und innerparteilicher Machtkampf in der CDU/CSU 1958–1969,* Munich: Oldenbourg. See also R.J. Granieri. 2003. *The Ambivalent Alliance: Konrad Adenauer, the CDU/CSU, and the West, 1949–1966,* New York: Berghahn; and E. Conze. 1996. *Die Gaullistische Herausforderung,* Munich: Oldenbourg.
3. 'Es geht um Deutschland und Europa: Dokumentation der Landesversammlung der Christlich-Sozialen Union in Bayern am 9. /10. April 1965 in München', Archiv für Christlich-Soziale Politik (hereafter ACSP) Nachlaß (NL) Franz Josef Strauß (FJS) Sammlung Kray RPT 65 (2).
4. Transcript in Bundesarchiv Koblenz (hereafter BAK) NL Guttenberg 1397, Band 47.
5. Monika Strauß Hohlmeier and Franz Georg Strauß, interview with the author, 1 Mar. 2008. For the irritation his independence caused among colleagues, see Gerhard Schröder, handwritten notes on meeting of the Kressbonner Kreis, 2 June 1969, Archiv für Christlich-Demokratische Politik (ACDP) NL Schröder 01-483-276.
6. The U.S. edition is F.J. Strauß. 1966. *The Grand Design: A European Approach to German Unification,* New York: Praeger.
7. Strauß, 'Mit Europa und mit Amerika', *Welt am Sonntag,* 21 Nov. 1965, ACDP NL Schröder 01-483-143/1.
8. Strauß speech in Milwaukee, 12 June 1964, ACSP, NL FJS Sammlung Kray RA 64 (1).
9. Strauß speech to CSU Landesversammlung, 30 June 1967, ACSP Sammlung Kray RPT 67 (1).
10. F.J. Strauß. 1965. 'An Alliance of Continents', *International Affairs* 42(2), 191–203. See also Bloemer to Strauß, 6 May 1965, ACSP NL FJS Büro PV 5690.
11. Strauß speech to the Kolpingtag, Saarbrücken, 4 July 1965, ACSP NL FJS Strauß Family 662.
12. Strauß, 'Zur außenpolitischen Lage der Bundesrepublik', ACSP Sammlung Kray A 65 (10).
13. Strauß speech to the CSU convention in Munich, 14 Dec.1968, *Dokumente zur Deutschland Politik* (hereafter *DzD*), Series V, vol. 2, 1599–1602.
14. R. Marcowitz. 1998. 'Yalta, or the Myth of the Division of the World', in C. Buffet and B. Heuser (eds), *Haunted by History: Myths in International Relations,* Oxford: Berghahn, 80–91.
15. Strauß interview with Gaus, 8 Sept. 1968, *DzD,* Series V, vol. 2, 1197–1209, esp. 1203–1205.

16. Strauß in Madrid, 30 Oct. 1967, ACSP CSU Landesgruppe (LG) 5, WP Folder 4/1, 25–28; Strauß speech to CSU Landesversammlung, 30 June 1967, ACSP Sammlung Kray RPT 67 (1).
17. Strauß, 'Es geht um Deutschland und Europa', ACSP Sammlung Kray RPT 65 (2).
18. Strauß speech in Milwaukee, 12 June 1964, ACSP NL FJS Sammlung Kray RA 64 (1).
19. 'Welche Wege führen die EWG aus der Krise?' *Sonntagsblatt*, 30 Jan. 1966, ACSP CSU LG 5, WP Folder 181. See also his comments to the CSU Landesgruppe on 24 Jan. 1966, ACSP CSU LG Minutes.
20. Strauß interview with Gaus, 8 Sept. 1968, *DzD*, Series V, vol. 2, 1201.
21. In addition to the above, see F.J. Strauß. 1966a. *Entwurf für Europa*, Stuttgart: Seewald, 122–124.
22. Strauß speech to the Kolpingtag, Saarbrücken, 4 July 1965. Text in ACSP NL FJS Strauß Family 662.
23. Strauß, *The Grand Design*, 103–104.
24. Strauß speech to CSU Landesversammlung, 30 June 1967, ACSP Sammlung Kray RPT 67; interview with Deutschlandfunk, 14 July 1967, summarized for Schröder by Brennecke on 14 July 1967, ACDP NL Schröder 01-483-276.
25. Strauß speech in Madrid, 30 Oct. 1967, ACSP CSU LG 5, WP Folder 4/1.
26. Blankenhorn to Strauß, 2 June 1969 and Strauß to Blankenhorn, 3 July 1969, ACSP NL FJS Bundesministerium für Finanzen (BMF) 32. See also Hans von der Groeben to Strauß, 30 May 1969 and Strauß to von der Groeben, 17 June 1969, ACSP NL FJS BMF 76.
27. 'Ganz g'scheit wir man erst im Jenseits', *Abendzeitung*, 3 Sept. 1965, ACSP NL FJS Sammlung Kray I 65 (13).
28. 'Healthy Nationalist Party a German Right: Herr Strauss Speaks to Bavaria Voters', *The Times*, 18 Nov. 1966, 8.
29. Interview with Sudwestfunk, 14 Aug. 1966, ACSP Sammlung Kray RU 66 (10). He believed that China would reach a position to challenge the existing powers by 2040. Strauß speech in Bundestag, 30 Nov. 1965, ACSP Sammlung Kray RB 65 (2).
30. 'Es geht um Deutschland und Europa', ACSP Sammlung Kray RPT 65 (2), especially 20–28; 'Die Zweierunion und die Europäisierung der deutschen Frage', 15 Oct. 1964, in F.J. Strauß. 1968. *Franz Josef Strauß: Bundestagsreden*, edited by L. Wagner, Bonn, Studio AZ, 217–224.
31. Strauß interview with *Die Zeit*, 8 Apr. 1966, *DzD*, Series IV, vol. 12, 435–442.
32. Strauß speech to the Royal Institute for International Affairs London, *DzD*, Series IV, vol. 12, 928ff.
33. Strauß speech to CSU Landesversammlung, 30 June 1967, ACSP Sammlung Kray RPT 67 (1).
34. Strauß, 'Nation mit neuem Auftrag', *Die Politische Meinung*, Oct. 1967. Excerpts in ACSP CSU LG 5, WP Folder 4/1.
35. Interview with Gaus, 8 Sept. 1968, *DzD*, Series V, vol. 2, 1207.
36. Strauß to Josef Klaus, 26 May 1966, ACSP CSU LG 5, WP Folder 139.
37. Interview with Sudwestfunk, 14 Aug. 1966, ACSP Sammlung Kray RU 66 (10).
38. Strauß, 'Gegenwartskonsum oder Zukunftsvorsorge', manuscript dated 1 Nov. 1965, ACSP Sammlung Kray A 65 (10). See also his Bundestag speech on 30 Nov.1965, ACSP Sammlung Kray RB 65 (2), 26–28.
39. J.-J. Servan-Schreiber. 1967. *Le Défi Américain*, Paris: Denoël; American edition: *The American Challenge*, New York: Athenaeum, 1968. See also R. Kuisel. 1993. *Seducing the French: The Dilemma of Americanization*, Berkeley: University of California Press, 154–184.
40. L. Armand. 1961. *Plaidoyer pour l'avenir*, Paris: Calmann-Lévy; L. Armand and M. Drancourt. 1968. *Le Pari Européen*, Paris: Fayard [published in English as *The European Chal-*

lenge, New York: Athenaeum, 1970]. Armand contributed a chapter to *The American Challenge.* Strauß spoke of the need to think on a 'continental scale' in his interview with Gaus, 8 Sept. 1968, *DzD,* Series V, vol. 2, 1206–1207.

41. Servan-Schreiber, *American Challenge,* 155–156, 177–178, 186, 228.

42. Servan-Schreiber says as much in his foreword to F.J. Strauß. 1968a. *Herausforderung und Antwort: Ein Programm für Europa,* Stuttgart: Seewald, 7.

43. Kuisel does not discuss the popularity of Servan-Schreiber's ideas elsewhere in Europe. Nor does R. Pells. 1997. *Not Like Us: Europeans and the USA,* New York: Basic Books.

44. See A. Schlesinger, Jr., Foreword to the American edition of *The American Challenge,* ix–x, and also the review by A. Campbell in *The New Republic* 159 (27 July 1968), 20.

45. J. Ney. 1969. *The European Surrender,* Boston: Little, Brown.

46. Strauß, foreword to Servan-Schreiber. 1968. *Die Amerikanische Herausforderung,* Stuttgart: Seewald, 17–18.

47. M. S. Milosch. 2006. *Modernizing Bavaria: The Politics of Franz Josef Strauß and the CSU, 1949–1969,* New York and Oxford: Berghahn. On Airbus, see Roussel to Strauß, 17 Mar. 1970 and Strauß to Roussel, 22 May 1970, ACSP NL FJS Büro Bonn 3634, and 'Wir haben den Fuß in der Tür', *Der Spiegel,* 9 May 1977, 115–118.

48. Strauß to Erhard, 5 July 1966, ACSP NL FJS Büro Bonn 3442.

49. 'Werden wir zu Arbeitern Amerikas?', *Bild,* 12 Aug. 1966. Enclosed in K. Schölzke to Strauß, 14 Aug. 1966, ACSP CSU-LG 5, WP Folder 149.

50. Strauß, *Herausforderung und Antwort;* English version, *Challenge and Response: A Program for Europe,* trans. by H. Fox, London: Weidenfeld and Nicolson, 1969 and New York: Athenaeum, 1970. See also Rieger to Seewald, 19 Feb. 1969, with the final draft of the postscript, ACSP NL FJS BMF 238.

51. See 'F. J. Strauß' Herausforderung', *Die andere Zeitung,* 5 Dec. 1968, 11; and H. Rasch. 1968. 'Strauß fordert heraus', *Blätter für deutsche und Internationale Politik* XIII (November), 1209–1210, ACSP NL FJS BMF 237.

52. T. Garton Ash. 1993. *In Europe's Name: Germany and the Divided Continent,* London: Jonathan Cape.

53. Strauß interview with Gaus, 8 Sept. 1968, *DzD,* Series V, vol. 2, 1208.

54. F.J. Strauß. 1989. *Erinnerungen,* Berlin: Goldmann, 612–628. See also Ronald J. Granieri. 2009. 'Odd Man Out? The CDU/CSU, Ostpolitik, and the Atlantic Alliance', in T.A. Schwartz and M. Schulz (eds), *The Strained Alliance: U.S.-European Relations from Nixon to Carter,* New York: Cambridge University Press, 83–101, esp. 97–101.

55. Strauß to Klaus, 26 May 1966, ACSP CSU-LG 5, WP Folder 139.

56. Strauß, *Challenge and Response,* 174.

Section IV

A HELSINKI VISION?

Chapter 8

A VERY BRITISH VISION OF DÉTENTE

The United Kingdom's Foreign Policy during the Helsinki Process, 1969–1975

Martin D. Brown

In late July 1975, delegations from thirty-three European counties, plus the United States and Canada, arrived in Helsinki to sign the Final Act of the Conference on Security and Cooperation in Europe (CSCE). The culmination of nearly six years of consultations, this moment proved to be the apogee of East-West détente. Over the thirty years since then, numerous commentators have argued that the act marked the beginning of the end of the Soviet bloc, the result of the inclusion of clauses legitimizing human rights as a subject for international negotiations. However, an examination of Britain's involvement undermines this 'visionary' interpretation of the Helsinki process.

Prime Minister Harold Wilson had been selected to make the opening address to the thousand or so delegates gathered in the auditorium of the newly completed Finlandia Hall.[1] In his speech he warmly welcomed the outcome of the talks, but he gave no indication that he envisaged them hastening the end of the Cold War, and he made no reference to human rights.[2] While Wilson's apparent lack of 'vision' sits somewhat uncomfortably with the theme of this volume, it provides a much-needed corrective to the retrospective glorification of the Final Act.

This chapter challenges the preeminence of human rights–based analyses of the CSCE through an examination of the formation of British foreign policy. It will demonstrate that between 1969 and 1975, consecutive British governments remained diffident about the expected outcomes of the process.[3] They engaged with the CSCE for a variety of reasons, foremost among them an inclination to preserve concord with their partners in the North Atlantic Treaty Organization (NATO) and the European Community (EC),[4] many of whom were far more enthusiastic proponents of détente. But while supportive of détente in general, London remained hesitant about the utility of the CSCE in particular. Second, the government acknowledged that limited political and economic advantages might be accrued. Still, it never made the Helsinki process a policy priority; various competing domestic and foreign concerns took precedence. Tellingly, British participation was neither instigated nor directed by senior political figures, unlike in the Federal Republic of Germany (FRG) or the Union of Soviet Socialist Republics (USSR). Instead, impetus emanated from a small coterie of middle-ranking Foreign and Commonwealth Office (FCO) officials. Overall, Britain's attitude towards the CSCE was hesitant and cautious, and there is little evidence of any 'visionary' expectations regarding its outcomes.

Before examining the formation of British policy, it is necessary to highlight the extent to which the human rights dimension of the CSCE (commonly referred to as Basket III of the negotiations) has come to dominate, and distort, our understanding of this subject.[5] Many secondary sources promote the thesis that the human rights clauses in the act functioned as a 'ticking time bomb' that later contributed, albeit obliquely, to the eventual implosion of the Soviet bloc.[6] This concept is sometimes expressed through the simplistic equation 'Final Act = Human Rights = Won the Cold War'.[7] While most serious authors eschew such reductive conclusions, they often still overemphasize the influence of Basket III and underemphasize the fact that the Final Act was a non-binding agreement, deliberately designed to avoid legal obligations.[8]

A reading of British and American media coverage from this era further undermines these arguments. These sources reveal that attention was focused on the rectitude of recognizing postwar Central European frontiers, on the development of multilateral security structures and on the free(r) movement of information and peoples, referred to as 'human contacts'[9] (especially Jewish emigration from the USSR).[10] The Final Act itself also was widely reported as a Soviet victory, or at the very best as a 'draw'.[11]

Few references to human rights are to be found in British official sources, not least compared to references to the aforementioned human contacts.[12] This is hardly surprising, as human rights were a problematic subject. As one memorandum noted, '[I]n the propaganda field we wish to be in a position to debate Czechoslovakia [after the Warsaw Pact invasion of 1968] but to prevent debate of Northern Ireland.'[13] From the British perspective human rights were not a universally accepted 'norm', but rather a double-edged sword, both sides used to score Cold War points – a game Whitehall had played diligently since the late 1940s.[14] Put bluntly, British governments had no more interest in accepting legal agreements

on human rights than the Soviets did.[15] In addition, the CSCE failed to establish any methods to monitor Basket III commitments until the 'human
dimension mechanism' was agreed to in 1989.[16] Equally, Britain resisted
enacting any domestic human rights legislation until 1998.[17]

The reason behind the prevalence of these interpretations lies in American reactions to the CSCE after 1975, principally in the retrospective re-
writing of Washington's involvement – not least by Henry Kissinger – and
in the categorization of the process as a zero-sum game.[18] Timothy Garton
Ash has argued that these influences, among others, have transformed
Helsinki into a mythologized shorthand for something that did not occur,
as has happened with the Yalta Conference.[19] Vojtech Mastny makes a similar point, maintaining that '[t]he CSCE is a textbook case of history read
backwards'.[20] Human rights were (and are) important, but they received
far less consideration in the period leading up to August 1975 than has subsequently been claimed. As Donald Cameron Watt might have observed,
the continued fixation with this issue reveals far more about Western discourses after 1975 than it does about the historic Helsinki process.[21]

Further clarification therefore depends on access to, and the study of,
primary rather than secondary materials. The relevant British documentation was released just over a decade ago, in parallel with the publication of
the third series of *Documents on British Policy Overseas* (*DBPO*). Research-
ers now have access to a growing selection of original materials, albeit
predominantly Western ones.[22] These resources have been used in a small
number of texts examining British involvement in the negotiations, notably works by Brian Fall and Keith Hamilton.[23] Nevertheless, a caveat
should be raised here, as over-reliance on official materials can lead to
problems.[24] It could be argued that the decision to devote an entire volume of the *DBPO* to the CSCE has overemphasized the relative importance of this process. Anne Deighton has pointed out that the Soviet Union
was not a British foreign policy priority in the late 1960s.[25] Archie Brown
has observed that these records fail to reveal the full range of opinions
within officialdom.[26] To compensate for these concerns, this chapter will
employ a broad range of sources, from which some conclusions about the
formation of British foreign policy can be teased.

The origins of the Helsinki process, and of the Final Act, lie in the messy
and confused conclusion of the Second World War, exacerbated by the
absence of any postwar peace conference (à la Paris in 1919 or Vienna in
1814–15) and by the Allies' hasty, and fractious, division of Germany and
Berlin.[27] Starting in the mid-1950s, a number of unsuccessful attempts were
made to craft a new security architecture designed to ameliorate these territorial tensions in Central Europe.[28] It was not until the mid-1960s, however, that détente flourished in a more receptive environment.[29] At this

point, the Warsaw Pact requested that a European Security Conference (ESC) be convened, and NATO tentatively agreed.[30] Progress was briefly delayed by the invasion of Czechoslovakia in August 1968, but NATO formally accepted proposals for an ESC in December 1969.[31] The CSCE process evolved out of these multilateral exchanges. Preparatory talks opened outside Helsinki on 22 November 1972 and led to agreement on the format, agenda and costs of the conference.[32] In July 1973 the first stage began with a meeting of foreign ministers in Helsinki.[33] A more protracted, and often more acrimonious, second stage began in Geneva in September 1973 and concluded on 21 July 1975.[34] The Final Act was signed in Helsinki on 1 August 1975.[35]

It is now clear that this process was initiated by decisions made in Moscow, Washington, Warsaw, Berlin and especially Bonn, where Willy Brandt's pursuit of Ostpolitik set the pace. Several of these participants, Brandt and the Soviet leader Leonid I. Brezhnev in particular, had their own 'visions' of what they hoped to achieve.[36] Conversely, London was conspicuously absent from this list of détente's 'movers and shakers', for the simple reason that the government was preoccupied with other matters.[37] East-West relations were a major concern, but – perhaps counterintuitively – the Cold War was not always the preeminent or only consideration in British foreign policy.

The general consensus within the FCO was that the CSCE was a Soviet ploy designed to undermine Western cohesion.[38] As one British diplomat later recalled, it was seen as 'a Russian propaganda initiative that we should treat with the utmost scepticism and care'.[39] Another remarked that they feared that 'if we go into a conference with the Russians, they are so much cleverer than we are that they will steal our trousers.'[40] These opinions were perhaps to be expected in the FCO, whose upper echelons clung to a Cold Warrior's world view at odds with the concept of détente.[41] These negative attitudes therefore raise a crucial paradox: why did British governments engage with the CSCE? The answer is to be found in the Cabinet conclusions of 11 December 1969:

> [I]t was pointed out that the United States had initiated talks on strategic arms limitation with the Soviet Union; the Federal Republic of Germany was having bilateral discussions with that country and other Warsaw Pact members; and the French had declared themselves in favour of a system of bilateral contacts. We did not appear to have taken any comparable initiative; and we therefore ran the risk of being accused of rigidity and a lack of enthusiasm for détente between East and West.[42]

Wilson's, and subsequently Edward Heath's, governments engaged with the ESC (then the CSCE) to keep in step with their allies and to be seen as fully engaged with détente.[43] There is little evidence of any genuine enthusiasm for the process.

Another motivating factor was Britain's multilateral obligations, particularly its membership of NATO and involvement (after 1972) with the EC's Davignon machinery, both organizations advocating continued dialogue with the Soviet bloc.[44] These commitments propelled Britain into ever-deeper engagement with the CSCE, a stance that sharpened interest in maintaining concord with these allies so as to prevent the Soviets from exploiting any internal disunity.[45] The resignation of French President General Charles de Gaulle in April 1969 and the closer relations that developed between Heath and Georges Pompidou finally led to the U.K.'s accession to the EC, thus placing greater emphasis on European Political Cooperation (EPC)[46] – so much so that London's negotiating tactics were more often than not in line with the positions taken by Paris and Bonn.[47]

The motivation provided by bilateral relations with the USSR and the United States is less apparent. During Heath's premiership, contacts with the Kremlin were strained as a result of the mass expulsion of Soviet 'spies' in 1971 – although by February 1975 they had improved sufficiently for Brezhnev to invite Wilson to Moscow for a good-natured visit.[48] The Soviets viewed the British, probably correctly, as reticent participants in the CSCE, but as the process progressed, relations were reported as having 'dramatically improved'.[49] The clarity of communications with Washington left much to be desired too. President Richard Nixon's administration was regarded as notoriously difficult to deal with, and Kissinger's self-proclaimed 'Year of Europe' was poorly received.[50] That having been said, both governments shared reservations about the utility of the process and kept in close contact throughout.[51] The two superpowers' contribution to the CSCE was vital, as no agreement could be achieved without them, but neither appears to have had a particularly positive impact on British participation.

By September 1971, these interrelated dynamics led the FCO to report to Heath: 'We lack enthusiasm for the idea of a conference and regard it as an event which may have to be accepted as a political inevitability. There is no reason, we think, to be afraid of an ESC *per se.*'[52] While this was hardly an enthusiastic endorsement, it did signal a resigned acceptance of this process. Hereafter, British policy, in line with Britain's allies (not least the French), was designed to use the negotiations to secure limited political, cultural and economic concessions from Moscow and, if possible, to loosen the Soviet Union's grip on its satellite states[53] – although not to an extent that might threaten the Soviet bloc's internal stability.[54] A Polish representative later explained that 'détente gives us room for manoeuvre', and this would seem to be the best summary of these goals, as opposed to any concerted attempt to destroy communist regimes from within.[55]

This leads us to the second motivating factor behind Britain's involvement with the CSCE: the advantages it expected the process to produce. In particular, it hoped it would ease passage of the talks on Mutual and Balanced Force Reduction (MBFR), which, after some early reservations, were regarded as more substantive.[56] This proved not to be the case, but the documents made repeated reference to the linkage between the two issues and encouraged further involvement with both.[57]

Britain also expressed a keen interest in the success of Ostpolitik. This was due, in part, to its military and financial commitments to the FRG, especially those related to the British Army on the Rhine (BAOR) and the four-power administration of Berlin.[58] Both Wilson and Heath welcomed Brandt's engagement with the German Democratic Republic (GDR) and the USSR, as well as the various bilateral treaties Bonn signed with its eastern neighbours in the early 1970s.[59] British support was most clearly demonstrated by the alacrity with which the U.K. recognized the GDR in December 1972.[60] Moreover, Whitehall expressly identified the finalization of these treaties, and the Quadripartite Agreement on Berlin, as prerequisites for its involvement with the CSCE.[61]

Equal emphasis was placed on the expectation that the conference, in conjunction with the MBFR, might help reduce defence expenditure and promote East-West trade.[62] The economic discussions conducted in Basket II are often overlooked, but the FCO regarded them as important enough to hold interdepartmental consultations with the Department of Trade and Industry and to send one of its officials, Michael Fielder, to Geneva.[63] These economic dimensions should not be overemphasized, having ultimately failed to deliver the expected rewards, but they were a factor, especially given the bleak economic circumstances of the early 1970s.[64]

Nevertheless, once the decision to take part in the CSCE had been made, it never became a foreign policy priority. A close reading of Cabinet discussions and Commons debates confirms this, as does the lower status accorded to the CSCE delegation compared to the one sent to the MBFR.[65] This was because the process generated very little public discussion in Britain (unlike in the United States),[66] with only the weekly magazine *The Economist* opposing the talks.[67] Also, the extended and intricate nature of the process meant that it failed to excite the electorate's interest or to generate much political capital. Members of Parliament were kept informed of developments, but no major debates were held on the subject until mid-July 1975.[68] Between 1969 and 1975, Whitehall spent far more time dealing with the economy and the worsening conflict in Northern Ireland than with the CSCE, while foreign affairs were dominated by events in the Commonwealth, the Mediterranean, and the Middle East, and by accession to the EC.[69] The signing of the Final Act itself was overshadowed by Britain's referendum on EC membership and by the political crisis in Portugal.[70]

This leads us to the third and final point regarding British policy formation: that these negotiations were conducted, and directed, by a small group of middle-ranking FCO diplomats. In the final analysis, ministers exerted relatively minor influence over what was a complex, convoluted and protracted round of multilateral negotiations. Direct ministerial involvement occurred precisely twice: during the foreign ministers' meetings in July 1973, and at the final ceremony in August 1975.[71] Moreover, the FCO was more than happy to keep its political masters at arm's length.[72] Consequently, British policy at the CSCE was shaped by professional diplomats, who in general are reluctant advocates of substantive change.

Although the FCO was generally hesitant about the CSCE, differences of opinion did exist between London-based staff and staff in embassies behind the Iron Curtain, between senior and junior officials, and among the three Foreign Secretaries Michael Stewart, Alec Douglas-Home and James Callaghan.[73] These divergent views might have hindered the development of a coherent policy, had it not been for the head of the Western Organisations Department (WOD), Crispin Tickell. His departmental remit covered politico-military affairs, NATO, the EC and the MBFR, as well as the proposed CSCE. In February 1972, Tickell submitted a memorandum arguing that dialogue with the Soviet bloc for its own sake could be advantageous, and that the CSCE might be used to wrestle a minor propaganda victory from the situation.[74] Although this was no 'visionary' statement of intent and contained no mention of human rights or of ending the Cold War, it did offer the possibility of using the conference to jostle for position and to prove Britain's pro-détente credentials. By happy coincidence, Tickell's well-timed memorandum provided just such a solution, and his department was best placed to implement it. Thus Tickell and the WOD took the lead in fashioning the coordinating machinery required to navigate through these discussions. The delegation was first led by Ambassador Anthony Elliot and then, after November 1974, by Ambassador David Hildyard. Day-to-day negotiations were handled by, among others, Charles Adams, Michael Alexander, Roger Beetham, Rodric Braithwaite, Brian Fall, Michael Pakenham and David Miller.[75] They ensured that a cautiously diplomatic approach prevailed, focused on preserving allied unity and on maintaining a consistent line with the Soviet bloc.[76]

The protracted course of British involvement with the CSCE has already been well documented, and there is no need to recount these events in detail again.[77] During the three stages of the conference, the British delegation worked closely with its NATO, EC and neutral partners. This cooperation ensured that the wording of the Final Act came as close as possible to providing the required outcomes on security issues, economic and scientific cooperation, human contacts and the proposed follow-up meetings. As we have already noted, discussion of human rights, as compared to the concern with human contacts, was infrequent. Cooperation with the French, Dutch, Swiss and West German delegations proved useful, while the Maltese were the most awkward of attendees.[78] The lack of any sustained American engagement at the outset of the process also raised concerns.[79] On the opposing side, only the Soviets were regarded as capable of serious negotiations, and Ambassador Lev I. Mendelevich was singled out for some little praise, while the delegations from the other satellite states were viewed as less useful partners.[80]

Ironically, Britain's crowning achievement in the final phases of the CSCE had nothing to do with the talents of its diplomatic team. Rather, the decision to select Wilson to give the opening speech in Stage III was simply down to the drawing of names in a lottery. 'The Prime Minister is presented with an unexpected opportunity to steal the headlines for the first day', Hildyard announced.[81] Wilson did not disappoint. According to one observer, it was 'a brilliant performance. It was excellent substantively, as well as rhetorically.'[82] But even after this unanticipated coup, the FCO's estimation of the conference's accomplishments remained subdued. Terence Garvey, the Ambassador in Moscow, sent a sober assessment to Callaghan in September 1975: 'The CSCE has given the Russians something that they have long wanted … But the Western Governments have gained also – in limiting and qualifying their endorsement of a situation they do not intend to change.'[83] For better or for worse, Garvey reported that the Cold War looked set to continue for the foreseeable future.

To conclude, British policy between 1969 and 1975 with regard to the Helsinki process was hesitant and diffident about the expected outcomes. High-level political interest in the process was sporadic, and the CSCE never became a foreign policy priority. Most of the substantive negotiations were carried out by middle-ranking FCO diplomats, who were focused on securing a narrow range of political, cultural and economic concessions from Moscow, in addition to proving Britain's credentials as a fully paid-up supporter of détente. Although the FCO ultimately wrestled a minor victory from what was widely regarded as a Soviet propaganda ploy, human rights played a smaller role and were far less apparent than many subsequent texts have suggested. Harold Wilson may well have stolen the limelight by giving the inaugural speech at the conference's finale, but his performance should not be taken as an indication of his interest in the process. The record is quite clear: the CSCE was never a primary consideration in U.K. foreign policy, and Britain's vision of its long-term effectiveness was at best limited.

Notes

1. United Kingdom National Archives (UKNA). Foreign and Commonwealth Office (hereafter, FCO) 41/1772, Hildyard to Helsinki, 17 July 1975; H. Wilson. 1979. *Final Term: The Labour Government, 1974–1976*, London: Weidenfeld and Nicolson, 173.

2. UKNA. Prime Minister's Office (hereafter, PREM) 16/392, Weston to Wright, 18 July 1975, PM's note, 23 July 1975; FCO 69/565, Wilson to Callaghan, 4 Aug. 1975; Wilson, *Final Term*, 290–294.

3. Harold Wilson, 1969–70, Edward Heath, 1970–74, and then Wilson again, 1974–75.

4. Especially via the process of European Political Cooperation (EPC); C. O'Neill. 2000. *Britain's Entry into the European Community: Report on the Negotiations of 1970–1972*, London: Frank Cass.

5. See K. Spohr Readman. 2006. 'National Interests and the Power of "Language": West German Diplomacy and the CSCE, 1972–1975', *Journal of Strategic Studies*, 29(6), 1080–1081.

6. For the prominence given to human rights and the 'ticking bomb' theory see J.L. Gaddis. 2006. *The Cold War: A New History*, London: Penguin, 188–190; E. Heath. 1998. *The Course of My Life: My Autobiography*, London: Hodder and Stoughton, 490; T. Judt. 2007. *Postwar: A History of Europe since 1945*, London: Pimlico, 501–503; D. Reynolds. 2000. *One World Divisible: A Global History since 1945*, London: Allen Lane, 337; M. Walker. 1993. *The Cold War and the Making of the Modern World*, London: Vintage, 237; V. Zubok. 2007. *A Failed Empire: The Soviet Union in the Cold War from Stalin to Gorbachev*, Chapel Hill: University of North Carolina Press, 238.

7. D. Fascell. 1979. 'The Helsinki Accord: A Case Study', *Annals of the American Academy of Political and Social Science*, 442(March), 69–76; R. Kagan and R. Cooper. 2008. 'Is Democracy Winning?', *Prospect*, 146(May), 24–25; M. Morgan, 'From Helsinki to Baghdad', *Wall Street Journal*, 1 Sept. 2005.

8. J. Donnelly. 2003. *Universal Human Rights in Theory and Practice*, London: Cornell University Press, 249; D. C. Thomas. 2005. 'Human Rights Ideas, the Demise of Communism, and the End of the Cold War', *Journal of Cold War Studies*, 7(2), 116–117; Thomas. 2001. *The Helsinki Effect: International Norms, Human Rights and the Demise of Communism*, Princeton, NJ: Princeton University Press, 220–256; cf. G. Edwards. 1985. 'Human Rights and Basket III Issues: Areas of Change and Continuity', *International Affairs*, 61(4), 631–642.

9. There are only eight references to 'human rights' in the Final Act, while 'human contacts' (the reunification of families and the freer exchange of information) is discussed at length under its own subheading; see *CSCE: Final Act*, Helsinki, August 1975, http://www.osce.org (accessed 29 Oct. 2010), 6–7, 38–42.

10. D. Cook. 1973. 'The European Security Conference', *Atlantic Monthly*, 232(4), 6–12; *The Observer*, 23 Sept. 1973; M. Palmer. 1972. 'A European Security Conference: Preparation and Procedure', *The World Today*, 28(January), 36–46; *The Times*, 17 and 26 Sept. 1973.

11. R. Davy. 1975. 'The CSCE Summit', *The World Today*, 31(September), 353; *The Economist*, 24 May 1975, 2 and 9 Aug. 1975; *The Guardian*, 1 and 2 Aug. 1975; *Time Magazine*, 4 Aug. 1975; *The Times*, 28 July 1975 and 2 Aug. 1975.

12. See the references for 'human contacts' (100) and 'human rights' (1) in the index of G. Bennett and K. Hamilton (eds). 1997. *Documents on British Policy Overseas* [hereafter, *DBPO*]: *The Conference of Security and Cooperation in Europe, 1972–1975*, series III, vol. II, London: Routledge, 499.

13. *DBFP*, vol. 2, 20; C. Townshend. 1986. 'Northern Ireland', in R. J. Vincent (ed.), *Foreign Policy and Human Rights: Issues and Responses*, Cambridge: Cambridge University Press, 132–137.

14. UKNA. Cabinet Office files (hereafter CAB) 129/25 CM (48) 72, Bevin memorandum, 3 Mar. 1948; E.G.H. Pedaliu. 2007. 'Human Rights and Foreign Policy: Wilson and the Greek Dictators, 1967–1970', *Diplomacy and Statecraft*, 18(1), 206.

15. Interview with Sir Brian Fall, 12 Sept. 2008 (hereafter, Fall interview); interview with Sir Paul Lever, 22 June 2009 (hereafter, Lever interview).

16. F. Baudet. 2001. 'The Origins of the CSCE Human Dimension Mechanism: A Case Study in Dutch Cold War Policy', *Helsinki Monitor*, 12(3), 185–196.

17. House of Commons Debates (hereafter, HC Deb.), 1997–98 session, vol. 317, col. 1368, 21 Oct. 1998.

18. R. Garthoff. 1994. *Détente and Confrontation: American–Soviet Relations from Nixon to Reagan*, Washington, DC: Brookings Institution, 475–479; R. Kagan. 1999. 'The Revisionist: How Henry Kissinger Won the Cold War, or So He Thinks', *The New Republic*, 220(25), 38–48; H. Kissinger. 1999. *Years of Renewal*, London: Simon and Schuster, 635, 639, 660; P. Williams. 1985. 'Détente and US Domestic Politics', *International Affairs*, 61(3), 431–447; cf. R. Davy. 2009. 'Helsinki Myths: Setting the Record Straight on the Final Act of the CSCE, 1975', *Cold War History*, 9(1), 1–22; C. G. Stefan. 2000. 'The Drafting of the Helsinki Final Act: A Personal View of the CSCE's Geneva Phase (September 1973 until July 1975)', *SHAFR Newsletter*, 31(2), 7–10.

19. T. Garton Ash. 1993. *In Europe's Name. Germany and the Divided Continent*, London: Jonathan Cape, 260, 364; R. Marcowitz. 1998. 'Yalta and the Myth of the Division of the World,' in C. Buffet and B. Heuser (eds), *Haunted by History: Myths in International Relations*, Oxford: Berghahn, 80–91.

20. V. Mastny and A. Wenger. 2008. 'New Perspectives in the Origins of the CSCE Process' in A. Wenger, V. Mastny and C. Nuenlist (eds), *Origins of the European Security System: The Helsinki Process Revisited, 1965–75*, London: Routledge, 3.

21. D.C. Watt. 1978. 'Rethinking the Cold War: A Letter to a British Historian', *The Political Quarterly*, 49(4), 446–448.

22. See *Foreign Relations of the United States* (hereafter, *FRUS*), *1969–1976: European Security*, vol. XXXIX, Washington, DC: U.S. Government Printing Office, 2008; *Cold War International History Project*; *Parallel History Project on Cooperative Security*; V. Mastny and M. Byrne (eds.). 2005. *A Cardboard Castle? An Inside History of the Warsaw Pact, 1955–1991*, Budapest: Central European University; Zubok, *A Failed Empire*, 192–274.

23. B. Fall. 1977. 'The Helsinki Conference, Belgrade and European Security', *International Security*, 2(1), 100–105; K. Hamilton, 'Introduction', *DBPO*, vol. II, v–xxxvi; Hamilton. 1999. 'The Last Cold Warriors: Britain, Détente and the CSCE, 1972–75', *European Interdependence Research Unit*, Oxford, Discussion Paper, EIUR/991, 1–27; Hamilton. 2007. 'Cold War by Other Means: British Diplomacy and the CSCE, 1972–1975,' in W. Loth and G. Soutou (eds.), *The Making of Détente: Eastern Europe and Western Europe in the Cold War, 1965–75*, London: Routledge, 168–182; P. Williams. 1986. 'Britain, Détente and the CSCE', and M. Clarke. 1986. 'Britain and European Political Cooperation in the CSCE' both in K. Dyson (ed.), *European Détente: Case Studies in the Politics of East-West Relations*, London: F. Pinter, 221–236, 237–243.

24. K. Wilson. 1996. 'Governments, Historians, and "Historical Engineering",' in K. Wilson (ed.), *Forging the Collective Memory: Government and International Historians through Two Great Wars*, Oxford: Berghahn, 1–23.

25. A. Deighton. 1998. 'Ostpolitik or Westpolitik? British Foreign Policy, 1968–75', *International Affairs*, 74(4), 900–901.

26. A. Brown. 1998. 'Glasnost at the FCO', *Prospect*, 32(July), 68–69.

27. The FCO's comprehension of the background to, and rationales for, the CSCE can be traced through the volume of documents it produced; see Foreign and Commonwealth Office. 1977. *Selected Documents Related to Problems of Security and Cooperation in Europe, 1954–77*, London: Her Majesty's Stationery Office.

28. U. Bar-Noi. 2008. *The Cold War and Soviet Mistrust of Churchill's Pursuit of Détente, 1951–1955*, Brighton: Sussex Academic Press; G. Bischof and S. Dockrill (eds). 2000. *Cold War Respite: The Geneva Summit of 1955*, Baton Rouge: Louisiana State University Press.

29. See J. Suri. 2003. *Power and Protest: Global Revolution and the Rise of Détente*, Cambridge, MA: Harvard University Press.

30. *The Harmel Report*, Ministerial Communiqué, North Atlantic Council, Brussels, 13–14 Dec. 1967; Declaration of the North Atlantic Council, Reykjavik, 24–25 June 1968, both at http://www.nato.int/ (accessed 21 Oct. 2010).

31. HC Deb., 5th series, vol. 799, cols. 30–31, 6 Apr. 1970; Declaration of the North Atlantic Council, Brussels, 4–5 Dec. 1969.

32. Interview with Roger Beetham, 8 Nov. 2007 (hereafter, Beetham interview) and Fall interview; 'Final Recommendations of the Helsinki Consultations', 8 June 1973; http://www.osce.org/ (accessed 20 Oct. 2010).

33. UKNA. PREM 15/2082 'Visit of the Secretary of State for Foreign and Commonwealth Affairs to Helsinki for the first stage of the CSCE', 3–7 July 1973.

34. *DBPO*, vol. II, 447–460.

35. UKNA. CAB 128/57 Cabinet conclusions, 24 July 1975, 3–5.

36. J. von Dannenberg. 2008. *The Foundations of Ostpolitik: The Making of the Moscow Treaty Between West Germany and the USSR*, Oxford: Oxford University Press, 16–66; Mastny and Byrne, *A Cardboard Castle?*, 330–331, 347–353; Zubok, *A Failed Empire*, 193–204.

37. Interview with Dick Leonard, 3 Jun. 2009; interview with Tony Benn, 8 Oct. 2009; S. Dockrill. 2002. *Britain's Retreat from East of Suez: The Choice Between Europe and the World?*, Basingstoke: Palgrave Macmillan, 198–199, 222; D. Greenhill. 1992. *More by Accident*, York: Wilton 65, 131; D. Healey. 1990. *The Time of My Life*, London: Penguin, 358.

38. Beetham interview; interview with George Walden, 27 Oct. 2009; M. Stewart, 'Memorandum on Relations with the Soviet Union and Eastern Europe', 17 June 1969, also D. Wilson to Stewart, 'The Soviet Attitude to West Europe', 14 July 1969, *DBPO: Britain and the Soviet Union, 1968–72*, vol. I, 1997, 48–57, 179–187.

39. *British Diplomatic Oral History Archive* (hereafter, *DOHP*) 36/1 C. Tickell, 9, http://www.chu.cam.ac.uk/archives/collections/BDOHP/ (accessed 20 Oct. 2010).

40. *DOHP* 30/1 R. Braithwaite, 11.

41. Hamilton, 'The Last Cold Warriors', 3–9; Hamilton, 'Cold War by Other Means', 170–171.

42. UKNA. CAB 128/44 Cabinet conclusions, 11 Dec. 1969.

43. See Stewart's reports to Cabinet on a possible ESC, 23 Jan. 1970, in T. Benn. 1988. *Office Without Power: Diaries 1968–72*, London: Hutchinson, 228.

44. *DBPO*, vol. I, 151–157, 171–178, 197–200, 316–317, 441–443; vol. II, 62–69; *The Harmel Report*, 13–14 Dec. 1967; Declaration of the North Atlantic Council, Reykjavik, 24–25

June 1968; 'The Davignon Report' (Luxembourg, 27 Oct. 1970), *Bulletin of the European Communities*, 11(November 1970), 9–14.

45. UKNA. FCO 41/1540-44 CSCE: European political co-operation, 1974; *DOHP* 34/1 M. Alexander, 13–14; *DBPO*, vol. II, 196–199.

46. UKNA. CAB 184/28 'The Kind of Europe We Want', 9–12 Oct. 1971; *DOHP* 63/1 R. Beetham, 23, Braithwaite, 10–11; *DBPO*, vol. II, 62–69; O'Neill, *Britain's Entry into the EC*, 432–439; Clarke, 'Britain and EPC in the CSCE', 241–251.

47. UKNA. CAB 133/429 conversation between Brandt and the PM, 21 Apr. 1972; Heath, *The Course of My Life*, 486–489; A. Romano. 2009. *From Détente in Europe to European Détente: How the West Shaped the Helsinki CSCE*, Brussels: Peter Lang, 153–155.

48. Interview with Sir Crispin Tickell, 29 Nov. 2007 (hereafter, Tickell interview); UKNA. FCO 41/1781 PM's conversation with Brezhnev, Moscow, 13–14 Feb. 1975; *DBPO*, vol. I, 292–425; A.A. Gromyko. 1989. *Memories*, London: Hutchinson, 158–159.

49. UKNA. CAB 128/57 Cabinet Conclusions, 27 July 1975, 5; FCO 41/1772 minutes of meeting of Soviet Ambassador with the PM, 16 June 1975; PREM 15/2082 Speaking note, on Brezhnev's complaints, 26 Feb. 1974.

50. Tickell interview; *DBPO: The Year of Europe: America, Europe and the Energy Crisis, 1972–1974*, vol. VI, 2006; Greenhill, *More by Accident*, 171, 175.

51. *DBPO*, vol. II, 56–57, 323–325, 335–336; *FRUS*, vol. XXXIX, 44–48, 249–251, 391–92, 856–58, 917.

52. UKNA. PREM 15/1522 Graham, to Roberts, 'Memorandum on the possibility of an ESC', 6 Sept. 1971.

53. UKNA. Department of Trade and Industry (hereafter, BT) 241/2665 FCO minute on the CSCE, 7 July 1972, 1–10; *DBPO*, vol. II, 40–42.

54. Romano, *From Détente in Europe to European Détente*, 95, 195.

55. UKNA. CAB 128/57 Cabinet Conclusions, 24 July 1974, 4.

56. UKNA. FCO 41/1504 'MBFR linkage with CSCE', various files, 1974; *DBPO*, vol. II, 43–45; *Détente in Europe, 1972–76*, vol. III, 2001, 1–53; *FRUS*, vol. XXXIX, 249–251, 258–269; Heath, *The Course of My Life*, 488–489.

57. Lever interview. Sir Paul Lever raised the intriguing counterfactual argument that had the MBFR talks been successful, and had NATO managed to get traction on the concessions it wanted, then the 'West' may have been willing to allow the Soviets greater leeway in the wording of the Final Act of the CSCE.

58. Beetham interview; HC Deb., vol. 895, cols. 1295–1296, 1309, 15 July 1975; Benn, *Office Without Power*, 143, 178; J. Garnett. 1970. 'BAOR and NATO', *International Affairs*, 46(4), 670–681.

59. UKNA. PREM 15/1522 Heath to Brandt, 11 Aug. 1970, Record of the PM's meeting with Scheel, 5 Feb. 1971, Record of the PM's meeting with Brandt, 20 and 21 Apr. 1972; Dannenberg, *The Foundations of Ostpolitik*, 238–259.

60. UKNA. FCO 33/224 Roberts to Brown, 13 Mar. 1968; Stewart memorandum, 25 July 1968; HC Deb., vol. 808, cols. 443–444, 457–460, 9 Dec. 1970; vol. 849, cols. 922–923, 29.1.1973.

61. Beetham interview; UKNA. CAB 128/50 Cabinet conclusions, 6 June 1972; FCO 33/2365 and 2366 'Quadripartite Rights and Responsibilities and the CSCE', July 1973 to December 1974; PREM 15/1522 FCO memorandum, 'The Soviet-Germany Treaty: A Preliminary Assessment', 17 Aug. 1970, 1–10; *DBPO*, vol. I, 376–377, 426–427; vol. II, 470–474; HC Deb., vol. 799, col. 30, 6 Apr. 1970; vol. 804, cols. 26–27, 20 July 1970; vol. 808, cols. 438–485, 9 Dec. 1970; vol. 817, cols. 875–877, 17 May 1971; M. Stewart. 1980. *Life and Labour: An Autobiography*, London: Sidgwick and Jackson, 159.

62. *DBPO*, vol. I, 207–210, 440–441; Benn, *Office Without Power*, 97; J. Callaghan. 1987. *Time and Change*, London: Collins, 366; Dockrill, *Britain's Retreat from East of Suez*, 168, 170–171, 197–198, 218; Heath, *The Course of My Life*, 486; Healey, *The Time of My Life*, 379, 411–415.

63. UKNA. BT 241/2665 Preston to Fielder, 19 Dec. 1972, Fall to DTI, 'The Economic Aspects of the CSCE', 10 Jan. 1973; FCO 69/565 Killick to Preston, DTI, 12 Aug. 1975; *DBPO*, vol. II, 444–447.

64. UKNA. CAB 128/56 Cabinet Conclusions, 20 Feb. 1975; 128/57 Cabinet Conclusions, 27 July 1975; P. Hanson. 1985. 'Economic Aspects of Helsinki', *International Affairs*, 61(4), 619–629.

65. Fall interview; UKNA. CAB 128/44 – 57 Cabinet conclusions, January 1969 to December 1975; HC Deb., vol. 799, 1970 to vol. 897, 1975.

66. M.D. Brown. 2009. 'Détente, British foreign policy and public opinion, 1969–75', paper presented at *Britain and the End of the Cold War*, conference organized by the Centre for Contemporary British History, University of London, 23–25 June 2009.

67. Interview with Richard Davy 18 June 2009; interview with Brian Beedham, 28 June 2009; *The Times*, 1969–1975; *Guardian*, 1969–1975; *The Economist*, 26 Apr. 1975, 64, 3 May 1975, 9, 7 June 1975, 32, 21 June 1975, 29, 12 July 1975, 13, 19 July 1975, 40, 26 July 1975, 55, 2 Aug. 1975, 9 and 49, 9 Aug. 1975, 12, 16 Aug. 1975, 40, 23 Aug. 1975, 37.

68. HC Deb., vol. 895, cols. 1274–1341, 15 July 1975.

69. *DOHP* 35/1 E. Fergusson, 7–10, Braithwaite, 15–17; *DBPO: The Southern Flank in Crisis, 1973–1976*, vol. V, 2006; Healey, *The Time of My Life*, 358.

70. HC Deb., vol. 897, cols. 230–245, 5 Aug. 1975; T. Benn. 1989. *Against the Tide: Diaries 1973–76*, London: Hutchinson, 142–143, 385–387.

71. UKNA. FCO 41/1773 Loader, 'Administrative plan for the United Kingdom delegation to the CSCE – Third Stage Helsinki, July 1975', 3 July 1975.

72. Beetham, Fall and Tickell interviews; *DOHP* Alexander, 16; M.D. Brown. 2006. *Dealing with Democrats: The British Foreign Office and the Czechoslovak Émigrés in Great Britain, 1939 to 1945*, Frankfurt am Main: Peter Lang, 27–32.

73. Beetham and Tickell interviews; Sir Christopher Mallaby interview (15 Nov. 2007); *DBPO*, vol. I, 40–57, 229–238, 467–471; Callaghan, *Time and Change*, 364–370; Stewart, *Life and Labour*, 146, 218, 227–228.

74. Beetham and Tickell interviews; *DBPO*, vol. II, 1–15.

75. *The Diplomatic Services List*, vols. 1972–77.

76. Romano, *From Détente in Europe to European Détente*, 128–130.

77. See note 23.

78. *DOHP* Beetham, 21–23, Tickell, 10–12; *DBPO*, vol. II, 317–326, 447–454; Hamilton, 'Cold War by Other Means', 168–182.

79. J. Hanhimäki. 2003. "'They can write in Swahili': Kissinger, the Soviets, and the Helsinki Accords. 1973–75', *Journal of Transatlantic Studies*, 1(1), 37–58.

80. UKNA. FCO 28/2455, 41/1582 to 1587 'Attitude and negotiating tactics of Soviet Union, Eastern European states, Federal Republic of Germany, Poland, Romania, Czechoslovakia, and Switzerland to CSCE', 1–31 Dec. 1974; *DBPO*, vol. II, 287.

81. UKNA. FCO 41/1772 Hildyard to Helsinki, 17 July 1975.

82. *FRUS*, vol. XXXIX, 966.

83. *DBPO*, vol. II, 479.

Chapter 9

THE EC NINE'S VISION AND ATTEMPTS AT ENDING THE COLD WAR

Angela Romano

Among those who attempted to promote visions of the end of the Cold War, the European Community (EC) Nine deserve a due place and a detailed analysis of their rationales and efforts.[1] This chapter will consider the EC Nine as a collective actor expressing a common vision on the issue.[2] It first describes the birth, nature and aims of such an actor, arguing that it emerged in the early 1970s from the interplay of European integration and East-West détente. The chapter then analyses the EC Nine's vision of overcoming the Cold War, exploring both its rationale and aims. The topic is inevitably intertwined with the preparations for the Conference on Security and Cooperation in Europe (CSCE),[3] for the CSCE immediately became the tool of the Nine's attempts to promote a common strategy and common actions. The fundamental question is whether there was indeed an EC Nine scheme to overcome the Cold War or whether the position of the Nine was just a lowest-common-denominator position. To answer this question, the chapter will consider the interaction of national visions in the making of a common strategy, as well as the debate about tactics and means. Finally, the essay briefly reports on and appraises the Nine's performance at the CSCE.

The Birth of the EC Nine as an International Actor

The resignation in 1969 of French President Charles de Gaulle unlocked the doors of the European Community to the membership of Britain, Ireland, Denmark and Norway. The new French leader, Georges Pompidou, linked enlargement to the completion and deepening of the EC, the ambitious so-called triptych of the Hague summit in December 1969. Enlargement was also pivotal in efforts to elaborate a common response to urgent international challenges, not least the marginality of Western Europe within global politics. The Community *à Neuf*, with its 253 million citizens and its status as the biggest trade power in the world, had additional weight in the international arena, as well as greater responsibility. The EC member countries faced challenges they could not manage effectively unless they united: East-West dialogue, commercial and monetary negotiations among industrialized countries, relations with developing countries. All of these issues needed both careful study to ascertain EC interests and the political definition of strategic goals and tactics. Hence, at the Hague summit, the EC member states also decided to initiate European Political Cooperation (EPC) – a mechanism designed to coordinate the foreign policy stances of the EC member states – in order 'to prepare the way for a united Europe capable of assuming its responsibilities in the world of tomorrow and of making a contribution commensurate with its tradition and its mission'.[4] This step also revealed the search for a specific European political identity. In structure, the EPC was purely intergovernmental: EC governments decided only to harmonize their views on foreign policy, coordinate national positions and, where possible and desirable, take common actions. They pledged to consult each other, not to reach agreement.[5]

The first EPC meeting in November 1970 focused on East-West relations, against a backdrop of intensifying détente pushed forward by West German Ostpolitik, increased dialogue between the superpowers, and the Warsaw Pact's call for a conference on security and cooperation in Europe. The topic was broadly debated, and the foreign ministers agreed to a Belgian proposal that the EPC should engage in elaborating a common policy on the pan-European conference.[6] The EC member states set up EPC working bodies expressly to deal with the CSCE, despite the fact that the Atlantic Alliance was already working on the issue. Indeed, the assertion of an autonomous European identity and role as proclaimed at the Hague summit necessitated a more visible role for the EC within the West. This was not intended to decouple Western Europe from the U.S., but rather to answer U.S. President Nixon's call for responsibility and burden sharing. Meanwhile, the EC member states suspected the Warsaw Pact's call for the immutability of frontiers and for a collective system of security of being an attempt to halt the development of the EC towards political integration. Furthermore, the proposal for pan-European economic cooperation, and particularly the reference to the elimination of trade discriminatory practices, could be designed to undermine the EC.[7] Although NATO allies would back the EC states, it was difficult to envisage all NATO members adopting a common stance on matters that primarily concerned the EC, particularly at a time when divergent economic interests were turning transatlantic relations increasingly competitive, if not sour.[8] Later on, the Nine were also encouraged to act together by growing suspicions that the White House and the Kremlin might make a deal over their heads, and concerns that the EC would be 'squeezed by the superpowers'.[9]

These motivations met the approval of the four candidate states, which were increasingly involved in the EPC, the difference between EC members and candidate states on the verge of membership being irrelevant in an intergovernmental mechanism.[10] Following a referendum rejecting EC membership, Norway left in September 1972. From that moment, it is accurate to speak of 'the Nine'. At the October 1972 Paris summit, which set the guidelines for the enlarged European Community, the Nine affirmed their resolution to promote their policy of détente with the East at the CSCE and to establish 'on a more solid basis, a wider economic and human cooperation'.[11]

The EC Countries' Vision of Overcoming the Iron Curtain

Since the mid-1960s most Western European governments had promoted a more or less successful policy of détente with the Soviet Union and the Eastern European countries.[12] The various national initiatives had been developed autonomously and through bilateral channels. The result was a sort of competition among allies that Moscow did not hesitate to nourish and exploit in order to weaken Western solidarity.[13] The new international climate and the relaunch of the European integration process in the early 1970s prompted the EC states to elaborate a unitary approach to East-West relations. Closer coordination on Eastern policy might also provide a means of including the German neue Ostpolitik into a wider Western approach.[14] This would help reassure those partners like Britain, who feared that the Federal Republic of Germany (FRG) might lurch towards neutrality, and those such as France, who wished to contain the FRG's growing political power.[15] So what was this common approach about?

The key word is détente, but the key element is the meaning of this term. For the superpowers, détente was a means of guaranteeing the bipolar order, which would secure their hegemonic role while reducing the costs and effort of confrontation.[16] For Western European governments détente was instead a means to start a gradual transformation of European relations aimed at overcoming the Cold War divide.[17] While preserving NATO so as to guarantee defence and security, they aimed at loosening bipolar restraints and deepening the mutual interdependence between the blocs. They therefore proposed to expand economic and cultural exchanges and to start mutually advantageous cooperation in several fields. In the short and medium term, détente was intended to improve the daily life of European citizens and promote wider human contacts and mutual knowledge, irrespective of political regime or military alliance. In the long run, the emergence of effective dialogue across the Iron Curtain would, it was hoped, engender reforms and liberalization amongst the communist regimes. As seen from the West, the real anomaly in the continent – and the lasting threat to European security – was the Soviet politico-military domination of Eastern Europe and the repression of individual rights and fundamental freedoms in half of the continent.[18]

In this connection the CSCE offered a real opportunity. The Nine aimed at making clear that they did not accept the Brezhnev doctrine, and that relations between states were to be based on principles incompatible with it. Furthermore, they wanted the CSCE to agree on practical measures to promote cooperation and the freer movement of peoples, ideas and information.

The Making of a Single Voice on the CSCE

Behind this common vision and goals, the Nine differed significantly in their enthusiasm about, and approach towards, the CSCE. Among the EC member states there were forerunners, mediators, sceptics and even one Cold Warrior. Generally speaking, the higher the value accorded to détente in each country's foreign policy, the more optimistic its attitude towards the CSCE, and the more cautious its tactics, phrasing and preferred content in each CSCE proposal.

Given Germany's position at the heart of the East-West divide, Bonn had the biggest national stake in the CSCE.[19] Not only did the FRG make the preservation of the possibility of peaceful frontier change a fundamental point of its strategy, but it also was strongly interested in the wider objectives of the CSCE: a higher degree of security, wider economic, scientific and technical cooperation, and greater freedom of movement for citizens.[20] According to Bonn, the most fruitful approach to the negotiation was a gradual and cautious one. The Germans feared the tendency of some NATO allies to regard the conference as an occasion for judicious political warfare with the Soviets, possibly moderate in tone but not in substance. This would wreck whatever chance the conference might have of improving East-West relations, from which the FRG wanted to benefit.[21] It was thus important not to create the impression in the Soviet Union that the West was trying to overthrow its regime. This applied most particularly to the issue of freer movement and its potential consequences on intra-

German relations. The matter was definitely too important to national interest to be handled in a confrontational way. The Germans preferred a step-by-step negotiation starting with less problematic issues such as cultural cooperation, instead of raising more controversial subjects such as human rights or freer movement.[22] German representatives therefore made determined efforts within the EPC to prevent proposals from being couched in overly ideological tones.[23]

For France, the CSCE offered a useful tool to promote its vision of a loosened bipolar order, since the conference had been specifically called as a meeting outside the bloc context. France also aimed at reasserting a visible role as the leader of a united Western Europe. What the French saw at the time was the danger that the superpowers might strike a bilateral deal on the CSCE, for both the U.S. and the USSR seemed reconciled, for different reasons, to a conference bringing no innovative and actual results.[24] The French government, on the contrary, intended to work for concrete achievements. In private talks with the British, French Foreign Minister Maurice Schumann suggested that the CSCE could let the West realize a sort of pacific rollback, induce a gradual loosening of Soviet control in Eastern Europe and favour a process of liberalization of communist regimes.[25] Consequently, the best tactic was to present sober proposals that might bring about gradual improvements, and to use such moderate terms so as to make it difficult for the communist countries to reject or dispute the Western European proposals.[26]

Belgium and Denmark came to be known as the 'wet front', for their ministers tended to believe that the conference was a good thing in itself and could negotiate a genuine détente. Consequently, they wanted to avoid provocative attitudes, especially on such issues as freer movement on which the Soviets were vulnerable. In the exploratory phase of bilateral contacts, the Belgian government moved further than its allies to promote the convening of the conference and constantly played the role of bridge-builder between East and West.[27] Denmark too had welcomed the CSCE idea. The Danish government attached high importance to the question of freer movement of peoples, ideas and information, without which détente was nonsense, as Foreign Minister Andersen clearly pointed out. Although they knew that the Soviet Union vigorously opposed advance on these issues, the Danes regarded even small progress in this field to be important and worthwhile.[28]

Britain emerged as a mediator. Its attitude towards the CSCE had long been perceived as negative, or at the very least extremely sceptical. In actuality, it was Soviet propaganda to target Britain's cautious pragmatism with polemical attacks. The British government, while certainly not enthusiastic about the CSCE, described its position as 'somewhere between the French [positive] and American [sceptical] position'. London considered the conference inevitable, not especially dangerous and likely to offer some good opportunities, the first of which was the chance to present a European common front.[29] According to Edward Heath's British government, the ability to influence international relations in the existing world required a stronger and more united Western Europe able to express its own identity.[30] This kind of Europe could only result from close political, economic and defence cooperation among its members.[31] The British government encouraged its EPC partners to adopt a common stance and speak with one voice.

As for negotiations with the East, London called on the EC to set two main goals. First, EC members should preserve the integration process from possible Soviet interference as long as Moscow regarded Europe as a battlefield in the global confrontation with Washington. Second, the EC and its member states should foster contacts and cooperation with Eastern European countries to the maximum extent possible, in order to lower artificial barriers and persuade the communist regimes eventually to recognize the European Community. These two goals were to be pursued in parallel, via a cautious but constructive approach, and through close coordination amongst the EC partners.[32] As for the CSCE, the British government underscored the risks of a merely defensive approach and attached high relevance to the freer movement question. Indeed, the British proposed to include the respect for human rights and fundamental freedoms among the principles guiding relations among states. Above all, the British government wanted the conference to debate practical measures to improve the quality of life of all Europeans. For this reason, it did not want to engage in an ideological wrangle with the communist delegations and fully supported the French proposals on tactics and phrasing.[33]

The Italian government had been the first to welcome the call for a CSCE. Nonetheless, Rome was seriously concerned about Soviet intentions and thought that Moscow aimed to use the conference to undermine the cohesion of Western Europe and the process of integration.[34] The Italian government defended the role of the EPC with growing conviction, all the more so as it perceived connivance between the superpowers. Political Director Roberto Ducci explicitly told French Ambassador Charles Lucet that the Italian government was increasingly concerned about an American-Soviet deal over the heads and interests of the Europeans. Were such suspicions confirmed, he added, the Italian government would consider withdrawing its delegation from the Helsinki preparatory talks.[35] Italy believed the human and cultural issues discussed at the CSCE to be fundamental elements likely to bring meaningful political consequences. Italian diplomats hence tended to have a firm attitude on the promotion of human contacts, stopping just short of intransigence.[36] Later on, due to the Soviet regime's campaign of repression targeting dissident intellectuals in September 1973, the Italian government slightly softened its position. Before the Italian House of Deputies, Foreign Minister Aldo Moro defined the Italian approach to the issue of freer movement of peoples and ideas as a balance between 'great determination and responsible prudence', thereby acknowledging the limits imposed by the reality of communist regimes.[37]

The odd man out was Holland, which approached the conference as a Cold Warrior. The Dutch had vigorously opposed the idea of a pan-European conference, which they considered useless and dangerous.[38] The Dutch government gave clear signs of regarding the CSCE as an opportunity for political warfare with the Soviet bloc. Within the EPC the Dutch delegates held ideological positions that hardly left room for dialogue and conciliation. The Dutch were much more inclined to prefer NATO coordination, where they could rely on strong American scepticism about the CSCE. Up to the start of the conference, the Dutch seemed to work more to slow down Western preparation than to actually contribute positively. They were reconciled with European partners only *in extremis*, and primarily due to their isolation rather than to a change of opinion.[39] Indeed, the Dutch remained stubbornly determined to adopt a tougher line towards the Soviets than anyone else.[40]

The Resulting Common Approach

Given this variety of national positions, it is hard to imagine what a lowest-common-denominator position might have been. Fortunately, however, it never proved necessary to find out. The Nine's approach to and action at the CSCE was much more the result of a clear prevailing majority in the EPC combined with an awareness on the part of the minority of the costs of destroying the unity of the Nine. The resulting strategy clearly rejected a confrontational attitude. It would have been not merely naïve but counterproductive to demand the elimination of existing barriers and abolition of communist regulations. As clearly emerged in the EPC debate, maximalist proposals would certainly have caused Soviet suspicion and rigidity, consequently prejudicing any chance of success on human contacts and in the conference itself. Furthermore, an open ideological challenge could only sharpen the Soviet craving for security, resulting in a tightening of control over Eastern European countries. Instead, the Nine's approach had to be realistic and recognize that the liberalization of communist regimes would only be gradual. The hope was that better and fruitful relations with the West would make Moscow less wary of close contacts and induce new thinking amongst Soviet leaders.[41]

The EC Nine thought it possible to engage the Soviets in a serious discussion by introducing specific proposals with reasonable argumentation and avoiding unnecessary polemics as far as possible.[42] Nonetheless, this went already much further than the cautious German approach. The intention was 'to see the question of freer movement permeate every aspect of the Conference', and the Nine presented a huge number of detailed and consistent proposals in almost every chapter of the CSCE agenda.[43] The Nine's common position struck a correct balance between avoiding ideological warfare and searching for meaningful actual change. All of the Western proposals revealed a double-track rationale. On the one hand, Western governments adopted a 'people first' approach to détente that was meant to bring actual benefits to European citizens without questioning political systems. On the other hand, they attempted to introduce measures likely to favour or engender, in the long run, the liberalization of the communist regimes from within.[44]

Given the rules of the EPC, the member states were not bound to reach a common position. Speaking with a single voice was not mandatory. Nevertheless, the socialization of diplomats and ministers, the growing practice of constructive consensus-seeking and the accumulation of a notable *acquis politique* all combined to make the EPC an 'interdiplomatic mobilisation process without supranational effects, but with increasingly binding character'.[45] In the case of the CSCE, no one was willing to accept anything less than a united, thoroughly conceived action. Not only did this meet the ambitious call of the Hague summit, it also meant safeguarding the EC's existence and future development. Ever since the first EPC meeting it was crystal clear that as long as the Cold War persisted, the EC could hardly hope to gain recognition from the communist countries.[46]

The EC member states scrupulously set up the EPC for dealing with every possible aspect of what was meant to be a common policy on détente and CSCE. Two special working groups were organized with this aim.[47] Senior national officials with expertise on NATO or Eastern Europe formed the subcommittee on the CSCE, which was mandated to investigate all aspects of the conference likely to interest the EC from a political point of view. A few months later, the member states established the ad hoc group on the CSCE, which was to involve the European Commission in dealing with the economic aspects of the negotiations.[48] Work on the CSCE developed intensively in Brussels, resulting in very detailed analyses of Soviet and Western goals, a string of proposals and suggestions as to the proper tactics of negotiation.[49] Moreover, national delegates and the Commission did not limit the scope of their work to the CSCE but also devoted attention to detailed analyses of East-West relations in general. This also led to the close coordination of EC members within NATO. In the course of 1972, EC governments established the Group of the Eight at the NATO Economic Committee, and the Political Sub-group of the Eight at the NATO Political Committee, which both worked in close coordination with EPC working bodies.[50] The EC member states had no intention of undermining NATO solidarity, but they were determined to promote their vision of the East-West relations and the role of the European Community on related issues.[51]

The lengthy preparations for the CSCE would have been in vain without the determination to defend agreed positions. The Nine set up a precise and complete discipline for the CSCE negotiations aimed at effectively presenting a unitary front. The nine delegations met daily to coordinate their positions. The delegation of the EC presidency provided the link with the EPC committees, which sat in permanent session. Foreign ministers dealt with fundamental political questions in their dual capacity as members of the EC Council of Ministers and national representatives within the EPC.[52] As a result, they kept a strict alignment and spoke with a single voice throughout the negotiations, as all CSCE participants recognized.[53]

This unitary, actual and thoroughly conceived action enabled the EC Nine to be quite successful in the promotion of their vision of overcoming the Cold War in Europe. Thanks to their determination, principle VII on respect of human rights featured in the Final Act, as did principle VIII on the self-determination of peoples, both implying a clear rejection of the Brezhnev doctrine. Furthermore, concrete measures were adopted to realize the freer movement of people, information and ideas.[54] Soviet Ambassador Yuri Kashlev has retrospectively affirmed that the CSCE results on this issue came from the pressure that the Western European governments put on the Soviets, also at the top level.[55] The Final Act was meant to be a legal tool for people within and outside the communist countries wishing to promote reforms and normalization in Europe.

Conclusions

In the late 1960s, most Western European governments had attempted to promote a policy of détente with the Soviet Union and the Eastern European countries. Due to the new approach of the U.S. administration to the international order and the relaunching of the European integration process at the Hague summit, the EC member and candidate states decided to closely coordinate their policy on East-West relations, particularly on the CSCE. Amongst the Nine EC members, there were sceptics, mediators and front-runners in terms of the approach and tactics to adopt on East-West relations and on the possibilities offered by the CSCE. However, most EC member states shared a similar conception of détente as a means to overcome the partition of Europe. Moreover, wishing to foster the EC role and its future development, all agreed that it would be better promoted in the absence of Cold War logic.

The nature of the CSCE and its agenda made common interests visible to the EC member states. Suspicions about Soviet intentions gave both the initial impulse and constant stimulus for common action. The U.S. indifference to the CSCE and Kissinger's numerous statements on the pointlessness of human contacts issues alienated the Europeans and further strengthened their cohesion and willingness to act together.[56] Finally, the socialization of diplomats and ministers within the EPC committees engendered a growing practice of consensus seeking, making the Europeans discover that they could actually work together and produce results even on foreign policy.[57]

All these factors combined in a perfect juncture enabling the Nine to elaborate a unitary vision, to align themselves on common action and to speak with a single voice. It was, however, a highly contingent juncture, as the Nine were unable to repeat their impressive performance under different circumstances. The (lack of a) European answer to the oil crisis in the same decade of the 1970s was emblematic of the weakness and limits of the EPC mechanism and of the willingness of the Nine to act as one.

Notes

1. The analysis is based on documents from the Historical Archives of the European Union (HAEU), the British National Archives (UKNA), the Archives du Ministère des Affaires étrangères, Paris (AMAE), and the Nixon Presidential Materials (NPM) at the National Archives and Records Administration of the US, Washington, DC (NA).
2. See P. Taylor. 1979. *When Europe Speaks with One Voice: The External Relations of the E.C.*, Westport, CT: Greenwood Press; D. Allen, R. Rummell and W. Wessels. 1982. *European Political Cooperation: Towards a Foreign Policy of Western Europe*, London: Butterworth Scientific; S.J. Nuttall. 1992. *European Political Cooperation*, Oxford: Clarendon Press, New York: Oxford University Press; C. Hill (ed.). 1996. *The Actors in Europe's Foreign Policy*, London: Routledge; D. Möckli. 2008. *European Foreign Policy during the Cold War*, London: Macmillan.
3. On the Helsinki CSCE see J. Maresca. 1985. *To Helsinki: The Conference on Security and Cooperation in Europe 1973–1975*, Durham, NC: Duke University Press; L.V. Ferraris. 1979. *Report on a Negotiation: Helsinki, Geneva, Helsinki 1972–75*, Alphen a/d Rijn: Sijthoff and Noordhoff; C. Meneguzzi Rostagni (ed.). 2005. *The Helsinki Process: A Historical Reappraisal*, Padua: Cedam; O. Bange and G. Niedhart (eds). 2008. *Helsinki 1975 and the Transformation of Europe*, New York: Berghahn; A. Romano. 2009. *From Détente in Europe to European Détente: How the West Shaped the Helsinki CSCE*, Brussels: Peter Lang; T. Fischer. 2009. *Neutral Power in the CSCE: The N+N States and the Making of the Helsinki Accords 1975*, Baden-Baden: Nomos; A. Wenger, V. Mastny and C. Nuenlist (eds). 2009. *Origins of the European Security System: The Helsinki Process Revisited, 1965–75*, London:

Routledge. Focused on the long-term consequences of the Helsinki CSCE see, for example, V. Mastny. 1992. *The Helsinki Process and the Reintegration of Europe, 1986–1991: Analysis and Documentation*, New York : New York University Press; D.C. Thomas. 2001. *The Helsinki Effect: International Norms, Human Rights, and the Demise of Communism*, Princeton, NJ: Princeton University Press; J. Andréani. 2005. *Le Piège, Helsinki et la chute du communisme*, Paris: Odile Jacob; S.B. Snyder. 2011. *Human Rights Activism and the End of the Cold War: A Transnational History of the Helsinki Network*, Cambridge: Cambridge University Press.

4. HAEU, FMM 37, The Hague Communiqué, 2 Dec. 1969.

5. HAEU, FMM 37, Rapporto dei Ministri degli Affari Esteri ai Capi di Stato o di Governo degli Stati membri delle Comunità Europee, 20 Jul. 1970.

6. AMAE, série: Europe 1944–70, sous-série: Organismes Internationaux et Grandes Questions Internationales (hereafter OIGQI), dossier 2031, 'Echanges de vues sur la CSE à la réunion ministérielle de Munich le 19 novembre (coop. Politique)', 17 Nov. 1970.

7. HAEU, FMM 36, Réunion des Ministres des Affaires étrangères de pays membres de la Communauté, 'L'Union Soviétique et l'Unité Européenne', Munich, 19 Nov. 1970; ibid., Groupe *ad hoc* sur la CSCE, Document de travail de la Présidence, 'Nature de la participation de la CEE (et des organes communautaires) à une CSCE', Rome, 6 Oct. 1971.

8. UKNA, FCO 28/1684, FCO to Peck, 12 May 1972; HAEU, KM 47, Commission, SEC(72) 2052, 'Remarques au sujet de certains documents préparés par le secrétariat général du Conseil Atlantique pour le Comité économique de ce Conseil', 7 June 1972.

9. UKNA, FCO 41/1061, Peck to Tickell, 29 Feb. 1972; AMAE, série: Europe 1971–juin 1976, sous-série: OIGQI , dossier 2925, Tél. No. 2107/2125, 8 Dec. 1972.

10. HAEU, FMM 52, 'Relations avec les pays de l'Est', 20 Mar. 1972.

11. HAEU, FMM 59, Final declaration of the Paris Summit, 20 Oct. 1972.

12. The literature is huge. See, for example, M. Vaïsse. 1998. *La grandeur. Politique étrangère du Général de Gaulle, 1958–1969*, Paris : Fayard; M.-P. Rey. 1991. *La tentation du rapprochement: France et URSS à l'heure de la détente (1964–1974)*, Paris: Publications de la Sorbonne; A. Varsori. 1998. *L'Italia nelle relazioni internazionali dal 1943 al 1992*, Rome: Laterza, 171–198; W. Loth. 2002. *Overcoming the Cold War*, London: Palgrave, 89–95; B. Bagnato. 2003. *Prove di Ostpolitik: politica ed economia nella strategia italiana verso l'Unione Sovietica: 1958–1963*, Florence: L. S. Olschki; A. Hofmann. 2007. *The Emergence of Détente in Europe: Brandt, Kennedy and the Formation of Ostpolitik*, London: Routledge; N.P. Ludlow (ed.). 2007. *European Integration and the Cold War: Ostpolitik-Westpolitik, 1965–1973*, London: Routledge; W. Loth and G.-H. Soutou (eds). 2008. *The Making of Détente: Eastern and Western Europe in the Cold War, 1965–75*, London: Routledge.

13. AMAE, série: Europe 1944–70, sous-série: OIGQI , dossier 2034, Tél. No. 6600/6608 – Moscow, 11 Dec. 1969; NA, NPM, NSC Country Files, box 683, folder 1, Research Memorandum, Dept. of State, 'West Germany/URSS: The Bahr-Gromyko Talks', 7 Apr. 1970. See also M.-P. Rey. 2008. 'The USSR and the Helsinki Process 1969–1975' in Wenger, Mastny and Nuenlist, *Origins of the European Security System*.

14. HAEU, FMM 50, 'IAI – Gruppo di studio sul vertice europeo', 18 May 1972.

15. See W. Wagner. 1971. 'Basic Requirements and Consequences of the Ostpolitik', *The Atlantic Community Quarterly*, 9(1), 20–33; G.-H. Soutou. 1996. *L'alliance incertaine. Les rapports politico-stratégiques franco-allemandes 1954–96*, Paris: Fayard, 311–349; M.-P. Rey. 2008a. 'France and the German Question in the Context of Ostpolitik and the CSCE, 1969–1974' in Bange and Niedhart, *Helsinki 1975 and the Transformation of Europe*.

16. See, e.g. R. Garthoff. 1985. *Détente and Confrontation: American-Soviet Relations from Nixon to Reagan*, Washington, DC: Brookings Institution. Also D. Geyer and D. Selvage (eds). 2007. *Soviet-American Relations: The Détente Years 1969–1972*, Washington, DC: U.S.

Government Printing Office; and 'Special Forum: U.S.-Soviet Relations in the Era of Détente', *Diplomatic History*, 33(4), 2009.

17. UKNA, FCO 28/1692, 'The European Community and the Conference on Security and Cooperation in Europe', 16 July 1972; Tickell to Wiggin, 6 Mar. 1972, Document No. 2 in G. Bennet and K.A. Hamilton (eds). 1997. *Documents on British Policy Overseas*, Series III, vol. II: *The Conference on Security and Cooperation in Europe 1972–75*, London: Routledge (hereafter *DBPO*).

18. AMAE, série: Europe 1971–76, sous-série: OIGQI , dossier 2900, Conseil de l'Atlantique du Nord, Document C-M (71) 75, 'Les tendences enregistrées en Union Soviétique et en Europe de l'Est – Leurs incidences dans le domaine politique', 29 Nov. 1971.

19. O. Bange. 2008. 'An Intricate Web: Ostpolitik, the European Security System, and German Unification', and G. Niedhart. 2008. 'Status Quo vs. Peaceful Change: The German Question during the ESC/CSCE Process', both in Bange and Niedhart, *Helsinki 1975 and the Transformation of Europe*.

20. UKNA, FCO 41/1070, Bonn to Tickell, 18 Apr. 1972.

21. *DBPO*, Document no. 8, Braithwaite to Allan 25 Apr. 1972.

22. P. Hakkarainen. 2005. 'A Monolithic Bloc or Individual Actors? West German Perceptions of the Warsaw Pact in the CSCE Process, 1969–72', in Meneguzzi Rostagni, *The Helsinki Process*, 72.

23. P. Hakkarainen. 2008. 'From Linkage to Freer Movement: The FRG and the Nexus between Western CSCE Preparations and Deutschlandpolitik, 1969–72' in Wenger, Mastny and Nuenlist, *Origins of the European Security System*.

24. AMAE, série: Europe 1971–juin 1976, sous-série: OIGQI , dossier 2925, Tél. No. 2107/2125, 8 Dec. 1972.

25. *DBPO*, Document no. 8, Braithwaite to Allan 25 Apr. 1972.

26. AMAE, série: Europe 1971–juin 1976, sous-série: OIGQI , dossier 2923, Sous-direction d'Europe orientale, Paris to Brussels, 'A/S :Discussion au Conseil atlantique sur le Chapitre de l'o.d.j. de la CSCE consacré à la coopération culturelle et aux contacts entre les hommes', 10 Apr. 1972.

27. UKNA, FCO 41/1061, Tel. from Peck to Tickell, 29 Feb. 1972.

28. AMAE, série: Europe 1971–juin 1976, sous-série: OIGQI , dossier 2924, Tél. No. 664/671, Copenhagen to Paris, 13 Oct. 1972.

29. NA, NPM, NSC Institutional "H" Files, box H-187, folder NSSM 138 (2 of 2), Tel. London to SecState, 19 Oct. 1971.

30. HAEU, FMM 50, Délégation de la Commission des C.E. à Londres, 'La relance institutionnelle. Points de vues britanniques', 14 Feb. 1972.

31. UKNA, CAB 184/28, Definition of the government's major objectives 10/9/71–12/10/71, 'The Kind of Europe We Want'.

32. HAEU, FMM 53, UK delegation to the EC, 'External Relations and Responsibility of the Community', 16 Mar. 1972.

33. UKNA, CAB 133/429, Record of the Brandt-Heath meeting, 21 Apr. 1972.

34. UKNA, FCO 30/1250, Italian paper, 'Une politique de la Communauté vis-à-vis des Pays de l'Europe de l'Est', 20 Mar. 1972.

35. AMAE, série: Europe 1971–juin 1976, sous-série: OIGQI , dossier 2926, Tél. No. 1395–96, Rome, 8 May 1973.

36. Ducci R., in Ferraris, *Report on a Negotiation*, xv–xix.

37. Camera dei Deputati. 1996. *Aldo Moro, Discorsi Parlamentari (1963–1977)*, vol. 2, Rome: Camera dei Deputati. 'Sul dissenso nell'Unione Sovietica', 27 Sept. 1973.

38. AMAE, série: Europe 1971–juin 1976, sous-série: Communautés Européennes, dossier 3799, Tél. No. 282/EU from The Hague, 23 Mar. 1972.

39. AMAE, série: Europe 1971–juin 1976, sous-série: OIGQI , dossier 2926, The Hague Note, 5 July 1973.
40. *DBPO*, Document no. 136, Hildyard to Callaghan, 25 July 1975.
41. UKNA, FCO 28/1678, UKDEL NATO, 28 Feb. 1972.
42. UKNA, FCO 30/1252, CP (72) 27, 'Rapport du Comité Politique sur la préparation de la CSCE', 3 Oct. 1972; ibid., Groupe *ad hoc* CSCE, 'Objectifs et Tactiques de l'Ouest au cours de la phase de préparation multilatérale', 3 Oct. 1972.
43. UKNA, FCO 30/1251, Record of the Anglo-Swedish Discussions on the CSCE, 24 Aug. 1972; FCO 13/504, CSCE Dossier on Freer Movement of People, 30 Mar. 1972.
44. UKNA, CAB 133/422, 'Visit of the Prime Minister to Paris 19–21 May 1971'; CAB 133/429, Record of the Brandt-Heath meeting, 21 Apr. 1972; AMAE, série: Europe 1971–juin 1976, sous-série: OIGQI , dossier 2923, Paris to Brussels, 'Discussion au Conseil atlantique sur le Chapitre de l'o.d.j. de la CSCE consacré à la coopération culturelle et aux contacts entre les hommes', 10 Apr. 1972.
45. See J. Øhrgaard. 1997. 'Less than Supranational, More than Intergovernmental: European Political Cooperation and the Dynamics of Intergovernmental Cooperation', *Millenium – Journal of International Studies*, 26(1), 1–29.
46. HAEU, FMM 36, 'Réunion des Ministres des Affaires étrangères à Munich', 19 Nov. 1970.
47. AMAE, série: Europe 1944–70, sous-série: OIGQI , dossier 2031, 'Echanges de vues sur la CSE à la réunion ministérielle de Munich le 19 novembre (Coop. Politique), 17 Nov. 1971.
48. HAEU, FMM 37, Commission, SEC(71) 2362 : 'Problèmes de la CSCE. Initiatives possibles des Communautés Européennes', 15 July 1971.
49. HAEU, FMM 36, 'Rapport du Comité politique sur la CSCE', 4 Nov. 1971; HAEU, FMM 36, Commission, SEC(72) 3304 final, 'Conférence sur la Sécurité et la Coopération en Europe. Proposition pour une position des Communautés Européennes (Principes politiques)', and Commission, SEC(72) 3304 final/2, 'Conférence sur la Sécurité et la Coopération en Europe. Proposition pour une position des Communautés Européennes (Volét coopération)', 9 Oct. 1972.
50. Peck to Douglas-Home, 17 Oct. 1972, Document No. 15 in *DBPO, Series III, vol. II*. The number of states involved reflected the fact that one EC member state, the Republic of Ireland, was not a member of NATO.
51. HAEU, KM 47, Commission, SEC(72) 2052, 'Remarques au sujet de certains documents préparés par le secrétariat général du Conseil Atlantique pour le Comité économique de ce Conseil', 7 June 1972; AMAE, série: Europe 1971–juin 1976, sous-série: OIGQI, dossier 2925, Tél. No. 414/420, 'Objet: CSCE et OTAN', 17 Nov. 1972.
52. D. Allen et. al.. *European Political Cooperation*.
53. Machiavelli Center and Cold War International History Project Oral History Conference, 'The Road to Helsinki: The early steps of the CSCE', Florence, 29–30 Sept. 2003, contributions of former ambassadors to CSCE negotiations.
54. A. Romano. 2007. 'The Nine and the Conference of Helsinki: A Challenging Game with the Soviets', in J. van der Harst (ed.), *Beyond the Customs Union: The European Community's Quest for Deepening, Widening and Completion, 1969–1975*, Brussels: Bruylant.
55. Contribution by Ambassador Kashlev to the Florence Conference, 29–30 Sept. 2003.
56. *DBPO*, Document No. 12, Brimelow to Wiggin: 'Talk with Dr. Kissinger in Washington, 10 August 1972. CSCE, MBFR, SALT', 14 Aug. 1972; Document No. 89, Tel. No. 350, Peck to Callaghan: 'Kissinger Briefing: CSCE', 4 July 1974.
57. NA, NPM, NSC Country files, box 687, folder 2, Sonnenfeldt to Kissinger, 'Subject: Von Staden on Year of Europe Problems', 2 Aug. 1973.

Section V

VISIONS AND DISSENT
IN THE 1970S

Chapter 10

'THE TRANSFORMATION OF THE OTHER SIDE'

Willy Brandt's Ostpolitik and
the Liberal Peace Concept

Gottfried Niedhart

Willy Brandt's Vision

When the Cold War led to dangerous confrontation over Berlin and Cuba between 1958 and 1962, Willy Brandt was mayor of West Berlin and experienced the crises first-hand. Looking for an interim solution in Berlin, he initiated a policy of 'small steps'.[1] By negotiating with the authorities in East Berlin he tried to ameliorate the life of the Berliners. Simultaneously he developed a vision of how to permeate the Iron Curtain and induce change in the East. Confronted with the Cold War, he conceived a long-term process of transforming it by increasing communication with the East.

Brandt was well aware of the Soviet threat. At the same time he was convinced of the inherent structural weakness of the Soviet system. Rather than being afraid of contacts with the East, he pleaded for the establishment of all sorts of contact. The West, not the East, would benefit from it. For Brandt, overcoming the Cold War meant the opening up of the communist East, thereby civilizing East-West antagonism. Over the years this vision became a strategy generally known as Ostpolitik. In a long-term perspective, Brandt's vision of overcoming the East-West conflict and eventually bringing it to an end was identical with his vision of overcoming the division of Europe and, in this framework, the division of Germany. As early as 1969 Brandt predicted that the East-West confrontation, which was then still uppermost in the minds of most Europeans, would come to be seen

---

as increasingly anachronistic. The true threat to world peace would stem from starvation and social inequality – from the North-South conflict.[2]

The purpose of this chapter is to explore Brandt's transformation strategy during his period in office, first as foreign minister and later as federal chancellor. In order to avoid a mere history of ideas and perceptions, it is necessary to look at the national and international context, describing Brandt's position with respect to détente as a general process in East-West relations and to the phases of Ostpolitik as the specific West German variant of this process. Brandt's Ostpolitik achieved a normalization in the Federal Republic of Germany (FRG)'s relationship with the East. But it led also to a kind of normalization in the relations between the FRG and its Western allies, because a more self-reliant West Germany approached the West and in particular the United States in a much more assertive way than before.[3] Washington was greatly irritated by 'the semi-Gaullist, seemingly more independent style'[4] of the Brandt government. Furthermore, Brandt's and Kissinger's views on international politics differed considerably. Consequently, Brandt's belief in the assumptions of the 'liberal' peace concept will be compared with Kissinger's 'realist' point of view. Against this background Brandt's concept of change in East-West relations will be outlined. The terms 'liberal' and 'realist' will be used as analytical categories. Brandt's wording was different, but his approach to international affairs, even if he never used its terminology, corresponded to a high degree with the liberal international theory as developed by political scientists.[5]

This essay focuses on Brandt. However, it has to be pointed out that the support for a new attitude towards the German question and for a 'new' Ostpolitik grew significantly in West German society at large from the mid-1960s onwards.[6] And one must not forget that Brandt was able to become chancellor thanks in no small part to the support given by the liberal party, the Free Democrats (FDP).[7] With respect to the conceptual work and also to the decision-making process, Brandt relied on a relatively small team of collaborators, among them, above all, Egon Bahr, his close aide in West Berlin as well as in Bonn. They did not agree on every detail, but essentially they were in full accordance. Hence, talking about Brandt means also talking about the Brandt-Bahr tandem.[8] Focusing on Brandt (and Bahr) is justifiable because they shaped the course of Ostpolitik. This does not mean, however, that variations on the issue of Ostpolitik did not exist within the SPD or in Brandt's cabinet. Notably Helmut Schmidt, minister of defence and later of finance and finally Brandt's successor as chancellor, had severe doubts about the appropriateness of the liberal school of thought and was much closer to Kissinger's 'realist' position.[9] Furthermore, Schmidt used to stress that politicians should do without visions, whereas Brandt, although starting from realities, always inspired (and provoked, often even irritated) his interlocutors by searching for a 'better' world. However, regarding concrete steps in foreign policy and particularly in Ostpolitik, Brandt and Schmidt did not differ that much.

Liberal vs. Realist Views of the East-West Conflict

When Willy Brandt became chancellor in October 1969, the FRG had already gone through the first phase of its 'new' Ostpolitik. The so-called grand coalition formed in 1966 by the Christian Democrats (CDU and CSU) and the Social Democrats (SPD) had given priority to a new departure in the West German attitude and policy towards the Warsaw Pact states. Chancellor Kurt Georg Kiesinger (CDU) and Foreign Minister Brandt (SPD), although differing over specific issues, were in fundamental agreement about the necessity of an alteration in West Germany's Eastern policy.[10] Basically, this first phase of Ostpolitik was about coming to terms with the postwar order in Europe and adapting to the overall trend of détente in East-West relations. Otherwise, given President de Gaulle's initiatives towards the East[11] and President Johnson's approach of 'bridge building',[12] the FRG would have been in danger of isolation within the Western alliance. By late 1969 the FRG was not only in step with its Western allies but was about to become the Western pace setter in the European détente process. The very basis of the new West German government, formed by the Social Democrats and the liberal Free Democrats with Brandt as chancellor and Walter Scheel as foreign minister, was the conviction that Ostpolitik should be pursued in a more vigorous way. The CDU/CSU opposition, in spite of its earlier involvement in Ostpolitik, launched a furious campaign against this because the social-liberal government seemed to be prepared to give up too much that was essential to German national interests.[13]

Equally severe doubts about the underlying assumptions of Ostpolitik could be heard amongst the FRG's allies, particularly in Washington and Paris. West Germany claimed to be a 'more independent ally'.[14] Brandt wanted the FRG to be 'more equal' than before,[15] keeping in close touch with its NATO partners but looking independently after its interests.[16] Given West German decision-makers' new self-reliance, President Nixon and his National Security Advisor Henry Kissinger were haunted by the question of whether German interests and NATO's interests fully coincided or whether there was a risk of endangering 'Germany's Western association'.[17] Similar anxieties were expressed by President Pompidou. He praised Brandt's preparedness to recognize the territorial status quo but he also feared that the FRG might detach itself from Western Europe. At the same time, however, he shared Brandt's view of détente as a process leading to a certain degree of liberalization in the East and thereby contributing to overcoming the East-West conflict.[18]

Consequently, Brandt had to cope with fierce opposition at home and had to be aware of the reservations of the FRG's main allies. As to his adversaries in Bonn, he was convinced that his Ostpolitik could induce a process of change in East-West relations, thereby serving the interests of the nation as a whole much more than the less flexible course advocated by his critics. Regarding Kissinger's or Pompidou's fears, Brandt practiced 'full loyalty' to the NATO alliance[19] and kept Germany's allies, in particular the United States, well informed. At the same time Brandt differed from Kissinger with respect to the notions of détente, power and security. In Brandt's view détente was more than looking for stability on the basis of the status quo and of the balance of power between East and West, power was not only military power and security was not only a matter of arms limitation treaties. Questioning the traditional approach, Brandt pleaded for a wider notion of security. The Harmel formula[20] was a move in the right direction that Brandt wanted not only to continue emphatically but also to develop further as far as the détente aspect was concerned. He wished to broaden the areas of cooperation, thereby civilizing the East-West conflict and gradually liberalizing the East. He envisaged what might be called a liberal turn in East-West relations.

This 'expansion of the meaning of security'[21] became apparent in 1973 when the CSCE negotiations were under way. The Soviet understanding of security was challenged by the Western Europeans, who sought to make borders more permeable through confidence-building measures, economic exchange and the freer movement of people and ideas. Whereas the traditional concept of security maintained that the balance of power and the recognition of spheres of interest and influence could best secure peace, the wider definition of security covered also economic and human security. American diplomats participated in the CSCE negotiations, but Kissinger himself moved only very slowly 'from indifference to interest'.[22] He wanted to do business with the Soviet Union on his own terms, which in fact to a great extent were compatible with the outlook of the Soviet leadership. From Kissinger's point of view, Brandt and other Western European leaders who were in favour of the CSCE embodied the Wilsonian approach to international affairs, something that Kissinger wished to avoid at all costs in his own conduct of American foreign policy. At the heart of Kissinger's reservations about Ostpolitik was his strong belief in the so-called realist theory of international relations, whereas Brandt's frame of mind was shaped by liberal theory. Kissinger doubted that the FRG could play a significant role in the big game of East-West relations.

When Brandt made it perfectly clear that exactly this was his intention, Kissinger and even more so Nixon regarded Ostpolitik as a 'dangerous affair'.[23] The explanation for their sceptical attitude is quite simple. The FRG, in Kissinger's 'realist' perspective, lacked an attribute he considered as being essential for the successful pursuit of an autonomous Ostpolitik, namely power.[24]

For Brandt and his advisors, power could not be reduced to one element only. In a most revealing exchange of views between Kissinger and Bahr in 1973, the difference between the 'realist' and the 'liberal' approach became apparent. For Bahr it went without saying that the military power of the United States was crucial for counterbalancing the Soviet superpower. Only the U.S. could provide security for Western Europe and particularly for the FRG in the foreseeable future. At the same time Bahr, for various reasons, declared the reduction of the military confrontation with the East to be a common goal of the U.S. and Western Europe. Reducing the weight of military forces would mean that political and economic factors would become more important in dealing with the East. Under these circumstances soft power, i.e., the power that was plentifully at the disposal of the FRG, would become more relevant than military power. What Kissinger regarded as a 'revolutionary conclusion'[25] was in fact the central rationale of Ostpolitik, as Bahr disclosed frankly. A carefully planned expansion of East-West economic relations would aggravate the internal inconsistencies in the Warsaw Pact countries and contribute to further modifications of the communist systems. In the light of the awful example of Czechoslovakia, Bahr conceived any change in the East as gradual change. The West had to make sure that such a development did not lead to an explosive and uncontrollable reversal.[26]

Kissinger and Nixon were both well aware of the relative decline of the U.S. as a superpower and of the danger of imperial overstretch; hence they looked for stability, as did Brezhnev, who had reached military parity but otherwise commanded a backward economy in need of Western technology and capital. Détente was their method to stabilize the international system. Brandt and Bahr's notion of détente was different. They wanted to transform the international system. Furthermore, they started from a psychologically much more comfortable basis. The FRG could look back on a political and economic success story. A quarter century after the end of the Second World War and total defeat, the West Germans perceived themselves as being back in the international arena and pursued their Ostpolitik from a position of mental, economic and political strength. Shortly after his appointment as foreign minister, Brandt received a note from Bahr reminding him that the time was ripe for putting into operation what had been conceived in Berlin in the early 1960s. A 'new' Ostpolitik should have one paramount goal, namely the transformation of the East-West conflict. The FRG had no interest whatsoever in preserving the status quo.[27]

The Liberal Peace Concept: Tools and Expectations

Bahr's reference to Brandt's 'early' Ostpolitik was absolutely appropriate.[28] The concept of Ostpolitik and the idea of how to reduce the tension between East and West had been developed since the late 1950s.[29] After the building of the Berlin Wall in 1961, a new constellation had emerged that demanded new answers to deal with the East-West conflict. For Brandt and Bahr it became absolutely clear that the traditional Cold War paradigm had to be substituted by a new approach. The shortest formula for this new approach was 'Wandel durch Annäherung' (change through rapprochement). The phrase was first used by Bahr in a speech in Tutzing, near Munich, in July 1963 at a conference that was attended by politicians and foreign policy experts. Brandt was also among the participants. Brandt's address was more statesmanlike, but both speeches complemented one another and can be summarized as follows:

1. Politics should be based on two principles: realism and communication. The realities of the postwar settlement have to be accepted. At the same time, there should be an increase in communication between East and West. Contact with the communist East might lead to its penetration by Western ideas, which would then engender gradual change.
2. Within the framework of President Kennedy's 'strategy of peace' and starting from the 'common security interests' of the West, the 'interests of the other side' should be acknowledged as legitimate. The realities of power politics could only be changed after they had first been accepted. The recognition of the status quo was the initial step to overcoming it.
3. The Soviet Union should be reassured of its predominance in Eastern Europe. Once Moscow had lost its fear of being pushed out of Germany and Eastern Europe, it could enter into a process of increasing communication with the West. A rapprochement between East and West might result in the 'transformation of the other side'. Communist rule was not to be abolished but changed.
4. The division of Germany would last as long as the division of Europe. The German question could only be solved through cooperation with the Soviet Union and not through antagonistic behaviour.[30]

Brandt and Bahr were ready to accept the status quo for the time being. Otherwise it would have been impossible to initiate a process of communication with the East. Of utmost importance in their concept of a new Ostpolitik was the term communication: 'We need as many points of real contact and as much meaningful communication as possible.'[31] In his handwritten notes for his first statement as foreign minister in the Bundestag, Brandt mentioned as the two sides of his European policy the advancement of the European Communities and 'communication with eastern Europe'.[32] Communication was not meant to harmonize fundamental antagonisms but to deescalate existing conflicts of interest. Communicative methods introduced a new element to East-West détente, providing for the exchange of information and thus introducing an element of greater precision to mutual perceptions.

Trade relations were regarded as a particularly promising field where the division of Europe could possibly be transformed into a commercial network. Trade with the East was something that had a long tradition in German foreign trade; even during the Adenauer era West German *Osthandel* had been allowed to develop.[33] Trade with the East was of economic importance for a number of West German companies, but it also had political functions. Economic diplomacy[34] could help to promote political relations. An outstanding example was the role of the Krupp manager Berthold Beitz, who was well acquainted with the Polish leadership. In 1969–70 he served as a messenger between Bonn and Warsaw.[35] In September 1971, when Brandt commented on the state of West German–Soviet relations – which in his view had improved significantly since the late 1960s and in particular since the Treaty of Moscow signed in August 1970 – he stressed the importance of trade: 'More trade and less polemics'.[36] The increase in trade seemed to indicate a clearly positive change in bilateral relations.

Brandt made these remarks after having returned from Oreanda, Brezhnev's summer resort in the Crimea, where an informal German-Soviet summit, itself a spectacular example of a new form of top-level communication, had just taken place. The Soviets had asked for economic cooperation on an unprecedented scale. In addition to the usual trade relations, the Germans were invited to develop certain underdeveloped regions in the Soviet Union.[37] This fit with German ideas of starting German-Soviet joint ventures and seeking the interconnections between national economies.[38] Clearly, this vision of economic interaction has to be seen in the context of a fundamentally liberal approach. Since the 1920s there had been much discussion in the West about whether the Soviet Union might be regained for the West with the help of economic incentives. During the Brezhnev era, when the Soviet Union no longer regarded economic cooperation with the West as a threat, there seemed to be a good chance of making the Soviet Union dependent on Western technology and products. This might lead, as a British observer concluded, to a 'kind of Finlandisation in reverse'.[39]

The establishment of new channels of communication was a common practice during the years of détente. However, the expectations of what effect an increase in communication might have varied considerably. Brandt had high expectations and envisaged the possibility of a 'transformation of the other side'.[40] Time and again he argued in this way during his period in office. He did not believe in the general theory of convergence, which stressed the similarities of industrial societies in the West and the East. Rather he adhered to an 'offensive approach to convergence',[41] maintaining that the transformation of the Soviet system could be achieved from outside. According to Brandt and Bahr the Soviet empire was in a state of erosion.[42] Given this assessment the West seemed well advised to take into consideration both the Soviet Union's military strength *and* its structural weakness. In Brandt's view the Soviets were dependent on closer contacts with the West.[43] He argued that the Soviet leadership 'will try for a greater degree of communication with the West'. This not only appeared to be a success for German Ostpolitik and Western détente in general, but also stemmed from the Soviet need 'for better contacts in trade and technology'. It seemed to Brandt 'to be almost a law governing all modern industrial states, whatever their political systems, that the development of science, technology and so on leads to greater contacts'. For Brandt, the Soviets were under an illusion if they believed 'that they can combine greater political discipline with freer contacts with the Western countries'.[44] He was sure that the Soviet Union could not have it both ways, moving towards a modern industrial society while keeping the centralized power structures intact.[45] And he had no doubts about the second effect of détente. A normalization in East-West relations would change the Warsaw Pact.[46]

When interviewers asked Brandt whether the policy of détente might induce a liberalization of Eastern societies, he imagined that a gradual change towards democracy was possible. He did not speculate on whether the immediate effects of détente – East-West trade, tourism, cultural exchange – would directly contribute to 'great changes' of the political systems. But these effects would not be damaging. 'They might help.'[47] Brandt's wording was imprecise, but for obvious reasons he had to take care to hide the offensive elements in his approach. It is most revealing that in one case Brandt asked an interviewer not to publish his view that détente would promote the liberalization of communist societies and foster the independence of the Warsaw Pact states.[48] As an acting statesman who wanted to work for a pan-European security system, Brandt had to guard against suspicions about the ultimate goal of Ostpolitik.

Behind closed doors it was not concealed that the FRG aimed at ending the Soviet grip on Eastern Europe. According to Bahr the strategic objective of Ostpolitik was the 'disintegration of the Soviet bloc'.[49] Brandt was less outspoken, but he foresaw a historical process. He anticipated that the Prague Spring would not remain a unique event but would recur in other countries, including the Soviet Union, hopefully under more favourable circumstances. One could not look into the future, and setbacks like the suppression of the Prague Spring could not be ruled out. The West could not give direct support to the East. However, the example of Czechoslovakia proved that the striving for more independence and more democracy was also present within the ruling communist classes. The Soviet leadership was hostile to the social democratic form of socialism, calling it *Sozialdemokratismus* and fearing infection by it. But the attraction of social democracy would increase, and the symptoms of this evolution were already apparent. Corroborative reports came 'not only from the Russian underground'. Many young people regarded the Soviet type of communism as too conservative.[50]

Vision and Reality: Taking Stock at the End of Brandt's Chancellorship

During Brandt's period in office it was a question of pure belief whether the liberalization of communist societies or the independence of the Warsaw Pact states would ever happen. Détente was by no means a linear process, and Brandt always warned against illusions. Nixon, when ranking him among the 'hopeless idealists' in March 1973, was a prisoner of his prejudices. He spoke plainly to Golda Meir when she congratulated Nixon on the achievement of détente: 'One thing you can do with your fellow Socialists. They are naïve and think we can all drop our defenses. It doesn't mean we're still in the Cold War, but we must be realistic.' As far as defence spending by the Brandt government was concerned, Nixon was simply out of touch with reality. But with respect to East-West relations he was nearer to the truth in perceiving a departure from the Cold War. 'We have changed the world because of this dialogue and these agreements. There are improved chances that confrontation will not explode into war.'[51]

The differentiation between Cold War and détente as two different forms of the East-West conflict[52] indicated that whereas the overarching conflict continued, an important change in conflict behaviour had occurred. The confrontation of the Cold War had been replaced by the antagonistic co-operation of the détente period. Berlin was a striking example. The Four Power Agreement was a product of détente, but this did not prevent endless disputes about the interpretation of the agreement. At the same time, the increase in communication enabled both sides to know 'where they agree, where a rapprochement is conceivable, and where they have differences'.[53] The explicit renunciation of force meant that images of the enemy disappeared and could no longer be used for internal purposes. Brandt regarded the 'peace order among states' in Europe as a precondition for a 'turn for the better'. In the long run, 'but only step by step', Europe would change.[54] In the short run, however, Brandt had to live with disappointment that Brezhnev did not feel compelled to modernize the Soviet system in a way that would start a process of convergence. Above all, détente did not result in any measures of disarmament and troop reductions in Europe. In particular the Mutual Balanced Force Reduction negotiations did not bring the desired result. On the contrary, in the late 1970s and early 1980s there was a 'crisis of détente'.[55] But what really mattered was that there was no relapse into the Cold War habits of the 'long' 1950s, either in the relationship between the two German states or in Europe generally.

Notes

1. W. Schmidt. 2001. *Kalter Krieg, Koexistenz und kleine Schritte. Willy Brandt und die Deutschlandpolitik 1948–1963*, Wiesbaden: Westdeutscher Verlag.
2. Statement for the Mexican paper *El Universal*, 8 May 1969. Willy Brandt Archiv im Archiv der sozialen Demokratie der Friedrich Ebert Stiftung, Bonn (hereafter WBA), A 3/306.
3. O. Bange. 2008a.'Ostpolitik as a Source of Intrabloc Tensions', in M.A. Heiss and S.V. Papacosma (eds), *NATO and the Warsaw Pact: Intrabloc Conflicts*, Kent, OH: Kent State University Press, 106–121.
4. W. Link. 2004. 'Détente German-Style and Adapting to America', in D. Junker (ed.), *The United States and Germany in the Era of the Cold War, 1945–1990, vol. 2: 1968–1990*, Cambridge: Cambridge University Press, 36.
5. In what follows I use the term liberal in a broad sense. 'Liberals' in politics as well as in political sciences, notwithstanding many differences with regard to concrete political steps, were resolved to escape the Cold War paradigm. They aimed at overcoming enemy images in East-West relations and the militarization of the East-West conflict by active coexistence. Trade, as a classical instrument of the liberal peace concept since the days of Immanuel Kant and Adam Smith, could serve this purpose but also other forms of cooperation. See J. Roosevelt (ed.). 1962. *The Liberal Papers*, Garden City, NY: Doubleday; D. Senghaas. 1966. 'Unilateralismus und Gradualismus. Zur Strategie des

Friedens', *Neue Politische Literatur* 11, 1–15; D. Senghaas et al. 1966a. 'Katechismus zur deutschen Frage', *Kursbuch* 4, 1–54; D. Eisermann. 1999. *Außenpolitik und Strategiediskussion. Die Deutsche Gesellschaft für Auswärtige Politik 1955 bis 1972*, Munich: Oldenbourg, 203–260; and C. Hauswedell. 1997. *Friedenswissenschaften im Kalten Krieg. Friedensforschung und friedenswissenschaftliche Initiativen in der Bundesrepublik Deutschland in den achtziger Jahren*, Baden-Baden: Nomos, 50–58.

6. M. Glaab. 1999. *Deutschlandpolitik in der öffentlichen Meinung. Einstellungen und Regierungspolitik in der Bundesrepublik Deutschland 1949 bis 1990*, Opladen: Leske & Budrich.

7. G. Niedhart. 1995. 'Friedens- und Interessenwahrung. Zur Ostpolitik der F.D.P. in Opposition und sozialliberaler Regierung 1968–1970', *Jahrbuch zur Liberalismus-Forschung*, 7, 106–126; M. Siekmeier. 1998. *Restauration oder Reform. Die FDP in den sechziger Jahren. Deutschland- und Ostpolitik zwischen Wiedervereinigung und Entspannung*, Cologne: Janus.

8. A. Vogtmeier. 1996. *Egon Bahr und die deutsche Frage. Zur Entwicklung der sozialdemokratischen Ost- und Deutschlandpolitik vom Kriegsende bis zur Vereinigung*, Bonn: Dietz, 65.

9. H. Soell. 2008. *Helmut Schmidt. Bd. 2: 1969-heute. Macht und Verantwortung*, Stuttgart: DVA.

10. O. Bange. 2004. *Ostpolitik und Détente: Die Anfänge 1966–1969* (unpublished manuscript, University of Mannheim); K. Schönhoven. 2004. *Wendejahre. Die Sozialdemokratie in der Zeit der Großen Koalition 1966–1969*, Bonn: Dietz; P. Gassert. 2006. *Kurt Georg Kiesinger 1904–1988. Kanzler zwischen den Zeiten*, Munich: DVA.

11. M.-P. Rey. 1991. *La tentation du rapprochement: France et URSS à l'heure de la détente (1964–1974)*, Paris: Publications de la Sorbonne; M. Vaïsse. 1998. *La grandeur: Politique étrangère du général de Gaulle 1958–1969*, Paris: Fayard.

12. T. Schwartz. 2003. *Lyndon Johnson and Europe: In the Shadow of Vietnam*, Cambridge, MA: Harvard University Press; M. Lerner. 2008. '"Trying to Find the Guy Who Invited Them": Lyndon Johnson, Bridge Building, and the End of the Prague Spring', *Diplomatic History*, 32(1), 77–103.

13. A. Grau. 2005. *Gegen den Strom. Die Reaktion der CDU/CSU-Opposition auf die Ost- und Deutschlandpolitik der sozial-liberalen Koalition 1969–1973*, Düsseldorf: Droste.

14. The phrase is Kenneth Rush's, U.S. ambassador in Bonn, in a letter to assistant secretary Marin Hillenbrand, 17 Nov. 1969. *Foreign Relations of the United States 1969–1976* (hereafter *FRUS*), vol. XL: Germany and Berlin 1969–1972, 121.

15. W. Brandt. 1989. *Erinnerungen*, Frankfurt: Propyläen, 189.

16. Brandt in Cabinet, 7 June 1970. *Akten zur Auswärtigen Politik der Bundesrepublik Deutschland* (hereafter *AAPD*) 1970, 921. For a similar statement by Brandt during a meeting of executives of the SPD, 2 Nov. 1968, see W. Brandt. 2005. *Ein Volk der guten Nachbarn. Außen- und Deutschlandpolitik 1966–1974*, edited by F. Fischer, Bonn: Dietz, 209–210. For a general assessment see G. Niedhart and O. Bange. 2004. 'Die "Relikte der Nachkriegszeit" beseitigen: Ostpolitik in der zweiten außenpolitischen Formationsphase der Bundesrepublik Deutschland im Übergang von den Sechziger- zu den Siebzigerjahren', *Archiv für Sozialgeschichte* 44, 415–448.

17. H. Kissinger. 1979. *White House Years*, Boston: Little, Brown, 408.

18. M.-P. Rey. 2008a. 'France and the German Question in the Context of Ostpolitik and the CSCE, 1969–1974', in O. Bange and G. Niedhart (eds), *Helsinki 1975 and the Transformation of Europe*, New York: Berghahn Books, 53–66. See also W. Loth. 2007. 'Détente and European Integration in the Policies of Willy Brandt and Georges Pompidou' in N. P. Ludlow (ed.), *European Integration and the Cold War: Ostpolitik – Westpolitik, 1965–1973*, London: Routledge, 53–66; G. Niedhart. 2004. 'Frankreich und die USA im Dialog über Détente und Ostpolitik 1969–1970', *Francia. Forschungen zur westeuropäischen Geschichte*, 31(3), 65–85.

19. Assurances were not only given to the Western allies. This was also underscored in talks with the Soviets. See, e.g., Brandt in his conversation with Brezhnev at Oreanda, 17 Sept. 1971. *AAPD 1971*, 1386. On the FRG as firmly tied to Western institutions see W. F. Hanrieder. 1995. *Deutschland, Europa, Amerika. Die Außenpolitik der Bundesrepublik Deutschland 1949–1994*, Paderborn: Schöningh, 448.
20. H. Haftendorn. 2008. 'The Harmel Report and Its Impact on German Ostpolitik', in W. Loth and G.-H. Soutou (eds), *The Making of Détente: Eastern and Western Europe in the Cold War, 1965–75*, London: Routledge, 103–116; A. Wenger. 2004. 'Crisis and Opportunity: NATO's Transformation and Multilateralization of Détente, 1966–1968', *Journal of Cold War Studies* 6, 22–74.
21. A. Wenger, V. Mastny and C. Nuenlist (eds.). 2008. *Origins of the European Security System: The Helsinki Process Revisited, 1965–75*, London: Routledge, xi.
22. M.C. Morgan, 'North America, Atlanticism, and the Making of the Helsinki Final Act', in Wenger, Mastny and Nuenlist, *Origins of the European Security System*, 30–34.
23. Nixon in conversation with Heath, 17 Dec. 1970. National Archives, Public Record Office (Kew) (UKNA), FCO 7/1842. For a detailed recent study see H. Klitzing. 2007. *The Nemesis of Stability: Henry A. Kissinger's Ambivalent Relationship with Germany*, Trier: Wissenschaftlicher Verlag.
24. Kissinger during a seminar with senior State Department staff, 8 Oct. 1969. National Archives and Records Administration (College Park) (NA), Nixon Presidential Materials (NPM), National Security Council (NSC), Presidential-HAK Memcons 1026.
25. H. Kissinger. 1982. *Years of Upheaval*, Boston: Little, Brown, 147.
26. Bahr to Kissinger, 14 Apr. 1973. Archiv der sozialen Demokratie der Friedrich-Ebert-Stiftung (Bonn) (AdsD), Dep. Bahr 439. Bahr tried to come back to this point two weeks later on the occasion of Brandt's visit to Washington, 30 Apr. 1973, but Kissinger did not respond. *AAPD 1973*, 611.
27. Bahr to Brandt, 30 Jan. 1967. AdsD, Dep. Bahr 299/3.
28. G. Niedhart. 2004a. 'The East-West Problem as Seen from Berlin: Willy Brandt's Early Ostpolitik' in W. Loth (ed.), *Europe, Cold War and Coexistence 1953–1965*, London: Frank Cass, 285–296. For the most recent account see A. Hofmann. 2007. *The Emergence of Détente in Europe: Brandt, Kennedy and the Formation of Ostpolitik*, London: Routledge.
29. W. Schmidt. 2003. 'Die Wurzeln der Entspannung: Der konzeptionelle Ursprung der Ost- und Entspannungspolitik Willy Brandts in den fünfziger Jahren', *Vierteljahrshefte für Zeitgeschichte* 51, 521–563.
30. Both speeches are printed in *Dokumente zur Deutschlandpolitik*, 4th series, vol. 9, 565–575.
31. Brandt in his speech at Tutzing (ibid., 567), referring to an earlier speech at Harvard in October 1962 printed in W. Brandt. 1963. *Koexistenz – Zwang zum Wagnis*, Stuttgart: DVA.
32. Notes by Brandt, 6 Dec. 1969. Printed in Brandt, *Ein Volk der guten Nachbarn*, 106.
33. R.M. Spaulding. 1996. '"Reconquering Our Old Position": West German Osthandel Strategies of the 1950s' in V.R. Berghahn (ed.), *Quest for Economic Empire: European Strategies of German Big Business in the Twentieth Century*, Providence: Berghahn Books, 123–143. See also R.M. Spaulding. 1997. *Osthandel and Ostpolitik: German Foreign Trade Policies in Eastern Europe from Bismarck to Adenauer*, Providence: Berghahn Books.
34. K. Rudolph. 2004. *Wirtschaftsdiplomatie im Kalten Krieg. Die Ostpolitik der westdeutschen Großindustrie 1945–1991*, Frankfurt/Main: Campus.
35. Brandt to Beitz, 4 June 1969. Brandt, *Ein Volk der guten Nachbarn*, 235; note by Brandt on the report given by Beitz, 15 June 1969. *AAPD 1969*, 706–707. Brandt to Cyrankiewicz, 25 Dec. 1969. *AAPD 1969*, 1471. The letter was delivered in Warsaw on 6 Jan. 1970. On

the background see M. Rakowski. 1993. 'Journalist und politischer Emissär zwischen Warschau und Bonn', in F. Pflüger and W. Lipscher (eds), *Feinde werden Freunde. Von den Schwierigkeiten der deutsch-polnischen Nachbarschaft*, Bonn: Bouvier, 154–159.

36. W. Brandt. 1976. *Begegnungen und Einsichten: die Jahre 1960-1975*, Hamburg: Hoffmann und Campe, 463.

37. Note by Bahr for Brandt, 11 Oct. 1971, giving an assessment of the talks. AdsD, Dep. Bahr 430.

38. See the correspondence between Ernst-Wolf Mommsen and Bahr between 1970 and 1972. AdsD, Dep. Bahr 109.

39. Minute by McNally, 11 Nov. 1975. *Documents on British Policy Overseas*, 3rd series, vol. 3, 404. See also J. Aunesluoma. 2008. 'Finlandisation in Reverse: The CSCE and the Rise and Fall of Economic Détente 1968–1975' in Bange and Niedhart, *Helsinki 1975*, 98–112.

40. Brandt in his Tutzing speech. *Dokumente*, 567.

41. For the term see G.-H. Soutou. 2008. 'Convergence Theories in France during the 1960s and 1970s', in Loth and Soutou, *Making of Détente*, 25–26.

42. Paper by Bahr for a conference of the Vereinigung Deutscher Wissenschaftler, 27 Oct. 1968. AdsD, Dep. Bahr 72. Bahr was invited by Carl Friedrich von Weizsäcker, the physicist, philosopher and peace researcher. Weizsäcker had advised Bahr to regard the Soviet intervention in Czechoslovakia as a sign of weakness and insecurity on the part of the Soviets. Conversation between Bahr and Weizsäcker, 17 Sept. 1968. Ibid. 399/3. The record of the conversation was seen by Brandt. For this view see also a memorandum by Bahr, 18 Sept. 1969. *AAPD 1969*, 1051 and E. Bahr. 1996. *Zu Meiner Zeit*, Munich: Karl Blessing Verlag, 244–245.

43. Brandt during a meeting of the executive of the SPD, 2 November 1968. Brandt, *Ein Volk der guten Nachbarn*, 214.

44. Conversation between Brandt and Heath, 6 Apr. 1971. UKNA, PREM 15/397. See also *AAPD 1971*, 596.

45. During the above-mentioned meeting of the executive of the SPD on 2 Nov. 1968, Brandt analysed the situation in the East that had emerged after the Soviet intervention in Czechoslovakia. He saw the Soviet leadership in a difficult position. Rather than having solved the problem that, in the Soviets' view, the Prague Spring had brought about, the Soviet Union was now confronted with 'new problems' (which in fact were old ones). Brandt, *Ein Volk der guten Nachbarn*, 214.

46. Note by Brandt in preparation of a Cabinet meeting, 7 June 1970. WBA, A8, 91. See also *AAPD 1970*, 921.

47. Brandt in a talk with Joseph Rovan, 22 Aug. 1973. Brandt, *Ein Volk der guten Nachbarn*, 491–494.

48. The interviewer was Golo Mann, who met Brandt on 23 Mar. 1972. U. Bitterli. 2004. *Golo Mann. Instanz und Aussenseiter. Eine Biographie*, Berlin: Kindler Verlag, 338.

49. Bahr during a meeting of the American, British and German planning staffs in Washington, 18 Apr. 1969. Report by R.A. Burroughs, 25 Apr. 1969. UKNA, FCO 49/265.

50. Brandt in the above-mentioned interview with Golo Mann. Schweizerisches Literaturarchiv (Bern), Golo Mann Papers, A-2-1972-6.

51. Nixon in conversation with Meir, 1 March 1973. NA, NPM, NSC, Presidential-HAK Memcons 1026.

52. See, e.g., Heath to Brandt, 27 Sept. 1971. WBA, A8, 52; Pompidou in conversation with Brandt, 10 Feb. 1972. *AAPD 1972*, 119; Pompidou to Brandt, 30 June 1973, on Brezhnev's remark that the ideology of the Cold War had come to an end. WBA, A 8, 51; Helmut Schmidt in a welcome address for George Shultz, 5 Oct. 1973. AdsD, Dep. Schmidt 5990. For an overview of recent literature see G. Niedhart. 2010. 'Der Ost-West-Konflikt.

Konfrontation im Kalten Krieg und Stufen der Deeskalation', *Archiv für Sozialgeschichte* 50, 557–594.

53. Notes by Brandt for a press communiqué after his meeting with Brezhnev in Oreanda, 18 Sept. 1971. WBA, A8/92. See also Brandt, *Begegnungen*, 471.

54. Handwritten draft for a speech, 15 Sept. 1973. WBA, A3/513. When Brandt gave the speech this paragraph was omitted.

55. L. Nuti (ed.). 2008. *The Crisis of Détente in Europe: From Helsinki to Gorbachev 1975–1985*, London: Routledge.

Chapter 11

NEITHER IN ONE BLOC, NOR IN THE OTHER
Berlinguer's Vision of the End of the Cold War

Laura Fasanaro

Historical debate on the political course envisaged by Enrico Berlinguer between the mid-1970s and the early 1980s has ranged from the enthusiastic to the hypercritical or, more recently, simply the sceptical. Berlinguer foresaw the democratic reform of Western European communist parties aiming to improve their role in capitalist countries and become the lever of a deeper socialist transformation. This chapter argues that Berlinguer, while seizing the chances offered by domestic political change, believed also in a broader, long-term transformation of the international system from rigid bipolarity to a world of many actors. The leader of the Italian Communist Party (PCI) interpreted this political development, however, not as the result of a rapid political break with the past, but instead as an evolution of international détente.

The chapter begins with a description of Eurocommunism and explains how this combined with the PCI's progressive detachment from Soviet foreign policy. In doing so, it highlights one essential element of Berlinguer's viewpoint: that the overcoming of military blocs would not necessarily result from the victory of one of the two systems over the other. The chapter then focuses on three aspects of Berlinguer's vision of overcoming the Cold War: his conception of détente, his desire to see the emergence of Europe as an international actor and the unyielding continuity of his policy as the international climate changed from détente to a reawakening of the Cold War. Based primarily on the many speeches, interviews and public statements Berlinguer made while he was secretary general of the PCI, and on the very recent literature on Eurocommunism by Italian and international scholars, this chapter describes the PCI leader's vision

---

Notes for this chapter begin on page 174.

of overcoming of the Cold War by combining an evolutionary approach to political change with ambitious Europeanism, high ideals and short-term pragmatism.

Berlinguer, Eurocommunism and Non-alignment

Enrico Berlinguer was secretary general of the PCI from 1972 until his death in 1984. A charismatic personality despite his notorious self-restraint, he led his party during a period of deep political and social tension in Italy.[1] In his political essays and countless interviews, he envisaged a reform of Western European communism and an ambitious role for the PCI both domestically and internationally.[2] Due to this broad political view, and also to his severe criticism of moral decline in Italian politics, he has been frequently pictured as a pure idealist. On the other hand, the ultimate failure of the PCI to turn so-called Eurocommunism into a widespread and solid political movement has also bred scepticism about the coherence and effectiveness of Berlinguer's strategy.[3] The fact, however, that the leader of the largest communist party in Western Europe repeatedly advocated the end of bloc alignment without creating a party split suggests the decline of a strictly dogmatic way of thinking within the PCI at least a decade before the end of the Cold War.

Berlinguer's ideas inspired the political and media phenomenon that the press named Eurocommunism. The term was then used to refer to the public positions of the Italian, French and Spanish communist parties.[4] Each of these parties retained distinctive national agendas, but they all shared a belief in domestic reform and a commitment to democratic change. Eurocommunists saw socialism in Western Europe as the eventual result of autonomous and national political courses. Their underlying principles were pluralism and respect for political liberties, leading Western communists to publicly criticize the Soviet Union and its allies for their disregard of these rights. Within the PCI, moreover, criticism of the shortcomings of Soviet socialism reflected a deeply felt internal political debate.[5]

In foreign policy Berlinguer championed the causes of détente and non-alignment. The latter gradually became one of Berlinguer's main foreign policy arguments. With the actual decline of détente, it turned into a distinctive element of his political vision. In 1975–76 the PCI leader still described the Soviet Union's 'peace politics' as a lever for international stability,[6] but in the following years his trust in Moscow's peace aims faded. Berlinguer then made an effort to distance his party from the Soviet Union's 'nervous expansionism',[7] despite the controversy this provoked within the party and its leadership. In the early 1980s the exacerbation of the international situation only increased the importance of keeping détente alive. From Berlinguer's perspective, reaching this goal largely depended on those political and social forces that for different reasons – their traditional approach to international politics, their spiritual authority or their national/regional priorities – could transcend bloc constraints:

> We need to reverse the current trend, to interrupt the spiral of violence responding to other violence, of action and retaliation. We must reopen the road to dialogue and negotiation. There are significant forces which are already discussing such steps and can act accordingly. In saying this we think for a start of the actions of that multitude of ordinary people who wish to live in peace, but also of the initiatives of the non-aligned states and of high spiritual authorities such as the Catholic Church. And above all we think of the irreplaceable role that can and must be played by this Europe of ours.[8]

As to the PCI, however, did Berlinguer ever intend to change it into a *non-aligned* political force? Certainly the years of Berlinguer's leadership were characterized by an increased and continuous search for ideological and political independence from Moscow, in spite of ongoing financial ties with the Communist Party of the Soviet Union (CPSU) that would persist at least until 1979.[9] While the continuity of this funding at a time of increasingly bitter relations between the CPSU and the PCI shows that the Italian party was far from achieving financial independence, at the same time the lack of a reconciliation between the two sister parties suggests that Moscow's strategy of seeking to reassert control over its reluctant ally through financial assistance was ultimately unsuccessful. The PCI's search for an autonomous stance in foreign policy was reflected in the party's new Europeanism, in its critical attitude towards Soviet intervention in Afghanistan, in its lack of support for Soviet-sponsored pacifist campaigns and, most of all, in its recognition that both superpowers were responsible for the decline of détente.[10] For the PCI, however, non-alignment meant *equidistance* from the two military blocs and their respective foreign policies. Berlinguer never questioned the overall superiority of socialism as an economic and social system over both capitalism and social democracy. But the realization of socialism in capitalist countries and membership of one bloc or the other were two separate problems rather than a single choice.

In its pursuit of the former, the PCI set out on a course that promised to be an alternative to the Soviet one, although Berlinguer could not grasp at that time what communists of his own generation would only realize after the end of the Cold War, namely that there were limits to the reform of communism beyond which a shift to social democracy would probably become inevitable.[11] Berlinguer argued in favour of a 'constant and gradual overcoming of capitalism in Italy and in Western Europe',[12] which was the substance of the theory of the '*terza via*' – or 'third way'.[13] Berlinguer used this expression to refer to a model of socialism that did not yet exist, either in the USSR or in other 'socialist' countries, but that would, he hoped, be implemented in Italy. This model would go beyond the Soviet model but preserve the legacy of two historical landmarks: the October revolution on the one hand, and the anti-Fascist alliance of the USSR with the Western democracies during the Second World War on the other.[14]

> The fact that the socialist experiments that have so far been carried out in various parts of the world do not represent an historically adequate and politically feasible solution for the West, i.e. in the high points of capitalism and hence also here in Italy, does not mean that we should abandon the objective of socialism and the struggle to build in Italy and in the other European capitalist countries a system of social and human relations superior to those produced by capitalism and its crisis. On the contrary, this makes it more urgent than ever for us to make the theoretical and practical effort so that the workers' movement, having reached a maturity and a new phase of its history, can decisively bring to bear its constructive and innovative strength.[15]

Certainly, the overall strategy had more than one flaw, the most evident being that it did not clarify how socialism would be realized in Italy, namely how social and economic reforms would lead to the overturning of capitalism and the establishment of socialism. Besides, this basically anti-capitalist approach was at odds with the deep-rooted reality of Italian and Western European capitalism.[16] Also, between idealism and pragmatism, this vision was unbalanced towards the former. Yet the PCI leadership also devised a concrete strategy in order to strengthen the party's position at home and gain international credibility. Berlinguer followed this strategy with unusual consistency: while defending the independence of the PCI, he prevented any breach with the Soviet Union, or with other Eastern European countries, at least until the end of détente brought his strategy to a crossroads.

Berlinguer's Vision of the End of the Cold War: An Evolution of Détente

In Berlinguer's political vision, the preservation of international détente was unquestionably the highest priority since it constituted the foundation for a gradual yet deep change in the international system. In order to maintain détente, however, it was necessary to keep the balance of power between the two military blocs unchanged for an indefinite period of time, until disarmament could be achieved by general assent. In one of his parliamentary speeches in February 1976, during a debate that was largely focused on the government crisis, Berlinguer added some significant remarks that showed how critical foreign policy was for Italian communists:

> our overall position is well-known: at the heart of our policy is the aim of keeping détente going and allowing Italy actively to contribute to it ... It is only in the context of the further progress of détente and international cooperation that we consider as realizable the gradual overcoming of opposing military blocs and disarmament. The main reason for our acceptance of the alliances that Italy has made is based upon our conviction that a unilateral breach of these alliances would alter the strategic balance between the two blocs, thereby bringing to an end an essential prerequisite for détente.[17]

Three underlying ideas were summed up in those words: the concept of détente as a dynamic process, the overcoming of the Cold War as its final development and the instrumental character of the PCI's acceptance of Italy's NATO membership. The first characteristic of Berlinguer's vision of the end of the Cold War, therefore, was this conception of détente as an evolutionary trend. As Silvio Pons has remarked, this was a crucial element of division between Berlinguer and Moscow, not least because the interpretation given by the PCI secretary had prevailed over the point of view of others within that party who, on the contrary, shared the Soviet static or 'conservative' idea of détente.[18] Berlinguer focused on the potential of this process without always perceiving its limits. One main reason for this confident approach was probably that he judged détente on the basis of the deep effect that it was exercising on Italy's domestic scene, where it favoured the extraordinary electoral rise of the PCI, eventually leading its members to high-level parliamentary positions and to the threshold of government in the summer of 1976. On the other hand, Berlinguer was aware of some of those limits. While he assumed that in the long term international power would be rebalanced and the superpowers would lose their central place, he was also very cautious about any move that could endanger détente in the short term. In other words, he knew very well from the peculiar Italian situation that there were political constraints due to bloc alignment and that ignoring them would seriously endanger domestic political balance. His foreign policy, therefore, was a moderated one, designed to balance relations with the two blocs. The PCI's acceptance of Italy's NATO membership should be interpreted as part of this strategy.

As Donald Sassoon has pointed out, while in 1968 the PCI was still in favour of bringing Italy out of the Atlantic pact, in the 1970s Berlinguer was aware that this request had become dangerously unrealistic. In spite of the new possibilities opened up by détente in Western Europe, he assumed that the autonomy of Italian governments (of any colour) in foreign policy was still very limited. He also knew that, at that time, Italy could take initiative only within two main forums: the Atlantic Alliance and the European Community.[19] Official recognition of Italy's NATO commitment, in other words, was compatible with the two short-term objectives mentioned above – increasing the chances of the PCI becoming a government party and preventing a possible right-wing backlash in Italy – but at the same time it was primarily intended to preserve détente. In an interview with the Italian journalist Giampaolo Pansa shortly before the national elections of June 1976, Berlinguer acknowledged that he felt more secure 'on this side', namely within NATO, rather than in the Warsaw Pact. He maintained that the fact that Italy was not in the Soviet bloc made it easier for Italian communists to follow a national path towards socialism than it was for their counterparts in other countries, although he also warned against the risk of the Atlantic allies' undue interference in Italy's domestic affairs.[20]

Berlinguer's argument, which sounds paradoxical, was raised within the context of an electoral campaign full of expectations and worries about the PCI. Those in the party who supported its participation in government believed that this was now possible; meanwhile, Italy's Atlantic allies put domestic Italian politics under the spotlight for the same reason. Given this context, Berlinguer's comment to Pansa should be regarded neither as a complete reversal of the PCI's international position, nor as a contradiction of what was affirmed above on its search for equidistance from both the Warsaw Pact and NATO. Berlinguer essentially meant to stress that were the PCI to take part in government after the elections, it would oppose any sudden change in Italy's international position.

Accordingly, the PCI also remained an active member of the international communist movement and improved diplomatic relations with those leaderships of Eastern Europe that proved more sympathetic towards the Italian situation: the Yugoslavs, who were traditional allies, but also the Hungarians and the East Germans (until 1979).[21] As a positive result, Berlinguer's talks with Janos Kádár in the autumn of 1977 helped keep the Hungarian leadership from supporting a formal ban on Eurocommunism at the meeting of party secretaries in Budapest in February 1978, an extreme measure suggested by the Soviets.[22] In the years of détente, therefore, balancing relations with the countries of the two blocs was a necessary step to preserve that process, with a view to a long-term emancipation from the whole bloc structure. As Berlinguer remarked in another interview in 1976: 'only gradually and only through détente will it be possible to definitively overcome military blocs and build up on a different basis security for all countries'.[23]

Berlinguer's background within the international communist movement, finally, helped broaden his focus on international developments.[24] Ever since the fourteenth PCI congress in 1975, Berlinguer had spoken of the wide-ranging objectives of 'international cooperation', which included the identification of 'global' challenges and allowed for the creation of a 'world government' that would also include the People's Republic of China and the United States.[25] This conception, which he himself admitted to be utopian, became more nuanced over time. It evolved into increased attention towards the North-South conflict in particular, something that became another leitmotif in Berlinguer's interviews and speeches, above all those addressed to the European Parliament:

> a European initiative is essential also in order to redefine the terms of North-South relations, and to fight against world starvation, which is also our Parliament's commitment. This commitment ... requires both a reduction of military expenditure and the building up of a new international order, able to use the task of lifting up the huge economically backward areas as a mechanism for creating a different kind of economic development, more rational and fair, in industrialized countries also.[26]

Berlinguer's confidence in an independent and extended international role for the European Community was the second element in his vision of overcoming the Iron Curtain. After the Brussels conference of European communist parties in January 1974, Italian communists formally recognized the importance of Italy's European policies; later on they would fully support the introduction of direct elections to the European Parliament (EP).[27] The PCI's Europeanism in the early 1970s originated, amongst other things, from an assessment of the advantages this would bring to the Western communists in terms of independence from the Soviet bloc. The Italian communists' commitment towards European integration became a characteristic of Eurocommunism, and then a boost to Berlinguer's appeals against nuclear weapons. 'With regard to Europe', he declared in the Italian parliament in early 1976, 'it should be clear to everyone that, while we wish to keep and develop our relations of friendship and cooperation with socialist countries, we also firmly support a new process of unification and democratic renovation within the European Economic Community and Western Europe'.[28]

Europe, then, was supposed to become a key actor in the transformation of the international system. Berlinguer's highest expectations involved the European Parliament, which he believed to be the best forum for the discussion for international issues, including disarmament and the problems of North-South relations. The PCI, however, also backed the reform of the EP because European elections would provide a new kind of democratic legitimization to Western European communists. At the same time, Berlinguer hoped to see European Political Cooperation (EPC) reinforced, although on this issue he was imprecise and sometimes contradictory. He certainly wished EC members to have a foreign policy more independent of the United States: 'It is necessary that Europe, without passively waiting for the trends of the Reagan administration, clearly states its own choice in favour of détente and of balanced and controlled disarmament.'[29] Yet he also stressed the need to respect international alliances in order to prevent a unilateral disruption of the nuclear balance of power between the two superpowers.[30] By and large, Berlinguer over-emphasized the real prospects of the early stages of European Political Cooperation. The actual stalemate within EPC, therefore, caused deep disappointment.

In the wake of the deployment of Soviet SS-20s, NATO's dual track decision and Soviet intervention in Afghanistan, Berlinguer's view of the international situation became gloomier. The end of détente threatened to push the PCI back into domestic isolation, particularly after the 'national solidarity' governments ended following the decline of political understanding with the Italian Christian Democrats and the decrease in electoral support for the communists revealed by the June 1979 Italian elections.[31] Against this backdrop of new Cold War tensions, Berlinguer revealed his frustration at the lack of a coordinated European foreign policy to defend détente and disarmament: 'As to Europe, the process of détente is stagnant, while at the same time right-wing forces advance aggressively in Britain, in the Federal Republic of Germany and elsewhere', he lamented in a speech to the Italian Chamber of Deputies on the eve of the Atlantic Council meeting in December 1979.[32]

His discontent was deeper still when he addressed the European Parliament. In Strasbourg, he overtly condemned Soviet politics in Afghanistan and blamed the Italian and other European governments for having been unable to adopt the proposal made by the PCI as an alternative to the dual track decision:

> Soviet intervention has worsened an international situation already heavy with tension. Today we are faced with a gloomy international scene, full of threats … [N]ot only are all negotiations on disarmament paralysed, but the ratification of existing agreements such as SALT II is also being reconsidered and the arms race is moving forward quantitatively and qualitatively. This is the result of the serious mistake made in Brussels by the NATO Council. Things would be different if the line we proposed together with other political forces and some European governments had prevailed: namely, deferring for a certain time all decisions on the production and deployment of new American missiles, while

at the same time asking the Soviet Union to stop the production and deployment of SS-20s, and opening immediately a negotiation between the two blocs in order to assess the real military balance and bring it to the lowest possible level.[33]

Most of all, he sharply criticized European institutions for being unable to stand up to the pressures the superpowers exerted on the international system: 'Up until now political cooperation among EEC countries ... has not been equal to the demands made by the gravity of the international situation ... We are still far not only from a common foreign policy, but even from an effective coordination of single initiatives'.[34]

At the same time, however, Berlinguer seemed to perceive no option other than to continue with the political course he had envisaged in the years of détente. Continuity, indeed, was the third characteristic of Berlinguer's vision of the end of the Cold War. In the new international context of the late 1970s, Berlinguer's foreign policy priorities remained unchanged: détente, European cooperation and disarmament. In his public speeches and interviews, he constantly appealed for the latter while simultaneously advocating closer European foreign policy cooperation from his seat at the EP.

> Certainly détente in Europe is our main objective. I agree, in this regard, with what has been affirmed at the Congress of the International Socialists in the last few days by some of its most influential representatives, who, addressing in part the new U.S. administration, underlined that détente is for us, as Europeans, a priority that cannot be ignored ... Here we see how important is an engagement of the Nine [EC member states] in order to make the Madrid meeting on security and cooperation progress ... and to reach concrete decisions above all on the convening of a pan-European conference on disarmament.[35]

The continuity was evident also in the PCI's quest for equidistance from the two superpowers: the reawakening of the Cold War did not bring the party back into line with the Soviet Union, not even with its pacifist campaign, on which Moscow expected full support from Western communists.[36] The PCI's reaction to the repression of Solidarność and its severe condemnation of the military government established in December 1981 in Poland, finally, were further opportunities to denounce bloc constraints.[37]

Berlinguer imagined two different phases in the process leading to the overcoming of the Cold War. Although he never outlined a clear 'schedule' for international change, one can argue that he differentiated between a long-term period, at the end of which the two military blocs would be disarmed and dissolved under the pressure of other political and social forces, and a short-term one, in which the international order would still rely upon the two superpowers and their military potential. In the latter, politics of moderation and equidistance was required, in order to prevent a unilateral shattering of the balance of power between the two. When asked by an Italian journalist for his opinion on the event of a final overcoming of the bipolar system, he made the following remarks:

> Undoubtedly we find ourselves confronted by a crisis of the bipolar system. But we should also consider that if the crisis of the bipolar system is translated into the chaotic rise of new challenges and of national interests, then it can develop into sharpened tensions, local conflicts and uncontrollable unrest. It would be wrong, therefore, to deny the essential task of the two great powers in preserving peace: any design of a new international economic and political order that leaves out of consideration the two great powers is overambitious. At the same time, we should not abandon autonomous initiatives of other countries and political groups ... The non-aligned front represents in this regard a positive element breaking the model of a rigid bipolar system, with its vertical leadership ... while not opposing in principle either of the two superpowers.[38]

The evident limitation of this vision was the lack of a clear strategy for the passage from a balanced bipolar system to the actual dismantling of the two blocs.

Conclusions

Enrico Berlinguer imagined the end of the Cold War, yet he neither foresaw the actual steps that would lead to that point, nor did he mean to destabilize the two blocs as a way to accelerate their crumbling. He held the leadership of the PCI at the time when international détente reached its high point, and he was still in power when it fell away under the threat of nuclear rearmament in Europe. Throughout this period, however, Berlinguer's political line – Eurocommunism – remained largely unchanged, as did his efforts to release the PCI from its allegiance to the Warsaw Pact. Accordingly, the way he imagined the end of the Cold War did not change either. The fundamental assumption underlying his vision, indeed, was that both blocs were experiencing different internal crises, yet both of them were capable of bringing about the transformation of the international system from its bipolar framework into a multi-polar one.

The Western bloc, according to the secretary general of the PCI, was facing a structural crisis due to the fundamental deficiencies of capitalism. The Soviet Union and socialist countries in Eastern Europe, meanwhile, were facing a historical stalemate.[39] Some of the principles and purposes of socialism, which Berlinguer still endorsed as the highest political, economic and social system, had been achieved in these countries; others remained unrealized. Moreover, Berlinguer's awareness that the Cold War had been a deterrent to the spread of socialism in Italy and in Western Europe only increased his reliance on international détente. In Berlinguer's perspective, the Cold War had encouraged the PCI's long-lasting isolation from government: détente, in theory, released this 'external' constraint on Italian politics and made a change in the Communist Party's position in Italy foreseeable. For all these reasons, détente was an absolute priority.

Berlinguer, then, envisaged the overcoming of the Cold War not as a revolutionary event, but instead as an evolution of international détente and military disarmament, and a consequence of the two superpowers' loss of supremacy in the international system. Among the other concurrent forces, Berlinguer looked with great anticipation to the directly elected European Parliament in its first mandate. An overestimation of its political potential and actual capability to react to the danger of nuclear rearmament in Europe was probably one of the flaws of Berlinguer's vision. Another was that he wrongly assumed that the other European governments would in general share the same dynamic conception of détente.

With the reawakening of the Cold War, Berlinguer's optimism faded away, yet his point of view on the international situation did not change substantially. He thought that nuclear rearmament was largely an outcome of the two blocs' internal crises and still believed that a solution to these tensions lay in the revival of détente and the acceleration of disarmament. Furthermore, he still argued in favour of a concerted effort by international and national non-aligned actors in order to reach those aims. The only alternative to this vision was catastrophe: as Berlinguer could not imagine permanent Cold War, the only other possibility he foresaw and feared was real war.[40]

It is not easy to assess the impact of Berlinguer's ideas and politics on the actual end of the Cold War. Although this event took place only a few years after his death and just a decade after the events of December 1979, the Iron Curtain fell in an international context that looked very different from that of ten years before. Probably Berlinguer would not have imagined such an acceleration of domestic reform in the USSR as that which took place under Mikhail Gorbachev, nor the sudden disintegration of the Soviet bloc. Paradoxically, Berlinguer imagined the end of the Cold War as a longer process and a less 'revolutionary' one. Besides, the overcoming of political and military confrontation was not, in his view, bound to end in the demise of socialist systems, but instead in the further spread of socialism in Western Europe. Accordingly, he underestimated the strength of capitalist systems. He also overemphasized the role of the European Parliament, in terms of both its independence from the constraints of the Cold War and most of all its capability to stimulate European Political Cooperation and make it an instrument of a non-aligned conception of security.

An echo of Berlinguer's ideas, however, remained alive in Eastern Europe and influenced Gorbachev and other young Soviet leaders.[41] Gorbachev would later on comment on Berlinguer's foreign policy as follows: 'Of course Berlinguer supported the end of East-West confrontation. Here too he gave his original contribution, which caused a sceptical reaction on the two sides of the barricade which at that time divided the world.'[42] Gorbachev praised the speech made by the Italian communist leader in Moscow in November 1977, and in the 1980s he concluded that the Soviet Union's opposition to the 'historical compromise' had been short-sighted. Analogies between Gorbachev's and Berlinguer's politics, however, apply not only to democratic reforms but also to the strong interest of both leaders – for different reasons and at different times – in European economic and political integration.[43]

More fundamentally, what Berlinguer envisaged was not a winner in the Cold War, but instead a profound transformation of Western and Eastern European societies and of their citizens' political demands that would affect the two blocs so much as to break their borders. In this sense, his vision anticipated the most recent reflections of the historians of the Cold War, who have turned their focus from the superpowers to underlying social forces in order to explain the events of 1989.

Notes

1. A. Guerra. 2009. *La solitudine di Berlinguer. Governo, etica e politica. Dal «no» a Mosca alla «questione morale»*, Rome: Ediesse; F. Barbagallo and A. Vittoria (eds). 2007. *Enrico Berlinguer, la politica italiana e la crisi mondiale*, Rome: Carocci; F. Barbagallo. 2006. *Enrico Berlinguer*, Rome: Carocci; S. Pons. 2006. *Berlinguer e la fine del comunismo*, Turin: Einaudi; C. Valentini. 1992. *Berlinguer. L'eredità difficile*, Rome: Editori Riuniti; G. Fiori. 1992. *Vita di Enrico Berlinguer*, Rome: Laterza. See also G. Chiarante. 2009. *La fine del PCI. Dall'alternativa democratica di Berlinguer all'ultimo Congresso (1979–1991)*, Rome: Carocci, 25–77.
2. E. Berlinguer. 1972. *Per un governo di svolta democratica*, Rome: Editori Riuniti; Berlinguer. 1976. *La politica internazionale dei comunisti italiani 1975–76*, Rome: Editori Riuniti; Berlinguer. 1977. *Austerità, occasione per trasformare l'Italia*, Rome: Editori Riuniti. See also Berlinguer's articles in *Rinascita*, some of them collected in Berlinguer. 1985. *La crisi italiana. Scritti su "Rinascita"*, Rome: Editrice l'Unità.
3. Examples of these two different approaches are Barbagallo, *Enrico Berlinguer* and Pons, *Berlinguer e la fine del comunismo*.
4. See in particular the two joint declarations of 1975 and 1977: Archivi PCI, Istituto Gramsci, Rome (hereafter Arch. PCI), Fondo Berlinguer, Mov. op. int., 129, 'Dichiarazione comune del PCI e del Partito Comunista Francese', 15 Nov. 1975; Mov. op. int., 146, 'Dichiarazione comune del Partito comunista di Spagna, del Partito comunista francese e del Partito comunista italiano', Madrid, 3 Mar.1977.

5. Tatò to Berlinguer, Mar. 1976, quoted in Fondazione Istituto Gramsci. 2003. *Caro Berlinguer. Note e appunti riservati di Antonio Tatò a Enrico Berlinguer,* Turin: Einaudi, 43–47 and Tatò's note to Berlinguer on his speech at the XV Congress of the PCI, 15 Mar. 1979, ibid., 100–104.
6. See for example Berlinguer's interview, *Europa,* 3 Feb. 1976, cited in A. Tatò (ed). 1984. *Conversazioni con Berlinguer,* Rome: Editori Riuniti, 57.
7. Arch. PCI, Fondo Berlinguer, Mov. op. int., n. 157, PCI Note on the Belgrade meeting between A. Grlickov, A. Minucci and R. Ledda, 7 June 1978.
8. Enrico Berlinguer's speech to the European Parliament, 16 Jan. 1980, in *L'Unità,* 17 Jan. 1980.
9. In 1979 direct CPSU funding to the PCI apparently ceased, although indirect channels supporting most pro-Soviet trends in Italy were kept open, mostly under cover of commercial actitives (see V. Zaslavsky. 2004. *Lo stalinismo e la sinistra italiana,* Milan: Mondadori, 137). On the broader issue of Soviet financial support to the PCI during the Cold War see M.-P. Rey. 2003. 'Le Département International du Comité central du PCUS, le MID et la politique extérieure soviétique', *Communisme,* 74/75, 179–215.
10. See for example the conversation between Berlinguer and SED Secretary for International Affairs Hermann Axen, Bundesarchiv, Stiftung Archiv der Parteien und Massenorganisationen der DDR, (hereafter BA, SAPMO), Büro Axen, IV 2/ 2.035/ 102, SED report on H. Axen's visit in Italy, 18–20 June 1980), 14–15; see also Berlinguer's speech to the Italian Chamber of Deputies, 16 Nov. 1983, in E. Berlinguer. 2001. *Discorsi parlamentari (1968–1984),* edited by M.L. Righi, Rome: Camera dei Deputati, 298–304; Barbagallo, *Enrico Berlinguer,* 406–407.
11. This last point is one of the main arguments of Pons, *Berlinguer e la fine del comunismo.*
12. Tatò to Berlinguer, Dec. 1981, in Tatò, *Caro Berlinguer,* 237.
13. E. Berlinguer. 1979. *Per il socialismo nella pace e nella democrazia,* Rome: Editori Riuniti.
14. Berlinguer's speech at the XV Congress of the PCI, Mar.–Apr. 1979, in *XV Congresso del PCI – Atti.* Rome: Editori Riuniti, 1977.
15. Berlinguer's interview with *Critica Marxista,* Spring 1981, in M. Gorbachev. 1994. *Le idee di Berlinguer ci servono ancora,* Rome: Sisifo, 35–55.
16. Pons, *Berlinguer,* 247–258.
17. Speech at the Italian Chamber of Deputies, 20 Feb. 1976, in Berlinguer, *Discorsi parlamentari (1968–1984),* 144–145.
18. Pons, *Berlinguer,* 75, 92, 110. On the superpowers' static conception of détente – or a 'mechanism for domestic fortification' against political and social change threatened by protest movements and political parties in the late 1960s and early 1970s, see J. Suri. 2003. *Power and Protest: Global Revolution and the Rise of Détente,* Cambridge, MA: Harvard University Press.
19. D. Sassoon, Introduction, in Berlinguer, *Discorsi parlamentari (1968–1984),* xxiv–xxv.
20. Berlinguer's interview with Giampaolo Pansa, *Corriere della Sera,* 15 June 1976.
21. On East German–Italian relations: C. Pöthig. 2000. *Italien und die DDR. Die politischen, ökonomischen und kulturellen Beziehungen von 1949 bis 1980,* Frankfurt: Peter Lang; L. Fasanaro. 2008. 'Eurocommunism. An East German Perspective', in L. Nuti (ed), *The Crisis of Detente in Europe: From Vietnam to Gorbachev, 1975–1985,* London: Routledge, 244–255.
22. Pons, *Berlinguer,* 112–113. For an East German account of the Budapest meeting, BA, SAPMO, Büro Axen, IV 2/ 2.035/ 22, 'Ausführungen des Genossen Axen: Zu aktuellen Problemen des Kampfes der Kommunistischen Bewegung', 1 Mar. 1978.
23. Interview by C. Casalegno for *Europa,* 3 Feb. 1976, quoted in Berlinguer, *La politica internazionale dei comunisti italiani,* 104.

24. D. Sassoon, Introduction, in Berlinguer, *Discorsi parlamentari*, xxiv–xxv.
25. Berlinguer, *La politica internazionale dei comunisti italiani*, 13–18.
26. Arch. PCI, Fondo Berlinguer, PE, n. 4, Berlinguer's speech at the European Parliament (hereafter EP), 19 Nov. 1980; PE, n. 6, Berlinguer at the EP, 16 Dec. 1981; Berlinguer's interview with *L'Unità*, 21 Feb. 1982, Gorbachev, *Le idee di Berlinguer*, 57–79. On the PCI's opening to the Third World and its policy in Africa, see P. Borruso. 2009. *Il PCI e l'Africa indipendente. Apogeo e crisi di un'utopia socialista (1956–1989)*, Florence: Le Monnier.
27. See P. Ferrari. 2007. *In cammino verso Occidente. Berlinguer, il PCI e la comunità europea negli anni '70*, Bologna: CLUEB; I. Poggiolini. 2005. 'Una partnership italo-britannica per il primo allargamento: convergenza tattica o comunanza di obiettivi (1969–1973)?', in F. Romero and A. Varsori (eds), *Nazione, interdipendenza, integrazione. Le relazioni internazionali dell'Italia (1917–1989)*, Rome: Carocci, 338; S. Pons. 2001. 'L'Italia e il PCI nella politica estera dell'URSS di Breznev', *Studi Storici*, 42(4), 941. An earlier 'conversion' of the PCI towards European integration has been identifed in D. Sassoon. 2001. 'La sinistra, l'Europa, il PCI', in R. Gualtieri (ed.), *Il PCI nell'Italia repubblicana*, Rome: Carocci, 223–249.
28. Speech at the Italian Chamber of Deputies, 20 Feb. 1976, in Berlinguer, *Discorsi parlamentari*, 144–145.
29. Interview with L. Barca, 'America after the Election of Reagan', in *Rinascita*, n. 47, 28 Nov. 1980.
30. Ibid.
31. Barbagallo, *Enrico Berlinguer*, 349–369.
32. Berlinguer's speech at the Chamber of Deputies, 5 Dec. 1979 in Berlinguer, *Discorsi parlamentari*, 188–203.
33. Berlinguer's speech to the EP, 16 Jan. 1980, in *L'Unità*, 7 Jan. 1980.
34. Arch. PCI, Fondo Berlinguer, PE, n. 4, Berlinguer's speech to the EP, 19 Nov. 1980.
35. Ibid.
36. BA, SAPMO, Büro Axen, DY 30/ IV 2/ 2.035/ 71, Axen to Honecker, 'Das ZK der KPdSU hat sich mit einem Schreiben an die kommunistischen und Arbeiterparteien Westeuropas gewandt', 9 Oct. 1979; later on, BA, SAPMO, Büro Axen, DY 30/ IV 2/ 2.035/ 71, 'Brief an die kommunistischen und Arbeiterparteien der nichtsozialistischen Länder', 3 Aug. 1982.
37. See G. Napolitano, 'Polonia, una vicenda cruciale', *Rinascita*, 18 Dec. 1981; also, Berlinguer's interview with *L'Unità*, 21 Feb. 1982, in Gorbachev, *Le idee di Berlinguer*, 57–79.
38. Interview by L. Barca, *Rinascita*, n. 47, 28 Nov. 1980.
39. Tatò to Berlinguer, Mar. 1976, in *Caro Berlinguer*, 43–47.
40. Berlinguer's speech to the EP, 16 Jan. 1980, in *L'Unità*, 17 Jan. 1980.
41. O.A. Westad. 2004. 'Beginnings of the End: How the Cold War Crumbled', in S. Pons and F. Romero, *Reinterpreting the End of the Cold War*, London: Frank Cass, 73. See also R.D. English. 2000. *Russia and the Idea of the West: Gorbachev, Intellectuals and the End of the Cold War*, New York: Columbia University Press.
42. Gorbachev, *Le idee di Berlinguer*, 16–20. Also, Barbagallo, *Enrico Berlinguer*, 310; A. Rubbi. 1994. *Il mondo di Berlinguer*, Rome: Napoleone, 108.
43. Historians who have reassessed the role played by the EC in the end of the Cold War have, accordingly, pointed out that the secretary general of the CPSU came to regard the EC as a necessary 'partner in reform': M. Cox. 2007. 'Another Transatlantic Split? American and European Narratives and the End of the Cold War', *Cold War History*, 7(1), 133.

Chapter 12

OVERCOMING BLOC DIVISION FROM BELOW
Jiří Hájek and the CSCE Appeal of Charter 77

Christian Domnitz

'This use of power is unjustifiable' – in these terms Czechoslovak Foreign Minister Jiří Steinich Hájek condemned the invasion of his country by Warsaw Pact troops in August 1968 to the United Nations Security Council.[1] These were harsh words coming from an understated functionary who was generally cautious in the choice of language. It is not widely known that this man had developed plans for European security structures to transcend the world's division into military blocs.

The diplomat and later dissident Hájek assessed world politics from an East-Central European perspective. As foreign minister of the Prague Spring government, he proposed closer cooperation between East and West, sought a way out of the confrontation of the military blocs and called for an East-West dialogue. After his demise as foreign minister and the revocation of his party membership, he co-founded the Charter 77 opposition movement.[2] Referring to the Conference on Security and Cooperation in Europe (CSCE), he formed Czech opposition with a focus on the future of Europe. In Charter 77, he participated in controversies about the meaning of peace between East and West and developed a concrete foreign policy strategy, which was unique for an Eastern dissident movement. Thus he was a main actor in the independent Eastern peace movements' struggle for a position in the global campaign for disarmament. In Hájek's view, the greatest threat to peace was the division of the European continent. Therefore he and the whole of Charter 77 pledged to overcome the Cold War through citizens' commitment 'from below' in both East and West. The dissident Hájek advocated an understanding of security and stability in Europe that was interconnected with civil rights guarantees.

Notes for this chapter begin on page 187.

Hájek's ideas on how to overcome the bloc division developed in the context of fast-changing East-West relations. After the mutual demonization of the 1950s, the Prague Spring of 1968 and the West German new Ostpolitik marked early asynchronous attempts at opening the East to the West and, later, the West to the East. These controversial reorientations both east and west of the Iron Curtain inspired Hájek and set the stage for his actions. The West German objective of 'change through rapprochement' and Eastern attempts at stabilizing the postwar order of Europe encouraged détente and led to the signing of the Helsinki Final Act at the CSCE in 1975. From the 1970s on, Hájek was a critical commentator on international politics and a human rights activist, becoming a leading figure in the citizens' struggle to overcome the Iron Curtain. In this process, Central European dissidents created networks with Western independent peace activists, diplomats and even government officials.[3]

Hájek experienced the limitations of the bloc confrontation personally. War and invasion shaped the biography and the political career of the social democrat, then Stalinist and, later, reform communist. In 1939 the National Socialists imprisoned him for his membership in Czechoslovak and international socialist youth associations. Later, the suppression of the Prague Spring of 1968 put an end to his career as a diplomat. These events transformed Czechoslovak foreign policies as well as the politician Hájek. They blurred his political actions, which had to suit different contexts. Representing a so-called small nation, he was caught in the constraints of power politics. Hájek's idea of overcoming bloc confrontation and limiting domination by the superpowers influenced his strategies and guided his actions in the different time periods. This chapter gives an overview of this idea, its context and its impact, reflecting upon how ideas affect historical change. It focuses on the relationship between ideas and their political and social contexts, especially on the transformation of actors' intentions in the face of given systemic structures and external responses. For this reason, attention is devoted to Hájek's own perception of the context. The chapter concludes that the impact of Hájek's struggle to overcome the bloc division was structural rather than ideational.

When Hitler, Chamberlain, Mussolini and Daladier decided to cut off the Sudeten German lands from Czechoslovakia, Hájek had just received his doctorate in law. At the start of his career as an academic, party functionary and diplomat, his early idea of Europe was based upon an anti-imperial world view rooted in his experience of occupation, imprisonment and war. In contrast to his later commitment to a unified Europe of peace and human rights, the young Hájek supported a Stalinist system that violated basic human rights principles. He considered Western imperialism a crucial problem in Europe's political geography and advocated a communist

'European postwar order'.[4] He described the Munich Agreement as a 'disastrous setback for peace, freedom, and progress for the whole of Europe'.[5] Hájek made light of his political roots, pursuing the incorporation of social democracy into the Communist Party.[6] Speaking to his students at Charles University, he claimed that the Czechs had survived German oppression only by being aware of the support of 'Great Stalin'.[7] His assessment of that time was that security and stability could be created only via the communist realignment of East Central Europe. Thus, Hájek was in line with those Czech intellectuals who already had been fascinated by the Soviet experiment during the interwar period.[8] Many of the later Czechoslovak reform communists shared Hájek's Stalinist socialization.[9] Later, a feeling of guilt encouraged them to search for a more human form of socialism.

Striving for Peace in Europe from an East-Central European Perspective

Appointed deputy foreign minister in 1958, Hájek distanced himself from Stalinist thought and saw a 'broader space' for a Czechoslovak foreign policy that could now set its own priorities beyond Soviet guidelines. As minister of education and culture, he advocated the slogan of 'struggle against conservatism and dogmatism' in 1965.[10] When the Communist Party decided upon the reformist 'action programme' of 1968, he felt 'things turn in the right direction'.[11] Although he had not been among the protagonists of the Prague Spring until then, he was appointed foreign minister and worked out concepts that connected the East and West. He favoured a European order in which small states had a broader scope of agency. The reformers hoped to create a benevolent European context for a specifically Czechoslovak path to socialism. They wanted to open their country to the West – without, however, questioning its integration into the Eastern bloc and with no active reference to Western concepts of Europe. The first steps towards a reform communist foreign policy were cautious. Hájek was afraid of 'doing anything that could be interpreted in a wrong way'. He remembered a conversation with Henry Kissinger in which he stated that the renovation of Czechoslovak socialism stabilized the socialist community and strengthened peaceful coexistence.[12]

Speaking to the Czechoslovak parliamentary commission for foreign affairs in June 1968, Hájek advocated 'pan-European cooperation' similar to that sought by Mikhail Gorbachev twenty years later.[13] In the Czechoslovak Communist Party's journal of Marxist-Leninist theory he wrote that a remodelled socialism should establish guarantees of citizens' rights and principles of democracy. In a think piece, he advocated 'more activist European policies' in Czechoslovakian foreign affairs and, distancing himself from purely anti-Western approaches, suggested 'differentiating between the inner powers of the Federal Republic of Germany' and establishing contacts with the Social Democrats.[14] Although this had already been proposed in the Communist Party's 'Action Programme' of April 1968, it was a controversial issue. The Prague Spring government envisaged re-establishing diplomatic contacts with West Germany, which was an important trading partner. According to Hájek's political memoirs, Germany's gradual retreat from the Hallstein doctrine under Foreign Minister Willy Brandt had made Czechoslovakian diplomats hopeful that an approach to the German government might encourage the development of a new Ostpolitik.[15] Discussing such considerations at the European communist parties' conference on security and cooperation in Karlovy Vary in 1967, the hosts had introduced an interpretation of 'Security and Cooperation' in Europe with distinctive Czechoslovak elements. Czechoslovakian foreign policy had thus distanced itself from that of Poland, the German Democratic Republic (GDR) and the Soviet Union.[16] Although he was not the original architect of this revised stance, Hájek was primarily responsible for presenting the new line in the international arena. Aware of the potential for conflict, he revised the key passages carefully in his manuscripts.[17] However, he positioned Czechoslovakia at the 'heart of Europe' in order to underline the new approach in a journal article.[18]

Ultimately, Czechoslovak considerations about a new order of peace and cooperation in Europe would not be finalized. After much hesitation and examination, work on the foreign policy conception of the Prague Spring started only two weeks before the invasion by Warsaw Pact troops. Hájek, whose earlier priority had been to contain the imperial ambitions of the West, was constrained by a military intervention from the East. The events of August 1968 caught him on holiday in Yugoslavia. He travelled first to Vienna to be briefed and then headed for New York, where he condemned the invasion in an emotional speech at the United Nations Security Council, referred to above. Meanwhile, the Prague government backed down under Soviet pressure. After Hájek's return, Premier Alexander Dubček and President Ludvík Svoboda advised him to resign from his post, explaining that 'Gromyko will not like to negotiate with you'.[19] Hájek's speech at the United Nations Security Council marked the end of his work within party structures and the diplomatic service. A short period of employment at the Academy of Sciences ended with his dismissal for political reasons and the revocation of his party membership.[20]

In 1968, Hájek and the reform communists' government had tested whether the Communist Party of the Soviet Union (CPSU) would accept new models of diplomatic relations between East and West. They proposed a dialogue not only between governments, but also among left-wing parties in the East and the West. The exchange was intended to support the democratization of socialism. The goal of the unfinished foreign policy of the Prague Spring was to transform Czechoslovakia from a frontier state in the East-West confrontation into a bridge between the blocs.[21]

Foreign Affairs as the Inspiration for Hájek's Commitment to Human Rights

The signing of the Helsinki Final Act in August 1975 demonstrated the will of both Eastern and Western European governments to preserve the achievements of détente. Promises of humanitarian exchange, included in the document and in negotiations on human rights at the CSCE follow-up conferences in Belgrade (1978) and Madrid (1982), soon encouraged opposition movements in the Eastern bloc.[22] Since the governments of the socialist states had to make national law compatible with the Final Act, invoking the CSCE was officially legitimate, and creating citizens' platforms was formally legal. Thus, the CSCE opened the way for civic engagement in the Eastern bloc by providing an instance of appeal for human rights. Ten years after his resignation as foreign minister, Hájek became one of the three speakers of Charter 77. He was among the first dissidents to realize the political potential of appealing to the Final Act.[23] For several months Hájek represented Charter 77 on his own, as the philosopher Jan Patočka had died following secret service interrogation and the writer Václav Havel was imprisoned. Acting as an independent intellectual, he saved the existence of Charter 77 in a critical period. Although the group had been created in accordance with the official law, its speakers and signatories were suppressed. Hájek experienced oppressive surveillance and harassment by the secret police.

Because of his experience, Hájek was considered a moral authority within Charter 77. It was a sensation that a former communist minister was among the first signatories of the founding document. Within the movement Hájek belonged to the faction of former communists, who shaped the platform to a great extent. The reform communist faction was sometimes called 'Eurocommunist' because its members followed the model of the Western European communists, pursuing a democratic path to communism and finding themselves in conflict with the CPSU as a result. It was the reform communists who put the issue of peace on the Charter 77 agenda. Other members of the group included socialists, social revolutionaries and religious-minded Chartists, who treated the former communists with respect but did not withhold criticism.[24]

As a member of Charter 77, Hájek continued to think in terms that interconnected the East with the West. He referred positively to German social democracy. He wrote letters regularly to the former German chancellor Willy Brandt. He thought that reform communist ideas of peace and Brandt's Ostpolitik were similar answers to the military threat, as they both involved approaching the opponent and initiating dialogue. 'I think my friends and I share your position on today's pivotal questions', Hájek wrote to Brandt.[25] In 1985, Hájek asserted that it was time to 'overcome black-and-white bipolar thinking'.[26] Hájek did not share the views of other dissidents who criticized deals between Western political elites and the state socialist governments as weakening the opposition movements.[27] He welcomed the prospect of rapprochement between East and West and asked West German social democrats to meet not only with governmental representatives but also with dissidents when visiting Czechoslovakia. 'Our friends and comrades outside', he wrote to Brandt, should 'show interest in our efforts that are focused on détente, too'.[28] Furthermore, Hájek occasionally corresponded with communists and social democrats in the West such as Austrian Chancellor Bruno Kreisky and the Austrian communist Georg Breuer. He also sought contacts with the Feltrinelli Foundation in Milan and the Istituto Gramsci in Bologna. To win the support of Western left-wing parties, Czech dissidents attempted to use communists who had emigrated after 1968 as intermediaries.[29] When Czechoslovak officials insisted that Brandt was not to meet any dissidents on a planned visit to Prague, Brandt delayed the visit and met the exiled Czech reform communists Zdeněk Mlynář and Jiří Pelikán in January 1985. When he finally visited Prague in November 1985, he sent his party colleague Peter Glotz to see Hájek.[30] Brandt avoided praising the opposition publicly because he was afraid of jeopardizing official East-West relations.

Hájek pleaded for a 'détente from below'. In his political memoirs, he argued that 'people on both sides of the dividing line should engage against bloc confrontation'. The citizens' engagement in security issues was to unify Europe from below. Hájek initially accepted the status quo of a divided continent, but he then became critical of 'political and ideational lethargy' and appealed to democratic civic consciousness. He saw Central Europe as a double periphery between East and West and never argued in explicitly anti-Soviet terms. A small nation like that of the Czechs and Slovaks, he stated, had to be subordinate to the superpowers for the sake of security.[31] Other dissidents and exiled writers, like the Czech author Milan Kundera, took more radical positions than Hájek. From exile in Paris, Kundera argued that Central Europe belonged culturally to the occident and had been politically kidnapped by the Soviets.[32]

Hájek considered the CSCE the most promising instrument for overcoming Europe's bloc division and appreciated the Final Act as the 'textual overcoming of bipolarity'. He saw it not only as a promoter of human rights guarantees but as a stimulus for change.[33] Hájek creatively searched for a more just order in European politics and within European societies. For him, 'Helsinki' represented the utopian objective of an ideal European order without the dominance of superpowers.[34] The 'spirit of Helsinki' that he wrote about included the equality of all European nations and their right to create a multilateral, not bipolar, political geography for the continent. For this reason, he also studied Western ideas of Europe, for instance, de Gaulle's 'Europe from the Atlantic to the Urals'. He was in favour of the concept because it allowed Europe to be imagined from the perspective of its nations and in a way that transcended the separation of East and West.[35] Hájek wrote essays and reports on the CSCE follow-up conferences. His high esteem for the CSCE spread to the rest of Charter 77. The platform continued to refer repeatedly to the CSCE, calling the Final Act a 'historic document' and underlining the necessity of compliance with it.[36]

Discussing the meaning and significance of peace had been another crucial issue in Charter 77. In the late, more confrontational phase of the Cold War, the military threat and the bloc division had become key topics in the growing European peace movements. The development of mobile Soviet SS-20 missiles, the NATO dual track decision in 1979 and the subsequent deployment of Pershing II missiles in Western Europe had created a tense situation. The question of how to deal with this threat under the conditions of dictatorship led to controversies in the movement. While the dissidents quickly agreed that it was not acceptable to sacrifice individual freedom for peace, the stance to adapt towards Western left-wing peace movements remained contentious. Chartists around Hájek argued that building links with Western campaigners offered a chance to debate a key point in world politics and criticize the official understanding of peace without freedom. Ladislav Hejdánek and members of the religious wing, however, criticized the contacts between Western peace activists and the communist governments.[37] The concept of the 'indivisibility of peace' was used to resolve this conflict. In several texts for the samizdat and for Western publications, Hájek promoted the concept and made it popular amongst the independent groups.[38] It combined peace between states with guaranteed human rights in their societies. The main argument was that sustained outer peace is impossible without inner freedom.[39] Hájek argued that Nazi power in Germany and the Second World War had confirmed this link *ex negativo* because the National Socialists had first suspended inner freedoms and then breached international peace.[40] Adding to his expertise in foreign affairs and international law, Hájek had become a human rights activist.

The Chartists made the 'indivisibility of peace' the basis for their dialogue with Western European peace movements. It served to bridge the gap between them and Western peace movements that they considered to be unduly idealistic. Eastern dissidents, however, rejected a narrow understanding of peace as the 'absence of war', as the official state socialist propaganda defined it.[41] Western and Eastern peace activists demonstrated their understanding of this point of view in the common memorandum 'Giving Real Life to the Helsinki Accords', issued to coincide with the 1986 start of the Vienna follow-up conference of the CSCE.[42] The 'indivisibility of peace' had thus facilitated the East-West networking of independent peace and human rights movements.[43]

Peace groups in both East and West started to focus on human rights commitments and citizens' participation. The transfer of human rights norms made people east of the Iron Curtain aware of their lack of rights and the necessity of participation.[44] The movement's 'Prague Appeal' of 1985 encouraged a transnational discussion about the bloc confrontation. The document was addressed to the fourth international conference of the movement for European Nuclear Disarmament (END) in Amsterdam, on the occasion of the fortieth anniversary of the Second World War's end. In his memoirs, Hájek attributes the authorship of the document to Jiří Dienstbier and Jaroslav Šabata, leaving his own role unclear.[45] The appeal nevertheless owes much to Hájek's thought. It claimed the CSCE process offered the opportunity to establish 'Europe as a community of equal partners ... that could be an example for the real and peaceful living together of its nations'. The artificial division of the continent was the biggest threat to peace in Europe. An 'association of free and independent nations in an all-European alliance' should transcend the structures of the blocs.[46] Opposition groups in East Germany and Poland soon answered the appeal.

At the end of the 1980s, however, dissidents questioned whether the mechanisms of security and cooperation in Europe could really provide the desired change. They became dissatisfied with the intergovernmental negotiations of the CSCE, which disregarded citizens' initiatives and non-governmental organizations. In particular, the course of the Vienna follow-up conference produced scepticism among both the Eastern bloc opposition groups and Western non-governmental organizations (NGOs) about the feasibility of a 'Helsinki from below'. Many dissidents, focused on the human rights aspects of the Helsinki Final Act, therefore questioned the CSCE's viability as an institutional actor for European unification.[47] At this time, a younger generation of Chartists around Václav Havel led value-oriented discussions about freedom and individuality that went beyond Hájek's juridical approach to human rights and security. They appealed to values such as truthfulness and the importance of the individual, pointing at the deficiencies of the state socialist societies. They hoped to establish such values by disseminating Kundera's concept of 'Central Europe' as a cultural region. In 1988 Hájek founded the independent Helsinki Committee, which promoted the human rights guarantees of the CSCE Final Act in Czechoslovakia. The group gave legal advice to those who were persecuted and disseminated information about human and civil rights.

Mikhail Gorbachev's perestroika encouraged some reform expectations in Czechoslovakia in the late 1980s. The exiled Czech communist Zdeněk Mlynář – a fellow student of Gorbachev and close friend of Hájek – was the first to see the potential for change here,[48] while many dissidents remained undecided in the first years of Gorbachev's rule. Only later did reform communists express their loyalty and hope in articles and in an open letter to Gorbachev.[49] In the documents of Charter 77, Gorbachev first appears in 1986 as someone to whom peace and human rights appeals could be directed. From 1987 onwards, Jiří Hájek, Jiří Dienstbier and Jaroslav Šabata also hoped Gorbachev's rhetoric of the 'Common European Home' would have positive effects on peace and human rights issues in Europe.[50] Before his visit to Prague, all the Chartists asked Gorbachev to comment upon the invasion of 1968,[51] but the Soviet leader avoided the topic – a response that led even years later to a dispute between Gorbachev and his student companion Mlynář.[52] Many writers in exile and dissidents in Czechoslovakia – Václav Havel and Václav Benda among them – saw in perestroika only an attempt to restabilize Soviet rule.[53]

In the autumn of 1989, observation and persecution ended for the Chartists, and for Hájek himself. His companions Václav Havel and Jiří Dienstbier became president and foreign minister. The 76-year-old Hájek led the official Czechoslovakian delegation at the Copenhagen CSCE human rights summit. He now debated European unification openly and in public.[54] His forum was the new magazine *Mezinárodní politika* (International Affairs), which former dissidents and reform communists had founded to foster European integration. He wanted to unify the whole of Europe, including the Soviet Union, and to that end continued to appeal to the CSCE for a relatively long time.[55] In his opinion, the integration of the dissolving empire into a Europe of East and West could stabilize change in Central and Eastern Europe. Until his death in 1993, Hájek only gradually withdrew from that view. Referring to the debate about Central Europe, he imitated his younger colleague Jiří Dienstbier in labelling his political viewpoint as 'Central European'.[56]

Conclusion: Hájek's Vision of the End of Cold War

Hájek's thinking about the European political order aimed at overcoming the bloc confrontation from the late 1950s onwards. He criticized the excessive influence of the superpowers and the resulting dividing line in the middle of Europe. Hájek integrated the antagonisms of the Cold War into his thought. He saw a lack of outer peace in the West and a lack of inner freedom in the East of the continent. On the one hand, he wanted to establish European structures of cooperative security that guaranteed a 'peaceful coexistence' of the states and their different political systems, in accord with communist propaganda. On the other hand, he sought a way to integrate citizens' rights into 'socialism with a human face'. Therefore he chose an intermediate approach between East and West and emancipated both foreign and home affairs from the terms of bloc confrontation. His ideas did not change, even as his surroundings were dramatically transformed. After the suppression of the Prague Spring, his ideas for overcoming the bloc confrontation ranged far beyond what was possible to articulate in the official sphere. Although they referred to official political slogans and law, Hájek's ideas were not in line with the official discourse. The philosopher Edgar Morin described an eccentric Europe that had historically been torn between the imperial use of power and the provision of human and civil rights. In this sense, Hájek can be regarded as a symbolic character of the Cold War's divided Europe who connected both extremes.[57]

In Central Europe, the bloc bipolarity had mentally been overcome long before the revolutions of 1989. Hájek's efforts to overcome the division of the continent and his participation in the European peace movement stimulated a debate in the societies east of the Iron Curtain. The samizdat publications of Charter 77 and of its individual members were read in neighbouring Poland and in the GDR. Charter 77 started a regular exchange of views with peace groupings such as the Polish Ruch Wolność i Pokój (Freedom and Peace Movement) and the East German Initiative Frieden und Menschenrechte (Initiative for Peace and Human Rights). However, there were also important differences between Hájek's quest to unify the whole of the continent through the CSCE and other Central European ideas about the end of the bloc confrontation. In Poland, for instance, independent samizdat writers published ideas of European culture and civilization that were dissociated from the official discourse on the CSCE. They stressed the importance of links between Poland and the West and pointed out that their nation was culturally a part of Western civilization. The Czechoslovak samizdat magazine *Střední Evropa* (Central Europe) took up Milan Kundera's idea of the Central European nations culturally belonging to the West.

Viewed in hindsight, Hájek's Europe also differed from the Europe that evolved through the enlargement of the European Union (EU) and NATO, and in the transfer of Western models of democracy and the market economy to the East. His hope of integrating the Soviet Union into a new Europe has met with little acceptance. Soviet foreign policy appeared incalculable during the military coup attempt in 1991, when Soviet tanks tried to suppress independence movements among the Baltic nations, and during the dissolution of the Soviet Union. Conceptualizing a united Europe with Russia was no longer convincing, for Central Europeans. The former dissidents who shaped Czechoslovak foreign affairs after 1989 preferred collective security in Western European structures over cooperative pan-European security. The significance of the CSCE and of Gorbachev's 'Common European Home' decreased because of competition from NATO and the EC/EU. When the political elites of Central Europe and the West agreed on NATO and EU accession perspectives for Czechoslovakia, Hájek's Europe of East and West became obsolete.

Hájek's ideas did not influence the political shape of post-1989 unified Europe. The impact of his commitment to an end of the Cold War was structural rather than ideational. His idea of overcoming the bloc confrontation 'from below' fostered structural change in the state socialist societies because it encouraged independent political activists to create sustainable and reliable networks of self-organization. Charter 77's attempts to democratize socialism through citizens' activity paved the way for more exchanges between East and West and enabled the development of transnational ties – first in the peace and human rights movements, and later in the societies of the eroding Eastern bloc. Transnationalism challenged the self-delimiting ideologies of state socialism. Continuing and broadening a tradition of independent civic engagement, mobilization from below initiated the dynamic events of 1989. In Czechoslovakia, Jiří Hájek and Charter 77 had prepared the ground for the democratic outbreak of a peaceful revolution.

Notes

1. J. Hájek. 1995. 'Pracovní text projevu J. Hájka, předneseného v Radě bezpečnosti OSN, s požadavkem plného obnovení svrchovanosti Československa (1968, 24. srpna, New York)', in J. Vondrová and J. Navrátil (eds), *Mezinárodní souvislosti československé krize 1967–1970: Prosinec 1967 – červenec 1968, Prameny k dějinám československé krize 1967–1970, vol. 4/1*, Prague: Doplněk.
2. As standard works on dissidence in Czechoslovakia, see B. Day. 1999. *The Velvet Philosophers*, London: Claridge Press; B. Falk. 2003. *The Dilemmas of Dissidence in East-Central*

Europe: Citizen Intellectuals and Philosopher Kings, Budapest: Central European University Press.

3. S.B. Snyder. 2009. 'The Rise of the Helsinki Network: "A Sort of Lifeline" for Eastern Europe', in P. Villaume and O.A. Westad (eds), *Perforating the Iron Curtain: European Détente, Transatlantic Relations and the Cold War*, Copenhagen: Museum Tusculanum Press.

4. J. Hájek. 1958. *Mnichov*, Prague: Státní nakladatelství politické literatury.

5. J. Hájek. 1958a. 'Historie Mnichova', *Nová mysl* 12(9), 790–803.

6. His works served as a pretext for purges among social democrats. Hájek claimed socialists and social democrats had betrayed the Czechoslovak nation by cooperating too closely with the West between the wars. See J. Hájek. 1954. *Zhoubná úloha pravicových socialistů v ČSR*, Prague: Státní nakladatelství politické literatury.

7. J. Hájek. 1954. *Projev na fakultním shromazdění mezinárodnich vztahů k výrocí umrti J. V. Stalina a K. Gottwalda*, A ÚSD AV ČR, Pozůstalost Jiřího Hájka, i.č. 558, kt.č. 15.

8. This also applied to many left-wing intellectuals. Cf. J. Křesťan. 2004. 'KSČ, Společnost pro hospodářské a kulturní styky s SSSR a obraz Sovětského svazu v prostředí české levicové inteligence (1925–1939)', in Z. Karník and M. Kopeček (eds), *Bolševismus, komunismus a radikální socialismus v Československu*, Prague: Dokořán.

9. B.F. Abrams. 2004. *The Struggle for the Soul of a Nation: Czech Culture and the Rise of Communism*, Lanham: Rowman & Littlefield.

10. J. Hájek. 1997. *Paměti*, Prague: Ústav mezinárodních vztahů, 202, 214, 241. See M. Kopeček. 2003. 'Obraz vnitřního nepřítele – revizionismus na stránkách „Otázek míru a socialismu" v letech 1958–1969', in Z. Karník and M. Kopeček (eds), *Bolševismus, komunismus a radikální socialismus v Československu*, Prague: Dokořán.

11. Hájek, *Paměti*, 241, 264.

12. Ibid., 267, 268.

13. The speech was published as J. Hájek. 1968a. 'Vytváříme podmínky pro úspěch obrodného procesu. Úkoly československé zahraniční politiky', *Rudé právo*.

14. 'K dalšimu postupu čs. zahraniční politiky vůčí Německé spolkové republice (3.5.1968)'. Reprinted in J. Vondrová and J. Navrátil (eds). 1995. *Mezinárodní souvislosti československé krize 1967–1970: Prosinec 1967 – červenec 1968, Prameny k dějinám československé krize 1967–1970, vol. 4/1*, Prague: ÚSD–Doplněk.

15. J. Hájek. 1987. *Begegnungen und Zusammenstöße. Erinnerungen des ehemaligen tschechoslowakischen Außenministers*, Freiburg im Breisgau: Herder, 165.

16. Ibid., 166.

17. J. Hájek. 1968. *Konstanty a nové prvky v zahraniční politice (k diskusi)*, A ÚSD AV ČR, Pozůstalost Jiřího Hájka, i.č. 671, kt.č. 15.

18. J. Hájek. 1968b. 'Konstanty a nové prvky v zahraniční politice', *Nová mysl* 22(8).

19. Hájek, *Paměti*, 267, 281, 292.

20. P. Blažek. 2002. 'Člen-korespondent ČSAV Jiří Hájek. Cesta z Ústředního výboru Komunistické strany Československa k Chartě 77 (1968–1976)', in A. Kostlán (ed.), *Věda v Československu v období normalizace (1970–1975)*, Prague: Výzkumné centrum pro dějiny vědy.

21. C. Reijnen. 2005. '"Hebben we een missie?" Over de Praagse Lente, de Koude Oorlog en Europa', *Nieuwste Tijd* 4(2/14).

22. D.C. Thomas. 2001. *The Helsinki Effect: International Norms, Human Rights, and the Demise of Communism*, Princeton, NJ: Princeton University Press.

23. 'Declaration of Charter 77', 6 Jan. 1977, *Archiv Libri Prohibiti*.

24. H.G. Skilling. 1981. *Charter 77 and Human Rights in Czechoslovakia*, London: Allen and Unwin, 26ff., 39ff.

25. A ÚSD AV ČR, Pozůstalost Jiřího Hájka, i.č. 52, kt.č. 2. Hájek to Brandt, 20 Mar. 1978.
26. A ÚSD AV ČR, Pozůstalost Jiřího Hájka, i.č. 52, kt.č. 2. Hájek to Brandt, 17 Dec. 1985.
27. Ladislav Hejdánek and other dissidents on Charter 77's religious wing were sceptical about Ostpolitik. Thus, they shared positions with Polish underground authors such as Zdzisław Najder. A samizdat special issue combined voices from the two countries: *Diskuse o východní politice* (=Komentáře, č. 7). Prague: Samizdat, 1986/87.
28. A ÚSD AV ČR, Pozůstalost Jiřího Hájka, i.č. 52, kt.č. 2. Hájek to Brandt, 25 Oct. 1984.
29. I am grateful for comments by Katja Hoyer, who is preparing a thesis on the political writings of Czechoslovak communists in exile.
30. P. Glotz. 2005. *Von Heimat zu Heimat. Erinnerungen eines Grenzgängers*, Berlin: Econ, 304. Brandt had done the same in a visit in 1977. Hájek, *Paměti*, 329.
31. Hájek, *Begegnungen und Zusammenstöße*, 208, 217, 220.
32. M. Kundera, 'The Tragedy of Central Europe', *New York Review of Books*, 26 Apr. 1984.
33. Hájek, *Begegnungen und Zusammenstöße*, 215.
34. Hájek, *Paměti*, 314, 326.
35. A ÚSD AV ČR, Pozůstalost Jiřího Hájka, i.č. 709, kt.č. 15. Hájek, 'De Gaulle jako hlasatel a průkopník celoevropské spolupráce', undated.
36. M. Hromádková and M. Rejchrt. 1980. 'Dopis Charty 77 prezidentovi republiky z 17.9.1980', *Informace o Chartě 77* 3(14).
37. J. Hájek. 1986. 'Helsinky a perspektivy vývoje k celoevropskému společenství', *Diskuse. Teoreticko-politický občasník* (40); L. Hejdánek. 1986. '"Milánská výzva" a co je kolem', *Diskuse. Teoreticko-politický občasník* (39). This was the resumption of an older controversy, see J. Kozlík, M.R. Křížková and A. Marvanová (eds). 1983. *Charta 77 o míru*, Prague: Samizdat.
38. Charter 77 stressed this nexus in Dokument Charty 77 č. 29/82. 1982. 'Dopis Charty 77 k pokračování madridských jednání signatářů helsinského závěrečného aktu konference o bezpečnosti a spolupráci v Evropě', *Informace o Chartě 77* (10).
39. J. Hájek. 1982. 'Die Achtung der Menschenrechte als Bestandteil einer Friedenspolitik', *Osteuropa* 42(3); J. Hájek. 1978. *Lidská práva, socialismus a mírové soužití*, Prague: Samizdat. Already during the Prague Spring he had stated that the development of socialist democracy would initiate a stronger commitment on the part of Czechoslovakia to international human rights protection: Hájek, 'Vytváříme podmínky'.
40. Hájek, 'Helsinky', 2.
41. V. Havel. 1985. *The Anatomy of a Reticence: Eastern European Dissidents and the Peace Movement in the West*, Stockholm: Charta 77 Foundation.
42. Europäisches Netzwerk für den Ost-West-Dialog (ed.). 1987. *Das Helsinki-Abkommen mit wirklichem Leben erfüllen (1986)*, Berlin.
43. A. Carter. 1992. *Peace Movements: International Protest and World Politics since 1945*, London: Longman, 183–213; P. Kenney. 2002. *A Carnival of Revolution: Central Europe 1989*, Princeton, NJ: Princeton University Press, 92–117.
44. On worldwide transfers of human rights norms see T. Risse, S.C. Ropp and K. Sikkink (eds). 1999. *The Power of Human Rights: International Norms and Domestic Change*, New York: Cambridge University Press.
45. Hájek, *Paměti*, 328.
46. Dokument Charty 77 č. 5/1985. 1985. 'Pražská výzva', *Informace o Chartě 77* 8(4).
47. Hejdánek, '"Milánská výzva"'.
48. Z. Mlynář, 'Il mio compagno di studi Mikhail Gorbaciov', *L'Unità*, 9 Apr. 1985.
49. A ÚSD AV ČR, Pozůstalost Jiřího Hájka, i.č. 476, kt.č. 12, Prague. 'Dopis skupiny byvalých představitelů KSČ M. Gorbačovovi na podporu jeho politiky', 5 Apr. 1987; J. Hájek and V. Kadlec. 1987. 'Přestavba také u nás?', *Listy* 17(2).

50. J. Hájek. 1988. 'Lidská práva v kontextu problematiky míru', *Informace o Chartě 77* 11(15).
51. Dokument Charty 77 č. 20/87. 1987. 'Dopis Michailu Gorbačovovi', *Informace o Chartě 77* 10(5).
52. M.S. Gorbachev and Z. Mlynář. 2002. *Conversations with Gorbachev: On Perestroika, the Prague Spring, and the Crossroads of Socialism*, New York: Columbia University Press.
53. V. Benda. 1986. 'Perspektivy politického vývoje v Československu a možná role Charty 77', *Informace o Chartě 77* 11(4), 12–15; V. Havel. 1999. 'Setkání s Gorbačovem (1987)', in V. Havel (ed.), *Spisy 4 – Eseje a jiné texty z let 1970–1989*, Prague: Torst.
54. M. Syruček, 'Jakou Evropu si přejme? Rozhovor s Jiřím Hájkem', *Tvorba*, 17 Jan. 1990.
55. J. Hájek. 1990. 'Československo a Evropa. Historická poučení pro dnešek', *Mezinárodní politika* (14).
56. J. Hájek. 1991. 'Rok nové čs. zahraniční politiky', *Mezinárodní politika* 1(15); J. Dienstbier. 1988. 'Mit den Augen eines Mitteleuropäers. Eine Strategie für Europa', *Neue Gesellschaft, Frankfurter Hefte* 35(4).
57. E. Morin. 1988. *Europa denken*, Frankfurt: Campus, 71ff., 128ff. and 141.

Section VI

VISION OR STATUS QUO IN THE 1970S

Chapter 13

HENRY KISSINGER
Vision or Status Quo?

Jussi Hanhimäki

In January 1989, as George H.W. Bush was about to take office, Henry Kissinger met with Mikhail Gorbachev. The former national security advisor and secretary of state proposed a tacit Soviet-American understanding: if the USSR would allow liberalization to proceed in Eastern Europe, the U.S. would not attempt to exploit this to its advantage by luring countries away from the Warsaw Pact.

The news of the 'backchannel' meeting leaked and caused a furore amongst commentators. Such luminaries as Zbigniew Brzezinski were quick to talk about 'Yalta II' or a 'new Yalta', drawing a parallel with the 1945 American-British-Soviet summit in the Crimea where President Franklin Roosevelt had, according to popular mythology if not entirely in tandem with actual facts, accepted Stalin's demands for Soviet control over East-Central Europe. To pre-empt accusations of another sell-out of Eastern Europe, incoming Secretary of State James Baker publicly disassociated the new administration from the meeting. Kissinger responded by criticizing Baker for both distorting his views and not engaging the USSR adequately. '[O]nce there is anarchy and the tanks roll it is too late for diplomacy', he warned in the *Washington Post* on 16 April 1989.[1]

As the events in Eastern Europe unravelled rapidly during the remaining months of 1989, however, Baker's dismissal of Kissinger's role and proposal appeared justified. By the end of the year, Eastern Europe was 'free'. Soon thereafter the Warsaw Pact was dissolved, Germany unified and the Soviet Union collapsed. Tanks did roll – not into Eastern Europe but into Beijing's Tianenmen Square, where a pro-democracy student protest was violently crushed in the summer of 1989. The People's Republic of China, which Kissinger had helped bring out of its self-imposed isolation some two decades earlier, remained politically under totalitarian control, even as its economy continued to experience a gradual liberalization.

The episode has more than anecdotal significance. It shows how ill-prepared Kissinger (and, in all honesty, many others) were for the collapse of the USSR in the late 1980s and early 1990s. Such a dramatic series of events simply did not accord with his world view: superpowers did not just wither and collapse. In fact, the main argument of this chapter is that Kissinger had rarely, if ever, considered the possibility of an international system without the Soviet Union. He certainly did not spend his time wondering how the Cold War conflict would end. Kissinger was not a visionary but a conservative. Perhaps because of his 'realist' background, Kissinger could not see how a superpower like the Soviet Union would ever give up power and influence voluntarily.[2]

There is of course a paradox: the Kissinger era did indeed set in motion or accelerate certain processes that brought about the end of the Cold War. Undoubtedly, the impact of the Conference on Security and Cooperation in Europe (CSCE) and the idea of human security ranked high in this regard. Détente and the emergence of Soviet-American summitry made possible the negotiations that diluted and eventually brought about an effective end to the Cold War nuclear arms rivalry. The end of American involvement in Vietnam signalled the end to large-scale U.S. military interventions in the name of anti-communism. And the opening to China enabled the beginning of an end to the extreme bipolarity of the Cold War.

But did Kissinger see these developments as elements that would undermine the Cold War international system? In my assessment the opposite is true. Kissinger in fact was working towards a very different goal: he wanted to restore stability, not to induce change. The argument that somehow the Nixon and Ford administrations foreshadowed Ronald Reagan and consciously 'started the ball rolling' towards the end of the Cold War is, as I see it, retrospective wisdom of the worst kind. Kissinger's grand design was a conservative one, aiming to restore battered American credibility abroad and based on the assumption that containment of the Soviet Union was the goal that would dominate American foreign policy for the rest of the twentieth century if not beyond. In short, there was no real 'vision thing' when it came to ending the Cold War. What Kissinger worked towards was changing the methods, not the goals, of American foreign policy.

Another paradox is important in understanding Kissinger's inability to predict the end of the Cold War. Although European by origin, the native of Bavaria adopted a heavily global outlook while in office. This was perfectly understandable: the 1970s were an era of global Cold War, a time when the events of the European continent were positively bor-

ing when compared to the upheavals in Asia and Africa.³ Kissinger, as
the NSC adviser and secretary of state, spent much of his energy in dealing with China, the Middle East, Africa and, of course, the Soviet Union.
While attempting to build a global equilibrium that benefited the United
States, however, Kissinger may have lost sight of the very real imbalance
of power between the two superpowers that was gradually but surely undermining the foundations of the bipolar order in Europe.

Kissinger and the Challenges of 1969

An emigrant from Nazi Germany, Kissinger came of age in the turmoil of
the Second World War – he served in the American occupying forces in his
former homeland – and the early Cold War as a student at Harvard University. In the early 1950s Kissinger embarked upon a high-profile career
that combined academic activities with consultancies to three administrations and, perhaps most importantly, to such presidential hopefuls as Nel-
son Rockefeller. He published numerous books, including the bestsellers
Nuclear Weapons and Foreign Policy and *A World Destroyed: Metternich, Castlereagh and the Problems of Peace.*⁴ Kissinger also wrote a series of articles
on topics ranging from the impact of non-alignment to the troubles of the
transatlantic alliance. During the Johnson administration, Kissinger began
his long engagement in secret negotiations by trying to find a settlement
for the Vietnam War. In short, by the late 1960s he had emerged as one of
the nation's top foreign policy intellectuals.⁵

Equally important, in 1968 Kissinger was one of the few well-established
academics who had a close association with the Republican Party. While
much has been made about the 'odd couple' – Kissinger and Richard
Nixon – that ran U.S. foreign policy in the early 1970s, the fact was that
Nixon faced a virtual dearth of talent within the Grand Old Party (GOP).
In 1969 Kissinger – an academic, a policy wonk, already an experienced
back channel negotiator – was an outstanding individual who brought an
aura of respectability to the new administration's foreign policy. While
few expected him to become a global celebrity, most thought that Nixon
had made a surprisingly excellent choice.

From a public relations perspective, choosing Kissinger as his national
security advisor was Nixon's master stroke. In February 1969, *Time* magazine ran a cover story of the man who would, in future years, become
a staple of American diplomacy. 'Bonn, London, and Paris may disagree
on a score of issues, but they are in happy unanimity in their respect for
him; even Moscow is not displeased', the article commented. It went on
to describe how Kissinger 'knows more foreign leaders than many State

Department careerists'. The article ended presciently with a quote from the nineteenth-century Austrian statesman Prince Metternich: 'I was born to make history, not to write novels'.[6]

When Kissinger took control over the National Security Council (NSC) he faced serious challenges. America was – not for the first or the last time – in decline. At the centre of American difficulties lay the Vietnam War. The Tet Offensive of February 1968 had exposed the hollow nature of Lyndon Johnson's assurances of late 1967 that the enemy's breaking point was about to be reached and that the war was coming to an end. Instead, the commander of U.S. forces in Vietnam, General William Westmoreland, had asked for another 200,000 troops to top up the half million already stationed in South Vietnam. That had been too much for Johnson, who had refused the request and announced, in late March, his decision not to seek a continuation of his presidency. Although he had ordered a bombing halt in late October, the Vietnam War presented mostly problems and few promising opportunities for the incoming administration in early 1969.

Aside from Vietnam, however, Kissinger and Nixon faced a whole host of other challenges and uncertainties. The relationship with the Soviet Union was at a crossroads as the Soviets approached nuclear parity. While their resources were far from equal to those of the United States, when it came down to other 'types' of power, the Kremlin's confidence appeared to have been boosted by the crackdown on Czechoslovakia in August 1968. The moderate response of the United States and its Western European allies to the arrival of thousands of Warsaw Pact troops in Prague could only have indicated to the Soviets that their 'sphere of influence' in East-Central Europe was secure. The inherent right of the USSR and its allies to 'defend socialism' in Eastern European countries by force if necessary – often referred to as the Brezhnev doctrine – had apparently been accepted in Washington. In addition, the Soviets continued to support militarily a number of Arab states, particularly Egypt and Syria, in their quest for retribution after Israeli victories in 1967's Six-Day War. The Soviet Union, in short, was casting its quest for influence far beyond East-Central Europe.

In 1969, America appeared besieged, and the Soviet Union ascendant. The end of the Cold War was nowhere in sight, much less envisaged. Kissinger, faced with additional challenges in the form of the frayed transatlantic alliance and volatility throughout the so-called Third World, had to focus on finding new ways to reinstate America's global pre-eminence. Or as Kissinger himself later put it, the task facing the new administration was vast indeed: 'Simultaneously we had to end a war, manage a global rivalry with the Soviet Union in the shadow of nuclear weapons, reinvigorate our alliance with industrial democracies, and integrate the new nations into a new world equilibrium.'[7]

Détente: Rivalry Through Different Means

As a policymaker Kissinger consistently emphasized the bipolar relationship between the United States and the Soviet Union as the key, and more or less permanent, feature of international relations. While Kissinger correctly stressed the limits of American power in the context of the Vietnam War (and other troubles), he was unable to break with some of the persistent paradigms of the Cold War. He operated, essentially, in the same bilateral framework as his predecessors had done, taking it as a given that containing Soviet power – if not communist ideology –should be the central goal of American foreign policy.

The real goal of détente was to manage the USSR. As he wrote to Nixon early on in the presidency: 'Moscow wants to engage us ... we should seek to utilize this Soviet interest, stemming as I think it does from anxiety, to induce them to come to grips with the real sources of tension, notably in the Middle East, but also in Vietnam. This approach also would require continued firmness on our part in Berlin.'[8] Indeed, while the sources of détente – as Andreas Wenger and Jeremi Suri have argued[9] – lay much deeper than the specific interests and tactical goals of a few policymakers, the actual practice of détente was, as is well known, a highly centralized matter in the Nixon administration. And at its base lay the strategy of linkage: the idea that one could create a web of relationships with the USSR and exchange, in effect, favours in one area (e.g., the SALT negotiations) for those made in another (say, the Vietnam peace talks).[10] In other words, while confronting Soviet power remained the key goal, the methods were to be changed because Kissinger was rather pessimistic about American power and how it could be deployed.

This meant that the role of diplomacy was magnified. Kissinger engaged the Soviets in a series of negotiations – over SALT, over Europe, over Berlin, over the Middle East, over almost all the issues that overshadowed the bilateral relationship. The end results were often impressive. Kissinger's time in office produced the various agreements on Germany and Berlin, the signing of the SALT I and ABM agreements at the Moscow summit of 1972, the Prevention of Nuclear War (PNW) agreement in 1973, and the tentative SALT II agreements of Vladivostok in 1974 (an agreement that Nixon – having bowed out of office in August 1974 – could only watch from the sidelines). After 1974, détente began to falter.[11] Under severe domestic attack from both the left and the right, Gerald Ford eventually banned the use of the word in his 1976 presidential campaign. But negotiations as a tool of U.S. policy towards the USSR were not to be shelved. As John Gaddis has pointed out, they became an 'institutionalized' form of Cold War competition.[12]

Another key ingredient in this new conception of containing the Soviet Union was the role that Kissinger's thinking assigned to the opening to China. It was clearly a diplomatic revolution and remains, arguably, the most substantial legacy of the Nixon-Kissinger era. One could easily argue that the emergence of China from isolation enabled its gradual rise towards the economic prowess it enjoys today. The opening surely heralded the splits that were evident in what had supposedly once been a communist monolith.[13]

But why did Kissinger and the Nixon administration pursue the opening to China? In order to accelerate the forthcoming collapse of the communist bloc? There is no evidence to indicate that this was the case. In fact, the opening to China was engineered as part of a relatively specific short-term strategy that had both international and domestic components. Internationally, the Kissinger and Nixon trips to China in 1971–72 launched the era of triangular diplomacy, enabling the United States to take advantage of the enmity between the USSR and China. And, it is important to emphasize, the advantages of this development were to be seen particularly in relations and negotiations with the Soviets: Kissinger and Nixon had a China card to play. It is another matter how effective this card was. The important point, though, is that the opening to China was to large extent not about China but about leverage vis-à-vis the Soviet Union. In this regard it was less of a revolution and more of a continuation of previous American policies.

This does not diminish the momentous long-term significance of the opening to China. If Kissinger and Nixon's foreign policy had a durable impact on the global arena, then surely it was their role in starting the long process of China's transformation from a backward and inward-looking virtual prison for 800 million of its citizens to the rapidly rising economic powerhouse we see today. The long-term interests of the United States and the international community at large would hardly have been better served if Kissinger had never feigned a stomach ache in Pakistan before his flight to Beijing in July 1971, or if Nixon had not embarked on his dramatic Journey of Peace in February 1972.[14]

In the near and medium term, however, the opening to China scarcely yielded as dramatic an end result as is often claimed. Most specifically, the new Sino-American relationship did not translate into a major diplomatic tool. After 1971 there were very few instances when the USSR practised restraint that could be directly attributed to its concern over a 'Washington-Beijing axis'. Although the China factor was not inconsequential in determining *American* policy (usually in favour of the Chinese), it seems to have given the USSR little incentive to act according to American desires. In some ways, it was almost the diplomatic equivalent of America's short-lived nuclear monopoly in the aftermath of the Second World War: the fact that the opening had taken place was important, but its practical application to other contexts was extremely difficult. And whatever role the opening to China may have played in bringing about the end of the Cold War, this was not something that the key players –Kissinger foremost among them – envisaged in those frantic days of international diplomacy in the early 1970s.

A Stable Europe vs Brandt's Ostpolitik

Europe was clearly not at the top of Kissinger's agenda in the 1970s. He did, however, focus on certain aspects of European policy. In particular, he worried about independent European policy initiatives towards détente and how they might negatively impact on the stability of the Cold War division by creating cleavages between Washington and its NATO allies. Undisputed American leadership over a united West was a central ingredient in Kissinger's overall strategy. Anything that might challenge this was, to him, an anathema.

Thus, Kissinger was particularly concerned over Willy Brandt's Ostpolitik. As early as 1963, Egon Bahr, Brandt's long-time associate and foreign policy adviser, had coined the notion of 'change through rapprochement' (*Wandel durch Annäherung*): the idea that a policy of engagement would bring about a gradual change in the division of Germany. After the Social Democrats won the September 1969 Bundestag election, Brandt and Bahr rapidly moved to put their ideas into practice. A number of treaties were signed: a Non-Aggression Pact with the USSR in August 1970, a West-German–Polish Treaty recognizing the Oder-Neisse line in December 1970, a four-power agreement on the status of Berlin in 1971 and, finally, the Basic Treaty between East and West Germany in 1972. In a span of a few years, the German question was transformed, laying the basis for further East-West détente in Europe. In 1971 Brandt even received the Nobel Peace Prize for his efforts.[15]

Kissinger was not a supporter of Brandt's diplomacy. Although pursuing détente with the Soviet Union himself, Kissinger thought that Ostpolitik might, if it proved successful as an independent West German policy, become a new form of 'Gaullism'.[16] As Kissinger put it in February 1970:

> assuming Brandt achieves a degree of normalization, he or his successor may discover before long that the hoped-for benefits fail to develop. Instead of ameliorating the division of Germany, recognition of the G[erman] D[emocratic] R[epublic] may boost its status and strengthen the Communist regime ... More fundamentally, the Soviets having achieved their first set of objectives may then

confront the FRG with the proposition that a real and lasting improvement in the FRG's relations with the GDR and other Eastern countries can only be achieved if Bonn loosens its Western ties.[17]

In other words, Kissinger worried that Brandt was pursuing a dangerous policy that was bound to give Moscow an edge in the Cold War confrontation.

By the spring of 1970, however, it was clear that the Brandt-Bahr Ostpolitik had claimed the forerunner's role in East-West détente. While Kissinger himself had been unable to make significant progress in his other backchannel negotiations with Soviet Ambassador Anatoly Dobrynin, the NSC adviser became increasingly concerned that the Soviets were playing an intricate balancing act of selective détente: deliberately stalling in their talks with the Americans while moving ahead with the Germans. Thus, when Brandt visited the United States in April 1970 hoping to get the Nixon administration's formal endorsement of Ostpolitik, Kissinger was distinctly recalcitrant and counselled Nixon against endorsing any specific element of Ostpolitik in public. The president, accordingly, insisted on coordination between Washington and Bonn on all matters.[18]

The American insistence on coordination and unity became even clearer after the signing of the Soviet–West German treaty in Moscow on 12 August 1970. Walter Scheel, Brandt's foreign minister and the head of the Free Democrats, had negotiated some important caveats in his July talks with Soviet Foreign Minister Andrei Gromyko. In particular, Gromyko agreed to an accompanying statement expressing support for German unification (through peaceful means). Moreover, the conclusion of a new agreement on Berlin – negotiated between the four occupying powers and the two Germanys – was understood to be a condition for the eventual FRG ratification of the treaty.[19]

The Berlin negotiations allowed Kissinger to get directly involved in the shaping of Ostpolitik via two sets of back channels that smoothed the way to the Berlin agreement of 3 September 1971. On the one hand Kissinger negotiated throughout the spring of 1971 on a weekly basis, and without the knowledge of the State Department, with Soviet Ambassador Anatoly Dobrynin. On the other hand, Kissinger engaged Kenneth Rush, the U.S. ambassador to Bonn, as his special link to Egon Bahr. Rush, to Kissinger's great satisfaction, managed to keep the rest of the State Department uninformed. By early June an agreement was basically ready. But in an ironic twist of fate, its finalization was postponed by two months until after Kissinger's secret foray to Beijing in July (creating the false impression that the opening to China resulted in Soviet accommodation on Berlin).[20]

While Kissinger would later overemphasize his own role in the Berlin negotiations, they were of some importance to transatlantic relations since the Americans and the West Germans cooperated closely throughout the negotiation process. As a result, by September of 1971 the concerns of an independent German-Soviet détente that would undermine Western unity no longer coloured American evaluations of the transatlantic relationship. The spectre of West German 'Gaullism' was gone. The key point to make is that Kissinger's approach towards West German Ostpolitik is an indication of a generally conservative outlook vis-à-vis Cold War Europe. Alliance unity clearly took precedence over everything else; Kissinger preferred strengthening the status quo to promoting change – including change through rapprochement.

In the second Nixon administration he would continue this general approach. In 1973 Kissinger launched the so-called Year of Europe initiative.[21] In public, the policy was not a great success, resulting in recriminations and complaints from various European capitals. But its key goal – strengthening Western unity in an era of détente and such challenges as the 1973 war in the Middle East and the oil crisis – was clearly achieved. Such strengthening of unity was, though, another reflection of Kissinger's essentially conservative outlook. The Soviet Union and the Warsaw Pact remained the primary long-term threat to American security. His vision remained one of stability and equilibrium based upon the premise that the Cold War was unlikely to wither away in the foreseeable future.

Writings in Swahili: Kissinger and the CSCE

What, then, about the CSCE? It seems that here we have in fact an example of an agreement that produced a revolutionary outcome by eroding Soviet domination in Eastern Europe. The 'Helsinki effect' – as one scholar calls it[22] – was surely the making of the Ford administration at a time when Kissinger, holding the positions of secretary of state and national security advisor, was the undisputed czar of American foreign policy. Kissinger was clearly present at the creation: he and Gerald Ford went to Helsinki in late July 1975 to participate in the signing ceremonies of the Helsinki Accords. In an interview in August 1997 Ford explained the 'time bomb' effect that the Helsinki Accords' human rights provisions – the so-called Basket III – had on the Soviet bloc:

> Well certainly the Soviet Union and the Warsaw pact nations did not recognize that the Human rights provision was a time bomb. We in the United States and our western allies I'm sure, were hopeful that that provision would bring about the kind of uprisings that did take place in the Warsaw pact nations, Hungary, Czechoslovakia, Poland and even in the Soviet Union itself. History I think is going to recognize that the Helsinki Accord was one of the great diplomatic achievements in the past, in this current century.[23]

Moreover, in the immediate aftermath of the signing of the Helsinki Accords in August 1975, Kissinger was already wondering whether the CSCE did mark a turning point for East-West relations. Rejecting the critical arguments of most American observers, he bemoaned the negative view of the CSCE as showing 'the moral collapse of our academic community'. In August 1975, he told the cabinet that the acknowledgement of the inviolability of borders – another important part of the Final Act (in Basket I) – was meaningless because 'the borders were legally established long ago'. Instead, Kissinger maintained, 'all the new things in the document are in our favor—peaceful change, human contacts, maneuver notification. At the conference … it was the West which was on the offensive'. He then summed the situation up by maintaining that 'relations with our allies are better than ever since the early Marshall Plan days', and no one 'observing from another planet would have thought Communism was the wave of the future'.[24] Kissinger, in short, appears as a true believer – perhaps the very first believer – in the so-called Helsinki effect.

The trouble with this assumption is that in previous years and later on, Kissinger was thoroughly dismissive towards the CSCE. He viewed the negotiations as a 'loser for the West' and summed up his assessment of the significance of the Helsinki Final Act in a quip during a staff meeting in December 1974: 'They can write in Swahili for all I care.'[25] Kissinger made incessant jokes about having the pope and Princess Grace of Monaco sit next to each other at the meeting. Throughout the process he had consistently opposed having a high-level summit – like the one in Helsinki – as its conclusion. If the CSCE negotiations had a function for Kissinger, it was far removed from the actual substance of the talks. As he said in an internal meeting of his staff in October 1974, the CSCE negotiations were a useful tool of linkage because the Soviets 'may not want to blow up the Middle East before the European Security Conference'.[26]

T.A.K. Elliott, the British ambassador to Finland and an active participant in the CSCE negotiations, offers some further insight into Kissinger's thinking about the CSCE. Elliott believed that Kissinger was probably correct in thinking that 'discussions in Geneva about increasing the number of kiosks at which foreign newspapers will be sold in the Soviet Union are no doubt insignificant in comparison with the issues of the strategic balance'. But, Elliott maintained, 'there is more to it than that. One thing the Conference has already achieved: to get it accepted for the first time by Communist states that relations between peoples – and therefore the attitudes of Governments towards their citizens – should be the subject of multilateral discussion.' '[E]xercising quiet pressure through the Conference', Elliott further predicted, may 'eventually be able to get the Soviet Union to lower, even a little, the barriers to human contacts and the flow of information and ideas between East and West.'[27]

Elliott's message effectively summarized the large gulf that separated the goals and views between Kissinger's realpolitik outlook on détente and the more 'idealistic' perception of a number of those diplomats, particularly Western Europeans but also some Americans, who were engaged in the CSCE negotiations in Geneva. To the negotiators, any concession by the Soviets was worth the wait because of the long-term consequences it could entail; to Kissinger, the CSCE was important only if it played a role in Soviet-American or, as it occasionally did, in transatlantic relations. Like many other issues – China, Vietnam, the Middle East – the CSCE mattered only in relation to the overriding strategic aims of American foreign policy.

The point, as with détente and with the opening to China, is the assumption of a continued adversarial relationship with the Soviet Union that would continue for the foreseeable future. While Kissinger may have defended the CSCE in both cabinet meetings and public speeches after he returned from Helsinki, the fact remains that he did not see it as a harbinger of Soviet decline, much less as a beginning of an end to the Cold War.

Unintended Consequences, Unforeseen Turning Points

The main argument of this chapter is straightforward. Henry Kissinger was not a visionary when it comes down to imagining how the Cold War would end or consciously setting in motion the processes that would cause this. He was, despite being a professor, a rather practical policymaker. As Kissinger put it in his memoirs: 'Once the oath of office has been taken there is no longer time for calm reflection. The policymaker is then like a man on a tightrope; he can avoid a precipitous drop only by moving forward.'[28] In 1968–69 Kissinger understood that American foreign policy was in trouble and things thus had to change. The United States could not, for example, keep its troops in Vietnam. Upon coming to office he considered the United States to be in a period of decline and sought means of restoring American power and influence. Thus, Kissinger proceeded – and arguably succeeded – in this task by using diplomacy and negotiations, rather than so-called hard power, as his major tools.

Most importantly, Kissinger – like almost everyone else around him – viewed the Soviet Union as not merely the main adversary of the United States at the time (which it obviously was) but as the only serious long-term adversary. Utterances about China's emergence as a 'decisive' player were mainly used as justifications for the opening to Beijing that, in turn, was intended to unleash new diplomatic opportunities for the Nixon administration. Kissinger summed it up in a post–Cold War interview: 'Well, it set up a triangular relationship between Russia, the United States and

China, in which we attempted to be closer to each of them than they were to each other, so we could calibrate our policy in relation to specific crises that arose in relation to our national interests.' Policies were clearly based on the assumption that the Cold War (and the Soviet Union) were not about to disappear in Kissinger's lifetime.

Yet, I would argue, the consequences of détente were more far-reaching and fundamental than its principal architects and practitioners, Kissinger among them, thought at the time. Détente changed the international system and unleashed many of the processes that helped bring an end to the Cold War in the 1980s. That this was not a conscious goal of those implementing détente is important to recognize. It shows that so-called historical turning points often, as Kissinger himself put it, 'pass unnoticed by contemporaries'.[29] In fact, there were plenty of intended and unintended consequences that, with the benefit of hindsight, can be said to translate into something of a revolutionary legacy.

One important consequence was the institutionalization of summitry at the superpower level. Détente did create an expectation that Soviet and American leaders could, should and would meet each other on a more or less regular basis to discuss ways of reducing the danger of nuclear war and developing other formal links. Even as tensions mounted in the 1980s, there would be no dramatic walkouts as in the case of Khrushchev during the 1960 Paris summit. As a result, both sides accepted a certain responsibility for the stability of the international system. Even as defence intellectuals and others fretted over the placement of new missile systems, détente had introduced a set of fundamental rules and assumptions that guided bilateral superpower relations. Détente gradually unleashed several other developments that fundamentally altered the Cold War system. East-West interaction became not only possible but, for the most part, irreversible. Regardless of the aim – increased but still limited East-West trade; the promise, if not always the reality, of freedom of movement; or added cultural interaction – détente enabled people, in a more fundamental sense than before, to see how the other side lived. This was, I would argue, particularly significant if we are to grasp the growing discontent within Eastern Europe in the 1980s that eventually climaxed in the events of 1989.

It may well be true that some of the policies Kissinger championed accelerated, or contributed to, the end of the Cold War. This was, ultimately, an unintended consequence of decisions adopted with a very different set of goals in mind. His primary ambition was more immediate: to find a new way of implementing containment. Kissinger's main contribution in this regard was enhanced diplomacy with the United States' main adversaries, the USSR and the People's Republic of China. But whether such policies contributed – or perhaps prolonged – the ending of the Cold War is impossible to determine. When it came to Europe, his role seems to have been more that of an interested observer, willing to yield short-term advantages to the Soviet Union but unable to fathom that true change could be in the air.

Even Kissinger himself offers little cause to believe that he had somehow consciously initiated policies that later brought about the collapse of the Soviet Union. After leaving office he remained an influential player in policymaking circles, repeatedly consulted by all subsequent presidents on grave matters of state. And he wrote – thousands upon thousands of pages. What is evident throughout all these writings, however, is that Kissinger's essentially realist outlook blinded him to the possible collapse of the USSR and the Cold War system in Europe. To be sure, he repeatedly spoke and wrote, as any former or serving American secretary of state would do, about the moral superiority of the free world. But his main concern in Europe in, for example, the 1980s tended to be the troubled state of the Atlantic alliance and the threat of 'pacifism and neutralism' among NATO countries.[30]

Nor was Kissinger's retrospective assessment of the end of the Cold War particularly groundbreaking. As he put it in an interview:

> The Soviet Union had undertaken something that was beyond its capacity: it had taken on the whole industrial world plus China, with a stagnant economic and a rigid political system, which had no capacity of rejuvenating itself. So the question really only was: at what point would the disparity between the Soviet Union and the outside world become intolerable?[31]

This much may be clear in retrospect. But while in office and all the way up to 1989, Kissinger could not foresee when or how that particular 'turning point' was about to occur. His vision was of stability rather than change, of an ongoing twilight struggle that could only end following some truly cataclysmic, and most likely violent, series of events. The peaceful revolutions that occurred throughout Eastern Europe and the lack of robust response from the Soviet leadership would hardly have qualified as such in Kissinger's essentially realpolitik outlook, which preferred the virtues of stability and status quo over unpredictability and change.

Notes

1. H. Kissinger, 'Reversing Yalta', *Washington Post*, 16 Apr. 1989; W. Isaacson. 1991. *Kissinger*, New York: Simon and Schuster, 727–729; M.R. Beschloss and S. Talbott. 1993. *At the Highest Levels: The Inside Story of the End of the Cold War*, Boston: Little, Brown, 13–17;

R. Garthoff. 1994a. *The Great Transition: American-Soviet Relations and the End of the Cold War,* Washington, DC: Brookings, 376–377; J.A. Baker, III. 1995. *The Politics of Diplomacy: Revolution, War and Peace, 1989–1992,* New York: Putnam, 39–40; G.H.W. Bush and B. Scowcroft. 1998. *A World Transformed,* New York: Knopf, 25–28.

2. For Kissinger's background see J.M. Hanhimäki. 2004. *The Flawed Architect: Henry Kissinger and American Foreign Policy,* New York: Oxford University Press; and J. Suri. 2007. *Henry Kissinger and the American Century,* Cambridge, MA: Harvard University Press.

3. See O.A. Westad. 2005. *The Global Cold War: Third World Interventions and the Making of Our Times,* Cambridge: Cambridge University Press.

4. H. Kissinger. 1957. *Nuclear Weapons and Foreign Policy,* New York: Doubleday; H. Kissinger. 1957a. *A World Destroyed: Metternich, Castlereagh and the Problems of Peace, 1812–1822,* Boston: Houghton Mifflin.

5. See Hanhimäki, *The Flawed Architect,* chap.1 and Suri, *Henry Kissinger and the American Century,* chaps. 1–3.

6. 'Presidential Adviser Kissinger: New Approaches to Friend and Foe', *Time,* 14 Feb. 1969.

7. H. Kissinger. 1979. *White House Years,* Boston: Little, Brown, 69–70.

8. Kissinger, *White House Years,* 143–144.

9. A. Wenger and J. Suri. 2001. 'At the Crossroads of Diplomatic and Social History: The Nuclear Revolution, Dissent and Détente', *Cold War History* 1(1), 1–42; J. Suri. 2003. *Power and Protest: Global Revolution and the Rise of Détente,* Cambridge, MA: Harvard University Press.

10. There is no need here to recount the 'coup d'état' that placed much of foreign policy decision-making in Kissinger's (and Nixon's) hands. See for example Hanhimäki, *Flawed Architect,* 17–32 or Isaacson, *Kissinger,* 151–156.

11. For an interesting set of documents on the Nixon administration's relationship with Afghanistan see the NSA web page, http://www.gwu.edu/~nsarchiv/.

12. The most exhaustive study dealing with Soviet-American détente remains R. Garthoff. 1994. *Détente and Confrontation: Soviet-American Relations from Nixon to Reagan,* Washington, DC: Brookings Institution. See also A. Preston and F. Logevall (eds). 2008. *Nixon in the World: American Foreign Policy, 1969–1977,* New York: Oxford University Press.

13. For the latest account of the opening to China see M. MacMillan. 2006. *Seize the Hour: When Nixon Met Mao,* London: Random House.

14. See MacMillan, *When Nixon Met Mao.* See also R. Accinelli (ed.). 2006. *Normalization of U.S.-China Relations: An International History,* Cambridge, MA: Harvard University Press.

15. For an outline of Ostpolitik see M. J. Sodaro. 1990. *Moscow, Germany, and the West from Khrushchev to Gorbachev,* Ithaca, NY: Cornell University Press.

16. G.A. Andrianopoulos. 1991. *Kissinger and Brzezinski,* Macmillan: London, 232.

17. Kissinger to Nixon, 16 Feb. 1970, NSC Country Files, box 683: Germany Vol. IV, Nixon Presidential Materials Project (NPMP), National Archives, Washington, DC (NA).

18. W. Brandt. 1992. *My Life in Politics,* New York: Viking, 176; Kissinger, *White House Years,* 416, 424. Rush to Rogers, 2 Apr. 1970; Kissinger to Nixon (drafted by Sonnenfeldt), 3 Apr. 1970, and Memcon: Brandt, Schmidt, Nixon, Rogers, Laird, Kissinger, 4 Apr. 1970, NSC, VIP Visits, box 917, NPMP, NA.

19. Sodrano, *Moscow, Germany, and the West,* 174–179, 183–185; W. Bundy. 1998. *A Tangled Web: The Making of Foreign Policy in the Nixon Administration,* New York: Hill and Wang, 173–179; Hanhimäki, *Flawed Architect,* 85–90.

20. Memcon: Dobrynin and Kissinger, 26 Apr. 1971, 'Dobrynin/Kissinger 1971, Vol. 5 part 1', box 490, NSC Files, NPMP, NA. Kissinger, *White House Years,* 823–833; E. Bahr. 1996.

Zu Meiner Zeit, Munich: Karl Blessing Verlag, 358–371; Garthoff, *Détente and Confrontation,* 136–139; Hanhimäki, *Flawed Architect,* 171–192.

21. The Year of Europe initiative has been discussed in detail elsewhere. For the latest see A. Horne. 2009. *Kissinger, 1973: The Crucial Year,* New York: Simon and Schuster, 106–121.

22. D.C. Thomas. 2001. *The Helsinki Effect: International Norms, Human Rights and the Demise of Communism,* Princeton, NJ: Princeton University Press.

23. National Security Archive interview with Gerald Ford, Beaver Creek, CO, 4 Aug. 1997. http://www.gwu.edu/~nsarchiv/coldwar/interviews/episode-16/ford1.html (accessed 6 Feb. 2009).

24. Cabinet Meeting, 8 Aug. 1975, Box 14, National Security Advisor, Memoranda of Conversations, Gerald Ford Library, Ann Arbor, Michigan.

25. Kissinger cited in W. Burr. 1999. *Kissinger Transcripts: The Top Secret Meetings with Moscow and Beijing,* New York: The New Press, 17 and 326. Although the American role in the CSCE has yet to be explored in detail, some key accounts include: J. Maresca. 1987. *To Helsinki: The Conference on Security and Co-operation in Europe, 1973–1975,* Durham, NC: Duke University Press; V. Mastny. 1986. *Helsinki, Human Rights, and European Security: Analysis and Documentation,* Durham, NC: Duke University Press; J. van Oudenaren. 1992. *European Detente,* Durham, NC: Duke University Press; J.E. Goodby. 1998. *Europe Undivided: The New Logic of Peace in U.S.-Russian Relations,* Washington, DC: United States Institute of Peace, esp. chap. 2. See also J.M. Hanhimäki. 2003. '"They Can Write it in Swahili": Kissinger, the Soviets, and the Helsinki Accords, 1973–1975', *Journal of Transatlantic Studies,* 1(1), 37–58.

26. Memcon: Kissinger, Brezhnev et al., 24 Oct. 1974, in Burr, *Kissinger Transcripts,* 327–342. Citation from 342.

27. Elliott to Callaghan, 29 Jul. 1974, in G. Bennet and K.A. Hamilton (eds). 1997. *Documents on British Policy Overseas,* Series III, Volume II, *The Conference on Security and Cooperation in Europe, 1972–1975,* London: Routledge, 317–326.

28. Kissinger, *White House Years,* 70.

29. H. Kissinger. 1999. *Years of Renewal,* New York: Simon and Schuster, 635.

30. 'A Plan to Reshape NATO', in H. Kissinger. 1985. *Observations: Selected Speeches and Essays 1982–1984,* London: Weidenfeld and Nicolson, 216.

31. National Security Archive interview with Henry Kissinger. http://www.gwu.edu/~nsarchiv/coldwar/interviews/episode-16/kissinger4.html (accessed 6 Feb. 2009).

Chapter 14

VALÉRY GISCARD D'ESTAING AND HIS VISION OF THE END OF THE COLD WAR

Georges-Henri Soutou

In 1995, on the twentieth anniversary of the Helsinki Accords, President Valéry Giscard d'Estaing stated his views about the end of the Cold War and its causes. Several factors were involved, he maintained, particularly the rampant decline of the Soviet economy under the pressure of arms and space competition with the United States. But the main factor, 'the beginning of everything', was the Helsinki Final Act, because 'it accelerated the fall and disruption of the Soviet Empire'. Helsinki gave more autonomy to the states of Eastern Europe vis-à-vis Moscow, and gave their opposition movements an internationally acknowledged legitimacy. Thus Helsinki created 'the instrument for the penetration of Western values into the Soviet system' and made possible the demise of that system.[1]

This view of an offensive, values-based end of the Cold War brought about by a clear-cut failure of Soviet communism may well, with all due respect for the former president, be slightly coloured *ex post* by hindsight. In contrast to Charles de Gaulle, who left an extensive amount of personally written notes, notations in the margins of draft documents and instructions to his ministers,[2] or Georges Pompidou, who annotated documents heavily,[3] Giscard left fewer really meaningful traces in his own archive, apart from some useful and revealing but usually rather general remarks made during cabinet meetings – although admittedly, one can see only a tiny percentage of them. A comparison, moreover, between his memoirs and those records so far released appears to reveal some discrepancies.

On top of that, Giscard fostered competitive views among his advisers, keeping his own counsel and not allowing anyone but himself to shape the debate and draw conclusions. Thus he had a very Gaullist diplomatic adviser at the Elysée, Gabriel Robin; a more informal but very important adviser for strategic matters and NATO relations, François de Rose, who was rather an Atlanticist; and a pro-European general secretary at the Quai d'Orsay, Jean-Marie Soutou, thus covering the three main directions of French foreign policy attitudes at the time – apart, of course, from the communists. And no adviser had the whole picture at any given time. Thus it is not easy to assess what Giscard's views really were, beyond the documents penned by his advisers, to which he seldom reacted – certainly not in writing and only infrequently verbally. He often remained an enigma to his own subordinates. The transcripts of his conversations with foreign leaders, particularly the Soviets, are indeed revealing, but they are not internal documents. All in all, it is not easy to describe his views about the possible outcome of the Cold War. Is it possible nevertheless to reconstruct Giscard's actual vision between 1974 and 1981, the period of his presidency?

Giscard d'Estaing's Own Vision of the End of the Cold War

This chapter will first try to assess Giscard's vision of the possible future of the Cold War, and its possible end, before turning to his actual strategy to overcome the Cold War divide. It must be understood that this description cannot but be partly hypothetical, since only systematic explanations by Giscard himself at the time or later could really enlighten us, but none were given.

A True Liberal in the French Meaning of the Word

Giscard's 1995 article about Helsinki was certainly not just an ex post facto reconstruction: Giscard was a true, proactive liberal (in the French, conservative, meaning of the word, stressing traditional personal freedoms and not American progressivism). The French president was certainly sincerely willing to use détente in order to promote a liberalization of Eastern Europe and better contacts between both halves of Europe. His speech in Helsinki in July 1975 stressed that the Final Act had not gone as far as France would have liked towards 'information exchange' and 'diverse forms of intellectual cooperation'.[4] He did not hesitate to order personally the strengthening of the communiqué that was to be issued after his meeting with Chancellor Schmidt in February 1977 about follow-up to Basket III, judging the first draft to be 'too weak'. A second draft prepared by the director of the European department at the Quai d'Orsay, Jacques Andreani, which explicitly stressed the need 'to let individuals directly benefit from the amelioration of contacts and information', elicited this marginal comment from Giscard: 'This is a good text'.[5] Generally speaking, the French were convinced that their attitude towards Basket III was much more active than the German one, and that Bonn was dragging its feet.[6] And Paris was convinced that the revival of contestation in Eastern Europe in 1976 was the result of Helsinki.[7]

Henri Froment-Meurice, French ambassador in Moscow from 1979 to 1981, is convinced that Giscard personally supported the Helsinki process, and particularly Basket III, rather more strongly than his predecessor Georges Pompidou had done.[8] Pompidou saw only one interesting feature in the Helsinki exercise: the opening of an international venue for Eastern Europe where it could express itself directly, despite the Brezhnev doctrine. He repeatedly calmed Soviet fears about possible Western encroachments in the name of human rights and certainly did not push the issue.[9] Giscard by contrast addressed the issue in his talks with Brezhnev, insisting for instance on a wider distribution of French newspapers in the Soviet Union,[10] even if he was very prudent, telling the Soviets in December 1974 that he saw a big difference between 'exchanging information and ideas' and 'trying to influence the way public opinion should develop'.[11] He told his cabinet on 2 May 1979, after a visit to Moscow, that the Soviets were making progress on human rights; the West should not pressure them, they had another regime, and one had to consider what could be reasonably asked of them.[12] He evidently believed in a long, incremental process.

Certainly Giscard was criticized at the time for refusing to meet Soviet dissidents at the Elysée Palace (contrary to President Carter, who did meet some of them at the White House). But the French embassy in Moscow was instructed not to be too squeamish in its dealings with dissidents, if only in order not to seem cooler towards them than other Western countries were.[13] This illustrates an important, if then largely unknown, feature of Giscard's policy towards Moscow: unpleasant things were to be said in private. In Giscard's view such discretion made French warnings or protests more, not less, effective.

Not a Harbinger of Soviet Communism's Demise

Jacques Andreani, generally and rightly considered to be one of the main architects of the CSCE on the French side, was not very sanguine in 1975 about the possible liberalizing effect of the Helsinki conference. He saw that conference much more as an instrument of East-West détente than as an instrument for transforming the East. The major aim of Basket III was not so much to 'achieve actual progress' in human rights matters, but to serve as a lever to put the East on the defensive and to counteract a Soviet attempt to exploit further the political advantages obtained in Helsinki. At the time Moscow was pressing strongly for an institutionalized follow-up to the CSCE and for disarmament measures detrimental to the West, and directing even stronger pressure towards Bonn.[14]

This prudent view was probably best expressed by Gabriel Robin, diplomatic adviser at the Elysée, in an April 1977 note criticizing Carter's immediate aggressively ideological approach to the Cold War in matters pertaining to human rights (of which the U.S. president was more aware than many contemporaries or historians even today) and recommending instead an incremental one: the ideological division of Europe was a fact that could not be reversed directly, but it should not prevent contacts, exchanges or cooperation. Still, one had to accept a dose of ambiguity and to avoid provocations. What was required was 'patience, continuity, subtlety'. Tangible results had already been achieved: the Berlin agreement, family rapprochements, and Soviet acceptance of terms that would have been unthinkable before. The West should thus seek to go on sowing apparently innocuous initiatives with long-term consequences, such as tourism and cultural exchanges. Such a strategy could be meaningful only in the long term, but it was promising.[15] In more contemporary language, one could speak of long-term constructive engagement.

Giscard himself was actually very prudent when he broached the subject with the Soviets. From his handwritten notes before meeting the Soviets in October 1975 we can guess what he had in mind: an incremental use of the Helsinki process, including the possibility of subscribing to foreign newspapers (meaning in practical terms that only institutions would be able to subscribe, not individuals); military confidence-building measures (which were to be an important feature of his disarmament proposals to the UN in 1978 and would ultimately lead to the Stockholm agreement to that effect in 1986); and a development of Franco-Soviet trade (with an eye to German competition).[16]

Giscard's Helsinki Strategy

Giscard was more prudent about the CSCE than Pompidou had eventually become. He could not undo Pompidou's support for a summit conference, but he did not accept what his predecessor had been willing to grant the Soviets: a permanent security organization in Europe, not just more or less regular conference meetings. A permanent security set-up was a very important aim for Moscow, with evident possible negative consequences for the cohesion of the Atlantic Alliance.

Giscard so heavily revised the draft of his Helsinki speech submitted by his staff that we can assume the speech he delivered on 31 July 1975 really expressed his own views. This assumption is also borne out by his subsequent behaviour on the issue. Three points stand out, besides his insistence on human rights. First Giscard insisted that balance, including military balance, was a precondition for progress towards détente and for peace. Second, ideological confrontation stood in contradiction to détente, which involved, according to the Helsinki Final Act, the recognition and acceptance of the fact that different political and social systems existed in Europe; the only way out this contradiction was to limit ideological confrontation to a form of competition devoid of intolerance or interference.[17] Third, Giscard referred in his speech in Helsinki to Talleyrand's policy in Vienna in 1815: the subtext was that it was necessary to return to some kind of European concert, resting on permanent negotiation and avoiding hurting the vital interests of any partner; once again, maintaining balance was of the essence.

Taken together this amounted to a two-level strategy: in the short and medium term, the emphasis should be upon a prudent approach, avoiding military confrontation without losing ground to the Soviets. Only in the very long term could one imagine change, to be achieved by working for a progressive change in the international system and by capitalizing on the problems of the Soviet bloc and the positive effects of East-West exchanges of all kinds.

Dealing with the Soviet Union

Giscard provided an important and significant overall view of the Soviet Union to the Council of Ministers on 2 May 1979, just after his return from Moscow. He explained that the Soviet economy was stagnant, that Brezhnev was obviously very ill, that its political system was bogged down, that China was their 'first problem' and that the Russians were disquieted about Carter. As for human rights, the Soviets were beginning to make concessions; American pressure was therefore 'most clumsy … The Soviets having a political regime different from our own, it was necessary to start by considering their regime, so as to see what could be asked of them'.[18]

This concise statement revealed much about French views. Paris was quite conscious of the long-term social and political problems of the USSR: beyond the economic slowdown they noted that the demographic differential, between a stagnating Russia and fast-growing Caucasian or Islamized Central Asian republics, would reinforce the peripheral republics' political quest for more autonomy.[19] Probably the real force for change resided, in Giscard's view, in the economic situation of the Soviet Union and its consequences. His advisers pointed out that the economic performance of the USSR was poor and its prospects for the 1980s quite dim.[20] But Giscard did not share the approach, popularized at the time by a famous book by Samuel Pisar, *Les Armes de la paix*.[21] The main thrust of the book was that the West's best chance to transform the East and establish peace was to develop trade with the communist countries. But Giscard did not believe this would work in the short term, and Paris was aware of the danger of excessive dependence on trade with the Soviet Union, particularly in the question of natural gas imports from Russia.[22] Such dependence would actually be the reverse of Pisar's ideas. At the same time, in his long-term strategy for détente, Giscard thought at one point of including Moscow in the great international economic agreements that were contemplated in that period of turmoil following the oil shock. These agreements, dubbed the 'Trilogue' in Paris at the time, aimed to establish a triangular relationship between the West, the oil-producing countries and the developing world, in which oil-producing countries would invest part of their huge revenues in the Third World in order to prevent the accumulation of short-term and unwisely invested capital.[23]

On the political side, the dissident movement could not be uprooted. On top of that, political problems, such as an ageing leadership, a top-heavy, ineffective system and the growing dissatisfaction of the younger generations with a static ideology that seemed less and less relevant, were weighing heavily upon Moscow, but only in the long term.[24] In the short term the more probable reaction of the Soviet Union to Western pressure would be to stiffen up. Once again, therefore, a distinction was made between a very prudent short-term approach and a more optimistic long-term (or rather very long-term) one.

Giscard d'Estaing was probably the first top French leader to realize that in Moscow power rested with the party, not with state officials and apparatus, and to encourage the French ambassador, Froment-Meurice, to visit members of the International Department of the Central Committee, and not to content himself with diplomats in the Ministry of Foreign Affairs (MID).[25] After all, for orthodox Gaullists, communist ideology and the party were just pretences, instruments of the perennial Russian state: thus de Gaulle and Pompidou dealt with Brezhnev because evidently he was the boss, but they and their advisers never understood that party precedence went all the way down the line. Meanwhile Giscard was not certain the party could retain full power. He realized that in the next few years a new generation of Soviet leaders would come to power, and he was convinced that the military was gaining more and more influence. In this unpredictable situation, which might evolve in the right way but then again might not or might even go far in the wrong direction, it was necessary not to 'provoke the USSR into an adventurist attitude', and to treat it gingerly.[26]

Giscard's Operational Concept of East-West Relations and Détente

Beyond vision and analysis of the situation, what was Giscard's operational concept? Again, his strategy is best viewed as a double-pronged one.

The Need for Prudent, Long-term Management of the Cold War

Giscard certainly believed that economic realities would ultimately push the USSR towards the West, and in the field of international relations he attributed more importance to economics than had de Gaulle. At the same time he ascribed great importance, as de Gaulle had done, to two other factors: the decline of communist ideology in the Soviet Union and the geopolitical consequences of Chinese pressures on Moscow. But he saw both as factors that would only have effects in the long-term, not in the short or medium-term as de Gaulle had expected. He encapsulated that view for the Council of Ministers on 6 February 1980, after the invasion of Afghanistan, and on that occasion described what we might call his overall strategy to overcome the Cold War through a vigilant and robust détente strategy:

> [Détente] had been a basic and sound political choice. It never made us abandon our distrust of Soviet expansionism ... The passing of time plays into the hands of the West and against the USSR, since that country's system has trouble adapting to the new economic trends and tends to get out of breath respective to its ideology. It is in this relatively vulnerable situation that the Soviet Union will have to confront the enormous problems that the evolution of Asia will pose.[27]

But actually Giscard's views were even more complex than this, at times verging on the contradictory. As far as Soviet ideology was concerned – which once again was an important factor in French evaluations of Soviet foreign policy at the time – he made a distinction between the 'danger of communism as an extension of Soviet foreign policy', which he saw as waning, and the danger presented by national communist parties coming to power, particularly in Western Europe, which he believed was increasing. (Only a few years had elapsed, after all, since the 1972 alliance between Socialists and Communists in France, and the two left-wing parties were widely believed to have a fighting chance of winning the 1978 general election).[28] At the same time, Giscard felt that in order to achieve power in the Western European democratic framework the communist parties would have to adapt, tactically at least, to the liberal institutions of the West. And Paris believed that Moscow and most Western European communist parties were drifting apart, and that Moscow did not want to risk endangering détente by seeing a communist party come to power in Western Europe.[29] An explanation for Giscard's view of a divergence between Moscow and Western European communist parties may be related to the opinion, then expressed frequently in French political circles, that Moscow would rather deal with conservative leaders of the Fifth Republic than with any eventual government including French communists. Giscard himself seems to have been convinced of this.[30] Indeed, Giscard's own fears in this regard were not directed towards Moscow but towards the Carter administration and its tendency to support the Socialist-Communist electoral alliance in France. He gave Carter a thorough upbraiding on this issue on 5 May 1977.[31]

On the international level, Giscard followed a twin-track policy, or possibly even a three-track one concerning ideology. On one side he sought to de-ideologize East-West relations – to extend détente to ideological matters. He told the Soviets as much during his speech at the state dinner on occasion of his visit to Moscow in October 1975, much to the Soviets' annoyance. (In response, Brezhnev snubbed Giscard by cancelling their second meeting, which had been arranged for the next day). 'A détente in the ideological competition was necessary in order to avoid the rivalry between economic and social systems, which differed because of the nature of their populations and their objective situation, leading to excessive tension'. Internal ideological quarrels should not be fought out at the international level.[32] At very least, ideological competition should not lead to intolerance and to interference in the internal affairs of the partner.[33]

French public opinion supported the president's stand in Moscow: 60 percent believed he had been right to lay a wreath in Lenin's Mausoleum at Red Square. The cancellation of the second talk with Brezhnev was not deemed a snub by 51 percent of those asked, and 69 percent believed that Giscard had been right not to curtail his trip. The president may well have been rather bemused by a public that was probably more lax towards Moscow than he was himself, but that at the same time believed (47 against 44 percent) that Moscow was not really interested in a true détente in Europe.[34]

Giscard d'Estaing did not wish to unleash an ideological battle. This was one of the major reasons for his deep disagreement with Carter, who was seen in Paris as too ready to interfere in Soviet internal affairs on human rights questions. As Giscard told *Newsweek* on 25 July 1977:

> What seems clear in Mr. Carter's foreign policy is that he has introduced a fresh ideological dimension. This undoubtedly met certain needs – such as non-proliferation, arms limitations and human rights – just as it met some of my own preoccupations, but it has compromised the process of Détente. The question

now arises whether or how new ideological themes can be applied without provoking negative reactions.[35]

In other words, Carter 'had broken the code of conduct of détente'. Giscard d'Estaing was much more conscious of the continuing ideological dimension of the East-West conflict than were many of his contemporaries, which is probably why he was so prudent in his dealings with Moscow. He was very aware of the constant Soviet military build-up, and of the new phase of Soviet expansionism since 1975. He repeatedly stated that the two systems were profoundly different; despite that fact he nevertheless believed that they should develop links so as to ensure stability and peace. The prospect of a societal transformation leading to a convergence of both systems, East and West – a popular view at the time – was only, for Giscard, a very long-term one.[36] Pressuring the Soviets into overhasty convergence would only lead to dangerous reactions on their part. Instead of attacking Soviet ideology head on, one had to prudently engage the Soviets in détente policies that they could accept, owing, as we shall see, to their geopolitical situation.

Giscard himself was deeply convinced that the more aggressive approach of the United States was counterproductive and even dangerous. He rejected explicitly the militant attitude that was gaining favour in France in the late 1970s, epitomized by the influential articles of Raymond Aron, who warned his readers against the reappearance of Soviet expansionism, or by the numerous brilliant essays by a younger generation of intellectuals. These included thinkers such as Alain Besançon, whose *Court traité de soviétologie* was published in 1976 – intellectuals who published frequently in *Contrepoint*, later *Commentaire*, or in *Politique internationale*, and who stressed the vitality of communist ideology and its radical hostility to the liberal West. Giscard alluded to those views at the Council of Ministers of 21 May 1980, lamenting 'the beginning and growth of a Cold War campaign which seeks confrontation with the Soviets without daring to go to the end: an armed conflict'. And then he asked: 'What do they want? Is it to isolate the USSR? That policy achieved brilliant results in 1920!'[37]

Aggressive Containment

This prudent approach did not, however, prevent Giscard from opposing Soviet expansion in Africa, sometimes by force of arms, as he did in Kolwezi (Zaire) in May 1978, when Katangan rebels, supported secretly by Moscow, tried to take over that mineral-rich territory.[38] As early as 2 April 1977, he told U.S. Secretary of State Cyrus Vance that 'twelve years ago not a single African country stood under Soviet influence, now it was half of them. If things go on like this, by around 1979 or 1980 all of Africa will be a Soviet satellite.'[39] Giscard constantly stressed the fact that détente should be 'global', that détente was 'indivisible' and could not be nurtured only between the two superpowers without concerning the rest of the world.[40] (This dictum applied also to the U.S. Hence, as we shall see, in 1980 Giscard reacted to save détente in Europe despite Afghanistan, in apparent contradiction to the 'indivisible détente' motto: he believed the U.S. was overreacting and not taking European interests into account).

Giscard also did not hesitate both to develop and considerably modernize French nuclear and conventional forces, even if this is not an issue that can be explored in depth in this chapter.[41] Suffice it to say that on 12 December 1980, the military staff of the Elysée were instructed to study the problems posed by Moscow and to suggest possible countermeasures against Soviet expansionism: what was the tolerable limit of dependence upon Soviet energy sources? (By the end of Giscard's term, preoccupation with Western Europe's dependence on Russian oil and gas was running high.[42]) And by what means, ranging from medicines to armaments, could France help the Afghan insurgents? How could such supplies ultimately be shipped to them?[43]

On 11 December 1980, Giscard warned the Soviet ambassador in Paris, Tchervonenko, that an eventual Soviet military intervention in Poland would have huge repercussions – a warning parallel to that from Carter delivered on 3 December, but one that remains largely unknown. But he added – and once again we see his peculiar, not to say clumsy mixture of containment and constructive engagement with the Soviet Union plus an 'Old European' attachment to the Concert of Europe – 'I know it is very difficult to reach a stabilization which would not pose a problem for Soviet security and which at the same time would allow the Poles to resume normal activity. This could be a theme for common reflection between the Soviet Union and its Western Partners.'[44]

The Overall Geopolitical Concept
of Valéry Giscard d'Estaing

The seeming inconsistencies or even contradictions identified in this chapter can be resolved by taking into account Giscard's overall geopolitical concept, in which the notion of 'balance' looms large. Thus, for Giscard a major force for change was the geopolitical situation of the USSR, confronted by the new militancy of American foreign policy under Carter, by a resurgent Germany and by China. But change would not come quickly: Moscow's first reaction was to reinforce the unity of the Eastern bloc

– Russia would not hesitate to crush any uprising by force – and to try harder than ever to drive a wedge between the United States and Western Europe. Prudence and balance were therefore the order of the day.[45]

This was particularly the case where China was concerned. Franco-Soviet relations under President Giscard d'Estaing had their ups and downs, but in 1979 there was a consensus in Paris that they had become much better and that this was largely due, according to the Elysée, to the growing Soviet fear of China, and to the fact that Paris did not try to play the Chinese card against the Soviet Union.[46] Apparently Giscard felt Carter was imprudent in this respect, particularly after the American establishment of diplomatic relations with Peking in 1978.[47]

Obviously the future of the Cold War, as both predicted and hoped for in Paris, had much to do with France's German policy. On 27 April 1979, Giscard told Brezhnev that France was opposed to German reunification because it would upset 'the European balance'.[48] He repeated exactly the same thing when he met Brezhnev in Warsaw on 19 May 1980, adding that the partition of Germany was one of the most important common interests between France and the Soviet Union.[49] Repeatedly Giscard stressed, with Soviet interlocutors as well as internally, the need to preserve the Franco-German balance as it was – by which he meant France having a margin of superiority over a divided Germany without nuclear weapons and with a conventional military establishment and an economy that were unlikely to become too much greater than those of France.[50] This revelation would come as a shock to naïve historians, victims of the media hype at the time, who believed in an intimate Giscard-Schmidt relationship. Prior to 1980 this relationship existed only in economic matters, but in 1980 it was extended to other topics because of the renewed Cold War – though not to the 'German question', i.e., the issue of Germany's partition. On this issue Giscard d'Estaing was much more adamant than de Gaulle, who could imagine some sort of German confederation, that Germany should remain divided. And he expressed himself with the Soviets much more bluntly and unequivocally on that topic than had de Gaulle or his other successors.[51]

Giscard's Soviet policy could therefore be defined as a mixture of containment and constructive engagement. The growing international problems caused by the Soviet invasion of Afghanistan in 1979 and the Polish crisis of 1980, as well as by Soviet policies and American reactions to them, were felt to vindicate this prudent approach, even though it was firmer than was often realized at the time. The common declaration issued after the encounter between Giscard and Schmidt on 6 February 1981 stressed the notions of 'balance in security', 'moderation in political attitudes', 'non-interference' and equal rights for all countries.[52] But this long-term approach to a kind of asymptotic convergence – this insistence on an East-West 'balance' – was not only dictated by prudence in a tense international context. It was also felt to be in the best interests of the French, for meanwhile, using both international tensions and that state of international balance, France could manoeuvre between Washington, Moscow and Bonn and enhance its own international role.[53] Valéry Giscard d'Estaing made this point to his ministers upon his return from Moscow at the end of April 1979.[54]

Indeed, one could go one step farther and assert that what was in the French interests was not to achieve full détente and full convergence between East and West, but only an asymptotic, never-ending process. As Gabriel Robin bluntly put it in 1977: 'The best would be a slow but steady process of unremarkable progress without bumps or back-sliding. Maybe one should be courageous enough to admit that we do not wish to see this process succeeding quickly and fully. Then at the end of it stands the reunification of Germany and the build-up at the centre of Europe of a first magnitude power.'[55]

Conclusion

Paris was of course aware of the changing world situation and believed that in the long term peace could safely rest only on the type of détente that would lead to some sort of East-West convergence, albeit one more complex than was frequently imagined at the time. Giscard was convinced that France could use such a détente strategy, which could be conceived as an asymptotic Cold War exit strategy, to good effect. Thus Paris positioned itself in the Cold War in such a way that the Russians considered, according to Giscard in May 1979, 'their relations with France to be the most stable of all Soviet foreign relations in the world'.[56]

Nevertheless, Valéry Giscard d'Estaing, despite his reputation at the time, was actually more prudent towards the USSR than most French politicians, including de Gaulle, who believed communist ideology was already moribund, and Mitterrand, who believed after 1985 that the historical divide between social democracy and communism could now be bridged. Giscard, by contrast, did not believe in a quick evolution of the USSR, despite its problems. At the same time, and in opposition to a widespread view at the time, Giscard did not believe in the inescapable convergence of both economic and social systems towards some social democratic middle ground. Convergence – through trade, through exchanges of all kind, through reform induced by economic necessities in the Soviet Union, through the encouraging of more freedom in Eastern Europe thanks to the Helsinki process – could only develop itself in the very long term. And convergence should only be very prudently encouraged for two reasons. First, if the Soviets were to feel too pressurized, their reaction might be very dangerous. And second, full convergence was probably not in the best interests of France. Giscard d'Estaing and his aides clearly realized what Pompidou had begun to suspect: that France was the great beneficiary of the balanced stalemate of the Cold War, because it kept Germany divided and the U.S. engaged in Europe. Complete convergence would only erode the special status of France and dissolve its world role.

Notes

1. V. Giscard d'Estaing. 1995. 'Le commencement de tout', *Politique internationale*, 68, 1–7.
2. Archives nationales (hereafter AN), 5AG 1. They are difficult to access, but many documents have been published in the *Lettres, Notes et Carnets* publication (by Plon).
3. As can be seen in AN, 5AG 2.
4. AN, 5AG3/917.
5. AN, 5AG3/AE 69, first draft, undated, and note by Andreani, 3 Feb. 1977.
6. AN. Note by Robin, 5 July 1974, 5AG3/823; note by Robin, 14 June 5AG3/826; note by Dutet, 25 July 1975, 5AG3/824.
7. Several notes by the Quai d'Orsay in Jan. 1977, AN, 5AG3/826.
8. H. Froment-Meurice. 1998. *Vu du Quai*, Paris: Fayard, 543.
9. G.-H. Soutou. 2007. 'President Pompidou, *Ostpolitik*, and the Strategy of Détente', in H. Haftendorn, G.-H. Soutou, S. Szabo and S. Wells (eds), *The Strategic Triangle: France, Germany, and the United States in the Shaping of the New Europe*, Washington, DC: Johns Hopkins UP and Woodrow Wilson Center Press, 229–257.
10. Meeting with Brezhnev in Moscow in Oct. 1975, AN, 5AG3/854.
11. AN, 5AG3/853, 6 Dec. 1974.
12. AN, 5AG3/858.
13. J.-M. Soutou to de Leusse, 16 Feb. 1977. Private collection.
14. Note from 3 July 1975, AN, 5AG3/826.
15. 1 Apr. 1977, AN, 5AG3/917.
16. AN, 5AG3/854.
17. AN, 5AG3/917.
18. AN, 5AG3/858.
19. See H. Carrère d'Encausse. 1978. *L'Empire éclaté: la révolte des nations en URSS*, Paris: Flammarion. It is unknown whether Giscard took any notice of this book, but it gained much attention at the time. It would seem that the French Secret Service remained sceptical.
20. Note by Dutet, 14 Feb. 1978, AN, 5AG3/857.
21. S. Pisar. 1970. *Les Armes de la paix. L'ouverture économique vers l'Est*, Paris: Denoël.
22. Notes by Panafieu, 5 Dec. 1980, and by Dutet, 14 Jan. 1981, AN, 5AG3/858 third part.

23. As explained by Giscard to Jean-Marie Soutou on 27 May 1977.
24. Note by Robin, 17 June 1977, and note from the Quai d'Orsay, 16 Nov. 1978, AN, 5AG3/856 and 858.
25. Froment-Meurice, *Vu du Quai*, 515.
26. Giscard to the Council of Ministers, 10 Jan. 1979, AN, 5AG3/858.
27. AN, 5AG3/AE 71.
28. *Newsweek*, 25 July 1977.
29. Such views were expressed to his American, British and German counterparts by Foreign Minister Jean Sauvagnargues at a meeting in Washington largely devoted to this issue, 12 Dec. 1975. *Documents of the National Security Council, 1947–1977*, Washington, DC: University Publications of America.
30. See the very perceptive and well informed historian P. Robrieux. 1982. *Histoire intérieure du parti communiste français*, vol. 3, Paris: Fayard, 422–423.
31. AN, 5AG3/AE 92.
32. Toast at the Kremlin dinner, 14 Oct. 1977; Press conference in Moscow, 17 Oct. 1977; AN, 5AG3/854.
33. Speech prepared by Giscard himself for the signing of the Final Act of Helsinki, 1 Aug. 1975, AN, 5AG3/917.
34. SOFRES poll, 16 Oct. 1975, AN, 5AG3/854.
35. *Newsweek*, 25 July 1977.
36. G.-H. Soutou. 2008. 'Convergence Theories in France during the 60s and 70s', in W. Loth and G.-H. Soutou (eds), *The Making of Détente: Eastern and Western Europe in the Cold War, 1965–75*, London: Routledge, 25–48.
37. AN, 5AG3/AE 136.
38. See M. Ledeen and W. Lewis. 1981. *Débacle. L'échec américain en Iran*, Paris: Albin Michel.
39. AN, 5AG3/AE 92.
40. Note on Franco-Soviet relations by the head of the European department at the Quai d'Orsay, 2 Feb. 1979, AN, 5AG3/858.
41. On 26 Mar. 1979, Robin noted that France had managed to modernize its nuclear forces, thereby certainly drawing Moscow's attention and grumblings but without excessive reactions from the Soviet side, AN, 5AG3/858. See also J. de Lespinois. 2001. *L'Armée de terre française: de la défense du sanctuaire à la projection*, Paris: L'Harmattan.
42. Panafieu note, 5 Dec. 1980; and Leclerq note, 14 Jan. 1981, AN, 5AG3/858 second part.
43. AN, 5AG3/858 second part.
44. AN, 5AG3/858 second part.
45. Ibid.
46. Robin note, 26 Mar. 1979, AN, 5AG3/858.
47. Foreign Minister Jean-François Poncet reported Giscard's opinion to that effect to a group of high-ranking diplomats on 9 Jan. 1979, private collection.
48. AN, 5AG3/AE 134.
49. AN, 5AG3/AE 135.
50. G.-H. Soutou. 2006. 'L'anneau et les deux triangles: les rapports franco-allemands dans la politique européenne et mondiale de 1974 à 1981', in S. Berstein and J.-F. Sirinelli (eds), *Les années Giscard. Valéry Giscard d'Estaing et l'Europe 1974–1981*, Paris: Armand Colin, 45–79.
51. G.-H. Soutou. 2008a. 'Staatspräsident Valéry Giscard d'Estaing und die deutsche Frage', in K. Hildebrand, U. Wengst and A. Wirsching (eds), *Geschichtswissenschaft und Zeiterkenntnis. Von der Aufklärung bis zum Gegenwart. Festschrift für Horst Möller*, Munich: Oldenbourg, 373–382.

52. AN, 5AG3/829.
53. Robin note, 17 June 1977, AN, 5AG3/856.
54. Council of Ministers, 2 May 1979, AN, 5AG3/AE 134.
55. 1 Feb. 1977, AN, 5AG3/917.
56. Giscard to the Council of Ministers, AN, 5AG3/858.

Section VII

EVOLUTIONARY VISIONS AND UNEXPECTED RESULTS IN THE 1980S

Chapter 15

ENDING THE COLD WAR, UNINTENTIONALLY

Gregory F. Domber

It is impossible to write about the end of the Cold War without discussing the democratic revolutions that swept Eastern Europe in 1989. While large-scale geopolitical and economic shifts in the superpower relationship, in East-West relations and within the Soviet Union and Soviet bloc all shaped the events of 1989, local populations and local conditions played the significant role in the course and outcomes of the revolutions. Whether it was coal miners striking in Silesia, citizens reburying a national hero, young workers fleeing to the West or protesters gathering in Wenceslas Square, people mobilized en masse to shape their own futures. As Padraic Kenney has shown, these mass displays were not simply spontaneous happenings but were expressions of organized social mobilization.[1] Moreover, these social movements did not simply materialize in 1989 but were based on political theories and tactics developed over the previous decades. In Barbara Falk's metaphor, 1989 was 'a peak in a mountain of activity glacial in development and proportion'.[2] In order to fully appreciate the end of the Cold War it is essential to know how the Eastern Europeans themselves viewed what they were doing.

This chapter is an attempt to summarize and analyse the concepts driving revolutionary events in Poland, particularly as these ideas pertain to envisaging an end to the Cold War. The Polish opposition movement, however, encompassed a wide range of political views, making it difficult to talk about any unified ideology or action programme. In addition, theoretical consistency was not a paramount goal; as one theorist wrote, 'total consistency is tantamount to fanaticism, while inconsistency is the source of tolerance.'[3] For the sake of brevity, this chapter focuses on one strain of Warsaw-area intellectuals who were connected first with the Committee

Notes for this chapter begin on page 236.

for Workers' Defence (Komitet Obrony Robotników, KOR), then the Free Trade Union movement and finally Solidarność. This group, including Leszek Kołakowski, Jacek Kuroń and Adam Michnik, represented generally left-centrist viewpoints and distinguished themselves for their continual relevance within the opposition and their high standing in society.

While this group's ideas played a central role in Poland's transformation in 1989, in reviewing their writings it becomes clear that ending the global Cold War was not their primary concern. They did not seek to overthrow the international order characterized by the East-West, Soviet-American superpower confrontation. Even a cursory review of underground literature from the 1980s proves that the democratic opposition focused its attention almost exclusively on internal concerns.[4] When they did discuss geopolitics and superpower affairs, the Cold War was characterized as a set of constraints to be manoeuvred around, not something to be overcome or overthrown. It was a nuisance best left untouched. In an irony of history, the Polish opposition did not strive to undermine the existing international Cold War order, but it nonetheless played a starring role in the events that led to this unintended consequence.

Self-limitation and Self-liberation

For Polish dissidents the defining characteristic of the Cold War world was not superpower relations, arms control or the threat of nuclear annihilation. All of these issues were secondary relative to the fact that Poland fell within the Soviet Union's sphere of influence. Their national fate had been sealed by the presence of Red Army troops at the end of the Second World War. Poles pointed to Soviet military interventions in East Germany in 1953, in Hungary in 1956 and in Czechoslovakia in 1968 as evidence that the Soviets were the fundamental force defining the limits of political change in Eastern Europe. As Kołakowski wrote in 1971, 'As experience has shown, Soviet military predominance will always be employed to crush local attempts at revolution.'[5] Or as Kuroń added in 1976, the stability of the totalitarian system was 'guaranteed by the readiness of the Soviet Union, which has been displayed three times already, to re-impose it by force on any nation attempting to free itself'.[6] For Michnik, 'The Soviet military and political presence in Poland is the factor that determines the limits of possible [political development].'[7] Even writing two days after Poles handed the Polish United Workers' Party (PZPR) an overwhelming electoral defeat on 4 June 1989, Michnik emphasized that 'Poland's geopolitical situation remains, after all, unchanged.... The fatal shots fired in Tblisi and Beijing show the dangers that we need to avoid.'[8]

Sitting far behind the Iron Curtain, Soviet military power was the starting point for all discussions about political transformation.

With this framework, the opposition drew lessons from history to understand the possibilities for change in Eastern Europe. The Soviet intervention in Hungary in November 1956 had shown that the communist system could not be wholly rejected; therefore, popular revolutionary change was out of the question. The elucidation of the Brezhnev doctrine following the Prague Spring proved that the Soviets would not allow deep reforms emanating from within the party either; thus, reform and revision from above were also impossible.[9] As Michnik summarized, 'It seems that the Soviet leaders invariably intervene militarily in their satellite states whenever power slips out of the hands of the local Communist party.'[10] Neither revolution nor revision provided a safe model for change.

To ensure that they did not provoke a Soviet intervention, the opposition needed to understand the boundaries of acceptable behaviour. As one part of their trinity of restrictions, the opposition stated that it was not their goal to 'subvert' the PZPR, to strive to remove them from political power or to deny the party's position in society.[11] Second, the movement did not question Poland's alliance with the Warsaw Pact or COMECON, because this system 'ensured that we had peace, secure borders and it is also the driving force behind the development of the economy. Therefore, this alliance and this cooperation are of primary importance to our national existence and security.'[12] This commitment to existing international agreements included an acceptance of Poland's postwar borders.[13] Third, the opposition understood that the PZPR should be allowed to maintain a monopoly on power 'in the police ... in the military, in foreign policy.'[14] Overall, the Polish opposition maintained a very cautious outlook. As Kuroń explained, 'No one can be sure when the critical point may come and it is certainly true that it is better to stop much too early than a moment too late.'[15] This predisposition to caution overlapped well with the movement's extended efforts to elucidate the parameters of its own actions. These parameters did not allow the opposition to draft a plan to overturn Communist Party power within Poland, let alone end the Cold War. Instead, their willing acceptance of these parameters set clear limits on Polish actions, earning the movement the label 'self-limiting' revolutionaries.[16]

Beyond the overwhelming issue of Soviet dominance in Eastern Europe, the democratic opposition looked at the global characteristics of the superpower confrontation as another limiting factor. First, these dissidents accepted that they could not count on the United States to liberate them. For Poles, Soviet domination was codified 'with the acquiescence of the countries of the Atlantic Alliance' in the Yalta agreements.[17] Moreover, the 'silence that greeted' the Hungarian revolution was a 'revealing sign that the Yalta agreements remained in force.'[18] After the Western response to the declaration of martial law in December 1981, Michnik wrote:

> I maintain that the Poles do not expect any help from outside. They do not place their faith in Reagan, or in the Pershing missiles – they have no hopes hanging on the outcome of negotiations in Geneva. Although they are happy to receive every gesture of solidarity made by the outside world, they are perfectly aware (and willing to say this to others) that they must, and will, place their faith only in themselves.[19]

The Polish opposition knew that they could not count on the outside to set them free.[20]

Buttressing their focus on 'faith only in themselves', the movement viewed improvements in the superpower relationship cynically. As one writer for *Tygodnik Mazowsze* – Solidarność's main underground publication in the Warsaw area – editorialized in June 1982, 'In the past few months it has become clear that Poland is one of the trump cards in the superpowers' game.'[21] Relations between Poland and the superpowers were not based only on bilateral concerns, but were manipulated by both superpowers to suit their desires. The opposition was additionally cynical about the efficacy of arms control agreements. According to Kuroń, 'The Soviet Union takes advantage of every arms control agreement.... All Western agreements with the Soviet Union create an obligation for only one side: the West.'[22]

After Mikhail Gorbachev's ascension to the general secretariat in 1985, Polish activists remained sceptical about change emanating from external sources, including from Gorbachev's summits with Ronald Reagan. Following the Geneva summit, opposition papers argued that the meeting did little to address the 'deepest and most chronic' issues in Poland's crisis and questioned the Soviet and Polish leaders' sincerity about reform: 'If the USSR really intends to accomplish a reversal in course (*zwrotu*), Jaruzelski's outfit is not generally prepared for it.'[23] Regarding the Reykjavik summit, the Poles lamented that 'Reagan kind of forgot his own principle that rockets are not the origin of tension, but their result.' They further argued that Reagan's interests in arms control took the focus away from the most important issue in East-West relations: building a peace 'based on respecting inalienable societal and natural rights.'[24] Critiques of the Washington summit combined this viewpoint with Kuroń's ideas about arms control: the INF treaty advantaged the Soviets in missile numbers, and the negotiations did not strengthen consensus on any other issues relevant to Poles.[25] Following the Moscow summit, *Tygodnik Mazowsze* announced that Washington was 'betting on perestroika' and that while Reagan had raised human rights concerns, the United States strove to buttress

Gorbachev against his internal competitors rather than pressure him to fundamentally change the Soviet system.[26] Although the opposition believed that decreased superpower tension could *possibly* improve Poland's situation, they were not impressed by superpower relations in actuality.

Finally, the Polish opposition consistently downplayed the importance of reform within the Soviet system because they were unconvinced of Gorbachev's sincerity. The editors of *Z Dnia na Dzien*, a Solidarność-affiliated publication from Wrocław, wrote that Gorbachev was one of a long line of Soviet reformers reaching back to Khrushchev and Brezhnev, explicitly making the point that reform movements in Moscow were easily reversed and rarely had positive outcomes for Poland.[27] In an article about the merits of perestroika, the reforms were not seen as a genuine redirection of Soviet policy but as 'a [political] manoeuvre, which will be turned against us.'[28] In 1987, Michnik labelled Gorbachev the 'Great Counter-Reformer', working to save the Soviet system.[29] Into 1988, he argued that the general secretary's primary motivation was to increase Soviet power: 'All the changes taking place from above in the Soviet Union are designed to maintain or modernize its empire. Gorbachev is not a man fighting for freedom. He instead wishes to make the Soviet Union more powerful.... He wants to defend the system by reforming it.'[30] As Warsaw intellectual and Solidarność advisor Bronisław Geremek retrospectively explained, democratic activists were reluctant to see Gorbachev as a positive force in Poland because they 'had the feeling that Gorbachev was weakening our resistance to the Communist regime. His special relationship with Jaruzelski was one of the last supports of this regime. So, we didn't think in terms of Gorbachev trying to create a good environment for transformation.'[31]

Interestingly, the opposition was not completely unconcerned with international forces: their writings included a nuanced subtext about the international dynamics of propagating change. Writing in 1965 before he had rejected the idea of popular revolution, Kuroń argued that upheaval in Poland would spread through the entire bloc, and that 'the possibilities of armed intervention on the part of the Soviet bureaucracy (if it is still in power) will not be measured by the number of its tanks and planes but by the degree of tension of class conflict within the USSR.'[32] Similarly, Michnik regularly confessed that he felt a sense of brotherhood with other dissidents – Andrei Sakharov in Moscow, Vaclav Havel in Prague and Janos Kis in Budapest – and drew inspiration from them.[33] Contacts between Charter 77 and KOR were particularly strong: representatives met on the Czech-Polish border three times from September to October 1978 and then again a decade later in 1988 and 1989.[34] Finally, while the Poles had little hope for perestroika in their own country, Michnik believed that it could open a Pandora's box of problems for Gorbachev. For Kuroń the unintended possibilities of perestroika were even more hopeful:

> With his attempts at reform Gorbachev is entering into conflict with his own apparatus. Because of this he will have to try and turn towards public opinion and to those social forces from which support for the reforms can be expected. This conflict will inevitably bring forth elements of pluralism, and will awaken Russian society and those of the other nations in the Soviet empire.[35]

Therefore, although they were sceptical about the superpower dynamics of the Cold War bringing positive domestic change, opposition activists understood that the futures of people behind the Iron Curtain were interlinked, and their writings contained muted strains of argumentation about the possibility for internationalizing self-liberation.

Overall, however, Polish activists believed that the geopolitical realities of the Cold War system offered little hope for change. Based on Poland's geographic position on the border of the Soviet Union, Poles had very little room to manoeuvre; they understood that taking provocative steps could lead directly to Soviet intervention. They also believed they could not count on the United States to free them, and they rejected the importance of improving superpower relations in the 1980s. Even signs of internal reforms in the Soviet Union were largely dismissed as irrelevant to the Polish experience. The foundations of the democratic opposition's model for change, therefore, were both self-limitation and self-liberation.

Crisis, Evolutionism and Self-organization

Self-liberation and self-limitation, however, did not provide an explanation of what was wrong with Polish society and how to improve it. Early in the development of opposition ideas, Kołakowski's essay 'Hope and Hopelessness' catalogued the mental and moral degradation, cycle of violent crises, and the 'disintegration of society' caused by the communist system and the PZPR's monopoly on power.[36] For Kuroń, who took a much more practical approach, Poland's problems were fundamentally reflected in the economic and social concerns of the 1970s. As he opened one essay from 1976, 'The depth of the current economic, political, and social crisis in Poland is now universally understood. The whole country suffers from shortages of food, particularly of meat and meat products, as well as of coal, electricity, etc.' Linking economic decline with growing social dissatisfaction, Kuroń continued: 'The country, deeply distrustful of the Government, is no longer willing to accept the conditions which have been forced on it [i.e., price increases]. The pressures inherent in such a situation threaten an immediate catastrophe and incalculable long-term consequences.'[37] Economic decline and mistrust of the government were the core components of the impending crisis because they were leading towards a national catastrophe.

With this fundamental concern about economic and social catastrophe, the opposition moved beyond the ideas of self-liberation and self-limitation to provide a specific guide for extricating Poland from the crisis. First the opposition turned its concept of international constraints on its head to argue that the opposition was not completely constrained from action. Noting that the Soviet Union would suffer huge international repercussions and would likely face a costly war of occupation if it intervened militarily, that intervention would 'signify dethronement' for the PZPR and that intervention would have obviously negative repercussions for the opposition, Michnik concluded that all three parties – the Kremlin, the PZPR, and the opposition – had 'concurrent interests' to keep intervention from happening.[38] Thereby, the opposition turned its predictions of impending catastrophe into its raison d'être. Kuroń believed that only a well-organized opposition movement could assure Poland's security: 'I believe that it is weakness and not the strength of the opposition that may result in an [Soviet] intervention. The most immediate danger lies in the possibility of total anarchy brought about by a collapse of authority.'[39] Together, these shared interests created the space necessary for the opposition to promote change within the existing system.

Once those in opposition had argued that there was space for action, they could define their objectives. A key starting point for defining their objectives was Michnik's concept of 'evolutionism', proposed in 1976. Building on earlier arguments by Kołakowski and by Kuroń, Michnik believed that both revolution and reform were 'unrealistic and dangerous', leaving open another path: 'an unceasing struggle for reform and evolution that seeks an expansion of civil liberties and human rights ... based on gradual and piecemeal change.' In order to drive these reforms, Michnik proposed mobilizing social pressure 'from below' to create what he called an 'independent public'.[40] Simplifying, Michnik proposed creating a social movement independent of the Communist Party that could seek slow, non-threatening changes based on pluralism, tolerance and humanism.[41]

Writing concurrently, Kuroń provided guidelines for how this independent public might take shape, based primarily on his idea of self-organization (*samoorganizacja*).[42] Kuroń advocated resistance in the form of 'open organized protest ... based on solidarity' between individuals and among different social groups.[43] This solidarity would lead to a larger movement, which he defined as 'a form of joint action in which every participant realizes his aims by acting in a small independent group, [but is] united by a common purpose ... to oppose successfully a government's attempt to control individual lives'.[44] As models of self-organized social movements that had not provoked Soviet intervention, Kuroń pointed to four examples from the postwar period: the peasants' movement, which had successfully resisted collectivization in 1956; the workers' protest movements, which had made economic gains following crises in 1956, 1970 and 1976; the Catholic Church, which functioned independently of communist control; and the independent writing and publishing movement, which was producing large collections of samizdat by the end of the 1970s.[45] Defining the path forward, Kuroń believed that creating social solidarity was 'more important than even demands' and that the opposition should focus its organizing efforts on four sections of society: industrial workers, peasants and landowning farmers, students and the independent publishing movement. Given intellectuals' prominent role in the opposition, promoting solidarity between intellectuals and all of these groups was inherently part of this strategy.[46]

On the theoretical front, both Michnik and Kuroń promoted two more concepts as essential characteristics of their 'independent, self-governing social institutions': non-violence and dialogue. In terms of practical considerations for non-violence, Michnik wrote, 'The USSR has such enormous military power that confrontation is simply unthinkable. In other words: we have no guns.'[47] More philosophically, Michnik – trained as a historian – reviewed the outcome of previous revolutions, particularly the French Revolution, and concluded that violent revolution only begat a new violent society, arguing succinctly, 'Whoever uses violence to gain power uses violence to maintain power.'[48] By renouncing the use of violent force, the opposition could pursue change only through compromise with the communists, a fact Kuroń recognized early on.[49] For Michnik, while it was essential that the movement remain 'independent and distinct' from the government, it was essential that the opposition work to foster a dialogue – defined as 'the communication and transfer of values ... whenever there is a readiness to understand the validity of someone else's position and to enter into a different way of thinking' – with the government.[50] Also, 'One can dislike the people in power, but they have to be accepted as partners in negotiations [to create] order based on compromise.'[51]

While Kuroń and Michnik provided a loose road map for moving forward, they were less clear about their end goals. In line with their mantra of self-limitation, their conflict with the authorities was 'not about who was in power but about methods of exercising power',[52] so they tended to provide visions of social organizations rather than political outcomes. Their goals were not utopian: 'We shouldn't fight for a perfect society that's free of conflicts, but for a conflictual society in which conflicts can be resolved within the rules of the democratic game.'[53] For Kuroń, it was 'a matter of a system in which the social structure can be established from below, while the decisions of principle are coordinated with the central authorities of the Communist party.'[54] Because it embodied the most practical mechanism for this goal, they strove for a parliamentary democracy with at least nominal independence from Soviet interference, although not necessarily a bourgeois, capitalist democracy.[55] In terms of a model for political transformation, the opposition remained (presumably purposefully) vague. In the 1970s and the early 1980s Kuroń pointed towards 'Finlandization' as a possibility, while Michnik invoked Spain's transition out of dictatorship.[56] However, neither took much time to fill in specific details. As late as April 1989, Michnik deflected questions about the road to democracy, saying only, 'I do not want to speculate on how Stalinist communism will crumble. That is a job for a prophet or a swindler.'[57]

Solidarność's Domestic Demands

Although in the 1970s Kuroń and Michnik held leadership positions in opposition groups – like KOR, the Committee for Social Self-Defence, the Flying University, the Student Solidarity Movement and underground publishing outlets – neither activist held an official position within Solidarność.[58] Nonetheless, their political theories deeply influenced the union. First and foremost, Solidarność accepted the doctrine of self-limitation. As stated in the August 1980 Gdańsk Agreements, which allowed for the creation of the Independent Self-Governing Trade Union Solidarność, 'The new unions ... have no intention of playing the role of a political party.... Acknowledging the leading role of the [PZPR] in Poland, and not impairing the existing system of international alliances, the new unions wish to provide the working people with the appropriate means of control, freedom of opinion, and protection of their interests.'[59] The union also embraced the concepts of non-violence and dialogue. According to the concluding document from Solidarność's national convention in October 1981, the union 'will not forgive anyone whose deeds ... lead to bloodshed', and any attempt to resolve Poland's current problem demanded 'the cooperation of the authorities and society.'[60] Finally, the union sought to improve Poland's situation by fostering 'social, ideological, and cultural pluralism' through free election of representatives to local institutions and the parliament.[61] Solidarność also appropriated Kuroń and Kołakowski's analysis of impending national crisis, focusing criticism on both social and economic problems.

Unlike Kuroń and Michnik, who shied away from enunciating specific demands, as a functioning trade union Solidarność was created to secure specific concessions from the government. Of the twenty-one demands that the striking Gdańsk workers made in August 1980, fifteen were purely economic, focused on compensation, health care, childcare, retirement and the availability of consumer goods. Three of the remaining articles tackled workers' rights (free unions, the right to strike and choice of management), and only two dealt with the overtly political issues of increasing freedom of the press and freeing political prisoners. Of course, in a centrally planned economy economic issues were inherently political, making it difficult to reconcile Solidarność's larger political agenda with its charter as a trade union.[62] Moreover, by October 1981, Solidarność had moved beyond labelling itself as a trade union to define itself as a social movement. According to proceedings from Solidarność's national convention, the movement was created to agitate for 'justice, democracy, truth, due process of law, human dignity, freedom of conscience, and a general moral reorientation of the Republic and not just with bread, butter, and sausage'.[63] Although workers often pursued more aggressive tactics and policies than the Warsaw intellectuals advocated, with Solidarność they created a real-world movement that reflected the ideas of Kołakowski, Kuroń and Michnik and maintained a purely domestic agenda, primarily focused on economic issues but including individual rights as well.

Throughout the 1980s, the PZPR confronted an increasingly difficult set of domestic economic problems: high inflation, decreasing productivity, lack of consumer goods, market disequilibrium, deficits in foreign trade, debt repayment problems and inefficiencies in the management system. Despite the PZPR's near-total control over the economic infrastructure, it did not pursue necessary, drastic economic reforms. Rather, the 'market reforms' announced in June 1986 as part of the 'Second Phase of Economic Reform' were merely superficial. As Maria Nowoczyk argues, 'In social consciousness, economic reform remained a slogan with no real consequences.... Implementing market mechanisms to the socialist economy was solely of a propaganda character and not an announcement of real activities.'[64]

More importantly, the communists understood that their cosmetic reforms were not lessening the chances of an impending crisis. As the PZPR reported in mid-August 1987:

> General anxiety is rising due to the prolonged economic crisis. An opinion is spreading that the economy instead of improving is getting worse. As a result there arises an ever greater dissonance between the so-called official optimism of the authorities ('after all it's better') and the feeling of society.... Social dissatisfaction is growing because of the cost of living.[65]

As Jaruzelski knew, political crises in 1956, 1970 and 1980, precipitated by social dissatisfaction – particularly among workers – had led to the removal of three general secretaries. When coal miners, shipyard workers and steel workers went on strike for the second time in four months in August 1988, it looked as if the established pattern of cyclical economic and political crises was repeating. Under this pressure, Jaruzelski decided that seeking a political agreement with Solidarność was better than risking further instability. As Polish historian Antoni Dudek summarizes,

> In the situation when the summer strikes were obviously stronger than the strikes in the spring, and Jaruzelski – despite being in charge of preparations – had not decided to introduce an exceptional state [*stan wyjątkowy*], initiating a dialogue with the moderate opposition appeared to be the optimal solution. 'It is a bold path, but it is the path forward,' he declared to the gathered members of the Politburo, adding simultaneously that 'tomorrow the situation will be worse'.[66]

On 31 August 1988, Interior Minister Czesław Kiszczak approached Wałęsa and proposed direct talks. Secret negotiations between Solidarność and the PZPR began less than two weeks later, leading to what became the round table negotiations.

These initial talks provided further evidence of the domestic sources of change and the powerful links between economic and political reforms. In his opening remarks, Kiszczak alluded to the PZPR's main concern: 'The "round table" could take a stance and eventually correct the economic model, which should ensure that reforms are effectively realized, achieve economic equilibrium, and dissolve the debt issue. The economic reform programme's success ... *depends upon the degree of its comprehension and social acceptance.'*[67] The PZPR understood that in order to get the public to accept painful reforms, it needed Solidarność's support. Rather than simply working with the PZPR, however, Wałęsa and his advisors argued that economic reforms would be insignificant without political change, linking any Solidarność support for economic policies to reforms in the political system.[68] Despite the fact that the movement was forced underground during most of the 1980s, Solidarność's foundation as a legitimate socio-economic movement with a strong domestic constituency created a new point for cooperation with the PZPR. With the communists' backs against the wall and impending social collapse raising its head in 1988, Solidarność's economic and social credibility as a politicized social movement forced the PZPR to accept the opposition's requests and led directly to the round table negotiations that allowed the opposition to take the reins of power through elections and adept political manoeuvring.

Once the ideas of Kołakowski, Kuroń and Michnik finally found expression in the mass, self-organized movement from below – Solidarność – that they had been advocating, the movement's power and political clout came from domestic sources. Jaruzelski chose to pursue negotiations in

August 1988 and ultimately accepted deep political reforms at the round table negotiations in spring 1989, because he feared a widespread domestic social crisis and needed Solidarność's support for the tough economic reforms that could save the economy from collapse. Overall, Poland's example is evidence of the centrality of domestic pressures and concerns in the revolutions of 1989. Importantly, political theorists' ideas and their model of provoking change had created a workable model for domestic protest. Self-limitation and self-liberation were purposefully designed to deemphasize and circumvent the global geopolitical realities of the Cold War. By working within the international system rather than attempting to subvert it or overturn it, the Polish opposition purposefully quarantined its economic and political demands from international concerns. This, in turn, created space for domestic forces and concerns to be paramount and unencumbered from international influences. The Polish opposition strove only to improve Poland's domestic social and economic conditions.

Of course, Poland's round table negotiations, semi-free elections, and Lech Wałęsa's brilliantly engineered political coup to create a Solidarność-led government very much led the way to the end of the Cold War system. Poland rode on the crest of the tidal wave of change that swept through Eastern Europe; however, the ultimate ends were unintentional consequences of its domestic agenda. Kuroń, Michnik and Kołakowski did not plan on overturning the existing international order, though they ended up moving the world in that direction. In terms of the grand narrative of the end of the Cold War, focusing on the Polish case highlights the centrality of economics and demonstrates that local concerns overshadowed international considerations. This group of Warsaw intellectuals sought to improve only Poland's domestic situation by increasing pluralism, tolerance and humanism and adopting more democratic institutions in their own country – not to undermine the entire communist system. Understanding that the Poles did not seek to overthrow the international order helps explain why the end of the Cold War surprised so many participants and spectators in 1989.

Notes

1. P. Kenney. 2002. *A Carnival of Revolution: Central Europe 1989*, Princeton, NJ: Princeton University Press.
2. B. Falk. 2003. *The Dilemmas of Dissidence in East-Central Europe*, Budapest: Central European University Press, 3.
3. L. Kołakowski. 1969. 'In Praise of Inconsistency', in Kolakowski, *Marxism and Beyond*, London: Pall Mall Publishers.

4. This view is based on a review of the complete run of *Tygodnik Mazowsze* (hereafter *TM*) from the 1980s, as well as other regional independent publications on file at the KARTA Foundation Archive, Warsaw.
5. L. Kołakowski. 1971. 'Hope and Hopelessness', *Survey* 17(3), 37.
6. J. Kuroń. 1977. 'Document on Contemporary Poland: Reflections on a Program of Action', *Polish Review* 22(3), 54.
7. A. Michnik. 1985. 'A New Evolutionism', in Michnik, *Letters from Prison and other Essays*, trans. by Maya Latynski, Berkeley: University of California Press, 143.
8. A. Michnik. 1998. 'Joy… and a Moment of Reflection', in I. Grudzinska Gross (ed.), *Letters from Freedom*, Berkeley: University of California Press, 126.
9. For a discussion on Kołakowski's positions regarding revolution and revisionism, which were adopted by Kuroń and Michnik, see Falk, *Dissidence*, 160–165.
10. Michnik. 1985a. 'The Prague Spring Ten Years Later', in Michnik, *Letters from Prison*, 159.
11. Michnik, 'Evolutionism', 142.
12. E. Lipinski. 1976. 'An Open Letter to Comrade Edward Gierek', *Survey* 22(2), 195.
13. T. Snyder. 2003. *The Reconstruction of Nations*, New Haven, CT: Yale University Press, 226–231.
14. 'Not to Lure the Wolves out of the Woods: An Interview with Jacek Kuroń', *Telos* 47 (Spring 1981), 97.
15. Kuroń, 'Reflections', 64.
16. The first use of this term is unclear, however, Michnik used it in August 1981 in 'A Year had Passed' in *Letters from Prison*, 130. The term gained popularity in the West as the title of J. Staniszkis. 1984. *Poland's Self-Limiting Revolution*, ed. Jan T. Gross, Princeton, NJ: Princeton University Press.
17. Michnik, 'A Time of Hope', in *Letters from Prison*, 106.
18. Michnik. 1981. 'What We Want To Do and What We Can Do', *Telos* 47(Spring), 69.
19. Michnik, 'Letter from the Gdańsk Prison', in *Letters from Prison*, 94.
20. This self-reliance runs counter to later triumphalist arguments about the centrality of Western, particularly American, support for Solidarność, arguments buttressed by statements Wałęsa made in an address to a joint session of Congress on a trip to the United States in early 1990. These were undoubtedly sincere words of thanks, but they may have been overstated based on political calculations to show American influence over events in Poland and the continued need for American economic support.
21. 'Moja Ocena Sytuacji: Gra Wielkich Mocarstw', *TM* 10 (23 June 1982), 2.
22. Kuroń, 'Jałta – i co Teraz?' *TM* 121 (14 Mar. 1985), 3.
23. K. Grodkowski [Kazimierz Dziewanowski], 'Genewski Słoń a Sprawa Polska', *TM* 148 (28 Nov. 1985), 2.
24. J. Białołęcki, 'Po Rekjaviku', *TM* 189 (26 Nov. 1986), 4.
25. Kass, 'Co załawiono w Waszyngtonie?', *TM* 232 (16 Nov. 1987), 1, 4.
26. J. Kolabiński, 'Warzyngton stawia na pierestrojkę', *TM* 253 (1 June 1988), 1, 3.
27. 'Co się dzieje w ZSSR', *Z Dnia na Dzień* 15/439 (20 Apr. 1987), 1. Also available at the KARTA Foundation Archive.
28. 'Czy da się wzkorzystać perestrojkę?', *TM* 218 (29 July 1987), 1.
29. Michnik. 1987. 'Gorbachev – as Seen from Warsaw', *East European Reporter* 2(4), 33.
30. Michnik, 'Towards a Civil Society: Hopes for Polish Democracy, Interview with Erica Blair', in *Letters from Freedom*, 96–97.
31. Author's interview with Geremek, 26 Jul. 2006.
32. Kuroń and K. Modzelewski. 1982. *Solidarność: The Missing Link? The Classic Open Letter to the Party*, London: Bookmark's Publishing Cooperative, 68.
33. See in particular Michnik, 'Notes from the Revolution', in *Letters from Freedom*, 141–150.

34. The group was known as Polish-Czech Solidarity. On the 1978 meetings see *Labour Focus on Eastern Europe* 2(5), November–December 1978.
35. Michnik, 'Gorbachev', 33.
36. Kołakowski, 'Hope and Hopelessness', 37–42.
37. Kuroń, 'Reflections', 51, 52.
38. Michnik, 'Evolutionism', 144.
39. Kuroń, 'Reflections', 64.
40. Michnik, 'Evolutionism', 142–143.
41. Michnik, 'A Time of Hope', 107.
42. See Falk, *Dissidence*, 187–190.
43. Kuroń, 'Reflections', 60.
44. Ibid., 60–61.
45. Ibid., 61–63.
46. Ibid., 67–69, quoted at 67.
47. Michnik, 'Letter from the Gdańsk Prison', 86.
48. Ibid., 86–88. Quote is from Michnik, 'Towards a Civil Society', 107.
49. Kuroń, 'Reflections', 66.
50. Falk, *Dissidence*, 172.
51. Michnik, 'Hope and Danger', in *Letters from Prison*, 116.
52. Michnik, 'The Polish War', in *Letters from Prison*, 35.
53. Michnik, 'Anti-Authoritarian Revolt', in *Letters from Freedom*, 64.
54. Kuroń, 'Not to Lure the Wolves', 95.
55. See for example, Kuroń, 'Reflections', 58; and Michnik, 'A Specter is Haunting Europe', in *Letters from Freedom*, 118.
56. On Kuroń see, 'Reflections', 69. On Michnik see 'What We Want To Do', 74; 'Towards a Civil Society', 103; and 'After the Round Table' in *Letters From Freedom*, 124.
57. Michnik, 'After the Round Table', 123.
58. Kołakowski left Poland for the West in the 1970s, so he was not directly involved in the organizations. On political developments in the 1970s see M. H. Bernhard. 1993. *The Origins of Democratization in Poland: Workers, Intellectuals, and Oppositional Politics, 1976–1980*, New York: Columbia University Press; and R. Zuzowski. 1992. *Political Dissent and Opposition in Poland: The Workers' Defense Committee "KOR"*, Westport, CT: Praeger.
59. 'The Gdańsk Agreement', in A. Paczkowski and M. Byrne (eds). 2008. *From Solidarity to Martial Law: The Polish Crisis of 1980–1981*, Budapest: Central European University Press, 70.
60. 'The Program of ISTU Solidarity', in L. Szymanski. 1982. *Candle for Poland*, San Bernardino, CA: The Borgo Press, 113 and 115.
61. Ibid., quoted at 114.
62. Staniszkis, *Poland's Self-Limiting Revolution*, 17.
63. Szymanski, *Candle for Poland*, 110.
64. M. Nowojczyk. 1994. 'Economic Reform as an Ideology in Poland during the 1980s', *History of European Ideas* 19(1–3), 321–322.
65. Report, 'A Synthesis of the Internal Situation and the West's Activity', dated 28 Aug. 1987, in P. Machcewicz. 2001. 'Poland 1986–1989: From "Cooptation" to "Negotiated Revolution": New Documents', *Cold War International History Project Bulletin*, no. 12–13, 98.
66. A. Dudek. 2004. *Reglamentowana rewolucja*, Kraków: Arcana Historii, 166. The term 'exceptional state' is a euphemism for imposing martial law.
67. 'Spotakanie Robocze w Magdalence, 16 września 1988 r., godz. 15.15–19.00' in K. Dubiński. 1990. *Magdalenka*, Warsaw: Sylwa, 19. Emphasis added.
68. Ibid., 20.

Chapter 16

COMMON SECURITY AS A WAY
TO OVERCOME THE (SECOND) COLD WAR?

Willy Brandt's Strategy for Peace in the 1980s

Bernd Rother

How Did Willy Brandt See the International Situation
During the 1980s?

When Willy Brandt was elected president of the Socialist International (SI) at the end of 1976, two years after having resigned as German chancellor, he was aware that détente, which he had helped to promote, was stagnating. In his acceptance speech, delivered to the SI congress in Geneva on 26 November 1976, he called for the continuation of détente without illusions. Brandt asked for the end of the arms race, which he called 'a marathon of irrationalism'. The Vienna talks on arms reductions in Europe should lead to 'a situation in which a military surprise attack will be impossible'.[1]

Instead, relations between the Soviet Union and the U.S. further deteriorated in these years. Ever since the Cuban intervention in Angola in 1975, the U.S. had accused the USSR of expanding its influence in the Third World, against the principles of détente. For Washington, the invasion of Afghanistan in 1979 seemed to be definite proof of Moscow's duplicity. The Soviet Union, for its part, perceived Jimmy Carter's foreign policy, which put human rights to the fore, as interference in domestic affairs and doubted that the U.S. was ready for cooperation. The election of Ronald Reagan, who rejected détente outright, was one more large step towards the worsening of superpower relations. Finally there came the Polish crisis: Solidarity destabilized the local communist authorities and potentially weakened communist power in the whole Eastern bloc. Even though the feared Soviet military intervention did not happen, the imposition of mar-

---

tial law on 13 December 1981 put additional pressure on the international situation.

Brandt was less convinced than ever that a strategy based only on keeping an equilibrium of deterrence could secure détente. This, he believed, would on the contrary only fuel the arms race. Instead he asked for a new effort at disarmament. In doing so he did not overlook how seriously the USSR's Afghanistan adventure endangered world peace. A few weeks after the invasion, he compared its effects to those of the Cuban crisis of 1962. But his motivation sprang rather from his preference for détente. 'We have to do what is humanly possible to help prevent a relapse into Cold War.'[2] According to Brandt, 'influential circles in the USA' were using the Soviet intervention 'as a welcome opportunity for translating fear of the Soviet Union into an accelerated arms build-up and the "cultivation" of the Cold War'.[3] It was obvious that in 1983 (when he wrote these lines) these 'influential circles' were actually the U.S. government.

The fresh arms race between the superpowers seemed to him not only to lead in the wrong direction in principle but also to constitute a short-term danger to world peace: 'the unscrupulous accumulation of weapons creates distrust. And whenever distrust mounts, miscalculations can result in intensified crisis and even in bellicose conflicts.'[4] It was of particular importance for Brandt to warn against the new source of danger, which came from the risk of a false alarm due to erroneous computer information. Given the extremely short duration of an alert – a particularly acute problem with medium-range missiles – there was no time for decision-makers to check such information. A war by mistake seemed to have become probable.[5]

In 1982 Brandt even spoke of the danger of a Third World War. The biggest problem 'for us Germans and a number of our neighbours' were the medium-range missiles, not the intercontinental missiles.[6] These missiles would destroy both German states (and other parts of Central Europe). Their extremely short warning times produced still greater insecurity for Europe, in contrast to the United States, which was menaced only by long-range missiles and was not so densely populated. According to Brandt (and many other European politicians), all of this together created a new sense of common responsibility for peace among governments and party leaders in both parts of the old continent.

How Did Brandt Define the 'Cold War'?

Today the overwhelming majority of politically informed people would define the end of the Cold War as the end of communist power in Europe and in the USSR. Twenty years ago this was far from clear. In 1988 both Margaret Thatcher and George Shultz declared the Cold War finished, and one year later Mikhail Gorbachev joined them.[7] It was not communist domination – still ongoing in 1988 – that constituted the 'Cold War' for Thatcher and others. What did Willy Brandt want to overcome in the 1980s? The acute political confrontation between the blocs, which from his point of view were on the verge of sliding into a military conflict? Or the communist domination of Eastern Europe?

When he spoke about overcoming the Cold War, he never had in mind the end of communist power. This could – perhaps – happen in a further stage, depending on the development of history. He defined 'Cold War' as a situation in which the superpowers constantly increased their arsenals, tried to gain military superiority and rarely talked to one another, each watching for a chance to enhance its influence at the expense of its rival. As a result the risk of a nuclear conflict grew. For Brandt, this situation had already been surmounted by the mid-1960s.[8] As the 1970s gave way to the 1980s, however, such an international constellation had arisen once more. Brandt largely avoided speaking of a new 'Cold War', but sometimes he could not help using this expression. In a speech delivered to the Academy of the Chinese Communist Party in Beijing in May 1984, he used the phrase 'In the light of the new cold war in which the two superpowers have got themselves bogged down....'[9] Only a year and a half later, in December 1985, he spoke of the 'phase of a new cold war which hopefully lies behind us', basing his hope on the first Reagan-Gorbachev summit in Geneva one month earlier.[10]

But Brandt was not always consistent in his terminology. In the summer of 1985 he even denied the existence of a second Cold War: 'The results of détente have contributed since the beginning of the 1980s to minimizing a new confrontation between the superpowers and to avoiding a remake of the Cold War.'[11] But this does not alter the point that for Brandt, the end of the Cold War did not imply the end of Communist Party dominance. Brandt made a difference between a possible long-term easing of Soviet control over Eastern Europe and a much more vague expectation of an end to communist power in the Soviet Union itself.

What Was Brandt's Vision of a Successful Policy of Détente, and How Did He Try to Achieve His Aims?

Once Reagan had taken office, new steps towards disarmament became illusory. Confronted with the new president's arms build-up and his aggressive Central American policy, proponents of détente like Brandt could only try to save as much as possible of their earlier achievements. Furthermore, it was an open question whether the new West German government formed by the CDU/CSU and FDP in October 1982 would continue with Ostpolitik or not. But Brandt did not confine himself to defensive efforts. He also participated in a debate amongst Western European Social Democrats about new concepts of peace and security on the continent. Later such ideas would become known as 'common security' or 'security partnership'. During this debate it seemed more and more that Brandt had greater problems with the U.S. policy of drastically increasing defence expenditure than with the policy of the USSR.

A few weeks after Helmut Kohl was elected chancellor, Willy Brandt outlined his ideas of a future détente policy in a speech to German and Soviet security experts in Bonn.[12] He still had not lost the hope of saving détente, but he warned against illusions. Détente, he argued, needed time and fresh impulses. One of the preconditions for there actually being a chance of preserving the current level of détente between East and West was, for Brandt, the continuation of dialogue between the two sides. In the following years this was the focus of Brandt's activities, especially as president of the Socialist International. The SI offered itself as a forum for talks between the U.S. and the Soviet Union, as well as with other interested parties such as the Non-Aligned Movement. Without communication between the superpowers, Brandt feared, mutual mistrust would further increase.

When he addressed the security conference in October 1982, Brandt made one more announcement. 'My party ... will also during its temporary opposition do its utmost for the progress of the state relations [between the Federal Republic and the Soviet Union].' This was the beginning of the so-called 'parallel foreign policy' (*Nebenaußenpolitik*) of the SPD. Its origins lay in the doubts about the new federal government's Eastern policy, but it was continued in the following years, even when it had become clear that Kohl and Hans-Dietrich Genscher, the foreign minister, intended to continue Brandt and Helmut Schmidt's Ostpolitik. In the following years the SPD agreed to establish joint working groups with most Eastern European communist parties and with the Communist Party of the Soviet Union (CPSU) to discuss international security issues.

The German social democrats' purpose was twofold. First, despite adverse international circumstances, they wanted to contribute on a party level to the continuance of a dialogue with the East, in order to reduce mutual mistrust and to search for a balance of interests. And second, the working groups of Social Democrats and Communists elaborated papers, and even actual draft treaties between governments, about new steps for détente in Central Europe. Thereby they wanted to demonstrate to the public and to the conservative government that there was scope for German initiatives designed to minimize the East-West confrontation, if there was political will. In 1988 Brandt characterized these activities with the words: 'We support and encourage the superpowers' decision-makers where common security is concerned.' This role, he admitted, was absolutely new for Social Democrats.[13]

Both of these steps – the dialogue in general and the talks about specific steps towards détente – concern the method of Brandt's reaction to the heated international situation. But what about the contents of Brandt's policies? Brandt's idea of a contribution to the revival of détente contained several key elements:

- The Federal Republic of Germany should stay inside NATO as long as the current military alliances remained unchanged. The neutralization of the country or even of the two German states would not help stabilize the situation.
- From a German and a European perspective, it was a solution to the problem of medium-range weapons that was paramount, not the issue of intercontinental missiles.
- Instead of a further arms build-up and an insistence on exact parity of weapons, the superpowers should agree upon an 'approximate balance at the lowest possible level'.[14]
- Local dissident movements should act with restraint where their struggle could threaten world peace.[15]
- In the medium term, East and West should build a security partnership. Peace could be secured only by a joint effort. Zones of lower weapons concentration along the bloc borders in Europe (nuclear-free zones, for instance) could be an important step in this direction.
- In the long run, a European peace order should be established to replace the competing alliances, NATO and the Warsaw Pact. With this, the ideological conflict between East and West could be demilitarized.
- The future European peace order should be a part of an international peace order organized by the UN. In this process, the UN must be significantly strengthened and enabled to secure the peace.
- Whether this process would lead to German unification or whether two German states would continue to exist was not foreseeable. The decision should be left to future generations.

In sum, it was in the long run a strategy for the gradual and mutually agreed demilitarization of the East-West conflict. But what progress was made towards the practical implementation of these elements?

As early as October 1982, Brandt proposed a dialogue between the two parties to the East German SED. As mentioned earlier, at this time it was still uncertain whether Kohl's new federal government would continue the social-liberal Ostpolitik. To make sure that intra-German contacts would not come to a standstill entirely, it seemed necessary for Brandt to approach the SED. After all, it was foreseeable that the deployment of Pershing II and cruise missiles in the Federal Republic would take place; thus it seemed likely, to Brandt, that East-West relations would continue to deteriorate. He wanted to discuss with the SED how inner-German relations could be improved.[16]

Brandt did not participate personally in the discussions but left his confidant Egon Bahr to play the leading role. He had fired the starting gun and now followed the progress of the talks as party chairman. In June 1985 a working group of the SED and SPD published a draft framework agreement for a chemical weapons–free zone in Europe; in October 1986 there followed common principles on the establishment of a nuclear weapons–free corridor in Central Europe. In 1987 talks began on 'conventional stability' in Europe, the results of which were available in July 1988.[17]

Contacts soon followed with the USSR, Poland, Hungary and Czechoslovakia. With the CPSU, the SPD discussed the reduction of military expenditure in favour of increased development aid from June 1984 to October 1987.[18] The 1984 to 1989 talks with the Polish PZPR concentrated initially on confidence-building measures and later on arms limitation in the Baltic Sea region.[19] With the Hungarian communists, dialogue centred upon economic cooperation between East and West. And discussions with the Czechoslovak communists focused on environmental issues.[20] In October 1987, there was also an agreement with the Bulgarian Communists; in this case the SPD wanted to debate new technologies.[21] In addition to the working groups, many visitors came to Bonn from Eastern European party headquarters – even from the Romanian Communist Party, which had been prevented from establishing joint working groups.[22] Over the years, the party contacts with the SED became so numerous at all levels of the SPD that in September 1987 the leadership of the Social Democrats enacted rules for the coordination of contacts with the second German state and its organizations.[23]

The novelty of these exchanges was their institutionalization in working groups. Never before, since the beginning of the Cold War, had such firm contacts existed between representatives of the German Social Democrats and Communists. They were more intensive than those with Western centrist or centre-right parties and even with most of the fraternal parties from the Socialist International. Mutual visits, which had already started in the 1970s, now reached an unprecedented scale. This historically unique step, started by Brandt but supported by the entire party leadership, only makes sense if we remember the all-encompassing fear for world peace that dominated the thinking of the Social Democrats in the first half of the 1980s. The outcome of these deliberations with the East was papers akin to treaties, which were sent to the governments of the participating sides for further use.

At the height of the fear of war, Brandt complemented the contacts between party delegations with a personal diplomatic offensive: between 1984 and 1985, he visited all party and government leaders of the Eastern bloc, again with the exception of Romania. He started with a trip to Bulgaria in December 1984, followed by one to the Soviet Union in May 1985 – where he met the newly elected CPSU General Secretary Mikhail Gorbachev for the first time – to Budapest in June, East Berlin in September, Prague in November and finally Warsaw in December 1985. Since peace could not be secured without the U.S. and Brandt had no doubt that the Federal Republic belonged to the West, he travelled to Washington in November 1985, where he spoke with Vice President George Bush but was not received by Reagan, who had also failed to find time for a meeting with Brandt during a visit to Germany in May 1985.[24]

The Socialist International, headed by Brandt, also participated in efforts to rescue or revive détente. In 1978, the Socialist International Advisory Council on Disarmament (SIDAC) had been founded (and only a year later was received by U.S. President Jimmy Carter[25]). Mainly, it sought to coordinate the security policies of SI member parties – a task that proved difficult – and to organize fact-finding missions to various capitals in East and West.[26] For Brandt, it was at the same time another instrument for coordinating, with Western partners, the discussions with Eastern European parties and governments. The SI's most important activity was the conference on disarmament held in Vienna in mid-October 1985 with the participation of official representatives of the United States, the Soviet Union, China, India (which at the time presided over the Non-Aligned Movement), and the United Nations.[27]

Finally, we should not forget Brandt's commitment to, and in, the German peace movement. Most famous is his speech to the rally in Bonn in October 1983.[28] A mobilization from below in favour of disarmament could help him win the governments over to his own ideas of peacekeeping. Brandt was certainly not one of the initiators of the peace movement, but he could not and did not ignore the strong involvement of his own party base. Not to lose contact with the new protest movement and to build bridges to the emerging Greens were other motives for this engagement.

Looking at the various initiatives taken by Brandt and his political allies in the SPD and in the SI from the early 1980s onwards, it is obvious that they were mainly directed towards the Soviet Union and its allies. This need not have been the case. Moscow, Warsaw and the other capitals of the Eastern bloc turned out to be places where Brandt could promote the security strategy of German social democracy, and where he was able to campaign for collective security and a European peace order. Meanwhile Reagan, for Brandt, was one of the politicians who bore the most responsibility for the escalation of international tension and therefore should have been amongst the first people addressed. But for the first time since 1945, the major Western governments proved to be more difficult partners than their Eastern counterparts. Mitterrand and Craxi opposed the security policy of the SPD, which they judged as pacifist. With Margaret Thatcher, there was no common basis for discussion; she never met Brandt. The same applied to Reagan. Repeatedly Brandt accused the U.S. government of not taking Soviet disarmament offers seriously but instead ignoring them totally and maintaining its own arms build-up.[29] The situation was quite different in the East. Reimund Seidelmann's comment on how the East treated SIDAC is also true for the other activities of the SPD: while 'the Reagan administration systematically snubbed it, working relations with the CPSU were controversial with regard to contents, but politically fruitful'.[30]

Results

What were the results of this strategy? From an international security perspective, they were of considerable range. Regularly, all of those involved, including Eastern German, Polish and Czechoslovak communists[31] as well as the representatives of the CPSU, committed themselves to the principle of common security, also called a security partnership. Specifically, this meant the acceptance of zones of reduced troops and weapons concentrations on the border between the two blocs in Central Europe (chemical and nuclear-free zones), the reduction in these areas of weapons suitable only for attack, the notification of major troop movements, the principle of mutual inspections and an effort to push forward balanced disarmament in the direction of ever lower force levels, without either side gaining the advantage. Compared with the results of the period of Ostpolitik, these were pioneering innovations. They did not simply reflect an improved climate between the two superpowers: the SPD-SED joint proposal to form a chemical weapon–free zone in Europe was finalized on 19 June 1985 at a time when Gorbachev had been general secretary for only a few weeks and when, on the American side, the prioritization of nuclear arms reduction had only just begun to prevail. Thus in the spring of 1985, the SPD and

SED were able to fix security principles that were still unusual in both East and West. Also noteworthy was the way in which the GDR demonstrated an independent interest in reducing the risk of war in Central Europe.

The summit meeting between Gorbachev and Reagan in Geneva in November 1985 gave further impetus to the SPD's talks with communist state parties. The negotiations at the Stockholm conference on confidence-building measures in Europe from January 1984 to September 1986 also had positive effects. In May 1986 the Communist Party of Czechoslovakia associated itself with the SPD and SED proposal for a chemical-free zone in Central Europe. The principles worked out between the SPD and the SED in October 1986 for a nuclear-free corridor in Central Europe mentioned the results of Stockholm but went far beyond them, as the only agreement reached in Stockholm had been over the announcement of major troop movements.

The joint declaration of the SPD fundamental values commission and the SED Central Committee's Academy of Social Sciences in August 1987 was a document of particular significance. Its title was 'The Conflict of Ideologies and Common Security', but it is also known as the SED-SPD paper. In this document the East German communists moved away from the claim of superiority of their ideology and their social order and declared themselves –on paper at least – ready for the peaceful competition of ideologies and systems on equal terms.[32] For communists, this was revolutionary. The survival of humanity, they conceded, allowed only evolutionary changes. The price the social democratic side had to pay was to refrain from declaring the other side to be illegitimate and undemocratic and to admit that the communists also pursued honest efforts for peace,[33] freedom and justice, although social democrats maintained their critique of the communist understanding of these terms and the realization of these objectives within the Soviet bloc. But the SED gave a lot more ground, conceding for instance that open discussion should be possible not only between systems, but also within them. The need for comprehensive information of citizens in East and West was a further point the East German communists admitted. This was more significant than the concession 'to develop living democracy', when the West knew well that the Eastern understanding of democracy was very different from its own.

The question does nevertheless arise: how seriously meant were the communist concessions in these papers? Formally, these were declarations by parties, which were then meant to be submitted as proposals to the respective governments – as if there were no unity of party and government in the East. It seems that we should differentiate between security issues and those of domestic policy. In the first case the Eastern partners actually wanted to introduce their commitments into subsequent intergovernmental negotiations. It is, however, an open question as to whether the positions of the East Germans, Poles or Czechs were coordinated with the CPSU. Since the beginning of the 1980s, a gradual emancipation of the Central European communist parties had occurred in matters of détente, starting in the GDR. This trend suggests that the security arrangements reached with the SPD were serious.

But this must not be confused with ideological softening. The programmatic concessions in the SED-SPD paper brought no reform to the GDR. They were no more than the theoretical deliberations of a small group of ideologues and scholars in the SED's academy, which the members of the politburo swallowed (like a bitter pill) in order to achieve the success of a joint paper with the SPD that might help legitimize its authority. But the unabridged version of the paper was published in the GDR (one of the few days when *Neues Deutschland* was sold out in the morning), and the incipient opposition used it for its arguments.

This touches upon a central point of the discussion about Brandt's strategy and its implementation by the SPD and the SI: what did this concept mean for the Eastern European civil rights movements? Only the SED-SPD paper addressed the internal constitution of the two societies, and this statement had resulted in no more than printed paper. The remaining documents, although written by political parties, concerned relations between governments. With a few exceptions they dealt only with security policy. And if the horizon was expanded to other policy areas, no mention was made of domestic dialogue. The joint statement of November 1985 by the SPD and the Polish Communists noted: 'Security partnership is based on the natural right of every state to determine its own way politically, socially and culturally.'[34] In other words, the state, rather than the people, was identified as the sovereign entity.

Perhaps the Eastern interlocutors would not have conceded more – although the SPD-SED document contained more, on paper at least. The Social Democrats, including Brandt, did not press harder, because in their eyes the current absolute priority was to preserve the endangered peace, especially in heavily armed Central Europe. The SED-SPD paper of 1987 reads: 'But only if peace is secured and history continues, can the argument about which social system is better be resolved.'[35] We should not forget: even in 1987, only two years prior to the epochal shift of 1989, signs of revolutionary change in the Soviet bloc were not sufficiently clear for the Social Democrats to feel compelled to abandon their current strategy. This was also the year of the first visit by the GDR head of state to the Federal Republic. After Honecker's visit to Bonn, 'the last inhibitions on the part of many Western politicians against personal contact with the SED Secretary-General fell. In 1987 the stream of prominent West German visitors to

East Berlin from all political camps swelled noticeably'.[36] At most, reform communism following the Gorbachev model seemed possible – the end of communism in general did not. Even in 1988 the state parties remained the SPD's principal interlocutors in the East. However, even within this horizon there was an option, as described by Janusz Reiter, who from 1990 to 1995 was the Polish ambassador to Bonn: 'You could have said to Solidarność and the other civil rights movements: "We cannot do much for you. There are limits of the possible, there are limits of realpolitik, let's call it. But, we are on your side, and of that there will be no doubt."'[37] And yet this was precisely what the SPD did not do.

Willy Brandt and the entire SPD leadership accorded absolute priority to the maintenance of peace. Solidarity in Poland, especially, was perceived more as a potential cause of unrest, instability and provocation to the Soviet Union than as a democratizing force. Brandt could not imagine that Solidarity would rather endanger communist power than peace. He returned to the lessons drawn from 1953, 1956 and 1968, namely that all Western promises of helping Eastern opposition movements would fail when confronted with Soviet military power. Brandt did not want to be responsible for inciting people to rise against communist dictatorships only to then abandon them if Moscow intervened. For the sake of world peace and for the sake of the fate of individuals in the East, he preferred a slow, evolutionary path.

Conclusions

Together with leading politicians of his own party and of sister parties, in the 1980s Willy Brandt developed extensive activities to counter the imminent risk of a nuclear war in and around Europe – a risk he and many others then perceived. He conceived – again with others, especially Egon Bahr and Olof Palme until the latter was killed in 1986 – advanced security concepts intended to overcome the confrontation of the blocs and lead to a security partnership. In the long run this would pave the way to a European peace order as part of a United Nations guaranteed world peace order.

Brandt tried to win decision-makers in East and West over to his concept. His ideas met with interest primarily in the East, though this did not mean automatically that the communist regimes changed their policy accordingly. At the same time Brandt always tried to maintain the dialogue with the governments of the West, which was not easy in the case of Washington and London. Brandt stuck to the principle he had developed in Berlin in the 1950s, namely that any step towards détente with the East was possible only on the basis of a firm anchoring of Germany in the Western alliance. He therefore always rejected the idea of German neutralization. On this point he was unwavering.

Brandt's concept was a consistent and fundamental alternative to the U.S. strategy during Reagan's first term – i.e., to secure peace through military superiority and an impenetrable defence network in space – but also an alternative to the USSR's strategy prior to Gorbachev, which demanded that the West disarm but was not ready to offer more than cosmetic curtailments itself. Brandt's proposal was also informed by his awareness that mutual distrust and misperceptions were major causes of the arms race – hence he insisted unrelentingly on dialogue between East and West and on personal contacts between decision-makers.[38]

Brandt pursued a strategy of realpolitik. His basic decision on the absolute priority of peace preservation sprang from clear moral principles but always took account of the interests of all states involved, suggesting a gradual approach that avoided idealistic objectives. With regard to Eastern Europe, Brandt concentrated on governments as the sole subjects of international policy, while inside the FRG the SPD chairman also cooperated with the peace movement – i.e., with a part of the civil society. Struggles for freedom and social justice in peripheral regions that did not endanger global peace could be tolerated (including, in Brandt's eyes, the liberation movements in Central America), but the Polish situation (and that of all Eastern European states) was so delicate that Brandt viewed anti-communist movements with moral sympathy but political mistrust.

So was Brandt in the 1980s a left-wing Metternich, a left-wing Bismarck, even a left-wing Kissinger? In any case his East-West policy was a left-wing, peace-oriented version of traditional diplomacy at its best – which unfortunately came at a moment when the peoples were about to enter the stage once again as in 1789, 1848 and 1917/1918. The new factor of the growing importance of civil rights movements in Eastern Europe, headed by Solidarity, was largely or even totally absent in Brandt's concept of common security until 1989. Janusz Reiter described the problem in 1993: 'Détente had always claimed to be realpolitik. But reality [had] changed, and you had to perceive the new reality.' Instead, advocates of détente 'ignored the new reality'.[39]

In the summer of 1989 Brandt too came to this conclusion – late, but earlier than many of his political allies. On 1 September 1989 he declared before the German Bundestag, 'I want to express openly my feelings … that a time comes to an end when our relations with the other German state were primarily about helping to preserve – by many kinds of small steps – the cohesion of separated families and thereby that of the nation.'[40] He now criticized his party chairman, Hans-Jochen Vogel, for rejecting any 'destabilization' of the GDR. Freedom could only be won, Brandt argued, by destabilizing entrenched structures.[41] This was the definite end for 'change through rapprochement' and 'small steps'. A new era had begun.

Notes

1. Brandt's speech in *Socialist Affairs* 27(1), 1977, 7.
2. W. Brandt. 2003. *Die Entspannung unzerstörbar machen. Internationale Beziehungen und deutsche Frage, 1974–1982*, ed. F. Fischer, Bonn: Dietz, 254 .
3. W. Brandt. 2009. *Gemeinsame Sicherheit. Internationale Beziehungen und Deutsche Frage*, ed. U. Mai, B. Rother and W. Schmidt, Bonn: Dietz (hereafter Brandt, *Berliner Ausgabe*, vol. 10), Doc. 3.
4. Ibid.
5. Ibid. For further similar declarations see Brandt, *Berliner Ausgabe*, vol. 10, Docs 7, 9 and 28.
6. Brandt, *Berliner Ausgabe*, vol. 10, Doc. 1.
7. Thatcher cited in P. Zelikow and C. Rice. 1997. *Sternstunde der Diplomatie*, Berlin: Propyläen, 47; G.P. Shultz. 1993. *Turmoil and Triumph: My Years as Secretary of State*, New York: Scribner, 1131, 1138; Gorbachev interview for Soviet TV before returning from Malta, 3 Dec. 1989, in *Europa-Archiv*, 45(2), 1990, D49–D52.
8. See for example Brandt's August 1967 article for *Außenpolitik*, published in W. Brandt. 2005. *Ein Volk der guten Nachbarn. Außen- und Deutschlandpolitik 1966–1974*, ed. F. Fischer, Bonn: Dietz, 130–137, esp. 131.
9. *Socialist Affairs*, 34(3), 1984, 33.
10. Brandt, *Berliner Ausgabe*, vol. 10, Doc. 29.
11. Brandt's statement on occasion of the tenth anniversary of the CSCE Final Act, 26 Oct. 1985, published in *Sozialdemokratischer Pressedienst*, no. 140, 1985, 1.
12. Brandt, *Berliner Ausgabe*, vol. 10, Doc. 1.
13. *Sozialdemokraten Service Presse Funk TV*, 28 May 1988.
14. Brandt, *Berliner Ausgabe*, vol. 10, Doc. 1.
15. See for this aspect especially Brandt's speech in Beijing, 30 May 1984: Brandt, *Berliner Ausgabe*, vol. 10, Doc. 12.
16. See R. Reißig. 2002. *Dialog durch die Mauer*, Frankfurt and New York: Campus, 28–30.
17. SPD. 1988. *Jahrbuch 86/87*, Bonn: Vorwärts, 622. For the declarations of the joint working-group: *Blätter für deutsche und internationale Politik*, July 1985, 892–896; ibid., Dec. 1986, 1511–1516; ibid., Aug. 1988, 1017–1019.
18. The result was published as *Sozialdemokraten Service Presse Funk TV*, no. 842/87, 13 Oct. 1987.
19. SPD-Parteivorstand (ed.). 1989. *Materialien. Frieden und Abrüstung in Europa. Ergebnisse der gemeinsamen Arbeitsgruppe SPD-PVAP*, Bonn: Vorwärts.
20. SPD. 1985. *Jahrbuch der Sozialdemokratischen Partei Deutschlands. 1984–1985*, Bonn: Vorwärts, 15.
21. *Sozialdemokraten Service Presse Funk TV*, no. 815/87, 5 Oct. 1987.
22. SPD, *Jahrbuch 86/87*, 608.
23. Ibid., 623.
24. Reagan was the first U.S. president in decades who did not meet Brandt.

25. *Socialist Affairs,* 29(4), 1979, 110–111.
26. R. Seidelmann. 1981. 'Die Sozialistische Internationale als Parteienbewegung und politischer Wegbereiter', *Europa-Archiv,* 36, 659–668.
27. P. Vittorelli. 1987. 'La Internacional Socialista por la paz en la ultima decada (1976–1986)', *Revista Internacional de Sociología. International Review of Sociology. Internationale Zeitschrift für Soziologie,* 45(3), 443–460, esp. 455.
28. The speech is published in W. Brandt. 2002. *Die Partei der Freiheit. Willy Brandt und die SPD 1972–1992,* ed. K. Rudolph, Bonn: Dietz, Doc. 92.
29. Ibid.
30. R. Seidelmann. 1990. 'Die Sozialistische Internationale und Osteuropa', *Europa-Archiv,* 45, 430.
31. The talks with Hungary and Bulgaria did not deal with security issues.
32. See Reißig, *Dialog durch die Mauer,* 393–398.
33. With regard to this particular field Brandt had already declared in 1978 that peace could only be secured 'if each side accepts that the other side is prepared to work toward peace'. Brandt's speech to the SI congress in Vancouver, 3–5 Nov. 1978, in *Socialist Affairs,* 29(1), 1979, 5–9, quote on 6.
34. *Blätter für deutsche und internationale Politik,* Dec. 1985, 1517.
35. Ibid., Oct. 1987, 1366.
36. H. Wentker. 2007. *Außenpolitik in engen Grenzen. Die DDR im internationalen System 1949–1989,* Munich: Oldenbourg, 518.
37. D. Dowe (ed.). 1993. *Die Ost- und Deutschlandpolitik der SPD in der Opposition 1982–1989,* Bonn: Friedrich-Ebert-Stiftung, 78–79.
38. For example, in Brandt's address to the SI Congress in Madrid, Nov. 1980: 'And what is the cold war if not a condition of flourishing mistrust?', *Socialist Affairs,* 31(1), 1981, 8–9.
39. Dowe, *Die Ost- und Deutschlandpolitik der SPD,* 77.
40. Brandt, *Berliner Ausgabe,* vol. 10, Doc. 51.
41. Brandt, *Berliner Ausgabe,* vol. 10, Doc. 53.

Chapter 17

WHICH SOCIALISM
AFTER THE COLD WAR?

Gorbachev's Vision and Its Impact on the French Left

Marie-Pierre Rey

When Mikhail Gorbachev came to power in March 1985, he aimed on the one hand to reform the Marxist-Leninist economic system to make it more efficient and better adapted to modernity, and on the other hand to promote a new foreign policy, less aggressive and less expensive, mainly in order to give back to the civil sphere the resources previously devoted to the military-industrial complex. But gradually, and in particular from 1988 onwards, his perspective became more ambitious and larger: for the new general secretary, glasnost was henceforth to be combined with perestroika and 'New Political Thinking', and his conception of socialism moved from an orthodox Marxist line to a more iconoclastic one. In August 1988, private property was de facto reintroduced; in February 1990, the Communist Party of the Soviet Union (CPSU) lost its leading role and the existence of other political parties was legalized; and finally, in July 1991, the Plenum of the CPSU adopted a social and economic programme that deleted any reference to class struggle, while at the same time Gorbachev called for the building of a 'Common European Home' based on respect for the Helsinki Final Act, human rights, freedom and social-democratic values.

Was this political, philosophical and psychological revolution perceived as a revolution in Western Europe, in particular by left-wing parties? Did these parties understand the true meaning of Gorbachev's views, and did they support and promote them, considering them an opportunity for Europe as a whole and for European socialism more specifically? Or were they sceptical, doubting the ability of the Soviet system to change and to adapt itself to new realities, new needs and new constraints?

Notes for this chapter begin on page 263.

To answer these questions is interesting for at least two reasons. First, as European questions assumed a growing importance in Gorbachev's own perceptions of the end of the Cold War from 1987 onwards, his views provoked strong reactions amongst Western European leftist parties at precisely the moment when he was in quest of support from Western Europeans. Second, as recently as the 1970s the Soviet experience with its dogma, ideology and practices remained a key model and a fundamental reference for all Western left-wing parties.[1] Thus the process in which Gorbachev was engaged – calling for the end of the Cold War and for a renewed socialism – raised questions for Western left-wing parties about their own destiny and identity.

This chapter will focus on the French case.[2] It will examine the political and intellectual relations that took place from 1985 to 1991 between Gorbachev and his advisers on the one hand and the French Socialist and Communist leaders on the other, and will identify two sub-periods: the years from 1985 to 1987, which were characterized by the fidelity of the French Communist Party, as opposed to the more reluctant attitude of the French Socialists; and the years between 1988 and 1991, which on the contrary were marked by enthusiastic support for Gorbachev from the French Socialists and distrust and anxiety amongst the French Communist leadership towards the revolution underway in the USSR.

1985–1987: The Weight of the Past

Gorbachev began to promote a new set of principles and guidelines immediately on arrival in office in 1985 and more clearly from February 1986 on, when the concept of New Political Thinking was officially launched during the twenty-seventh CPSU congress. This new approach to international relations was based on a few key ideas: the fear of nuclear danger shared by all peoples, the interdependence of the problems faced by humanity and the necessity to answer these questions in a multilateral way, without the concepts of ideology and class struggle in Soviet foreign policy.[3] From these general principles, concrete ideas emerged: peaceful coexistence had to be cooperative, security had to be mutual and the true priority had to be given to disarmament and in particular to nuclear disarmament.

For Gorbachev indeed, it was crucial to slow down the nuclear arms race. This position was largely motivated by his fear of a nuclear catastrophe, a fear deepened by the Chernobyl accident, which to some extent transformed the phantasmagorical imagined nightmare into reality. But it was also motivated by the 'insane cost of the nuclear arms races', as Gorbachev used to say. In his *Memoirs*, he insists on this last point, describing the negative impact of the Euromissiles crisis in terms of the increasing nuclear threat and the increasing financial burden on the Soviet economy. Consequently, in 1985–86, Gorbachev, who was launching his domestic reforms and needed peace and disarmament, focused on a narrow definition of the Cold War, conceived as a military competition between the two superpowers, and on the way this might be overcome. At the same time, in the general framework of the 'New Thinking', Gorbachev began to promote the concept of a Common European Home, even though at the time he in fact attached very limited importance to European questions, instead giving priority to the U.S.-Soviet dialogue. The Common European Home was given no true content yet: it was mainly a way to seduce Western European states and public opinion, and to look to them for support for his new diplomatic initiatives, particularly on nuclear disarmament.

With this opportunistic approach in mind, Gorbachev and his advisers, Anatoly Chernyaev and Vadim Zagladin in particular, began to look for help among the parties of the Western left, trying both to rely upon their natural allies, the communist parties, and to get close to the social democratic parties. As early as spring 1986, Chernyaev insisted, in a report to Gorbachev, on the necessity of a rapprochement with the social democratic parties, which could be useful in the promotion of the New Thinking due to their reputed pacifism.[4] Throughout 1987, Soviet leaders sent several signals to Western European socialist opinion-makers and parties, especially those in France: in June 1987, a couple of French members of the board of the Socialist International were invited to Moscow for disarmament discussions;[5] in September a delegation of the Socialist Party (PS), led by General Secretary Lionel Jospin, was invited to Moscow; and in November 1987, Gorbachev publicly expressed himself in favour of a new policy of rapprochement towards the social democrats in his speech to the Plenum of the Central Committee:

> Another point which, we believe, deserves wide discussion, is the cooperation of Communists with more diverse parties, with social democratic movements, the Socialists, and more generally, with all left-wing democratic movements. [In spite of our divergences], we are united by the greatest and the sincerest aspiration to prevent nuclear war, by the perception of the terrible danger generated for all peoples by global problems, by respect for human beings, the struggle for their rights, for a better life, for social progress and development. The CPSU believes in these: in the struggle against the threat of war, for the sake of the preservation of the world security, for the solution of global problems, for social progress, for the destiny of human beings, the largest coalition is possible and essential.[6]

Concomitantly, in November 1987, the Soviet leader organized an international conference in Moscow that, for the first time since 1976, brought together communist, socialist and social democratic parties from all over the world.[7]

However, the willingness in these years to initiate a rapprochement with social democratic parties remained predominantly an opportunistic move, as Gorbachev was still sceptical about its potential effect. Remembering his first contact with the members of the Socialist International in March 1985 as the leader of the Soviet delegation at the Advisory Council on Disarmament, Gorbachev wrote several years later: 'The question was about how to avoid a nuclear disaster. I declared that we were ready to cooperate actively with the member parties of the Socialist International. But at the same time, I was wondering: can we really conduct a dialogue with social democrats?'[8]

And on 2 September 1985, in his conversation with Georges Marchais, the leader of the French Communist Party (PCF), who was visiting Moscow, he asserted quite abruptly that the emergence of schismatic tendencies inside Western European communist parties was preoccupying. Then, focusing on the Italian situation, he declared to his interlocutor that he was disappointed by the Italian Communist Party's drift towards social democracy, a statement that clearly showed the opportunistic dimension of his general openness towards socialists: 'In practice the question is about the drift of the Italian Communist Party toward social democracy. *But can we really find anything new in social democratic positions? We will not find anything.* But this is thinking out loud, not a definitive conclusion.'[9]

What were the results of these first attempts at rapprochement with the French left? As far as French communist perceptions of Gorbachev's policies were concerned, they evolved from cautious support in March 1985 to more enthusiastic backing as of August–September 1985. By 1987, harmony, agreement and confidence were at their zenith between the French and the Soviet communists.

In 1985, the PCF was once more characterized by an unquestioning but also painful loyalty to the Soviet model and to the Soviet leadership after having earlier tried, without success, to distance itself from CPSU tutelage.[10] In March 1985, the first contacts between the PCF and the new Soviet leaders showed French communists' cautious support for the first signs of perestroika. The conversation between Vadim Zagladin and two members of the politburo of the PCF, Etienne Fajon and Francis Cohen, suggested the clear alignment of the French communist leaders,[11] but at the same time, and with some bitterness, Cohen noted an echo in Gorbachev's views of ideas defended eight years earlier by the French communists and condemned at that time by the CPSU: 'I am glad to see that some of the steps now undertaken by comrade Gorbachev coincide with the thoughts that some of your sincere French friends (and I personally) expressed in our time.'[12] So for Cohen, past grudges and wounds had thus not entirely disappeared by March 1985.

However, five months later, in August, the support was much more enthusiastic: the conversation between Leonid Zamyatin and Paul Laurent, another PCF politburo member and secretary of the central committee, who was spending his vacation in the USSR,[13] emphasized the French communist leaders' complete alignment with Soviet views.[14] Paul Laurent insisted on the fact that all levels of French society were deeply interested in perestroika and New Thinking. He also gave Gorbachev some advice on the attitude to adopt during his approaching visit to France,[15] suggesting the visit be used to promote a large-scale propaganda operation against anti-Sovietism and anti-Communism, and to give a press conference and a speech on French TV. The Soviet leader accepted both suggestions.

On 2 September 1985, less than a month before Gorbachev's official visit to Paris, Marchais was in Moscow, where he met Gorbachev. Their conversation was meaningful,[16] and Gorbachev gave Marchais a detailed lecture on the objectives of perestroika: peace, peaceful coexistence, the strengthening of the Soviet Union and the promotion of a new, fairer and more humane socialism. He then turned to the worrying situation of the international communist movement,[17] insisting on the one hand on the necessity for the communist parties to be independent from each other, and on the other hand on the idea that unity must prevail on the international scene: 'The struggle for peace is a common goal which must rely on a common struggle.'[18]

Eighteen months later, on the eve of French Prime Minister Jacques Chirac's trip to the USSR,[19] Marchais and Gorbachev met again in Moscow in May 1987.[20] Marchais was accompanied by André Lajoinie, the PCF candidate in the coming presidential elections, and by Maxime Gremetz, a reputedly conservative figure in the party. Gorbachev, who declared he was speaking 'without taboos', related the historical origins of perestroika before acknowledging its inner difficulties for the first time in his conversations with French communists. The general tone was friendly and candid, and when he came back to France Marchais issued a press release that assured Gorbachev of the unconditional support of the PCF for all his initiatives, in particular those on arms control.[21]

These different meetings clearly show that in 1987, the French Communist Party, fully aligned with Soviet theses, dutifully played its roles as adviser on French questions and as supporter of perestroika and New Thinking. The PCF leaders shared Gorbachev's views on disarmament; they also were very critical of Mitterrand's Atlanticism and did their best to promote Gorbachev's vision of strategic dialogue in their newspapers and amongst the French media in general. Finally, they encouraged Gorbachev to proceed, to go further, hoping that Soviet success would benefit the French party also.

By contrast, relations with the French PS during this same period remained much more ambiguous and suspicious, weighed down by hostile stereotypes and reciprocal mistrust. This mutual mistrust was perceptible during the rare meetings that took place between the two parties. During a four-day trip to the Soviet Union in September 1987,[22] Lionel Jospin was expecting to meet Gorbachev;[23] in fact he was only received by Egor Ligachev,[24] Anatoly Dobrynin[25] and Vadim Zagladin;[26] and during his conversations with his interlocutors, he solemnly reaffirmed the socialists' attachment to the French independent deterrent.

Similar distance was perceptible in the correspondence between the two party apparatuses. Of course, the French socialist leaders acknowledged perceptible changes and improvements: when Jean-Louis Joseph came back from a couple of days in the Soviet Union in May 1985, he reported – on the basis of his conversation with Yuri Joukov, a member of the Central Committee and president of the Soviet-French parliamentary group – that the Soviet leaders wanted to develop their links with the French socialists, on foreign policy questions in particular.[27] This latter point was further demonstrated by the letters successively addressed by the CPSU to the PS leaders in the course of 1986, which tried to convince them to support Soviet initiatives on disarmament. However, these first expectations were quickly disappointed, since throughout the 1985–87 period the PS stuck to the positions it had adopted in 1982–83; which were, in a general context of distrust towards the Soviet political regime and suspicion about superpower arms negotiations, namely an attachment to a defensive French nuclear force, a willingness to build European defence structures, a refusal to subscribe to the pacifist theses of the new Soviet leader and a denunciation of the Soviet attitude towards human rights and freedom in general.

At that time, these positions were strongly influenced by President Mitterrand's own perceptions.[28] For François Mitterrand, Gorbachev's intellectual qualities were supposed to lead him to push for changes on the diplomatic as well as the economic level, but these changes remained strictly within the margin of manoeuvre that the 'system' allowed him. To Mitterrand, Gorbachev appeared as the brilliant product of a system that had not fundamentally changed; consequently, Western European leaders had to remain cautious. In much the same vein, Mitterrand did not pay serious attention to the concept of the Common European Home in 1985–87, and in that respect the first Soviet attempt to conduct a rapprochement towards the French Socialists was a complete failure. However, from 1988 on the picture was to evolve markedly, largely because Gorbachev's perspective on the end of the Cold War evolved also, becoming much more ambitious.

1988–1991: The French Left Torn between Socialist Support and Communist Anxiety

It is clear from the archives of the Gorbachev Foundation that from 1988 onwards, Gorbachev's objective was not only to put an end to the strategic and military competition between the two superpowers but, more deeply and more fundamentally, to put an end to the ideological competition between them, thereby bringing a new 'civilization' to a reconciled Europe. In Gorbachev's mind, the Common European Home was to become a goal in itself: because in the short term it could contribute to ending the bipolarity of the world and to overcoming the Cold War by bringing peace and security to the continent, and because on a longer time scale, it could help solve the German question and would provide a framework within which the reformed USSR and its reformed Eastern satellites could grow. Such a framework would allow the building of a 'socialism with a human face' – a socialism that would be tolerant, respectful of others' values and based on the principles of renunciation of force and freedom of choice, two principles that Gorbachev emphasized on 7 December 1988 in his address to the forty-third session of the UN General Assembly.[29] In 1988, V. Lukin, a Soviet Foreign Ministry official, shared and clearly expressed Gorbachev's perception, writing in *Moskovskie Novosti*:

> By Europe, we should understand not only the political phenomenon, but also a definite method as to how to live, think, communicate with other people…. The 'Common European Home' is the home of a civilization of which we have been at the periphery for a long time. The processes that are going on today in our country, and in a number of socialist countries in Eastern Europe, have besides everything else a similar historical dimension – the dimension of a movement towards a *return to Europe* in the civilizational meaning of the term.[30]

The theme of the Common European Home thus reflected a real and deliberate choice to return to Europe, as well as a utopia that would offer a new order for the European continent. This order was to be first a diplomatic one based on the Helsinki process;[31] it could at the same time maintain some of the former links uniting the Eastern European countries and bring the two parts of Europe closer to each other.[32] Last but not least, it would also be a societal order that could be influenced by social democratic values. Indeed, the decisions taken by Gorbachev on the domestic scene attest to the fact that he was moving from an orthodox Marxist-

Leninist line to a much more iconoclastic one, paving the way for a true political and social revolution. In November 1990, the Soviet state's signature of the Charter of the New Europe expressed Gorbachev's intention to 'return to Europe'– accepting most Western principles and values such as the respect for human rights and pluralism – and consequently to overcome the Cold War forever. So from 1988 on, the appeal to Western European social democrats, far from being circumstantial as in the previous years, became essential[33] because it reflected the Soviet regime's willingness to evolve in its values and identity.[34] Characteristically, in September 1991, in his talk with the French Socialist Pierre Mauroy, vice-president of the Socialist International, Gorbachev emphasized his attachment 'to democracy, glasnost, to human rights and freedom, and to the socialist idea',[35] all principles that would characterize the future of the European home.

In response to Gorbachev's new position, the French Communists began to take more guarded and even hostile positions. As early as December 1988, Marchais abruptly declared in *L'Humanité*: 'What is happening in the Soviet Union cannot serve as a model for other Communist parties.'[36] From this date forward, the French communist leaders became more and more irritated by the extent of the political and mental revolution launched by Gorbachev and by some of his new principles and attitudes. First, largely traumatized by the electoral failure that had followed its political alliance with the PS, the PCF was now reluctant to accept the idea of increasing cooperation with socialists. Second, perestroika led part of the French Communist apparatus, the 'renovators', to question and to criticize the authority of the leadership, which was not acceptable to the communist hierarchy. Last but not least, the French Communist leadership was increasingly anxious about the destabilizing aspects of perestroika, particularly the evolution of the Soviet leadership towards social democracy and its growing rejection of communist ideological orthodoxy. For French Communists, Gorbachev was going too far in his ideological and philosophical revolution, and it was not possible to support him without denying their own identity, culture and historical heritage. In March 1989, in his discussion with Vadim Zagladin, René Andrieu, chief editor of *L'Humanité*, acknowledged that 'there are inside the PCF various opinions on Perestroika' – specifying, however, that 'in the majority, the PC still saw in Perestroika a hope for the future'.[37] He did not hide the difficult situation of the French party, stuck between the impossibility of existing by itself and the impossibility of uniting with the Socialist Party, given the electoral risks involved. Last, he emphasized the leadership's reluctance to ask the right questions and make a serious diagnosis, stating that '[We have to advance.] Your Perestroika helps us understand this. But seeing you going to the very limit did not help us. And as for us, we are not in a hurry to assimilate creative methods.'[38]

One year later, in January 1990, a meeting between Zagladin and Roland Leroy, director of *L'Humanité*, further emphasized the existence of growing doubts and hesitations within the French Communist apparatus towards the iconoclastic and uncontrollable dimensions of perestroika. Zagladin characteristically reported:

> Roland Leroy ... did not hide his ambivalence towards this policy [perestroika]. On the one hand, he resolutely supports the evolution of the CPSU; he emphasized that for a long time the PCF has been thinking that democracy is the key that will solve the problems of the contemporary society. But on the other hand, he said with anguish that democracy implies discipline, tolerance and responsibility – all things which the USSR is lacking, because for generations people have been used to passive obedience. In these conditions, implementing Perestroika is extremely difficult – but not implementing Perestroika is impossible.[39]

And on 25 December 1991, when Georges Marchais wrote to Gorbachev, who was resigning, in addition to words of sympathy and comfort he offered a true demonstration of fidelity to communist axioms, aimed at distinguishing himself from the Soviet leader:

> I also want to assure you of our resolution to always do better to make Communist identity and choices alive in contemporary conditions.... We have made the choice to be and to remain Communists.
> We do so by pursuing our efforts at renewal so as to respond better to what our people expect, which, as our congress has demonstrated, permits our party to be neither Stalinist nor social democratic, but Communist, hence democratic, modern, innovative, and *revolutionary*.[40]

All these extracts show that from 1988 onwards, the French Communist Party entered a phase of disillusionment with Gorbachev's initiatives, perceiving them as destabilizing for the French party and the international communist movement as a whole. By contrast, the French Socialists began to welcome the new direction in which Gorbachev was moving, which they viewed as decisive progress towards democracy and the reconciliation of the European continent, as an instrument that would allow Russia to join the European democratic arena and as a way to overcome the Cold War.

As of 1988, the French Socialists appeared reassured by the way the USSR was going and ready to believe in the capacity of the Communist leadership in Moscow to open up to democracy and the respect for individual freedom. The conviction that the USSR would evolve in its practices, as well as its principles and values, was clearly perceptible in a number of interviews given by Jospin and by Mitterrand himself. For example, on France Inter radio in November 1988 the French president reaffirmed his confidence in Gorbachev and in the positive changes the USSR was undergoing:

> As I said elsewhere and on other occasions, one indeed senses that the Soviets are experiencing – the words are difficult to use because they may appear excessive – an air of freedom: they are talking more, expressing themselves more freely, there are writings that circulate, you hear protests. Finally, Soviet television and radio are now revealing more of the real problems that are being posed to all the Republics.[41]

Later, the French president and the Socialist leaders did not fail to support the Soviet leader, praising his fight for liberty in the USSR as well as his decisive non-intervention in the changes underway in Eastern Europe. So convinced were they of the reality of this progress and the gradual evolution of the USSR towards a state of law that Mitterrand and the Socialist Party, starting in 1988, came also to adopt a benevolent position regarding Gorbachev's idea of the Common European Home. And from December 1989 on, Gorbachev's views appeared to resonate with Mitterrand and his project of pan-European confederation.[42] For the French Socialists and for Mitterrand, the Common European Home – like the European Confederation – could become a propitious framework for peaceful international relations, one that allowed the settlement of difficult issues like German reunification. But it also promised to be the privileged site for the apprenticeship of a renewed and reformist socialism grounded in ideas of democracy, the rule of law, and human rights. In this Common European Home, a renovated and reformist USSR would naturally have a full place, and the French Socialist leaders congratulated themselves on this prospect at the end of 1990, when the USSR signed the Charter for the New Europe.

However, for the French Socialist leaders, this signature was not an aim in itself but rather the foundation for a more ambitious dream of seeing French reforming socialism expand over the whole European continent. On 17 September 1991 during a meeting in Moscow between Gorbachev and Mauroy, then first secretary of the PS and vice-president of the Socialist International, Mauroy recalled his attachment to social-democratic ideas and affirmed that the 'Common European Home can be solidly built on Socialist foundations'. Echoing his theses, Gorbachev in turn underlined his 'attachment to the Socialist idea'.[43] Thus it was with increasingly marked sympathy that the French Socialist leaders perceived the themes Gorbachev was promoting in 1990–91. This was as much for geopolitical reasons – a shared desire to see the construction of a pan-European body – as for ideological reasons, especially the hope of seeing the USSR under

Gorbachev evolve towards a social democratic model. Ironically, meanwhile, the leadership of the PCF expressed growing disapproval of Soviet 'adventurism'.

Ultimately, nothing concrete emerged from these new political and ideological affinities that might perhaps have contributed to the emergence of a new European map: neither the plan for a Common European Home nor the plan for a European Confederation would see the light of day. This reflected the hostility of new Eastern states, which had decided to finish with the socialist idea and protect themselves from their Soviet neighbour by adhering to NATO rather than to a hypothetical European confederation, and the criticism levelled by American diplomacy, which was little inclined to accept the birth of a pan-European structure in which the U.S. was not actively involved.[44] Mitterrand's plan for a confederation was aborted at the end of June 1991, after the failure of the Prague conference. So between the French Socialists and Gorbachev there remained only the dream of a new European humanistic civilization to be shared, a dream that would, with the collapse of the Soviet Union, become a missed opportunity.

Notes

1. This was true even for those who wanted to distance themselves from this model – like the Eurocommunists – or who fully rejected it, as was the case of the French Socialists after their 1971 congress.
2. This reflects the author's access to Soviet and French archives. But a study could be extended to other Western European left-wing parties. A comparative study would certainly lead to a better view of the whole picture.
3. See M. -P. Rey. 2004. 'Europe Is Our Common Home: A Study of Gorbachev's Diplomatic Concept', *Cold War History*, 4(2), 33–66.
4. Chernyaev's report to Gorbachev 'On the International Department', 11 Apr. 1986, in Gorbachev Foundation Archives (GFA), collection n°2 (Chernyaev collection), opis n°1.
5. See J.M. Boucheron's report on his mission to Moscow, 3 June 1987, Archives of the Secretariat of the French Socialist Party for International Questions (ASFSP), 401 RI 6, AFJJ.
6. Extract of Gorbachev's report to the Plenum of the Central Committee, Nov. 1987, in GFA, collection n°3 (Zagladin collection), document n°7108.
7. 4–5 Nov. 1987. See the note by Lomme, the French Socialist delegate at this conference, 5 Nov. 1987. ASFSP, AFJJ.
8. M. Gorbachev. 1999. *Social Democracy on the Eve of the XXst Century*, Moscow: RAN, 85.
9. Meeting between Gorbachev and Marchais, 2 Sept. 1985. In GFA, coll n°3, document n°4780 (extract) and coll n°2 for the full text: document 85sep 02.doc. Emphasis added.
10. This took place within the framework of Eurocommunism.

11. Zagladin's report on his meeting with the members of the French Communist Party, Fajon and Cohen, 11 May 1985, in GFA, coll n°3, document n°4762.
12. Ibid.
13. This was an old tradition for the members of the PCF.
14. Zamyatin's report on his meeting with Paul Laurent, Aug. 1985, in GFA, coll. n°3, document n°4773.
15. This role of 'adviser' on foreign policy questions had existed in previous years as well. See M.-P. Rey. 2004a. 'The Western Communist Parties in the Cold War, 1957–1968', in W. Loth (ed.), *Europe, Cold War and Coexistence, 1953–1965,* London: Frank Cass, 202–215.
16. Meeting between Gorbachev and Marchais, 2 Sept. 1985. GFA, coll n°3, document n°4780 (extract) and coll n°2 for the full text: document 85sep 02.doc.
17. As Gorbachev put it: '[During recent years], Socialism has suffered from the pressure of its [capitalist] adversary; difficulties have appeared in its own ranks.' In document n°4780.
18. Meeting between Gorbachev and Marchais, 2 Sept. 1985, GFA, coll n°3, document n°4780.
19. The French legislative elections had led to the victory of the right-wing parties and to the constitution of a right-wing government, 'cohabiting' with Mitterrand, who remained president.
20. Meeting between Gorbachev and Marchais, 4 May 1987, GFA, coll n°2, document 87 May04.doc
21. *Le Monde,* 7 May 1987.
22. From 22 to 26 September 1987.
23. The Soviet secretary-general was in Yalta at the time.
24. Ligachev was then considered the number two of the regime.
25. Secretary of the International Department of the Central Committee.
26. Then not only Gorbachev's adviser but also vice-secretary of the International Department of the Central Committee.
27. Jean-Louis Joseph's report to Jospin, 10 May 1985, ASFSP, 401 RI URSS 4, Relations PSF/PCUS, 1985.
28. See F. Bozo. 2005. *Mitterrand, la fin de la guerre froide et l'unification allemande, de Yalta à Maastricht,* Paris: Odile Jacob ; and Rey, 'Europe Is Our Common Home'.
29. See his address in the *CWIHP Bulletin,* no. 12/13, 2001, 29.
30. V. Lukin in *Moskovskie Novosti,* 1988, n° 38. Quoted in N. Malcolm (ed). 1994. *Russia and Europe: An End to Confrontation?,* London: Pinter, 14.
31. In mid-November 1989, Gorbachev told Fabius: 'We need a Helsinki II, we need to bring the Helsinki process to a much higher level, that is, to build the Common European Home. Realistic politicians must frame the question as follows: we should not disrupt the creation of a system of international relations in Europe, but rather develop this system on the basis of new ideas and transform the existing institutions, on the basis of mutual understanding, into true tools for cooperation', Gorbachev to Fabius, 17 Nov. 1989, GFA, coll n°1 (collection Gorbachev), opis n°1.
32. In a conversation with Andreotti, Gorbachev stated: 'it is best to bind the two unification processes together so as to lead to a single pan-European process, to build a Common European Home, the objective of which is the new Europe.' Gorbachev to Andreotti, 30 Nov. 1989, GFA, coll n°1, opis n°1.
33. The necessity to cooperate with social democrats was also defended by the Direction of the Italian Communist Party; see Zagladin's meeting with Natta, 29 Mar. 1988. GFA, coll n°3, document n°7125.

34. See M.-P. Rey. 2008b. 'Gorbachev's New Thinking and Europe, 1985–1991', in F. Bozo et al., *Europe and the End of the Cold War: A Reappraisal,* London: Routledge.
35. Gorbachev to Mauroy, 17 Sept. 1991, GFA, coll n°1, opis n°1.
36. *L'Humanité,* 2 Dec. 1988, quoted by M. Lazar and S. Courtois. 1995. *Histoire du Parti Communiste Français,* Paris: PUF, 427.
37. Zagladin's report on his meeting with René Andrieu, 13 Mar. 1989, GFA, coll n°3, document n°7200.
38. Ibid.
39. Ibid.
40. Emphasis added. A copy of this letter sent by Marchais to Gorbachev was given to me by Vadim Zagladin. I am very grateful.
41. France Inter, 30 Nov. 1988. Private source.
42. See Rey, 'Gorbachev's New Thinking and Europe', 33.
43. Meeting between Gorbachev and Mauroy, 17 Sept. 1991, GFA, coll n°1, opis n°1.
44. See H. Vedrine. 1996. *Les mondes de François Mitterrand. A l'Elysée, 1981–1995,* Paris: Fayard, 448.

Chapter 18

THATCHER'S DOUBLE-TRACK ROAD TO THE END OF THE COLD WAR

The Irreconcilability of Liberalization and Preservation

Ilaria Poggiolini

Margaret Thatcher's policy towards Eastern Europe was inspired by a vision of communism's end – a unique blend of liberalization and preservation, facilitating the progressive liberalization of Iron Curtain states. As her leadership came to an end in 1990, her post-détente Ostpolitik revealed its main contradictory assumption: that communism's defeat could live inside the Cold War's geopolitical architecture. This chapter is a first attempt at an interpretation of Thatcher's Eastern policy, relying on Freedom of Information Act (FOIA) requests, published and online sources, memoirs and protagonists' voices.[1]

The central argument of the chapter is that Thatcher was the most significant political actor in shaping British Ostpolitik in the 1980s, itself an important factor in East-West relations before the Cold War's end. Thatcher 'had her own vision of how East-West relations should be shaped', particularly in her second term, when she expressed 'public support for liberal change in Eastern Europe'[2] and endorsed the idea that Soviet decline and Eastern European transformation could gradually subvert Europe's status quo. Secondly, Thatcher envisaged progressive change in the East, not a radical, swift transformation. The tools at her disposal were thus limited: increased trade with Eastern Europe, and incentives to economic pluralism in the expectation of political liberalization. Thirdly, Thatcher's Ostpolitik sprang both from her anti-communism and her realist approach to international relations. This combination allowed the exercise of pressure on Eastern political leaderships but also support for opposition movements.[3]

Notes for this chapter begin on page 276.

Finally, the chapter will argue that Thatcher's diplomacy towards Eastern Europe did not pass the test of the acceleration of history in the late 1980s. As change quickened, it became increasingly difficult to harmonize her responses to the new challenges with those of her European and Atlantic partners. Her vision of what Ostpolitik could achieve was at odds with the Cold War's rapid ending. She blamed her European Community (EC) partners for pursuing supranational goals and for not containing Germany economically, politically or strategically. Accustomed to difficulties in relations with her continental partners, she found herself this time in a much more isolated position, given the sharp decline of her influence on the U.S. administration and her estrangement from the Foreign and Commonwealth Office (FCO), whose previous support had been an essential precondition for the development of both her Westpolitik and Ostpolitik. Thatcher forcefully opposed the swift reunification of Germany. This final choice sealed her fate and that of her Eastern policy.

Winds of Change

Michael Clarke argues that 'during the early 1980s, when East-West relations were extremely poor and the Reagan administration was reinforcing all Mrs Thatcher's anti-Soviet instincts, the problems of balancing Atlantic against European priorities were essentially tactical'.[4] Thatcher increasingly concentrated on signs of decline in the Soviet Union, and claimed credit for her open stance towards the East after general elections in Britain in 1983.[5] According to a recent insider's account, 'the point at which this change in British policy took place was a two-day seminar held at the prime minister's country residence of Chequers on 8–9 September 1983',[6] focusing on Britain's relations with and policy towards the Eastern bloc. She emerged with an enhanced knowledge of the power structure in the USSR and with the expectation that her Ostpolitik would assist a long-term transformation from inside in the East.[7]

This marked a shift from Thatcher's early years as Conservative leader, when she had rejected the Heathite tradition of bipartisan consensus on détente. The new détente of her second term, and that which had characterized the 1970s, stemmed from radically different security considerations. From the mid-1970s onwards, the British New Right viewed détente sceptically; after the Conservatives' victory in 1979, bipartisan consensus on détente declined (to reemerge in the later 1980s) and the foreign policy debate instead centred upon the independent nuclear deterrent and relations with the U.S.

The pro-European Conservative government of the early 1970s had joined the effort to develop a European strategy in Eastern Europe, including the liberalization of economic relations and the pursuit of cultural and political exchanges with Eastern Europe. An important FCO document, 'FCO Future Policy towards Eastern Europe',[8] had argued that Western Europe could play a role in Eastern Europe 'by showing sympathy and patience' while remembering that 'the impulse for change in Eastern Europe is autonomous and Western European policies can do little to control its effect or to inhibit the major constraint or progress'.[9]

In the 1980s, Thatcher's expectations that the Western example, along with a mixture of pressures and incentives, could help defeat communism[10] were compatible with the advice of British diplomacy. More difficult was the reconciliation of the FCO's outlook with Thatcher's hostility towards continental views of European integration. Equally problematic was the harmonization of FCO ideas of East-West detente with Thatcher's pursuit of liberalization in Eastern Europe, if her unfaltering belief in bipolarity and the need for nuclear deterrence were not to be called into question. Even in the late 1980s she refused to abandon her Cold War posture, thus provoking marginalization from the international decision-making process.

In the first half of the decade, however, Thatcher carved a relevant role for herself in East-West relations by giving impetus to British Ostpolitik and pursuing close transatlantic relations. This allowed her to criticize Reagan's Strategic Defense Initiative and oppose the president's 'unattainable dream' to 'disinvent' nuclear weapons[11] without straining their political and personal closeness. Until the Cold War's end, good transatlantic relations,[12] when strained, were easily mended, as at the G7 in London in June 1984, following the U.S. decision to invade the Caribbean island of Grenada (a Commonwealth member) so as to pre-empt the seizure of power by a Marxist military leadership.[13]

Almost the opposite applied to relations with her European partners, which were never easy to manage and proved almost impossible to mend after a rift. A revealing example of this was the attempt to overcome tensions with EC partners made by the U.K. delegation at the Fontainebleau summit of 25–26 June 1984. Thatcher and the FCO surprised the participants, still shaken by the negotiation over the British budgetary contribution to the EC, with a document called 'Europe-the future' that displayed a startling willingness to engage openly on fundamental issues in the EC.[14]

This gesture of reconciliation was part of a diplomatic offensive aimed at trading cooperation for influence on future decisions. The main targets of the British relaunch were harmonization, flexibility, freedom of movement for European citizens and the example of the United States in job creation.[15] These goals were largely compatible with the collective aspiration of her partners to create a single market. Priorities, however, diverged. For Thatcher, the single market was the summit of her European vision, assuming that 'such a word could be aptly applied to her continental attitudes'.[16] If not a vision by continental standards, it was at least a coherent project and an attempt at achieving reconciliation.

It did not last long. Soon after the Single European Act's signing in 1986, Thatcher began to doubt that her partners shared her goal of implementing the single market. She believed herself its solitary upholder. A single market in the West, increased volumes of East-West trade and the re-creation of 'political links across the European divide' constituted the pillars of her concept of European liberalization.[17] Between 1984 and 1988, the balance between her involvement in European integration and her aspiration for the 'return' of a wider Europe tilted towards the latter. Her visit to Hungary in 1984 and good teamwork with the FCO in the name of British long-term involvement with liberalization in Eastern Europe contributed to this trend.[18]

Active Engagement

The visit to Hungary contributed significantly to a major shift towards active engagement in Eastern Europe. It reinforced Thatcher's impression that 'it was through Eastern Europe that we would have to work' and her belief that the Hungarian example of economic reforms and political relaxation could be emulated elsewhere.[19] Was this due to FCO pressures? Or was it the natural evolution of her growing self-confidence in her second term? Indeed, after the Falklands war and her second electoral victory, she took a close interest in foreign policy and felt more confident, but she also engaged in productive collaboration with the FCO. Changes and pressures, such as the rise of Gorbachev in the USSR or the need to expand British commercial interests in Eastern Europe, also played a role in shaping her approach. Thatcher's Eastern policy was nuanced, based on realism, long-term expectations of change and belief in the potential of Ostpolitik, particularly the support it could provide to both ruling elites and opposition movements.[20]

Thatcher was particularly interested in Hungary because it deviated from Moscow's line in economic policy and wished to build a society 'Central rather than Eastern European in character'.[21] The FCO described Hungary as 'an active practitioner of East/West dialogue'.[22] Thatcher agreed.

Meeting Gyorgy Lazar, the Hungarian prime minister, she proposed to expand British-Hungarian trade relations within the European framework and agreed 'that security between the two blocks should be guaranteed at the lower level of armaments'.[23] Talking to the Hungarian Communist Party General Secretary Janos Kádár, Thatcher tackled the Soviet role in East-West relations, arguing that international stability should be upheld by 'smaller nations' such as Hungary and Britain. This was not an obvious association for Kádár, but he in turn surprised his guest by characterizing Khrushchev as 'impulsive', Brezhnev as 'emotional', and Andropov as 'ill and no longer a child'.[24]

Thatcher also believed that her experience of walking in Budapest in 1984 had given her an insight into the minds of 'Hungarian shoppers'. She felt they 'retained a thirst for liberty' and sympathized with her open stand against communism.[25] Looking back at her choice of Hungary as her first visit in Eastern Europe, she celebrated it as 'the first foray in what became a distinctive British diplomacy towards the captive nations of Eastern Europe'. She was convinced that greater economic and commercial links between the West and the existing regimes in Eastern Europe could reduce dependence on the closed Council for Mutual Economic Assistance (COMECON) system. Increasing Western demands to uphold human rights could follow later. Finally, Thatcher foresaw a terminal decay of Soviet control in Eastern Europe and the opportunity for the West to trade internal political reforms for Western aid.[26]

After Gorbachev came to power, she believed it only a question of time before the governments in the Eastern bloc embraced the Kremlin's reformist agenda. In Poland this potential choice between reformism and conservative communism was apparent in 1985, as reported in the British embassy's annual review. The image of the Polish government improved after General Jaruzelski's address to the UN General Assembly, but the economic crisis was still unchecked,[27] the trial of Father Popiełuszko's murderers revived dark memories[28] and the opposition remained marginalized. Still, the British ambassador described Poland as 'the most liberal regime in Eastern Europe' and advised the government to schedule more 'high-level, hard working visits from the UK'.[29] The German Democratic Republic (GDR), by contrast, was ruled by hardliners little inclined to change, as reported in 1984[30] and 1985.[31] In 1986 the coolness of relations between Gorbachev and Erich Honecker was central to the annual report of British Ambassador John Everard.[32] His counterpart in Prague, John Barrett, signalled to London that 'The dinosaurs in the Presidium do not behave as if they fear extinction from a comet called Gorbachev' but described Gustav Husàk, the general secretary of the Czechoslovak Communist Party, as not 'entirely immobilista'.[33]

The annual reports of the ambassadors in Eastern Europe bear witness to the early years of transformation in Eastern Europe and to the active engagement of the FCO in the development of Ostpolitik. Even before Gorbachev's ascendancy, the British embassy in Poland suggested improved contacts with both General Jaruzelski and the opposition, and advanced the view that 'Poland could not be governed over the opposition of the Vatican'. This early message, pointing to a long balancing act of engagement with both government and opposition in Poland in the name of the vitality of its civil society, coincided with Thatcher's view. However, she continued to expect her Eastern policy would take time to upset the existing stasis in countries like Hungary and Poland, which more than others saw an alternation between rigid control by the government and phases of dissident forces' extreme vitality and visibility.[34]

In March 1985 Geoffrey Howe, Thatcher's foreign secretary since 1983, accompanied her to Konstantin Chernenko's funeral. The prime minister again met Gorbachev, who now was the Soviet leader, in a friendly atmosphere, though neither 'ever completely lowered their guard'.[35] The foreign secretary continued his journey in the spring of 1985, visiting East Berlin, Czechoslovakia and Poland. He exchanged views with Polish leaders, including Jaruzelski, and paid respects at the grave of Father Popieluszko, signalling the importance Thatcher attached to human rights. During martial law in Poland, the political element took centre stage in British-Polish relations; reports from the British embassy in Warsaw reveal the complexity of the battle for reformism.[36]

Thatcher's government carried on a dialogue with both government and Solidarity to support the emerging reformist voices. She was adamant that political breakdown in Poland could be avoided if the West showed unity. She asked Reagan to open a dialogue with the U.K., Germany, France and Italy in order to replace U.S. unilateral sanctions with shared measures.[37] According to the American president, this facilitated the creation of new consensus in the West and a commitment by the United States to modify sanctions.[38]

Thatcher's policy after 1983 significantly expanded the volume of trade in comparison with the 1970s, following a tendency she shared with the other main actors in the EC to pursue independent trade policies in Eastern Europe.[39] The commercial side of Thatcher's Eastern policy was based on a combination of trade expansion, the opening of a line of credit and incentives to private investors.[40] Politically, the goal was equally clear: to contribute to the development of economic pluralism in Eastern Europe in the expectation that this would ultimately produce political liberalization.[41] She believed that a combination of economic and political incentives could expose existing contradictions. Her expectation was a progressive transformation that could be gradually embraced and managed by local elites or even by their oppositions – not an uncontrolled destabilization with direct repercussion on East-West relations.

The confrontation between Jaruzelski and Solidarność took centre stage again in 1986, and the country edged towards a 'worst case' scenario.[42] Thatcher had endorsed the struggle of the Polish opposition but also expected that dialogue with the government would continue. The British ambassador in Warsaw signalled that the situation could spin out of control and that the consequences for 'Poland's relations with the West and thus for East-West relations, for Mr Gorbachev's own reform programme and for human rights in Poland would be very serious.'[43]

At this time the West was exerting unprecedented pressure on Jaruzelski to move from a limited to a full amnesty of political prisoners. The question whether the main source of pressure on Jaruzelski came from Western Europe or the U.S. has been reassessed on the basis of documentary evidence.[44] The European request to release all Solidarity prisoners, advanced by the British ambassador on the EC's behalf, sent a clear message: non-compliance would directly affect European-Polish relations. It has been argued that the Politburo of the PZPR (Polish United Workers' Party) responded to European, not U.S., pressures.[45] The Polish decision was of great consequence, for it meant that a crackdown on the opposition had become unlikely.[46] Resisting pressure from some of her diplomatic representatives, Thatcher remained reluctant to exert strong pressure on Poland at the bilateral level and felt that in the last instance it all depended on Gorbachev's success in the Soviet Union and Eastern Europe. As the British ambassador in the GDR reminded her, distrust of Gorbachev's policies of perestroika and glasnost was still an issue.[47] Thatcher would soon discover that when it came to encouraging reformism in Eastern Europe, her expectation that it would flourish slowly but steadily, in line with Gorbachev's success as Soviet leader, would be challenged by events.[48]

The Shortening of the Long Term

The common European initiative to release Solidarity prisoners was launched under the British presidency of the EC. This success showed that EC partners could take a common approach to the acceleration of the process of liberalization in Eastern Europe.[49] As observed before, this consensus did not apply to the implications of the Single European Act (SEA), particularly regarding institutional change and an increase of qualified majority voting. Thatcher was very much at odds with President of the European Commission Jacques Delors and his energetic initiative, epitomized by the Delors Report on EMU (Economic and Monetary Union) in April 1989 and the Social Charter in May 1989. By contrast, Thatcher had prioritized agreement on a record number of single-market measures at the European Council in London under her presidency in December 1986.[50] Her dislike of Delors reached its zenith in 1988, following two of his speeches. Speaking to the European Parliament in July 1988, he announced that in ten years' time, 80 per cent of legislation in the economic, financial and social fields would come from Brussels. Then, at the Trade Unions Congress (TUC) conference in September 1988, Delors spoke of the need to improve workers' protection at the European level. Thatcher felt directly challenged by this; particularly since the 1987 general elections in Britain[51] her fight 'to raise the flag of national sovereignty, free trade and free enterprise' had been reenergized.[52]

In the meantime, the structure of European security changed because of direct superpower cooperation and liberalization in Eastern Europe, and Britain's role in the triangular relationship with Moscow and Washington was markedly reduced. Thatcher's instincts remained to play the Atlantic card, whereas her European partners were more determined than ever to pursue common initiatives on the future of Eastern Europe. She remained active in Eastern Europe with an increasingly personal Ostpolitik. In November of 1988 she visited Poland, starting in Warsaw with a meeting with Jaruzelski, then moving on to Gdansk to see Lech Wałęsa.[53] After her visit, Wałęsa's public profile grew;[54] meanwhile, the Polish economy remained in disarray and required ever more support from the West.[55]

Before her Polish trip, Thatcher gave a controversial speech at the College of Europe in Bruges. With words only partly tamed by the FCO,[56] she expressed her distrust of federalism and of the EC. Idealism, not a centralized Community, was at the heart of the hopes of Eastern Europeans: 'Arguably, it was the Czechs, Poles and Hungarians who were the real – indeed the last – European "idealists", for them Europe represented a precommunist past, an idea which symbolized the liberal values and national cultures that Marxism had sought unsuccessfully to snuff out'.[57] Though controversial on the issue of European integration, Thatcher's Bruges speech made absolutely clear her belief that 'East of the Iron Curtain, people who once enjoyed a full share of European culture, freedom and identity have been cut off from their roots. We shall always look on Warsaw, Prague and Budapest as great European cities'.[58]

The speech in favour of the liberation of Eastern Europe and its 'return' to the West pitched her directly against the 'European superstate'. She believed that the reality of the EC, as she perceived it, contradicted the Eastern Europeans' dreams of freedom as well as her own vision of an open market and society. At a time of revival of national identity in the East,

Thatcher asserted that 'to try to suppress nationhood and concentrate power at the centre of a European conglomerate would be highly damaging and would jeopardise the objective we seek to achieve'.[59] Her subsequent visit to Poland seemed to leave her more in tune with the Pope than with her European partners, though her meeting with Jaruzelski left her under the impression that the conversion of Poland to reformism could be managed on the basis of a realist approach. She believed Jaruzelski was 'close to Mr. Gorbachev' and that he understood her reasons for supporting Solidarity.[60]

Acceleration of change in the Eastern bloc in 1989 shortened the timescale on which Thatcher was operating. She reacted by attempting to slow down the pace of events and groping for answers in the economic sphere: the £25 million 'Know-How-Fund', announced when Jaruzelski was visiting the U.K. in June, was one of them.[61] The U.K. doubled its contribution to the International Monetary Fund's Stabilization Fund just before welcoming Wałęsa to the U.K. in November.[62] The balancing act of the British government in Poland had now merged de facto into one policy: consolidating the coalition government of Mazowiecki, which merged old and new.

It has been argued that 'the emergence of the new détente of the 1980s seemed at first to suit Britain's natural diplomatic strengths in security policy but then gradually undermined the basis on which those policies rested.'[63] A second paradox was that when the EC emerged as a key institutional actor in integrating Eastern Europe in the West, that Thatcher had no intention of joining this process or accepting this new reality. In December 1989 she admitted she was unable to reconcile the inclination of her head 'towards the commercial significance of the EC' with her heart still beating for 'the political/social ethos of the United States'.[64] This was damaging politically for Thatcher and for Britain, as the end of East-West division seemed to erase the distinction between the limited goals of European institutions and the global dimension of Atlanticism. Thatcher welcomed changes in Eastern Europe, but she opposed the strengthening of the role of the EC in the transition to a new international order. This opposition was based on two interrelated motives: her resistance to the expansion of the political and regional-security dimension of European collaboration, and her opposition to the reunification of Germany. The latter grew when the U.S. administration began to see Germany as a 'partner in leadership' within a new European framework.[65]

According to the pro-European Hugo Young, 'attempting to stop German unification was one of the more bizarre initiatives in the Thatcher foreign policy record'.[66] Indeed, her 'ruinously outspoken' hostility towards Germany damaged her public image and did not reflect the view of

British voters, who according to opinion polls were 70 per cent in favour of the reunification of the former enemy.[67] However, Thatcher saw two good reasons to stop, or delay as much as possible, the return of a unified Germany: first, her mistrust of Helmut Kohl and his pro-European motives; and second, her concern that the future domination of the EC in an economic, political and – most dangerously – strategic post–Cold War European scenario would benefit a great deal from Germany unity.

Endorsement of the Thatcher position or a debate on what Germany could be in the future was the purpose of a seminar that was organized at Chequers in March 1990. Patrick Salmon has argued that Thatcher 'did not like German unification or the speed at which it was proceeding but she did nothing to stop it or slow it down'.[68] Yet, as Salmon points out, many held the view that Thatcher's hostility towards a united Germany made the FCO's task in advising her extremely difficult.[69] Recently released British documents on German unification (1989–1990) show that senior officials in the Foreign Office repeatedly warned Thatcher of the severe damage her hostility towards the post–Cold War future of Germany could do to British transatlantic and European relations.[70]

The Chequers seminar did not endorse Thatcher's strong aversion to a reunified Germany. It provided one overall, simple message: be nice to the Germans.[71] Indeed, the seminar at Chequers, which had opened with a discussion of the 'evil' dimension of Germany in the past, ended with a strong emphasis on the benignity of contemporary and future German identity. Nobody among the guests, except Thatcher, expected that unification could be stopped, as the release of new documents shows. They also show that pressures on Thatcher intensified 'to turn the necessity of acceptance of the principle of reunification into a virtue', but to no avail.[72] In July, Dominic Lawson wrote an article for *The Spectator* based on an interview with Trade and Industry Secretary Nicholas Ridley, who spoke of the EC as a 'German racket designed to take over Europe' and went so far as to argue that deciding to give up national sovereignty in favour of European institutions was unacceptable: 'you might just as well give it to Adolf Hitler, frankly'.[73] The article caused such a strong reaction that Ridley was forced to resign. Thatcher was suspected of similar feelings against both the EC and Germany in Europe: this convinced many Tory MPs of her ineligibility to be a leader who could guarantee them a fourth election victory. According to Malcolm Rifkind, then secretary of state for Scotland, Thatcher did not grasp how the disappearance of East Germany and the reunification of Germany were 'historically inevitable' and 'morally justified', but he concludes that 'that error does not diminish the historical importance of the wider contribution that Britain, led by her, made to the most momentous achievements of the late twentieth century'.[74]

The extent of that contribution is the focus of this essay. The contrast between liberalization and preservation in Thatcher's Eastern policy at the end of the Cold War finally tilted to the side of preservation in a self-defeating attempt at opposing, and then slowing down, the inevitable consequences of the end of the Cold War. With the demise of the expectation of progressive change, Thatcher's role mediating between the Soviet Union and the United States diminished sharply, while her uncompromising attitude in domestic and international affairs grew alarmingly. A well-informed British diplomat views the shift from the early years of her premiership to her attitude in the late 1980s as striking: 'from being combative and opinionated, but fresh, open and approachable, she had gone to being tired, closed and cut-off from outside advice'.[75] However, her early vision of Ostpolitik was a fundamental factor in the creation of a Western dialogue with the Eastern bloc that eventually was reciprocated by the Westpolitik of the Eastern Europeans. It was a vision of the end of communism that Thatcher shared in different degrees with her European partners and with the United States. Her vision, however, did not pass the test posed by the acceleration of history at the end of the Cold War and was proved wrong in its prediction of a unified Federal Germany taking on an overpoweringly dominant role in Europe.

Notes

1. Archival documentation, when released, will make it possible to verify or amend this interpretation.
2. R. Braithwaite. 2010. 'Thatcher's Role as an Interpreter of Gorbachev 1984–1991', *Journal of European Integration History*, 16 (1), 31–44.
3. See M. Thatcher. 1993. *The Downing Street Years*, London: Harper Collins, 456–467.
4. M. Clarke. 1992. 'A British View', in R. Davy (ed.), *European Détente: A Reappraisal*, London: Sage Publications, 104.
5. M. Rifkind. 2005. 'Britain Restored in the World', in S. Roy and J. Clarke (eds), *Margaret Thatcher's Revolution*, London: Continuum Press, 31.
6. A. Brown. 2008. 'The Change to Engagement in Britain's Cold War Policy: The Origins of the Thatcher-Gorbachev Relationship', *Journal of Cold War Studies*, 10(3), 4–12.
7. Clarke, 'A British View', 102–107.
8. FCO Future Policy towards Eastern Europe, Jan 1974 FCO 30/2493. UK National Archives, London (UKNA).
9. Ibid.
10. 'But the example of Western Europe is one of the incentives to change in Eastern Europe', ibid.
11. Thatcher, *The Downing Street Years*, 463–466.

12. See, e.g., Reagan to Price, Jul. 31, 1984, see http://www.margaretthatcher.org (accessed 5 June 2010); 'Margaret Thatcher as Foreign Policy Maker', *The Economist*, 30 June 1984.
13. The London Economic Declaration, 9 June 1984, US Department of State Bulletin, No 2089, Aug. 1984, 2–4.
14. 'Europe-the future' was the work of Robin Renwick, with inputs from Michael Butler in Brussels and David Williamson in the Cabinet Office. The editor was Julian Bullard, political director of the FO. Wall states that Thatcher 'read it and approved it, and if she agreed to it that means she agreed with it'. The main purpose of the pamphlet was to clarify British vision for the future of the EEC. See S. Wall. 2008. *A Stranger in Europe: Britain and the EU from Thatcher to Blair*, Oxford: Oxford University Press, 41–42.
15. Ibid. See also D. Gowland and A. Turner. 2000. *Britain and European Integration 1945–1998: A Documentary History*, London: Routledge, 173–174.
16. H. Young. 1999. *This Blessed Plot: Britain and Europe from Churchill to Blair*, London: Macmillan, 326.
17. Thatcher, *The Downing Street Years*, 536–537.
18. FCO Future Policy towards Eastern Europe, Jan. 1974 FCO 30/2493, UKNA.
19. Thatcher, *The Downing Street Years*, 454–455.
20. See M. Clark. 1988, 'The Soviet Union and Eastern Europe', in P. Byrd (ed.), *British Foreign Policy under Thatcher*, Oxford: Philip Allan/St Martin's Press.
21. FCO Steering Brief, 10 January 1984. Prime Minister's visit to Hungary, 2–4 Feb. 1984, FOIA request by the Machiavelli Center, I. Poggiolini – 2007.
22. Ibid.
23. Record of Plenary talks between the Prime Minister and the Hungarian Prime Minister on 3 Feb. 1984, FOIA request by the Machiavelli Center, I. Poggiolini – 2007.
24. Record of Conversation between the Prime Minister and the First Secretary Kádár, 4 Feb. 1984, FOIA request by the Machiavelli Center, I. Poggiolini – 2007; now in http://www.margaretthatcher.org (accessed 5 June 2010).
25. J. O'Sullivan. 2006. *The President, the Pope and the Prime Minister*, Washington, DC: Regnery Publishing, 291; Thatcher, *The Downing Street Years*, 456.
26. Thatcher, *The Downing Street Years*, 457–458.
27. The Paris Club agreement on rescheduling of debts due to Western governments in 1982–84 was finally signed in July 1985.
28. Jerzy Popiełuszko was a priest close to the Solidarity movement. He was murdered by three Security Police officers after being kidnapped in October 1984.
29. Poland: Annual Review for 1985, Her Majesty's Ambassador at Warsaw to the Secretary of State for Foreign and Commonwealth Affairs, 10 Jan. 1986, FOIA by the Machiavelli Center, I. Poggiolini – 2007; now in http://www.margaretthatcher.org (accessed 5 June 2010).
30. German Democratic Republic: Annual Review for 1984, Her Majesty's Ambassador at East Berlin to the Secretary of State for Foreign and Commonwealth Affairs, 2 Jan. 1985, T J Everard, ibid.
31. German Democratic Republic: Annual Review for 1985, Her Majesty's Ambassador at East Berlin to the Secretary of State for Foreign and Commonwealth Affairs, 22 Jan. 1986, J Everard, ibid.
32. German Democratic Republic: Annual Review for 1986, Her Majesty's Ambassador at East Berlin to the Secretary of State for Foreign and Commonwealth Affairs, 12 Jan. 1987, T J Everard, ibid.
33. Czechoslovakia: Annual Review for 1986, Her Majesty's Ambassador at Prague to the Secretary of State for Foreign and Commonwealth Affairs, 5 Jan. 1987, S J Barrett, ibid.

34. Poland: Annual Review for 1982, Her Majesty's Ambassador at Warsaw to the Secretary of State for Foreign and Commonwealth Affairs, 31 Dec. 1982, C M James, ibid.
35. Howe was British foreign secretary from 1983 to 1989; on the meeting between Thatcher and Gorbachev see G. Howe. 1994. *Conflict of Loyalty,* London: Pan Books, 430.
36. Poland: Annual Review for 1981, Her Majesty's Ambassador at Warsaw to the Secretary of State for Foreign and Commonwealth Affairs, 30 Dec. 1981, C M James, FOIA request by the Machiavelli Center, I. Poggiolini – 2007; now in http://www.margaretthatcher.org (accessed 5 June 2010). See also O'Sullivan, *The President, The Pope and the Prime Minister,* 295.
37. Thatcher to Reagan, Dec. 22 1981; Haig to Reagan, Jan. 29, 1982; Reagan to Thatcher, July 2, 1982, see http://www.margaretthatcher.org (accessed 5 June 2010).
38. Reagan to Thatcher, Nov. 12, 1982, see http://www.margaretthatcher.org (accessed 5 June 2010).
39. See K.E. Smith. 2004. *The Making of EU Foreign Policy: The Case of Eastern Europe,* Basingstoke: Palgrave Macmillan, 52–65.
40. Poland: Annual Review for 1983, Her Majesty's Ambassador at Warsaw to the Secretary of State for Foreign and Commonwealth Affairs, 31 Dec. 1983, J A L Morgan, FOIA request by the Machiavelli Center, I. Poggiolini – 2007; now in http://www.margaret thatcher.org (accessed 5 June 2010).
41. Broomfield minute on Chequers Soviet Seminar, Sept. 7, 1983, FOIA request by the Machiavelli Center, I. Poggiolini – 2007; now in http://www.margaretthatcher.org (accessed 5 June 2010).
42. Poland: Annual Review for 1986, Her Majesty's Ambassador at Warsaw to the Secretary of State for Foreign and Commonwealth Affairs, 21 Jan. 1987, B L Barder, FOIA request by the Machiavelli Center, I. Poggiolini – 2007; now in http://www.margaretthatcher.org (accessed 5 June 2010).
43. Poland: Annual Review for 1983, Her Majesty's Ambassador at Warsaw to the Secretary of State for Foreign and Commonwealth Affairs, 31 Dec. 1983, J A L Morgan, FOIA request by the Machiavelli Center, I. Poggiolini – 2007; now in http://www.margaret thatcher.org (accessed 5 June 2010).
44. G.F. Domber. 2008. 'Rumblings in Eastern Europe: Western Pressure on Poland's Moves towards Democratic Transformation', in F. Bozo et al. (eds), *Europe and the End of the Cold War: A Reappraisal,* London: Routledge, 51–63.
45. Ibid., 57–58.
46. Poland: Annual Review for 1987, Her Majesty's Ambassador at Warsaw to the Secretary of State for Foreign and Commonwealth Affairs, 20 Jan. 1988, B L Barder, FOIA request by the Machiavelli Center, I. Poggiolini – 2007; now in http://www.margaretthatcher.org (accessed 5 June 2010).
47. German Democratic Republic: Annual Review for 1988, Her Majesty's Ambassador at East Berlin to the Secretary of State for Foreign and Commonwealth Affairs, 4 Jan. 1989, N.H.R.A. Broomfield, ibid.
48. Poland: Annual Review for 1987, Her Majesty's Ambassador at Warsaw to the Secretary of State for Foreign and Commonwealth Affairs, 20 Jan. 1988, B L Barder, ibid.
49. Indeed, 'the basic objectives (support for economic and political reform) and principles/ norms (specificity, conditionality) of the common policy were made fairly clear before the revolutions swept through Eastern Europe'. Smith, *The Making of EU Foreign Policy,* 65.
50. Howe, *Conflict of Loyalty,* 521.
51. Wall, *A Stranger in Europe,* 74–75.
52. Thatcher, *The Downing Street Years,* 728.

53. For a poignant description of Thatcher's visit, see Chris Collins's conversation with Lord Powell at his office in London, 12 Sept. 2007, http://www.margaretthatcher.org (accessed 5 June 2010).

54. Poland: Annual Review for 1988, Her Majesty's Ambassador at Warsaw to the Secretary of State for Foreign and Commonwealth Affairs, 10 Jan. 1989, S G Barrett, FOIA request by the Machiavelli Center, I. Poggiolini – 2007; now in http://www.margaretthatcher.org (accessed 5 June 2010). See also the case of Czechoslovakia.

55. See P. Machcewicz. 2001. 'Poland 1986–1989: From "Cooptation" to "Negotiated Revolution"', *Cold War International History Project Bulletin*, no. 12–13, 93–128; A. Paczkowski. 2003. *The Spring Will Be Ours: Poland and Poles from Occupation to Freedom*, Pennsylvania: Penn State University Press, 482–491.

56. Wall, *A Stranger in Europe*, 78–81.

57. Thatcher, *The Downing Street Years*, 744.

58. Thatcher, Speech to the College of Europe (The Bruges Speech), Sept. 20, 1988, Margaret Thatcher Foundation, http://www.margaretthatcher.org (accessed 5 June 2010).

59. Ibid.

60. Thatcher, *The Downing Street Years*, 782.

61. L. Borhi. 2008. 'The International Context of Hungarian Transition, 1989: The View from Budapest', in Bozo et al., *Europe and the End of the Cold War*, 85–89.

62. On the conditionality of IMF aid in 1988 see V. Sobell, RFE research, RAD Background Report/75. Eastern Europe, 2 May 1988. 'New moves by the IMF in Hungary and Poland', Open Society Archives, CEU, Budapest, country: Hungary, Box 37, Folder 5, Report 28.

63. Clarke, 'A British View', 109.

64. J. Rogaly, 'Head in Europe, Heart in the US', *Financial Times*, 12 Dec. 1989.

65. German Democratic Republic: Annual Review for 1989, Her Majesty's Ambassador at East Berlin to the Secretary of State for Foreign and Commonwealth Affairs, 4 Jan. 1990, N.H.R.A. Broomfield, FOIA request by the Machiavelli Center, I. Poggiolini – 2007; now in http:/www.margaretthatcher.org (accessed 5 June 2010).

66. Young, *This Blessed Plot*, 359.

67. Ibid.

68. P. Salmon. 2008. 'The United Kingdom and German Unification', in Bozo et al., *Europe and the End of the Cold War*, 179.

69. Ibid., 180; Powell to Garton Ash, Meeting at Chequers on 19 Mar. 1990, in http://www.margaretthatcher.org (accessed 5 June 2010).

70. P. Salmon, K. Hamilton and S. Twigge (eds). 2009. *Documents on British Policy Overseas, German Unification 1989–1990*, Series III, Volume VI, London: Routledge.

71. Chequers Seminar on Germany, March 24: Summary Record, in http://www.margaretthatcher.org (accessed 5 June 2010).

72. Submission from Mr Synnott to Mr Weston, with Minute by Mr Weston. The German Question: German Views about Britain, 1 February 1990, in Salmon et al., *Documents on British Policy Overseas, German Unification*, 239–241.

73. *The Spectator*, 14 July 1990.

74. Rifkind, 'Britain Restored in the World', 32–33.

75. Wall, *A Stranger in Europe*, 85.

Chapter 19

MITTERRAND'S VISION AND THE END OF THE COLD WAR

Frédéric Bozo

France's role and President François Mitterrand's personal record at the end of the Cold War have been widely debated since the events of 1989–91. It is often affirmed in the dominant literature that the part France played in that period was limited in comparison with that of other key actors, foremost the United States, the USSR and Germany. Most accounts maintain that the French president essentially failed to anticipate the chain of events that led to the overcoming of the East-West conflict, namely the peaceful liberation of Eastern Europe, the unification of Germany and the breakup of the Soviet Union. It is generally assumed that Mitterrand's France was caught off guard by the 'acceleration of history' in the late 1980s and early 1990s and, worse yet, reacted obstructively to it. Paris allegedly tried to slow down or impede these events outright, especially German unification.[1]

This rendering of French policy at the end of the Cold War is intriguing. It is, to begin with, at odds with the role that French diplomacy, ever since the 1960s, had claimed under the impulse of General Charles de Gaulle: that of a challenger to the bloc system and 'Yalta'. Moreover, it contrasts with Mitterrand's adherence to the Gaullist legacy in foreign policy even before his coming to power in 1981 and his willingness, once elected president, to carry on a policy of overcoming the Cold War status quo. Finally, it contradicts what we now know of France's actual role in the events of 1989–91 thanks to archive-based research, a role that was, by and large, in accordance with the Gaullist (and the Mitterrandian) vision of overcoming the Cold War.[2]

It is therefore worth exploring what that vision was, before the revolutionary years 1989–91 provided the ultimate test of its validity, and evalu-

---

Notes for this chapter begin on page 291.

ating how it met that test. The first section of this chapter sketches out Mitterrand's concept of the end of the Cold War in the early years of his presidency. His vision, in line with de Gaulle's, was one of overcoming 'Yalta' as a long-term objective. While this seemed a somewhat rhetorical aspiration as the 'new' Cold War was culminating in the early 1980s, Gorbachev's coming to power in 1985 gave it renewed credence. The second section looks at Mitterrand's vision on the eve of the dramatic events of the autumn of 1989. With the confirmation of Gorbachev's readiness to break with past Soviet policies, especially starting in 1988, ending the Cold War became a more concrete possibility, at least in the medium term. By 1989, it is fair to say that Mitterrand, perhaps more than other Western leaders, had a clear vision of how to overcome 'Yalta'. The final section looks at the confrontation between Mitterrand's vision of a progressive ending of the East-West conflict and the 'acceleration of history' that occurred in 1989–91. While there is no denying that the actual unfolding of the end of the Cold War did not match earlier French anticipations and preferences, the vision was eventually reconciled with the reality.

De Gaulle, Mitterrand and 'Overcoming Yalta'

It would be impossible to explain Mitterrand's concept for overcoming the Cold War in the 1980s without taking into account the enduring influence of the Gaullist legacy. In the 1960s, President Charles de Gaulle had been the first Western statesman to articulate a far-reaching (and in many ways dissident) vision of going beyond the East-West conflict. At a time when the dominant Western approach postulated that the end of the Cold War would result from a preponderance of the West over the East, de Gaulle's central premise was that the Cold War stalemate – 'Yalta', in de Gaulle's parlance – could only be overcome by calling into question the very logic of 'blocs'. This presupposed the USSR's progressive abandonment of coercion in the East and confrontation with the West (a scenario that by the mid-1960s seemed plausible in de Gaulle's eyes, at least in the medium term), as well as the gradual withdrawal of the U.S. from the continent (which he believed to be unavoidable in the long term). Meanwhile, the strengthening of European unity, which would lead to the emergence of a Western Europe more autonomous from the U.S. (and therefore in a better position to intensify relations with the East and the Soviet Union), would stimulate the softening of the Soviet grip and the emancipation of Eastern Europe. Eventually, these evolutions would allow for the emergence of a 'greater Europe' stretching 'from the Atlantic to the Urals' and free of the divisions imposed by the Cold War, leading to a pan-European settlement with a reunified Germany at its core – an outcome, he reckoned, that would require a 'generation'.[3]

In spite of the brutal confirmation of the East-West status quo that took place in the wake of the 1968 Soviet-led invasion of Czechoslovakia, the Gaullist vision had essentially remained at the core of French diplomacy ever since. By the time of his election in May 1981, Mitterrand – although a socialist and a longtime opponent of de Gaulle – had all but espoused it: 'All that contributes to the exit from Yalta is good', he declared typically on New Year's Eve 1982.[4] His long-term expectations were in line with de Gaulle's, in particular with regard to evolutions in the East. He later reported that after his election he had instructed his staff to 'articulate our foreign policy conceptions around a major hypothesis: by 2000, the Soviet empire would be over'.[5] The 'Soviet empire' would be critically weakened within 'fifteen years', he confided to a sceptical West German Chancellor Helmut Schmidt in the autumn of 1981, adding (like de Gaulle) that this would make a German reunification possible within a 'generation'.[6] Regarding Eastern Europe, the Elysée was convinced as early as 1981 that the Soviet grip was now weakened and that the popular democracies would eventually become, as it were, 'Finlandized'.[7] 'A national liberal trend is developing' there, Mitterrand told U.S. President Ronald Reagan three years later.[8]

So how could one exploit these underlying trends and overcome 'Yalta'? Mitterrand's approach, here also, was a continuation of that of de Gaulle and his successors. The French president saw the pursuit of European integration and the build-up of a more autonomous Western Europe as the most powerful lever to move beyond the status quo: 'If we manage to give Europe a political will', he told the newly elected chancellor Helmut Kohl in 1982 (with whom he would quickly establish a close personal relationship), 'we will have accomplished a historic task'.[9] And although it was for him a matter of lesser urgency, Mitterrand saw the pursuit of the pan-European process as an important component of the strategy to overcome the logic of blocs: 'Helsinki', it was thought in the Elysée, was an avenue that could well lead, in the long run, to an 'exit from Yalta'.[10]

Yet in the early 1980s all this seemed quite distant. With the 'new' Cold War culminating in those years (as the Euromissile crisis, Afghanistan and Poland loomed in the background), the objective of ending the East-West confrontation, let alone of overcoming the Iron Curtain, was a long-term goal at best. Mitterrand, in fact, had initially pursued tough policies towards the East, as illustrated by his famous January 1983 Bundestag speech on Intermediate Nuclear Forces (INF). Still, if an exit from the Cold War in the wider sense was a speculative scenario early in the decade, Mitterrand soon proved eager to overcome the 'new' Cold War. His aim, starting in 1983–84, was to restore an East-West climate more conducive to France's long-term goals. One should be ready to resume dialogue with the Soviets 'on the inevitable day when [they] want to discuss things', he told President Reagan in March 1984 before going to Moscow.[11]

The coming to power of Mikhail Gorbachev one year later was a turning point. 'The Soviet Union might at long last exit from its immobility', the Elysée now hoped.[12] To be sure, Mitterrand was at first under no illusions as to the profound consequences of the change of leadership in Moscow on Soviet policies, let alone on the very structure of the Cold War system, at least in the foreseeable future. Gorbachev's coming to power, he told his ministers after his first encounter with the new secretary general in March 1985, marked a generational change and 'the passage from one era to another' – but, he added, although the Soviet leader had shown himself 'charming and smiling', this did not mean he would 'renounce' past Soviet policies.[13] Still, because it heralded less confrontational policies and a more serene East-West climate, Gorbachev's advent offered Mitterrand an opportunity to return to a more actively Gaullist foreign policy and to emphasize long-term aims again. 'If new possibilities of a modus vivendi with the Soviet Union open up this would be a good thing', he told Gorbachev during his October 1985 visit to France (his first foreign trip as secretary general), stressing that 'strengthening Western Europe' was for him a major perspective that Moscow should welcome.[14]

The French president then sketched out a long-term vision of East-West relations: 'There is a situation in Europe inherited from the war', he recognized, but one might 'correct' this situation by 'expanding' relations between Eastern Europe and Western Europe, he affirmed, encouraging the Soviets to 'take the hand' of the European Community (EC).[15] Shortly after Gorbachev's visit, he made a lyrical public presentation of his East-West concept: 'We are living in the era of Yalta', he said, but this situation was not satisfactory. '[T]he gradual affirmation of Western Europe's autonomous personality, the promotion of its complementarities with Eastern Europe, the obligation of the USSR to re-establish a more trusting climate with Community countries in order to stimulate its exchanges and to foster its development', he maintained, 'all this will slowly displace the immobile horizon of the last forty years' and give rise to 'awareness after a half century of ignorance of [our] belonging to the same continent, expressing the same civilization', thus hastening 'the hour of Europe, the true Europe, that of history and of geography'.[16]

During the three years that followed the advent of Gorbachev, this scenario for overcoming the Cold War nevertheless remained by and large what it had been since de Gaulle, i.e., a long-term vision. By 1988, however, its main premise – the Soviet Union's profound evolution – was beginning to gain credence. Hence, in the wake of his reelection to a second presidential term in the spring, Mitterrand decided to vigorously revive France's dormant *politique à l'Est* through a series of high-profile visits to Eastern countries, a decision that was predicated on his belief that Moscow had now renounced the use of force in Eastern Europe.[17] Political developments in Moscow confirmed Mitterrand's intuition. The nineteenth Communist Party of the Soviet Union (CPSU) conference in June and the changes that Gorbachev imposed within the party apparatus over the summer considerably reinforced his internal power, allowing him to make a quantum leap in his 'New Thinking'. By autumn, French diplomacy believed that the USSR had in effect renounced a 'messianic' foreign policy based on class struggle applied to international relations in favour of the search for 'the common interests of all mankind'.[18] As seen from Paris, Gorbachev's speech at the United Nations in December 1988 confirmed this, marking a clean break with the 'revolutionary' inspiration of Soviet policy.[19] (Gorbachev's entourage agreed: 'Your UN speech', Anatoly Chernyaev wrote to him, 'brought us to a new level in world politics. Now we can't afford concessions to the policies of the past.'[20]) The changes in Soviet policy in the last months of 1988 were so dramatic that by the early weeks of 1989, French diplomats believed that a forty-year status quo was now in effect drawing to an end. 'Everyone feels', wrote the Quai d'Orsay political director, 'that the organization of Europe born of the Second World War is being replaced by something new although we don't know clearly where we are going'.[21] The time had come to effectively look beyond 'Yalta'.

Before the Wall: Mitterrand's Vision in 1989

By the early months of 1989, therefore, it was clear to President Mitterrand and French diplomacy that the Cold War was drawing to an end and a new era was in the making. The Gaullist-Mitterrandian vision, in other words, was beginning to be validated by events. As a result, what had been, during the past twenty-five years or so, a long-term, hypothetical perspective was in essence becoming a medium-term, plausible scenario – although it was clearly not yet a short-term political reality. So what was Mitterrand's script for overcoming 'Yalta' in the months preceding the dramatic events of the autumn of 1989? What were the French expectations or assumptions regarding the ongoing evolutions in the East? What were their preferred Western responses to these evolutions? And how, as seen from Paris, would East-West relations move from conflict to cooperation and to a new European order?[22]

More than ever, ending the Cold War was premised, in French eyes, on the continued transformation of Soviet policies. By early 1989, this seemed to be a safe bet. The Quai d'Orsay predicted that the evolutions that had been triggered in Moscow in 1988 would be 'prolonged' and even 'amplified' the following year.[23] This, in turn, made an acceleration of change in Eastern Europe likely. By spring 1989, the French believed that the old 'status quo' had now been replaced by increased 'fluidity' inside the Soviet sphere and that this tendency could but intensify in the near future.[24] Mitterrand's 1981 prediction seemed confirmed: 'The Soviet empire', he assured U.S. President George H. W. Bush in May, will 'unravel'.[25] Yet Mitterrand's vision of the future evolution of Eastern Europe was not one of a radical rupture. Of course, by 1989 the French president was convinced that the end of 'Yalta' would come about primarily as a result of the generalization of the democratic process already under way in countries like Hungary and Poland (which, he suggested, might become associate members in the Council of Europe).[26] But he also seemed to assume that in the foreseeable future these countries would remain somehow 'socialist' in socio-economic terms and that they would wish one way or another to remain linked to the Soviet Union in geopolitical terms. This might take place within a revamped, 'politicized' Warsaw Pact in which they would regain their full international sovereignty (by spring 1989, Gorbachev's all but complete refutation of the 'Brezhnev doctrine' seemed to validate this scenario).[27] Poland, where Mitterrand paid a visit in mid-June – in between the two rounds of the first free elections held in that country since 1947 – seemed to offer the best illustration of what the French president considered the right mix between internal democratization and geopolitical continuity: the transition in Poland, Mitterrand told General Wojtech Jaruzelski, 'took facts into account, but in order to change them'.[28]

In 1989 the Mitterrandian vision of the future of East-West relations beyond 'Yalta', therefore, was one of a smooth rapprochement between the two halves of the divided continent, and not one of a rapid and dramatic collapse of the post-1945 European order. In geopolitical terms, the Elysée wagered on a progressive effacement of the logic of military blocs (thanks in particular to the pursuit of disarmament), but not on a complete disappearance of the dividing line between the military alliances, at least in the short or medium term.[29] In political and socio-economic terms, the vision was also one of a progressive convergence between the two systems, with Eastern Europe steadily becoming more liberal democratic and Western Europe more social democratic: 'The Eastern countries must make progress toward individual liberties', Mitterrand told the Hungarian leader Karoly Grosz in November 1988, 'and the Western countries must make progress toward collective social liberties'.[30] All this, the French believed, would make it possible to progressively overcome Europe's Cold War divisions in the years and decades to come. The transformations in Eastern Europe and, to begin with, the internal democratization of the former Soviet satellites and their political emancipation from Moscow, the Elysée anticipated, would help restore throughout the continent 'a real fluidity both in political relations between states as well as in contacts of all kinds between individuals', thereby helping to surmount in concrete terms the forty-year division of the continent.[31] Last but not least, these evolutions would create a European context more conducive to the emergence of a practical solution to the German problem. The intensification of rapprochement between East and West, French diplomats believed – a reasoning not unlike that which remained in the background of West Germany's Ostpolitik – would indeed open the way to rapprochement between the two Germanys, which would thus be able to 'surmount if not the political division, then at least the human division from which the German people suffers'.[32]

The Mitterrandian concept for the future evolution of European 'architecture' beyond the Cold War was in accordance with the foregoing. On the pan-European level, the Helsinki process was of course seen as pivotal in the 1989 context. In the short or medium term, the director of political affairs at the Quai d'Orsay noted in the early weeks of the year, 'The pan-European dimension will in all likelihood become more prominent'.[33] The CSCE framework, Mitterrand confirmed in June 1989, was a necessity in order to 'overcome the divisions that separate European nations and truly establish confidence among them'.[34] Yet the CSCE was no panacea. Although it was seen as a useful framework in order to help assuage the logic of blocs thanks in particular to the linkages between its three baskets, French diplomacy remained somewhat fearful of a transformation of the CSCE into a pan-European collective security body, which had long been a traditional Soviet aim. Moreover, by 1989 the CSCE was seen as an inadequate framework for the intensified pan-European cooperation that Mitterrand wanted to encourage in areas such as energy, technology or culture in order to overcome the East-West divide through concrete projects and promote a truly 'European' Europe – i.e., a Europe free of the outside influence of the superpowers. 'The Europe of which we might dream in the long term', his diplomatic adviser Hubert Védrine wrote in November 1988, was 'a Europe at 32 (i.e., Western Europe without the U.S. and Canada plus Eastern Europe without Russia)'.[35] One year before the fall of the Berlin Wall, in a context characterized by Gorbachev's propagation of his own 'common home' concept, Mitterrand and his entourage were already thinking along the lines of what would become the 'European confederation' proposal of 31 December 1989.[36]

Yet by 1989 the Western European dimension was no doubt the dominant one in the French vision of European architecture beyond 'Yalta'. 'The Twelve [EC member states]', noted Védrine typically, 'are the best placed to conceive and implement ... a regular, constant and smooth reestablishment of links between the two Europes'.[37] For French diplomacy, it was up to the EC to foster the 'gradual rapprochement' between Western and Eastern Europe and thus to serve 'as magnet to the various parcels of a Soviet Empire on its way to being Ottomanized'. The EC was also seen as the most appropriate framework for the gradual rapprochement between the two Germanys: 'Managing the German problem', the Quai underlined, meant first of all 'tying the Federal Republic strongly to the Community, with Franco-German relations being the privileged means' to that end.[38] Overall, therefore, a strong European Community appeared to Mitterrand's diplomacy on the eve of the events of the autumn as the key condition of a stable transition toward post–Cold War Europe. Inversely, the end of 'Yalta' was perceived as an opportunity to make the EC the cornerstone of a Europe beyond blocs. 'Pursuing the construction of the Europe of Twelve and working to re-establish the unity of our continent', in short, were 'two projects that, far from being opposite, complement[ed] and reinforce[d] each other'.[39] The bottom line was clear: as seen from Paris, the strengthening of the EC and of its cohesion had become 'an absolute priority'.[40]

Clearly, Mitterrand and his advisors saw the ongoing transition as a progressive, incremental process. Although the overcoming of 'Yalta' had certainly become a shorter-term possibility in their vision than it had been years or even months before, the French did not visualize as rapid a departure from the status quo as would indeed take place in the autumn of 1989. This was, first of all, a predictive position. For French diplomats, the tendencies that would lead 'from the Europe of today to that of tomorrow' were not likely to yield dramatic results, at least not immediately; rather, they had to be appraised in a 'medium to long term' perspective, i.e., within a ten- to twenty-year period.[41] Mitterrand's own predictions were quite similar, in particular regarding the weakening of the Soviet Union and the intra-German rapprochement and their respective paces (in his view, those two processes were closely interrelated). Reiterating to Bush in May 1989 his conviction that the Soviet empire would sooner or later collapse and that this would make German unification possible, he estimated that these two events 'would not happen in the next ten years' and emphasized that 'the USSR will not accept [German unification] as long as it remains strong'.[42] Yet this was also a prescriptive position. For Mitterrand's diplomacy, the end of the Cold War in Europe was indeed a desirable perspective, but it also carried the danger, if poorly managed, of a return of instability in the East, not least as a consequence of a return of ethnic conflict: 'One may wish the desegregation of the [Soviet] empire, which should not last very long', he declared in July 1988, 'but one may also fear the consequences'.[43] By 1989, French diplomacy was both upbeat about the intensification of change in the East and wary of it gaining too much pace: 'we have no interest in an excessive acceleration', the Quai d'Orsay believed.[44]

The Fall of the Wall and the 'Acceleration of History'

Yet, starting in the summer of 1989, a dramatic acceleration did occur. The GDR refugee crisis, which culminated in September, marked a turning point. To be sure, the French continued to believe in the validity of their scenario: the 'extraordinary events' that were unfolding, Védrine wrote in September against the backdrop of the refugee crisis, announced 'the progressive overcoming of Yalta' and the emergence of a 'greater Europe' through a 'continued and controlled evolution in the East'. This evolution, he emphasized, was 'in line with what has happened since 1985', i.e., since the advent of Gorbachev.[45] A month later, in spite of yet another and even more dramatic acceleration in the East signalled by the downfall of Erich Honecker on October 18, his analysis remained essentially in the same vein. True, Védrine wrote, events in East Berlin did confirm the 'inevitability' of the ongoing rapprochement between the two Germanys, but this would in all likelihood remain an open-ended process both in terms of pace (it would take place step by step) and outcome (although the re-creation of a single German state could not be ruled out in the end, other, intermediary solutions for unification were also conceivable). 'Everything would remain manageable', Védrine believed, 'if the process of ending the division of Germany [did] not go faster than the process of European construction and the overall abolition of barriers between Eastern Europe and Western Europe'. European integration, therefore, had to be accelerated and be used as a 'magnet' in order to stabilize Eastern Europe; meanwhile, the military alliances would continue to guarantee European stability for an 'intermediary period' that could well prove to be 'rather long'. 'The issue of the relative rhythms [of these processes]', Mitterrand's strategic advisor concluded pointedly, 'is of the essence'.[46]

Yet the fall of the Berlin Wall on 9 November 1989 – which of course no one had foreseen in Bonn, Washington, Moscow or Paris – shattered all previous assumptions and expectations. Until then, the French had believed that the evolutions in the East were essentially validating their preferred scenario for the end of the Cold War. Now, things were becoming unpredictable. Because of their suddenness and of their magnitude, events contradicted the anticipation of a step-by-step convergence between Europe's two halves that would require years if not decades, rather than the months or weeks that indeed would be the case. Events simply no longer followed the script. Like all other diplomacies – but perhaps even more so, precisely because it had a well-written script – French diplomacy was caught off guard by what amounted to the eruption of the peoples on a scene once dominated by diplomats and statesmen: 'This is a phenomenal acceleration', the head of the European directorate at the Quai d'Orsay commented in the following days, speaking of a 'reawakening of history'.[47]

As seen from Paris, the fall of the Wall and the ensuing events challenged the heretofore privileged scenario for ending the Cold War in at least two important ways. First, the acceleration of events would – from the announcement of Kohl's ten-point plan for German unification in the Bundestag on 28 November 1989 to Moscow's 'green light' in late January 1990 – become even more 'phenomenal', leading to a unified and sovereign Germany on 3 October 1990, i.e., in barely 329 days, according to Horst Teltschik's famous reckoning.[48] This was hardly the kind of 'progressive' scenario that, until the late weeks of 1989, had been anticipated in Paris and elsewhere. Second, the 'rush' toward German unity meant that contrary to earlier French predictions or preferences, the German and the wider European evolutions (meaning in particular Western European integration and the pan-European process) would not be easily reconciled, with the former taking clear precedence over the latter. Mitterrand acknowledged as much in February 1990, confiding to the Italian Premier Giulio Andreotti that Western European integration was but 'a local train' in comparison with the 'express train' of German unification.[49] The 'relative rhythms' of German unification and Europe's transformation, as feared in Paris, had in effect diverged.

One week before the fall of the Berlin Wall, the French president, asked how he felt about the acceleration of events, famously responded that he did not 'fear' German unification: 'I do not ask myself this kind of questions as history moves forward. History is there. I take it as it is', he said, adding that France would 'adapt its policies' accordingly.[50] So how did Mitterrand's diplomacy 'adapt' to the new situation in the critical months that followed the fall of the Wall? Clearly not by trying to slow down, let alone block German unification, as has often – and wrongly – been said.[51] Although the French president did not conceal his nervousness about what he considered to be Kohl's excessive precipitation with regard to German unification, he stuck to the line he had announced publicly as early as July 1989: German unification was legitimate, provided it took

place 'peacefully and democratically'.[52] 'Whether I like it or not, unification is for me a historic reality which it would be unfair and foolish to
oppose', he told Kohl in early January 1990, meanwhile recognizing that
'if [I] were German, I would be in favour of as quick a reunification as
possible'.[53] Mitterrand fully understood that running against the course of
history would destroy the achievement of four decades of Franco-German
reconciliation and European unification. 'I am not saying no to German
reunification. This would be stupid and unrealistic', he told British Prime
Minister Margaret Thatcher at the end of January.[54]

Mitterrand's approach was in fact the opposite of Thatcher's. Rather
than try to slow down unification, French diplomacy, in 1989–90, essentially strove to reconcile the European agenda with the German agenda.
This was done in two ways. The first was to embed German unity within
an international and a European framework in order to manage its geopolitical consequences and ensure its 'pacific' and 'democratic' character:
while 'the national consequences' of German unification were the business of the Germans, 'the international consequences' had to be discussed
in an international framework, Mitterrand told Kohl in February 1990.[55]
To that effect, Paris sought to make the best of the '2 + 4' talks in spring
and summer 1990, insisting in particular on the need to settle the German-
Polish border issue as a prerequisite to German unification.[56] Most of all,
Mitterrand's priority was to firmly anchor a unified Germany in European
and international institutions – particularly, in France's ascending order of
preference, the CSCE, the Atlantic Alliance and, above all, the European
Community – a policy that culminated at the December 1989 European
Council in Strasbourg, when the French president obtained the German
chancellor's definitive acceptance of the Economic and Monetary Union
(EMU) project and the insurance that a unified Germany would thus remain tightly integrated into the EC.[57]

Inversely, Mitterrand was determined to promote his vision of the post-
'Yalta' organization of the continent beyond German unification, a vision
that of course had European integration at its core. This effort culminated,
in the spring of 1990, in a fresh Franco-German impulse to relaunch European construction, leading to the signing of the Maastricht treaty some
eighteen months later. This was a direct consequence of German unification, and of Mitterrand's and Kohl's determination to build on its momentum in order to promote their long-standing European objectives and
to 'face up to [their] joint responsibility with regard to European unification'.[58] Maastricht was thus the endpoint of France's management of the
transition toward a post–Cold War European order. It was, Mitterrand
commented, 'one of the most important events of the past half century'
and one that 'prepares the next century'.[59]

To be sure, France's vision was only partially fulfilled in the following decade. The Maastricht treaty notwithstanding, Europe after 'Yalta' was not – at least not yet – what the French had imagined and wished for. The failure of Mitterrand's European confederation project in spring 1991 was an illustration. Announced in December 1989, the project was premised on the anticipation that the convergence between the two halves of the divided continent would be progressive and that the post–Cold War order would be fixed around a Western Europe that would become its cornerstone. It collapsed because Eastern and Central European countries were now intent on joining Western institutions (European or Atlantic) as quickly as possible.[60] Another setback was the limited rebalancing of the transatlantic relationship that French diplomacy was able to obtain in the immediate aftermath of the end of the Cold War. The demise of the Soviet empire and indeed of the USSR did not lead, at least not immediately, to an American disengagement from the old continent, as anticipated since de Gaulle. Yet in hindsight, the decisions made in 1989–91 eventually opened the way to the sort of post–Cold War Europe that had been envisaged in Paris since the 1960s. Since 11 September 2001, the U.S. has effectively begun to disengage from the Old Continent. Meanwhile the European Union, now with twenty-seven member states, has emerged as the privileged framework for the reunification of Europe at large. In retrospect, then, those decisions – Maastricht to begin with – have laid the groundwork for today's Europe, in some ways vindicating the vision of a 'European' Europe that had been at the centre of French diplomacy for decades.

Notes

1. For a general discussion, see F. Bozo. 2007. 'Mitterrand's France, the End of the Cold War and German Unification: A Reappraisal', *Cold War History*, 7(4), 455–478.
2. See F. Bozo. 2005. *Mitterrand, la fin de la guerre froide et l'unification allemande. De Yalta à Maastricht* Paris: Odile Jacob. (Published in English as *Mitterrand, The End of the Cold War, and German Unification*, New York: Berghahn, 2009.)
3. For an analysis of de Gaulle's Cold War policies and post–Cold War vision, see F. Bozo. 2010. 'France, "Gaullism", and the Cold War', in M.P. Leffler and O.A. Westad (eds), *Cambridge History of the Cold War*, vol. 2, Cambridge: Cambridge University Press.
4. Mitterrand's New Year address, 31 Dec. 1981, *Politique étrangère de la France*, Nov.–Dec. 1981, 85.
5. F. Mitterrand. 1996. *De l'Allemagne, de la France*, Paris: Odile Jacob, 12–13.
6. Minutes of the meeting between Mitterrand and Schmidt, Latché, 7 Oct. 1981, private papers.
7. Jean-Michel Gaillard, handwritten note for Hubert Védrine, undated (May 1981), Archives nationales (AN), 5AG4/11386.

8. Minutes of the meeting between Mitterrand and Reagan, Washington, 22 and 23 Mar. 1984, private papers.
9. Minutes of the meeting between Mitterrand and Kohl, Paris, 14 Oct. 1982, private papers.
10. Pierre Morel, note pour Monsieur le Président, 'Le sommet de Versailles, le sommet de Bonn et les relations Est-Ouest', 1 June 1982, AN, 5AG4/2266.
11. Minutes of the meeting between Mitterrand and Reagan, Washington, 22 and 23 Mar. 1984, private papers.
12. Hubert Védrine, note pour le président de la République, 'Obsèques de M. Tchernenko', 12 Mar. 1985, private papers.
13. Record of the council of ministers, 14 Mar. 1985, private papers.
14. Minutes of the meeting between Mitterrand and Gorbachev, Paris, 2 Oct. 1985, private papers.
15. Minutes of the meeting between Mitterrand and Gorbachev, Paris, 4 Oct. 1985, private papers.
16. F. Mitterrand. 1986. *Réflexions sur la politique étrangère de la France*, Paris: Fayard.
17. P. Favier and M. Martin Roland. 1996. *La Décennie Mitterrand*, vol. 3, Paris: Seuil, 167.
18. Ministère des affaires étrangères (MAE), Centre d'analyse et de prévision, note, 'Entretiens de planification franco-soviétiques', 29 Sept. 1988, Archives diplomatiques (AD), Europe 1986–1990, URSS, box 6674.
19. MAE, Sous-direction d'Europe orientale, note, 'Discours de M. Gorbatchev devant l'AGNU', 7 Dec. 1988, AD, Europe 1986–1990, URSS, box 6649.
20. A. S. Chernyaev. 2000. *My Six Years with Gorbachev*, University Park: Penn State University Press, 148.
21. MAE, le directeur des affaires politiques (B. Dufourcq), note, 'De l'Europe d'aujourd'hui à celle de demain', 20 Feb. 1989, AD, Directeur politique, box 305.
22. For analysis of Mitterrand's vision on the eve of the dramatic events of 1989, see Bozo, *Mitterrand*, 94–102.
23. MAE, Direction d'Europe, Le directeur adjoint, note, 'Visite officielle de M. Qian Qichen', 3 Jan. 1989, AD, Europe 1986–1990, box 6097.
24. MAE, Direction d'Europe, sous-direction d'Europe orientale, note, 'L'URSS et ses alliés est-européens', 8 Mar. 1989, AD, Europe 1986–1990, box 6092.
25. Minutes of the meeting between Mitterrand and Bush, Kennebunkport, 21 May 1989, private papers.
26. Mitterrand's address on the fortieth anniversary of the Council of Europe, 5 May 1989, *Politique étrangère de la France*, May–June 1989, 8–11.
27. On this see Bozo, *Mitterrand*, 95–96.
28. Minutes of the meeting between Mitterrand and Jaruzelski, Warsaw, 14 June 1989, private papers.
29. 'Argumentaire à propos de la visite de François Mitterrrand en Tchécoslovaquie', Dec. 1988, private papers.
30. Minutes of the meeting between Mitterrand and Grosz, Budapest, 18 Nov. 1988, private papers.
31. 'Argumentaire', Dec. 1988, private papers.
32. MAE, le directeur des affaires politiques, note, 'De l'Europe d'aujourd'hui', 20 Feb. 1989.
33. MAE, le directeur des affaires politiques, note, 'De l'Europe d'aujourd'hui', 20 Feb. 1989.
34. Mitterrand interview with *Moscow News*, 1 June 1989, private papers.
35. Hubert Védrine, note pour le président de la République, 19 Nov. 1988, private papers.

36. On this see F. Bozo. 2008. 'The Failure of a Grand Design: Mitterrand's European Confederation (1989–1991)', *Contemporary European History*, 17(3), 391–412; and M.- P. Rey. 2004. '"Europe is our Common Home": A Study of Gorbachev's Diplomatic Concept', *Cold War History*, 4(2), 63–65.
37. Hubert Védrine, note pour le président de la République, 6 Apr. 1989, private papers.
38. MAE, le directeur des affaires politiques, note, 'De l'Europe d'aujourd'hui', 20 Feb. 1989.
39. MAE, dossier de synthèse, 'a.s. Visite de M. Gorbatchev (4–6 juillet 1989)', AD, URSS, Europe 1986–1990, box 6685.
40. MAE, le directeur des affaires politiques, note, 'De l'Europe d'aujourd'hui', 20 Feb. 1989.
41. MAE, le directeur des affaires politiques, note, 'De l'Europe d'aujourd'hui', 20 Feb. 1989.
42. Minutes of the meeting between Mitterrand and Bush, Kennebunkport, 21 May 1989.
43. Transcript of a meeting of the Defence council, 20 July 1988, private papers.
44. MAE, le directeur des affaires politiques, note, 'De l'Europe d'aujourd'hui', 20 Feb. 1989.
45. Hubert Védrine, note pour le président de la République, 13 Sept. 1980, private papers.
46. Hubert Védrine, note, 'Réflexions sur la question allemande', 18 Oct. 1989, private papers.
47. MAE, note du directeur d'Europe, 'Le réveil de l'histoire', 16 Nov. 1989, AN, 5AG4/7708.
48. See H. Teltschik. 1991. *329 Tage. Innenansichten der Einigung*, Berlin: Siedler.
49. Minutes of the meeting between Mitterrand and Andreotti, Paris, 13 Feb. 1990, private papers.
50. Kohl-Mitterrand joint press conference, Bonn, 3 Nov. 1989, *Politique étrangère de la France*, Nov.–Dec. 1989, 4–6.
51. For an archivally based refutation of the narrative of France's opposition to German unification, see Bozo, *Mitterrand*, and 'Mitterrand's France'.
52. Interview with five European newspapers, 27 July 1989, *Politique étrangère de la France*, Jul.–Aug. 1989, 78–82.
53. Gespräch des Bundeskanzlers Kohl mit Staatspräsident Mitterrand, Latché, 4. Januar 1990, in H. J. Küsters and D. Hofmann (eds.). 1998. *Deutsche Einheit. Sonderedition aus den Akten des Bundeskanzleramtes 1989/90*, Munich: R. Oldenburg, 682–690.
54. Minutes of the meeting between Mitterrand and Thatcher, 20 Jan. 1990, private papers.
55. Gespräch des Bundeskanzlers Kohl mit Staatspräsident Mitterrand, Paris, 15. Februar 1990, in Küsters and Hofmann, *Deutsche Einheit*, 851–2.
56. On this, see F. Bozo, *Mitterrand*, 212ff.
57. On this, see F. Bozo. 2008a. 'France, German Unification, and European Integration', in F. Bozo, M.-P. Rey, L. Nuti and N.P. Ludlow (eds), *Europe and the End of the Cold War: A Reappraisal*, London: Routledge.
58. J. Bitterlich. 1998. 'In memoriam Werner Rouget. Frankreichs (und Europas) Weg nach Maastricht im Jahr der deutschen Einheit', in W. Rouget (ed.), *Schwierige Nachbarschaft am Rhein: Frankreich-Deutschland*, Bonn: Bouvier.
59. Interview on TF1, 15 Dec. 1991, *Politique étrangère de la France*, Nov.–Dec. 1991, 151–158.
60. On this see Bozo, 'The Failure of a Grand Design'; and V. Mastny. 2008. 'Eastern Europe and the Early Prospects for EC/EU and NATO Membership', in Bozo et al., *Europe and the End of the Cold War*.

Chapter 20

VISIONS OF ENDING
THE COLD WAR
Triumphalism and U.S. Soviet Policy in the 1980s

Beth A. Fischer

Just as there are many explanations about why the Cold War began, there are various points of view about why the Cold War ended. Some have argued that Washington was largely irrelevant, as Mikhail Gorbachev drove the process of ending the conflict. Others maintain that the United States was an impediment, slowing down the process through hard-line policies, the Strategic Defense Initiative and a flat-footed response to Gorbachev's initiatives.[1] In the United States the dominant view is that the Reagan administration brought about the end of the Cold War by forcing the Soviet Union to surrender and, ultimately, collapse. This perspective is frequently referred to as 'triumphalism'. In this view, the Reagan administration intended to defeat the Soviet Union through a combination of tough rhetoric and a renewed arms race. The Soviet Union would not be able to match this newfound American strength, Reagan officials reasoned, and would be forced to concede. In the triumphalist view, Reagan's greatest success actually came after he left office – on 25 December 1991, when the Soviet Union lowered its flag for the last time.[2]

Triumphalism has become a dominant narrative in the United States. But to what extent is it historically accurate? A careful consideration of this question is beyond the scope of a single chapter. In keeping with the theme of this volume, then, this chapter will focus on the Reagan administration's views on superpower relations during the 1980s. Did the Reagan White House set out to vanquish the USSR? Does triumphalism accurately explain the intentions of the Reagan administration?

Notes for this chapter begin on page 306.

Reagan's Views on Soviet Sustainability

In 1977 Ronald Reagan famously commented to Richard Allen, 'My idea of American policy toward the Soviet Union is simple, and some would say, simplistic. It is this: We win and they lose.'[3] In fact, Reagan's views were more complex than his quip suggested.

Reagan had long believed that the Soviet system was not sustainable. A government that systematically suppressed human freedom carried the seeds of its own demise, he reasoned. Ultimately, Soviet citizens would rebel against economic, political and social repression. While Reagan did not indicate that the collapse of the Soviet system was imminent, throughout the 1970s and 1980s he seemed to be thinking about such a geopolitical earthquake to a greater extent than many so-called 'foreign policy experts'.[4] 'Communism is neither an economic or a political system – it is a form of insanity', Reagan asserted during a May 1975 radio address that he wrote himself. '[It is] a temporary aberration which will one day disappear from the earth because it is contrary to human nature.'[5]

In another address that year, Reagan contended that the Achilles heel of the Soviet system was its economy and questioned whether the sale of American grain to the USSR was in the best interest of the West. 'If we believe the Soviet Union is hostile to the free world … then are we not adding to our own danger by helping the troubled Soviet economy?' Reagan asked. 'Are we not helping a Godless tyranny maintain its hold on millions of helpless people? Wouldn't those helpless victims have a better chance of becoming free if their slave masters' regime collapsed economically?' Reagan concluded, 'Maybe there is an answer. We simply do what's morally right. Stop doing business with them. Let their system collapse but in the meantime buy our farmers' wheat ourselves and have it on hand to feed the Russian people when they finally become free.'[6] Two years later Reagan reiterated his view that the USSR could fall from within. 'The Soviet Union is building the most massive military machine the world has ever seen and is denying its people all kinds of consumer products to do it', he explained. 'We might have an unexpected ally if citizen Ivan is becoming discontented enough to start talking back. Maybe we should drop a few million typical mail order catalogues on Minsk and Pinsk and Moscow to whet their appetites.'[7]

Before becoming president, Reagan had also suggested that the arms race might ultimately bankrupt the Soviet Union. In a September 1979 radio address condemning the second Strategic Arms Limitation Treaty (SALT II), Reagan asked, '[W]hich is worse?… An unrestrained arms race which the US could not possibly lose given our industrial superiority, or a treaty [SALT II] which says that the arms race is over and that we have lost it.' Reagan's remark implied that one way to win the Cold War would be to step up the arms race, although it is uncertain whether he was actually calling for such a course of action.[8]

Once in the White House, Reagan's personal views about the weakness of the Soviet system found their way into policy statements, particularly during his first term. 'The West won't contain communism, it will transcend communism', Reagan asserted during a 1981 commencement speech. 'It will dismiss [communism] as some bizarre chapter in human history whose last pages are even now being written.'[9] During an address to the British parliament the following year, the president predicted that 'the march of freedom and democracy ... will leave Marxism-Leninism on the ash heap of history'.[10]

He also held fast to his views that the Soviet economic system was unsustainable. The president recalled in his memoirs that in 1982,

> I had been given a briefing on the astonishing Soviet arms build up, which left me amazed at its scale, cost, and breadth and the danger it posed to our country.... Several days later, I had another briefing, this time on the Soviet economy. The latest figures provided additional evidence that it was a basket case, and even if I hadn't majored in economics in college, it would have been plain to me that Communism was doomed as a failed economic system. The situation was so bad that if Western countries got together and cut off credits to it, we could bring it to its knees. How could the Soviets afford their huge arms build up?[11]

'President Reagan just had an innate sense that the Soviet Union would not, or could not survive', recalled Secretary of State George Shultz after leaving office. 'That feeling was not based on a detailed learned knowledge of the Soviet Union; it was just instinct.'[12]

Advisers' Views on Soviet Strength

Despite the president's strong beliefs, there was no consensus within the executive branch regarding the strength of the Soviet Union. On the one hand, there was great concern about Soviet military capabilities. Members of the administration repeatedly argued that the Soviet Union had been engaged in an unequalled military build-up as part of a quest for world domination. The Soviets had even attained military superiority, some suggested. Analyses from the Central Intelligence Agency (CIA) were influenced by this concern and contributed to it in turn. Throughout the early 1980s the CIA overemphasized most dimensions of the Soviet military threat.[13] Douglas MacEachin, director of the Office of Soviet Analysis in the CIA between 1984 and 1989, has recalled that the agency overestimated both the accuracy of Soviet missiles and the quality of their equipment.[14]

On the other hand, the administration was aware of weaknesses in the Soviet economy and health care systems, as well as social unrest within the Eastern bloc. However, it was uncertain as to the magnitude or meaning of these problems.[15] During the early 1980s, the CIA characterized the problem as one of slow economic decline rather than crisis.[16] Fritz Ermath, the former chairman of the National Intelligence Council, recalls that the CIA did not recognize the heavy toll that defence spending was taking on the Soviet economy until 1985, 'a date that was embarrassingly late'.[17]

Many members of the administration dismissed Moscow's economic problems, finding it incomprehensible that the superpower could not overcome them. '[T]he principal figures [in the Reagan administration] – Al Haig notably – had cut their teeth at a time when the prevailing view in the United States was that even if the Soviet Union had a dysfunctional economy, it still had sufficient capital resources to waste them forever and still be quite powerful', Robert McFarlane, Reagan's national security advisor from 1983 to 1985, recalled in 1998. 'And so, even in the beginning of the 1980s national security thinking was quite driven by the view that it didn't matter if the Soviet Union was totally chaotic, that it was so wealthy that it could go on forever. [This was] an underlying premise of détente.'[18] The president disagreed with his advisers' assessments, however. 'Reagan had a very different view', McFarlane explained. 'He didn't subscribe to that notion and instead believed that a more aggressive – well, that's the wrong word – a more energetic competition could impose such burdens as to bring down the Soviet Union.... [H]owever, many in his own Cabinet at the time didn't agree with him.'[19] MacEachin elaborates,

> [B]asically two views existed [within the Reagan administration]. One was 'Oh well, the old Stalinist methodology ... will enable this thing to be kept in the box [i.e., under control].' Another argument was 'Sooner or later it's going to have to be confronted by the political leadership, but when is not certain and the result is not certain.' That was where we kind of stood on the eve of Gorbachev's election [in 1985].[20]

Despite the president's suspicions regarding the sustainability of the Soviet system, the Reagan administration did not aim to bring about the collapse of the USSR. The notion that the Reagan administration planned to bankrupt or destroy the Soviet Union is misguided.

To be sure, between 1981 and 1983, the administration had a hard-line approach to the Soviet Union. Reagan officials insisted that the Soviet Union posed a grave and growing military threat, and focused on addressing this perceived vulnerability through the largest peacetime military build-up in U.S. history. Such a build-up was necessary to correct a perceived imbalance and to better counter Soviet expansionism, they reasoned. 'We maintain peace through our strength', the president explained. '[W]eakness only invites aggression.'[21] 'Peace through strength' was the president's mantra. However, there was little else of substance to U.S. policy during this period. Owing to organizational battles, ideological rifts and a pressing economic agenda, U.S. policy was little more than a military build-up combined with belligerent public statements. The priority – to the extent that there was one – was to rebuild American strength and resolve.

By 1983 the military build-up was taking hold, yet relations between the superpowers had seriously deteriorated. The arrival of U.S. Pershing missiles in Europe that autumn led the Soviets to storm out of all ongoing arms talks and at the same time invigorated peace activists in Europe. The year ended on a note of fear and loathing. 'The second cold war has begun', proclaimed the Italian newsweekly *Panorama*. French President Francois Mitterrand, warned that the situation was as grave as the Cuban Missile Crisis of 1962.[22] The Vatican even tried to mediate the growing rift between the superpowers. After a visit to Washington, however, the Vatican secretary of state was pessimistic. 'I do not believe that reaching very conciliatory results is possible', he solemnly concluded.[23]

Seeking Cooperation and Disarmament

As has been well documented, in January 1984 the Reagan administration shifted to a far more cooperative approach to the Soviet Union.[24] President Reagan unveiled the new policy in a 16 January 1984 address. 'I believe that 1984 finds the United States in its strongest position in years to establish a constructive and realistic working relationship with the Soviet Union', the president began.

> We must and will engage the Soviets in a dialogue as serious and constructive as possible, a dialogue that will serve to promote peace in the troubled regions of the world, reduce the level of arms, and build a constructive working relationship.... There is no rational alternative but to steer a course which I call credible deterrence and peaceful competition; and if we do so, we might find areas in which we could engage in constructive cooperation.... [We must] establish a better working relationship with each other, one marked by greater cooperation and understanding.... [W]e want more than deterrence; we seek genuine cooperation; we seek progress for peace.

The president's calls for constructive cooperation and the reduction of nuclear arsenals became the dominant themes in U.S. policy. Over and over again, the administration called for a better working relationship. These remarks were not simply for public consumption. The administration worked behind the scenes to underscore its desire to improve superpower relations. For example, in December 1983 President Reagan wrote a letter to Soviet leader Yuri Andropov in which he called attention to the cooperative tone of his upcoming address. 'I continue to believe that despite the profound differences between our two nations, there are opportunities – indeed a necessity – for us to work together to prevent conflicts, to expand our dialogue, and to place our relationship on a more stable and constructive footing', Reagan wrote. '[W]e do not seek to challenge the security of the Soviet Union and its people.'[25] Since the president's letters to his Soviet counterparts were the only confidential channel of communication between the two capitals, the administration had hoped that this letter would underline American intentions to improve relations.

When Andropov passed away six weeks later, Reagan immediately wrote a letter to his successor, Konstantin Chernenko, reiterating the same themes. 'Chairman Andropov had written to me on January 28, 1984 about the Soviet Government's concern for world peace and your willingness to pursue dialogue', Reagan began. 'I believe that this dialogue is so important that we should proceed with it as soon as your government is ready to do so.' The letter continued:

> As I made clear in my January 16 address, I have no higher goal than the establishment of a relationship between our two great nations characterized by constructive cooperation. Differences in our political beliefs and in our perspectives on international problems should not be an obstacle to efforts aimed at strengthening peace and building a productive working relationship. Indeed, in the nuclear age, they make such efforts indispensable.... Let me conclude by seeking to lay to rest some misunderstandings which may have arisen. The United States fully intends to defend our interests and those of our allies, but we do not seek to challenge the security of the Soviet Union and its people. We are prepared to deal with you in a manner that could establish the basis for mutually acceptable and mutually advantageous solutions to some of our problems.[26]

The president's aim was to engage the USSR, not to destroy it. Jack Matlock, the director of Soviet Affairs on the National Security Council (NSC) Staff at the time, recalled, '[T]he president's speech of January 16, 1984 set forward the parameters on which the Cold War was eventually eliminated. What we envisioned at that time was a process which we hoped conceivably could end in the end of the Cold War, but we couldn't be confident that it would.'[27]

Moreover, Reagan officials have repeatedly rejected the notion that they were seeking to vanquish or bankrupt the Soviet Union. Officials recall that they recognized Moscow's economic difficulties and sought to place pressure on these weaknesses. However, they deny that the administration was consciously seeking to defeat the Soviet Union. 'We imposed costs [on the Soviet Union], and put pressure on them through the USIA [US Information Agency] and so forth', McFarlane explained in 1995. 'But 80–90% of what happened to the USSR was because Marxism was a dumb idea. At most the Reagan administration accelerated its decline by 5–15 years.'[28] Jack Matlock agrees that the White House did not aim to bankrupt the Soviet Union. 'I think we recognized the difficulties with the Soviet economy', Matlock recalled in 1998.

> If you're going to negotiate, any rational negotiator tries to position things so your negotiating position will be advantageous.... There was no contradiction whatsoever in bringing pressure to bear on the Soviet system, particularly since we knew they needed to end the arms race [for domestic reasons].... [But] I would say that none of the key players [in foreign policy making] were operating from the assumption that we were going to do the Soviet Union in, or that the purpose of the pressure was to bring them down.... [T]hat's all thinking after the fact. Our goal was always to give the Soviets incentives to bring the Cold War to an end.[29]

Others within the administration have echoed these sentiments. For instance, Richard Pipes, Matlock's notoriously hard-line predecessor at the National Security Council, has explained that the administration was not interested in '"busting the Soviet Union", but rather, "creating difficulties for [the Soviets], and pushing them" in the direction of internal reform. [The White House] intended that, under US pressure "their economic condition" would become "so aggravate[d] that they would undertake reforms." Pipes added that he "didn't expect these reforms to bring down the Soviet Union," but "thought they would lead to very far-reaching changes in the Soviet system and Soviet policy."'[30] Secretary of State Alexander Haig did not think that a policy of 'trying to exploit and exacerbate internal Soviet weaknesses was either viable or wise'.[31] While he believed the Soviet system had serious flaws, he did not share Reagan's view that it was bound to fail, or that it might do so in response to American pressure. Like many others within the administration, Haig believed the superpower would be able to overcome any economic or political difficulties.

Haig's successor agreed. George Shultz favoured a policy of engagement and rejected the notion that the United States could exhaust the Soviet Union. For example, on 19 January 1983 Shultz sent a letter to President Reagan outlining a plan for U.S.-Soviet relations during the coming year. The secretary proposed a strategy for 'an intensified dialogue with Moscow to test whether an improvement in the US-Soviet relationship is possible.' Shultz noted the 'enduring features of US-Soviet competition' and admitted that 'there is no realistic scenario for a breakthrough to amicable relations with the Soviet Union.... If this dialogue does not result in improved US-Soviet relations, the onus will rest clearly on Moscow; if it leads to actual improvement, all the better.' Commenting on the health of the Soviet government, Shultz remarked, 'To be sure, the Soviet system is beset by serious weaknesses. But it would be a mistake to assume that the Soviet capacity for competition with us will diminish at any time during your presidency.'[32] Shultz's remarks indicate that the administration's long-term goal was to improve superpower relations – not to vanquish the Soviet Union. Moreover, the secretary dismissed the idea that the United States was even capable of bankrupting the USSR.

The administration's first definitive statement of its policy towards the Soviet Union also contained no suggestion that the administration sought to force the collapse of the USSR. The document, entitled 'US Relations with the USSR', began by stating that 'US policy toward the Soviet Union will consist of three elements: external resistance to Soviet imperialism; internal pressure on the USSR to weaken the sources of Soviet imperialism; and negotiations to eliminate, on the basis of strict reciprocity, outstanding disagreements.' The document continued that the administration's aim was to 'promote, within the narrow limits available to us, the process of change in the Soviet Union toward a more pluralistic political and economic system.... The US recognizes that Soviet aggressiveness has deep roots in the internal system, and that relations with the USSR should therefore take into account whether or not they help to strengthen this system and its capacity to engage in aggression.'[33] The aim, therefore, was not to weaken the Soviet system, but rather to avoid strengthening it further.

In November 1983 Secretary Shultz began chairing a series of Saturday morning meetings on Soviet policy for senior officials. After the first meeting Matlock jotted down notes summarizing the proceedings. '[T]here was general agreement on American goals', Matlock observed, but 'sharp differences regarding the specific steps that should be taken to reach those goals'. Notably, '[N]obody argued that the United States should try to bring the Soviet Union down. All recognized that the Soviet leaders faced mounting problems, but understood that US attempts to exploit them would strengthen Soviet resistance to change rather than diminish it. President Reagan was in favor of bringing pressure to bear on the Soviet Union, but his objective was to induce the Soviet leaders to negotiate reasonable agreements, not to break up the country.'[34] Ultimately, the group agreed upon three objectives. First, the United States should seek to 'reduce the use and threat of force in international relations'. Second, Washington should seek to 'lower high levels of armaments by equitable and verifiable agreements'. Finally, it should 'establish minimal trust' on a variety of issues. 'Our policy should *not* include the following goals', a document from the proceedings stated. First, 'challenging the legitimacy of the Soviet system'. Second, seeking 'military superiority', and finally, 'forcing the collapse of the Soviet system (as distinct from exerting pressure on Soviets to live up to agreements and abide by civilized standards of behavior.'[35]

Even Secretary of Defense, Caspar Weinberger, one of the more hawkish members of the administration, has suggested that the White House did not seek to force the collapse of the USSR. In explaining the rationale for the administration's military build-up, Weinberger stressed that the aim was to place the United States in a stronger position so as to negotiate arms reductions and peace. 'In order for a negotiation to succeed you have to have something to give up', Weinberger explained in 1995, 'and when the president entered office we had nothing to give up.'[36] As the president said time and again, the motive behind the build-up was to place the United States in a better position so as to negotiate a lasting peace.

To be sure, elements of U.S. defence policy were designed in part to place pressure on Moscow. For example, the primary intent of the U.S. build-up was to correct a perceived military imbalance vis-à-vis the Soviet Union. But there was also the potential side benefit that Moscow might be enticed into a costly build-up of its own, thus increasing the strain on its weak economy. In addition, the Defense Department sought to invest in areas of comparative advantage rather than simply try to match or mimic the Soviet arsenal.[37] However, as Matlock noted earlier, such policies constitute clever negotiating tactics, but they do not add up to a policy intended to bring down the Soviet Union. Moreover, by 1985 the military build-up was running out of steam as both Congress and the American public were no longer willing to support major increases in military expenditures, nor ever-growing arsenals. Any pressure on Moscow was therefore easing.

The Strategic Defense Initiative

Furthermore, the Reagan administration did not introduce SDI for the purpose of bankrupting the Soviet Union, as some triumphalists insist. Its origins lay in the president's antipathy for Mutual Assured Destruction, in which peace was maintained through each superpower possessing the ability to respond to a nuclear strike with a retaliatory nuclear attack of its own. Reagan abhorred nuclear weapons and rejected this 'balance of terror'. Instead, he favoured building defences against a nuclear attack. If such defences could be built, he reasoned, nuclear weapons would become obsolete, thus paving the way for their eventual elimination. SDI was one step towards the president's dream of a nuclear-free world.

When the president introduced SDI in March 1983, he explained his desire to 'break out of a future that relies solely on offensive retaliation for our security' and asked, '[w]hat if free people could live secure in the knowledge that their security did not rest upon the threat of instant US retaliation to deter a Soviet attack, that we could intercept and destroy strategic ballistic missiles before they reached our own soil and that of our allies?' In closing, the president succinctly stated his intentions: it was his hope that SDI research would 'begin to achieve our ultimate aim of eliminating the threat posed by nuclear strategic missiles. This could pave the way for arms control measures to eliminate the weapons themselves. We seek neither military superiority nor political advantage. Our only purpose – one all people share – is to search for ways to reduce the danger of nuclear war.'[38] Reagan reiterated this message in a handwritten note to Gorbachev shortly after the Geneva summit. '[T]he truth is that the United States has no intention of using its strategic defense program to gain any advantage…. Our goal is to eliminate any possibility of a first strike from either side.'[39]

'I was present at many, if not most, of the discussions on [SDI]', Lieutenant General Edward L. Rowny explained in 1998. 'As the archives are opened, I would be greatly surprised if you find any serious talk about [spending the Soviets into the ground] at all. I think it did come up once or twice in passing, but by and large, throughout the period, President Reagan's idea was "Let's defend the people of the United States."'[40]

Most of Reagan's advisers did not share his vision of a nuclear-free world, nor did they believe that a comprehensive defensive system was feasible, much less wise. Initially, most were unenthusiastic about the project. Nonetheless, they came to support it – oftentimes reluctantly – for other reasons. For one thing, Reagan was so wedded to SDI they had no choice but to go along. For another, it offered a solution to a strategic dilemma: the Soviets had far more land-based intercontinental ballistic missiles (ICBMs) than did the U.S., and the Reagan administration did not believe Congress would support a massive American build-up to match the Soviet arsenal. An effective defensive system could render this Soviet advantage meaningless.[41] Finally, Gorbachev's unrelenting objections to SDI led many of Reagan's advisers to conclude that it was a valuable bargaining chip. McFarlane came to view SDI in this manner and hoped Moscow would agree to significant cuts in its arsenal of ICBMs in exchange for restrictions on SDI.[42] Consequently, much of the internal debate over SDI focused on whether and how to trade it away in exchange for Soviet arms reductions.

The president never viewed SDI as a bargaining chip. For Reagan, SDI was about protecting the American people, pure and simple. 'I met with George Shultz about the [upcoming Geneva] summit', Reagan noted in his diary on 11 September 1985. 'I sense he and Bud [McFarlane] feel that Defense is going to be uncooperative and not want to settle anything with the Soviets. I can't quite agree on that. One thing I do know is I won't trade our SDI off for some offer of weapons reductions.'[43] A year later the president was still encountering resistance regarding his decision that SDI would not be bargained away. During discussions with his foreign policy advisers in July 1986, Reagan recalled that

> some of our arms control and State Department experts wanted me to hint to the Soviets that we might be willing to trade SDI for greater Soviet concessions on offensive weapons. Cap Weinberger, the chief evangelist, after me, of the strategic Defense Initiative, said that if the Soviets heard about this split in the administration and decided I was wavering on SDI, it would send the wrong signals to Moscow and weaken our bargaining position. I think he was also worried that I might be persuaded by those advocating possible concessions on the SDI, but he needn't have worried. I was committed to the search for an alternative to the MAD policy and said it as emphatically and as often as I could, privately and publicly: *The SDI is not a bargaining chip.*[44]

In fact, President Reagan was so enamoured of the idea of protecting people from a nuclear attack that he repeatedly offered to share SDI technology with the Soviets. Reagan was sincere in these offers, although his Soviet interlocutors did not think so. Aleksandr Bessmertnykh, Gorbachev's aide and eventual Soviet foreign minister, recalls that 'the part about sharing technology, visiting each others' labs and so forth. We didn't trust it. We didn't trust it at all. And all our specialists said that that was absolutely impossible that the Americans would really let us see those things developing in their laboratories. So there was no trust at all about it. It was considered a ploy.'[45] Shultz recalls, 'I remember Gorbachev saying to [Reagan] once, "You won't even sell us milk machines. How can I accept that you are going to [share SDI]?"'[46]

'President Reagan was not only a true believer in SDI, he was definitely a true believer in sharing', Matlock explained in 1993. '[T]his was something that most of the bureaucracy, virtually the entire bureaucracy … said we can't do'.[47] Frank Carlucci, who served as both Reagan's national security adviser and secretary of defense, recalls, '[The president] did, as best I could tell, sincerely believe that he could give [SDI] to the Russians and everything would be fine. And I and others tried to explain to him that technically that just was not feasible. And the only thing that finally convinced him, I remember [was] one day I said to him, "Mr. President, you have just got to stop saying that because Gorbachev, among others, doesn't believe you." And he said, "Well, I guess you are right. He really doesn't believe me." … But it took a number of years to get him to that realization.'[48]

In short, the administration did not embark on SDI for the purpose of causing the Soviet Union to collapse. The president's intent was to protect civilians from nuclear annihilation. This explains his steadfast refusal to abandon or even restrict the project as Gorbachev so often insisted he should. Other members of the administration valued SDI as a bargaining chip. For them, SDI was not a means to bankrupt Moscow but rather something to be traded away in exchange for arms reductions. The bulk of internal discussions about SDI focused on the conditions under which SDI research might be restricted, and how the president might be persuaded to support such a strategy. If the administration's intent had been to use SDI as a means to bankrupt the USSR, there would have been no discussion about trading it away; the plan would have been to move forward with the programme until Moscow conceded. Moreover, if Reagan had been seeking to bankrupt the USSR, he would not have repeatedly offered to share this research with the Kremlin. Sharing this technology would have removed any incentive for Moscow to invest in it itself. Finally, a counterfactual is instructive: if SDI had been cheap, would Reagan have still pursued it? If it held no prospect of placing financial pressure on the USSR, would Reagan still have embraced it? The answer, of course, is 'absolutely'. Even if the program had had no prospect of engaging the USSR in a costly arms race, the president still would have embraced the idea of building a defensive system. For him, SDI was about ending the scourge of MAD, and any other positive benefits would simply be icing on the cake.

Conclusions

What was the Reagan administration's perspective on the ending of the Cold War? Triumphalism maintains that the Reagan administration set out to vanquish the Soviet Union through a hard-line policy based on a costly military build-up and tough rhetoric. In this view, the administration sought to end the Cold War by destroying the Soviet Union, and President Reagan's greatest success was the collapse of the USSR.

However, triumphalism is based on many myths, some of which were considered in this chapter. One fallacy is that the administration actively sought to bankrupt or 'do in' the USSR. Although the president intuitively believed the Soviet system was doomed to fail at some point, there was no consensus on this view within his administration, and most rejected the notion outright. A second triumphalist myth contends that the Reagan administration's hard-line policy brought about the collapse of the USSR. However, Reagan had abandoned this approach by 1984. Beginning in January of that year, the administration sought 'constructive cooperation' with Moscow, which included nuclear disarmament, summit meetings and confidence-building gestures. Thus, it was the ending of the Cold War – not the collapse of the Soviet Union – that was Reagan's real triumph.

Notes

1. For examples, see R.G. Kaiser. 1992. *Why Gorbachev Happened: His Triumph, His Failure, and His Fall*, New York: Simon and Schuster; W.D. Jackson. 1999. 'Soviet Reassessment of Ronald Reagan, 1985–1988', *Political Science Quarterly*, 113(4), 623–624; and C. W. Kegley, Jr. 1994. 'How Did the Cold War Die? Principles for an Autopsy', *Merhson International Studies Review* 38, 14–15. For a longer discussion of these contending views see B.A. Fischer. 2004. 'The United States and the Transformation of the Cold War', in O. Njolstad (ed.), *The Last Decade of the Cold War: From Conflict Escalation to Conflict Transformation*, New York: Frank Cass, 226–240.
2. Examples of triumphalist arguments can be found in P. Schweizer. 1996. *Victory: The Reagan Administration's Secret Strategy that Hastened the Collapse of the Cold War*, New York: Atlantic Monthly Press; C. Weinberger. 1990. *Fighting for Peace*, New York: Warner Books; and R.M. Gates. 1996. *From the Shadows: The Ultimate Insider's Story of Five Presidents and How They Won the Cold War*, New York: Simon & Schuster. The notion that President Reagan had a hard-line policy towards the Soviet Union throughout his two terms in office is one of the fundamental myths of triumphalism. In fact, the president had jettisoned this approach by 1984 and adopted a more conciliatory posture. For more on the many myths surrounding triumphalism, see B.A. Fischer. Forthcoming. *Triumph? The Reagan Legacy and American Foreign Policy Today*.
3. R.V. Allen, 'The Man Who Won the Cold War', *Hoover Digest*, 30 Jan. 2000. Available at http://www.hoover.org/publications/hoover-digest/article/7398.
4. For Reagan's views before becoming president see K.K. Skinner, A. Anderson and M. Anderson (eds). 2001. *Reagan, In His Own Hand*, New York: The Free Press.
5. Ibid., 12.
6. Ibid., 31.
7. Reagan, 'Soviet Workers', 25 May 1977, ibid., 146–147.
8. Reagan,'Salt II', 11 Sept. 1979, ibid., 63. Reagan was quoting journalist Ben Stein.
9. R. Reagan, Commencement Address at Notre Dame, 17 May 1981, *Weekly Compilation of Presidential Documents* (*WCPD*) 17, 532.
10. R. Reagan, Speech to Members of the British Parliament, 8 June 1982, *Department of State Bulletin* (July 1982), 27.
11. R. Reagan. 1990. *An American Life*, New York: Pocket Books, 551–552.

12. As quoted in P. Schweizer, *Victory,* xiii.
13. See comments by Raymond Garthoff and Doug MacEachin in S.F. Wells, Jr. 2003. 'Reagan, Euromissiles, and Europe', in E. Brownlee and H. Graham (eds), *The Reagan Presidency: Pragmatic Conservatism and Its Legacies,* University of Kansas Press, 139. See also R.L. Garthoff. 1994. *The Great Transition: American-Soviet Relations and the End of the Cold War,* Washington, DC: Brookings Institution, 504–508.
14. Ibid.
15. For example, see NSDD-32, 20 May 1982. National Security Decision Directives are available at the Ronald Reagan Presidential Library in Simi Valley, CA (henceforward RRPL), or online at www.fas.org/irp/offdocs/nsdd.index.html
16. This was not necessarily an inaccurate assessment: some contend that it was Gorbachev's post-1986 reforms that brought the USSR to a crisis point. Absent these reforms, the Soviet Union could have continued in a slow decline for many years.
17. As quoted in Wells, 'Reagan, Euromissiles, and Europe', 139.
18. McFarlane remarks in Nina Tannenwald (ed.), 'Understanding the End of the Cold War, 1980–1987', an oral history conference sponsored by the Watson Institute, Brown University, 7–10 May 1998, 31–32. (Henceforth 'Brown Conference'.)
19. McFarlane in Tannenwald, Brown Conference, 32.
20. Douglas MacEachin in Tannenwald, Brown Conference, 12–13.
21. Ronald Reagan, Address to the Nation, 23 Mar. 1983, *Weekly Compilation of Presidential Documents 1983,* 442–448.
22. G.L. Church, 'Time's Men of the Year', *Time,* 2 Jan. 1984, 8.
23. H. Kamm, 'Vatican Seeks to Mediate US and Soviet Rift', *New York Times,* 5 Dec. 1983, A3.
24. On this more cooperative policy see B.A. Fischer. 1997. *The Reagan Reversal: Foreign Policy Change and the Ending of the Cold War,* Columbia, MO: University of Missouri Press; D. Oberdorfer. 1991. *The Turn: From Cold War to a New Era,* New York: Poseidon Press; Garthoff, *Great Transition.*
25. Reagan letter to Andropov, 23 Dec. 1983. (Draft dated 19 Dec. 1983.) Jack Matlock Collection: Head of State Correspondence (US-USSR, December 1983), Box 25, RRPL.
26. Reagan letter to Chernenko, 11 Feb. 1984. Executive Secretariat, National Security Council: Head of State File, USSR: General Secretary Chernenko, Box 39, Ronald Reagan Presidential Library, Simi Valley, CA.
27. Matlock in Tannenewald, Brown Conference, 85.
28. McFarlane interview with author, 7 July 1995.
29. Matlock remarks in Tannenwald, Brown Conference, 86, 88.
30. Richard Pipes, as quoted in P. Lettow. 2005. *Ronald Reagan and His Quest to Abolish Nuclear Weapons,* New York: Random House, 78.
31. Lettow, *Quest,* 55.
32. George P. Shultz, "US-Soviet Relations," 19 Jan. 1983, memo to President Reagan. In Tannenwald, Brown Conference, Document 2.
33. "US Relations with the USSR," National Security Decision Directive 75, 17 Jan. 1983. All NSDDs from the Reagan years are available at www.fas.org/irp/offdocs/nsdd
34. J. Matlock. 2004. *Reagan and Gorbachev: How the Cold War Ended,* New York: Random House, 75–76.
35. US Policy Guidance, 19 Nov. 1983 as reproduced in Matlock, *Reagan and Gorbachev,* 76. Emphasis in the original.
36. Weinberger interview with author, 31 July 1995.
37. See Richard Halloran's discussion of the Defense Guidance of 1982 in Halloran, 'Pentagon Draws Up First Strategy for Fighting a Long Nuclear War', *New York Times,* 30 May 1982, 12.

38. Ronald Reagan, Address to the Nation on National Security, 23 Mar. 1983, *Public Papers of the Presidents of the United States, Ronald Reagan, 1983,* Washington, DC: Government Printing Office, 1984, 442–443.
39. Reagan letter to Gorbachev, 28 Nov. 1985. National Security Affairs, Head of State File: USSR: General Secretary Gorbachev, Box 40, RRPL.
40. Ed Rowny in Tannenwald, Brown Conference, 63.
41. R.C. McFarlane, 'Consider What Star Wars Accomplished', *New York Times,* 24 Aug. 1993.
42. McFarlane in Tannenwald, Brown Conference, 47.
43. D. Brinkley. 2007. *The Reagan Diaries,* New York: Harper Collins, 352.
44. Reagan, *An American Life,* 665–666. Emphasis in original.
45. Bessmertnykh remarks in 'A Retrospective on the End of the Cold War', Oral History Conference sponsored by the Woodrow Wilson School of Public and International Affairs, Princeton University, 26–27 Feb. 1993, Session II, 95. (Henceforth 'Princeton Conference.')
46. Shultz remarks, Princeton Conference, Session II, 54.
47. Matlock remarks, Princeton Conference, Session II, 81–82.
48. Carlucci remarks, Princeton Conference, Session II, 54.

Chapter 21

THE POWER OF IMAGINATION
How Reagan's SDI Inadvertently Contributed to the End of the Cold War

Marilena Gala

The literature of the last decades has tended to characterize the Reagan administration as, above all else, the clear manifestation of a new era in American public discourse.[1] Reaganism has thus been interpreted as marking the beginning of a discontinuous but progressive emancipation from the traditional path the U.S. government had followed since the end of the Second World War on both domestic and international issues. According to most of the recent international historiography, those eight years of Republican dominance remain momentous in American and global history as, on the one hand, they led to the end of the Cold War, and on the other they sanctioned the rise and consolidation of conservatism in the U.S. Indeed, Ronald Reagan's powerful political instinct emerged as the hallmark of an administration that coincided with a real turning point for the whole world, which was eventually freed of a long-lasting bipolar confrontation. Therefore, President Reagan's contribution to the end of the Cold War deserves a careful analysis that emphasizes the role played by his own political credo – to be differentiated from that or those existing elsewhere in his administration – in reshaping U.S. foreign and Soviet policy and contributing to such an utterly unexpected result.

Ever since the mid-1990s, historians and political scientists have been debating the consequences of the Cold War's demise for the future of the international system without stopping to investigate its possible causes, and thus its main initiator. According to the 'Reagan victory school', the U.S. president's assertiveness in the early 1980s, and especially his decision to carry out a massive military build-up, hastened the collapse of the Soviet Union and forced the Soviets to succumb after almost fifty years of contest. This pattern of interpretation seems to imply that Ronald Reagan had a clear scheme to end the Cold War when he entered the White House.[2]

The main alternative approach constitutes almost a mirror image and is based upon the conviction that the only active protagonist of the deep transformations that occurred after 1985 was the Soviet leader Mikhail Gorbachev, whose reform project – labelled 'New Thinking' – reversed Soviet domestic policy as well as its international course of action. In this case, emphasis is placed on an autonomous decision taken by a Soviet leader who had the unprecedented capability – within the Kremlin – of imagining an entirely new world, freed of the zero-sum game the bipolar confrontation had heretofore established.[3]

To work out a synthesis between these two alternative interpretations is beyond the scope of this essay. Rather, its purpose is to investigate the meaning that the nuclear arsenal – as the core of the U.S. military build-up and modernization throughout the early 1980s – acquired in Reagan's beliefs and consequent political decisions. The goal is to figure out if and when the symbolic and material relevance of nuclear weapons had become part of an alternative vision of the future the White House was able to evoke against the perpetuation of the Cold War. In particular, this essay will try to define the importance that Reagan's instinctive refusal of the main tenets of deterrence had for the development of a different vision of strategic matters, which eventually contributed to the end of the Cold War.

Reagan's Dilemma

Reagan's launch of his 'star wars' idea broke with all previous strategic doctrine during the East-West confrontation, based as it had been on the principle of deterrence inherent in containment. Throughout the Cold War, atomic build-up itself had added to mutual fear, starting a process of emancipation from actual military needs that ascribed a sort of 'ontological' value to the nuclear arsenal. In other words, nuclear weapons had become the core of a language both superpowers spoke to regulate their relationship – be it either in terms of claiming a moral superiority and fighting an ideological confrontation, or recognizing the legitimacy of an opponent they had come to perceive as less aggressive, as happened during the period of détente. When Reagan took office, this language gradually changed.

Reagan's election in 1980 was the result of a mounting right-wing tide underway since the mid-1960s, within which anti-communism remained crucial. Yet Reagan's 'conservatism' cannot be easily characterized, as it constituted a synthesis of right-wing ideas difficult to label. On the one hand he kept – in words, more than in deeds – most of the 'old right' stance of deep distrust of the federal government; on the other, he took a militant standpoint in foreign policy, which owed more to neoconservative tenets than to those of the traditional conservative movement.

Reagan brought to the White House a philosophy of history that had not changed over the previous decades, although he effectively managed to carry it over into a new context. In these terms, his optimistic temperament and rhetorical skills made it possible to 'turn right-wing Republicanism into Reaganism'.[4] As a religious man familiar with the Calvinist language of election and predestination, he had made central to his philosophy the belief that America was part of God's progressive plan, standing up for protection of the superior moral objectives of freedom, equality and individualism. One of the images Reagan most liked to evoke when talking about the United States was that of a 'city upon a Hill', to emphasize the exceptional sense of hope that emanated from such a place in a world of darkness.[5] By contrast, the Soviet Union was doomed to collapse, as the message it conveyed to human beings was a big lie.

Because of its intrinsic innocence, America could not be effectively protected against Soviet expansionism and aggressiveness in a situation of strategic parity. Facing an adversary that sought to prevail and defeat freedom and democracy, the United States had to aim at military superiority in order to preserve peace. From this standpoint, Reagan was not a warmonger, but a Cold Warrior who believed in peace through strength.[6] He also rejected the logic of détente as outrageous to American values and principles. In fact, Reagan had harshly criticized the arms control process as it had been conducted over the last decade and in particular the SALT II agreement, which, he argued, had 'allowed the Soviet Union to double their nuclear capacity, giving the Soviets a definite margin of superiority'.[7] Nevertheless, he also possessed a remarkable capacity to imagine a future derived from an uncomplicated reading of international political issues, which enabled him to develop an instinctive vision of Russians and Americans one day living in peace and friendship.

Indeed, the new president was an optimist, as had been shown during the presidential campaign and restated in his inaugural address, which urged Americans to 'believe in ourselves and to believe in our capacity to perform great deeds'.[8] But more than anything else, Ronald Reagan was one of those provincials who 'attempt what sophisticates consider naïve', as Richard Rhodes points out.[9] Over the whole period of his presidency, he remained oblivious to many details his advisers kept setting out in memos he was supposed to read attentively. He never became interested in the minutiae of policy, while he preserved unchanged an ideological stance based on a few firm beliefs that eventually turned out to be his main political strength even in dealing with the Soviets.

As an optimist he believed in an almost mystical power of science, and in U.S. science and technology in particular.[10] As a provincial, he was captured by the idea that U.S. technology could produce the miracle of a ballistic defence missile system that would be thoroughly reliable and provide total protection of U.S. territory from any strategic threat. To him, the Soviet-American nuclear stand-off of mutual assured destruction (MAD) was simply unacceptable because, even after having spent billions of dollars on offensive weapons, the United States remained with no options other than surrender or mutual suicide in the case of a Soviet missile attack. Moreover, MAD implied the acceptance of strategic parity as the principle guiding arms control negotiations between the two superpowers – an idea that Reagan strongly resisted.

According to the president and his main advisers within the National Security Council (NSC), previous administrations had been wrong to think that 'the Soviets, like we, did not want first strike capability'. Therefore, as Reagan made quite clear during the same NSC meeting in April 1982, the United States 'should not have a negotiation position taking an approach linked to SALT'.[11] This meant that the next round of bilateral talks in Geneva, officially opened in June 1982, had to advance on an entirely different course aimed at removing what Washington considered the most destabilizing factor for the strategic balance.

While preparing for the Strategic Arms Reduction Talks (START), the U.S. administration affirmed as part of its national security strategy that the goal 'the United States sets for itself in strategic arms negotiations is to enhance deterrence and to achieve stability through significant reductions in the most destabilizing nuclear systems – ballistic missiles – and especially ICBMs, while maintaining an overall level of strategic nuclear capability sufficient to deter conflict'.[12] If arms control agreements were not an end but merely, as a subsequent National Security Decision Directive confirmed in January 1983, 'an important means for enhancing national security and global stability', negotiations with the Soviets had to be clearly subordinate to the condition that they would 'serve US national security objectives'.[13]

From critics of arms control such as the Committee on the Present Danger, the Reagan administration had inherited the concept that American national security necessarily required a deep reduction of the strategic advantage that the Soviet Union enjoyed in terms of missile throw-weight, because this condition would allow the Soviets to destabilize the strategic balance and even attempt a counter-force first strike against the U.S.

nuclear force.[14] Given that heavy ICBMs had always been the core of the Soviet deterrence capability, however, such a stance entailed an almost un-negotiable proposal at the bilateral discussions in Geneva.[15] As the first crucial stages of negotiations for strategic (and theatre) forces reduction loomed closer, the U.S. president was gradually caught in an inextricable dilemma: on the one hand he had been substituting military pressure for diplomacy, yielding to the one-sided approach to arms control suggested by Assistant Secretary of Defense Richard Perle; on the other, he could not simply forgo any attempt to prevent nuclear holocaust and world destruction.

In fact, as his correspondence with Soviet leaders reveals,[16] Reagan's main motivation in arms control matters since his first months in office was his visceral horror of nuclear war, an outcome he was determined to avert. He had developed the idea that Armageddon was coming and it could not be avoided using deterrence strategies based on a balanced capability of reciprocal annihilation.[17] In other words, the U.S. president could not achieve his ultimate purpose of setting his country and the world free of nuclear threat without urging the Soviets to be cooperative; at the same time, an accommodating attitude towards Moscow contrasted with his Soviet policy – which was grounded on the tenet of inherent Soviet aggressiveness – and openly contradicted by the consequent American military build-up he had decided upon.

Such a dilemma, however, did not produce a dispiriting effect on Reagan; on the contrary, his powerful political instincts eventually overlooked the clear contradiction between the goals he had set and some of their crucial preconditions, and further enhanced the president's determination to reshape American security policy around a seductively strong idea that he was able to present as his own conception: a defensive anti-ballistic system. According to what has become a sort of mythology of Ronald Reagan, the U.S. president had started fostering a deep interest in defensive systems in 1979, after he toured the North American Aerospace Defense Command headquarters in Colorado, where he was told that there was nothing the United States' forces could do to prevent a nuclear missile from hitting its territory.[18] Although there is no reason to believe that this is not a true story, it must be said that the Republican Party platform had included a call to develop an American anti-ballistic missile system in 1980 as an outcome, after the anti-ballistic missile (ABM) treaty was signed in 1972, of a rather well-established opinion among the conservative defence experts that the Soviet Union had already devised a defensive shield to which the United States had to respond in kind.[19]

Still, when Reagan announced that the United States would undertake a programme for research and development of a nationwide, ballistic-missile defence system – subsequently dubbed 'star wars'– he started an entirely new process to mobilize American ingenuity and technical prowess for a grandiose scheme that was bound to affect U.S.-Soviet relations over the next crucial years of bipolar confrontation. In fact, in March 1983, the U.S. president pointed out that he was trying to allow his people to 'live secure in the knowledge that their security did not rest upon the threat of instant US retaliation to deter Soviet attack'. Hence, he went on, 'I'm taking an important first step … to achieve our ultimate goal of eliminating the threat posed by strategic nuclear missiles. This could pave the way for arms control measures to eliminate the weapons themselves'.[20]

SDI: A Programme to Step Up or End the Cold War?

To the American leader, the words solemnly pronounced in March 1983 were not just a declaratory statement; he really meant what he said. Moreover, as for the need to abolish nuclear arsenals, Reagan would reiterate his deep conviction time and again during NSC meetings summoned to discuss and define the administration's line on the so called Strategic Defense Initiative (SDI) and START. Clearly assuming – if not claiming – that the United States was not an aggressive power, in November 1983 he explained that 'if the US is first to have both offense and defense, we could put the nuclear genie back into the bottle by volunteering to eliminate offensive weapons'.[21] This was an objective he felt the United Stated could realistically pursue because Americans 'have never believed that we would find ourselves at war with Russia, except to defend ourselves against attack'. At the same NSC meeting, on 4 December 1984, the U.S. president also noted that 'everything [the Soviets] have says that they are looking at a first-strike'; and, although it was doubtful that Moscow 'had in mind Pearl Harbor', it could be expected that 'they believe that they would be so powerful that they could coerce us into achieving their objectives peacefully'.[22]

Indeed, since entering the White House, Reagan had never ceased to look at the current situation as 'a duel between two gunfighters', and in spite of the fact that the (shared) 'policy of MAD could get us both killed', he was able to note that 'Chernenko and Gromyko had quoted his words supporting the goal of the ultimate elimination of nuclear weapons'.[23] Sticking to this ambitious aim at NSC discussions with his main advisers in mid-December 1984, the U.S. president was to state 'his belief that international control for world protection might be possible at some point with SDI and that SDI would help alleviate the dangers associated with the impossible job of verification'.[24]

However unfeasible the idea of an anti-ballistic defence system to verify compliance with international treaties might have been, it was just one of several hypotheses circulated about the different options theoretically available, were SDI to go ahead. Indeed, the programme Reagan presented to the American public was soon to be exploited for a series of political objectives totally different from the ones the president had announced. Although Reagan eventually managed to ignore all contrary opinions – even those of his secretary of defense, Caspar Weinberger[25] – SDI turned out to be a very useful tool to those in the Pentagon, including Weinberger, who primarily wanted to pursue an American strategic build-up. In fact, the idea of a nationwide defence system promised to be quite helpful in countering the nuclear freeze movement, which sought to promote nuclear disarmament by means of a nuclear arms race stand-off between the two superpowers. Since the nuclear freeze movement further enhanced the risk that Congress would reject the expensive MX programme, the feasibility of which was widely doubted, a research programme that could assure an effective protection against any Soviet missile aggression allowed the U.S. government to achieve a twofold objective: it allayed the fears of those who charged the administration with warmongering and, at the same time, provided a way out of the MX debate, which risked jeopardizing the centrepiece of the American strategic modernization programme.[26] Moreover, other important members of the Reagan administration, like Secretary of State George Shultz, INF negotiator Paul Nitze and National Security Advisor Robert McFarlane, thought that SDI would be a potential bargaining chip in the START negotiations, as Soviets could be persuaded to make significant reductions in their ICBM arsenal in exchange for a promise to restrict the development of SDI. On the other hand, there were those who, like Perle, strongly opposed any arms reduction; for them, to champion the early deployment of a ballistic missile defence would be to undermine any chance of a START agreement, since it would discourage the Kremlin from accepting deep cuts in their nuclear arsenal.[27]

The Reagan administration remained highly inconsistent regarding both the role that SDI would play in U.S. national security policy, and the effects it hoped the policy might have upon the Soviet Union. Thus the National Security Decision Directive 172 of May 1985 affirmed on the one hand that 'the overriding, long-term importance of SDI is that it offers the possibility of reversing the dangerous military trends ... by moving to a better, more stable basis for deterrence, and by providing new and compelling incentives to the Soviet Union for seriously negotiating reductions in existing offensive nuclear arsenals.' On the other hand, the very same directive also focused on a quite different – and much less reassuring in terms of a stable deterrence – aspect of SDI, namely that 'its emphasis [is placed] on options which provide the basis for eliminating the general threat posed by ballistic missiles'.[28]

Indeed, it is undeniable that from a conceptual standpoint, SDI had several shortcomings. Even overlooking analyses that estimated that it would be much cheaper to develop effective means of destroying space-based systems than to develop the systems themselves, 'the net effect of deploying such a system would not be to provide an escape from mutual deterrence, but to make that relationship less stable', because each side would have an incentive to strike first.[29] Nonetheless, Reagan's attachment to SDI could not be undermined by intricate reasoning. His approach was not aimed at elaborating any consistent strategic doctrine but was that of a visionary leader who believes in the power of his visions. He thus intended to lead his country and the whole world away from Armageddon.

In the run-up to the Geneva summit, where he was to meet the new Soviet general secretary, Mikhail Gorbachev, the U.S. president openly declared that he was prepared 'once any of our SDI programs proved out … to tell to the world that we were ready to consult and negotiate on integrating these weapons in a new defense philosophy, and to state that we are ready to internationalize these systems'.[30] This was a statement he was to reiterate and enhance before his Soviet interlocutor later in November, when Reagan plainly spoke of the idea of 'both our governments agreeing that both conduct relevant research and that both share the results of such research'. Gorbachev, who was another provincial, and 'in his own way an idealist determined to push beyond the status quo',[31] countered that 'to a certain extent he could understand the President on a human level; he could understand that the idea of strategic defense had captivated the President's imagination. However, as a political leader he could not possibly agree with the President with regard to this concept.'[32] According to Gorbachev, SDI could 'lead to an arms race in space, and not just a defensive arms race but an offensive arms race with space weapons … harder to verify [which] will feed suspicions and mistrust'. Instead, to Reagan such a programme had the purpose 'to find out if there were a means to stop nuclear missiles. He had said that if such a means existed, the US would share it with other countries so as to make nuclear weapons unnecessary.'[33] The U.S. leader persisted in claiming that the two superpowers had to reduce offensive weapons by 50 per cent 'and to determine if defense was possible. We could then sit down', he went on, 'and decide if deployment was desirable. We would share our findings.' The rather naïve approach shown by President Reagan eventually prompted the Soviet leader not only to reply that he 'felt inappropriate in their conversation to inject banalities more in keeping with press conferences', but also to warn the president 'not to treat the Soviets as simple people'.[34]

In spite of the evident differences that still hampered the negotiation process, in Geneva Reagan and Gorbachev also perceived unexpected and encouraging similarities in their shared willingness to engage in a constructive dialogue with the adversary, which turned out to be crucial to the development of a close human relationship between the two of them. Their first meeting to talk about arms reduction, therefore, marked a turning point in Soviet-American relations and offered an important opportunity to break the long-lasting stalemate in bilateral negotiations. In fact, both leaders really wanted to improve relations and remove the causes of distrust, but an important obstacle remained in their path: no change in U.S.-Soviet relations could disregard the strategic balance that had symbolized, militarily and politically, their reciprocal confrontation over the whole Cold War period.

In order to achieve this goal and promote the deep cuts both Washington and Moscow were now willing to make in their strategic arsenals, Reagan and Gorbachev had to come to terms with the factor of discontinuity that the U.S. president had introduced into the consolidated equilibrium of deterrence. Indeed, it was a factor difficult to defuse or neglect, since it derived from Reagan's stubborn stance, reiterated at the NSC meeting on 3 February 1986, that 'SDI is not for the US alone – we seek a mutual shift from sole reliance on offensive weapons to an offense-defense mix'.[35] From this standpoint, SDI was still 'a strategic necessity and a crucial part of [the U.S.] three part response to the Soviet strategic threat: modernizing [U.S.] retaliatory forces, negotiating deep equitable and verifiable reductions of nuclear weapons, and taking steps now to provide future options for the possible introduction of strategic defenses'.[36]

Because of these premises based on a consolidated pattern of Cold War distrust, which neither the U.S. president nor the Soviet general secretary had yet entirely dispelled when they met again in Reykjavik on 11 and 12 October 1986, agreement on strategic arms control measures proved not to be close at hand. The dramatic proposal the Soviet leader presented in mid-January for liquidating nuclear weapons throughout the world within the next fifteen years[37] – a move that clearly emphasizes Gorbachev's commitment to developing a direct dialogue with his American counterpart so as to turn his own country away from militarism – did not ultimately result in any progress at the negotiation table. Despite the fact that Reagan's opening remarks on the shared ambition 'to see a world without nuclear missiles' looked promising, discussions in Iceland ended up in a plain deadlock. SDI and the related interpretation of the ABM treaty were still the principal bone of contention between the two superpowers: while Gorbachev kept warning of the danger of 'creating new weapons which would destabilize the strategic situation', Reagan responded that 'SDI was

born as an idea which would give a chance to all of us to completely eliminate strategic weapons'.[38] At Reykjavik the abolition of nuclear arsenals
was to remain unreachable. For the Kremlin, both START and INF agreements had to be conditional on the provision that 'the ABM treaty will
be observed during the period of the process of eliminating [those weap-
ons]', a requirement the White House firmly rejected since, according to
Reagan, it would confine research and development to the laboratory and
thus 'destroy the possibility of proceeding with SDI'.[39]

In October 1986 the two superpowers came very close to accomplishing
a historic task. In Gorbachev's own words, Reykjavik was the first time
'the real leaders got together and really talked about important subjects'.[40]
Indeed, as the related memoranda of conversations underline – and Soviet
economic constraints cannot but corroborate – it was the Soviet general
secretary who eventually made the most important concessions and presented the boldest proposal for abolishing nuclear arsenals. In fact, SDI
remained only a temporary obstacle, as Gorbachev – who had feared that
any U.S. defence system would encourage the Soviet military apparatus
to ask for further defence spending in a country that instead needed badly
to implement economic reforms – decided in 1987 to move ahead, overlooking that issue. As Soviet scientists had explained to the Kremlin, any
strategic defence system promised to be highly unreliable and could be
easily countered with a modest increase in national offensive capabilities.
This encouraging analysis, which urged the Soviet leader not to be too
obsessed by the strategic balance, enabled him to announce on 1 March
1987 that negotiations on the so-called Euromissiles would finally proceed
untied from SDI. It was the signal that a thoroughly new era had started:
beginning with a negotiation aimed at eliminating not only intermediate
but also short-range nuclear forces in Europe, the two superpowers were
already on the path leading to the end of the Cold War.

Conclusions

This result – unanticipated by either Reagan or Gorbachev – clearly
stemmed from their shared and stubbornly pursued goal of 'putting the
nuclear genie back into the bottle'. From this standpoint, the two leaders
who (partially) succeeded in their attempt, though equally crucial, cannot
be equally credited with the political risks they were ready to take and
the boldness of challenges each of them posed to an otherwise 'predict-
able' future. As Gorbachev reasonably claimed in a letter he wrote to the
U.S. president in September 1986, just a month before the planned summit
in Iceland, 'it is a fact, after all, that despite vigorous efforts by the So-

viet side we have still not moved an inch closer to an agreement on arms control'.[41]

An international system freed of bipolar confrontation was not necessarily what Ronald Reagan imagined as he strove for the abolition of all nuclear weapons, although his instinctive and relatively uncomplicated approach to international affairs did allow the idea of Americans and Soviets living together in a peaceful future world to emerge from time to time. Once the dialogue had definitely started in Geneva, this opened into a brighter perspective of cooperation to 'make the difference in the future course of world events'.[42] Still, throughout the whole negotiation process he conducted with his Soviet counterpart up to the INF treaty, the U.S. president never entirely escaped from his Cold Warrior mindset, even when he reiterated his offer to share defence system technology with other countries, including the Soviet Union. In fact, this proposal stemmed primarily from Reagan's instinctive refusal of the concept of a national defence based on the theoretical acceptance of holocaust, coupled with his obliviousness and indifference to specific strategic matters. Rather, SDI absolved the U.S. president of the responsibility to take a trustful stance toward the Soviets and work out the dilemma he had been caught in since the first crucial stages of bilateral arms control negotiations. As a matter of fact, it is the very idea of defence inherent in the SDI programme, together with the way such a programme was tenaciously excluded from any genuine negotiations with the Soviets, that shows that Ronald Reagan had not developed a real vision of the end of the Cold War. For Reagan, the elimination of the strategic arsenals and menace did not necessarily entail a consequential demise of the bipolar international system, so American security could not simply depend on the abolition of nuclear arsenals agreed with Moscow, as Gorbachev had proposed in Geneva and Reykjavik.

On the other hand, the White House's commitment to arms control negotiations – up to the point of imagining a world without a nuclear threat – had been significantly strengthened by the possibility of a shift in U.S. defence from a policy based on offensive weapons and the related deterrence to a policy built around the idea of lessening the enormous threat posed by nuclear arms while keeping American technological prowess unchanged. Nonetheless, the SDI programme remained above all a basic shift that the U.S. president inserted in the superpowers' language, whose rules had been consolidating for decades since the Second World War. In this sense, Reagan introduced a momentous change potentially tantamount to imagining – no matter how inadvertently – a transformed international system. The radical alteration of jargon Reagan imposed through his almost dogmatic stance on SDI, therefore, had the essential merit of setting in motion a new process of dialogue where the 'strict' rules of deterrence were to be replaced by a more flexible language the two superpowers could develop together. However, without Gorbachev's willingness to embark upon – and to remain committed to – a new Soviet course, neither Washington nor Moscow would have succeeded in finding a compromise on arms controls and from there proceeded to make history.

Notes

1. The Reagan administration's legacy is the focus of many recent studies; see esp. W.E. Brownlee and H.D. Graham (eds). 2003. *The Reagan Presidency: Pragmatic Conservatism and Its Legacies*, Lawrence: University Press of Kansas; J. Ehrman. 2005. *The Eighties: America in the Age of Reagan*, New Haven, CT: Yale University Press; M. Schaller. 2007. *Right Turn: American Life in the Reagan-Bush Era*, New York, Oxford University Press; S. Wilentz. 2008. *The Age of Reagan: A History 1974–2008*, New York: HarperCollins.
2. One of the most zealous in subscribing this interpretation is P. Schweizer. 1996. *Victory: The Reagan Administration's Secret Strategy That Hastened the Collapse of the Soviet Union*, Boston: Atlantic Monthly; see also A.E. Busch. 1997. 'Ronald Reagan and the Defeat of the Soviet Empire', *Presidential Studies Quarterly*, 27, 451–466; R. Gates. 1996. *From the Shadows: The Ultimate Inside Story of Five Presidents and How They Won the Cold War*, New York: Simon and Schuster; C. Weinberger. 1990. *Fighting for Peace*, New York: Warner Books. For refutations of this account that nonetheless invariably underline the crucial role played by the U.S. president in contributing to the ending of the Cold War, see B.A. Fischer. 1997. *The Reagan Reversal: Foreign Policy and the End of the Cold War*, Columbia and London: University of Missouri Press; J. Matlock. 2004. *Reagan and Gorbachev: How the Cold War Ended*, New York: Random House.
3. See R. L. Garthoff. 2004. 'The US Role in Winding Down the Cold War, 1980–90', in O. Njolstad (ed.), *The Last Decade of the Cold War: From Conflict Escalation to Conflict Transformation*, London: Frank Cass, 179–195; see also: W.D. Jackson. 1999. 'Soviet Reassessment of Ronald Reagan, 1985–1988', *Political Science Quarterly*, 113(4), 617–644.
4. Wilentz, *The Age of Reagan*, 137.
5. To get a sense of Reagan's personality see L. Cannon. 2000. *President Reagan: The Role of a Lifetime*, New York: PublicAffairs.
6. This is one of the theses clearly developed in M. Leffler. 2007. *For the Soul of Mankind: The United States, the Soviet Union and the Cold War*, New York: Hill and Wang, 339–345.
7. R.E. Powaski. 2000. *Return to Armageddon: The United States and the Nuclear Arms Race, 1981–1999*, New York: Oxford University Press, 15. It was not by chance that 32 of the 182 members of the Committee on the Present Danger were appointed to positions in the Reagan administration.
8. J.T. Patterson. 2005. *Restless Giant: The United States from Watergate to Bush v. Gore*, New York: Oxford University Press, 152.
9. R. Rhodes. 2007. *Arsenals of Folly: The Making of the Nuclear Arms Race*, London and New York: Simon and Schuster, 187.
10. Ibid., 179.
11. www.thereaganfiles.com, NSC Meetings, National Security Council Meeting, 21 Apr. 1982, subject: Strategic Arms Reduction Talks.

12. Ronald Reagan Library (hereafter RRL), National Security Decision Directives, box 1, folder NSDDs 31–40, 20 May 1982, NSDD 32.
13. RRL, De Graffenreid Kenneth files, box 91072, folder NSDD 75 operation, 17 Jan. 1983, NSDD 75.
14. The Reagan administration would try to equalize missile throw-weight at a ceiling of about 4 million pounds, since total U.S. throw-weight was about 4.2 million pounds in 1982 and the Soviet Union's was about 11.2; see Powaski, *Return to Armageddon*, 22.
15. For a detailed description of the first phase of the START negotiations, see S. Talbott. 1984. *Deadly Gambits: The Reagan Administration and the Stalemate in Nuclear Arms Control*, New York: Alfred A. Knopf, 209–352.
16. See M. Anderson and A. Anderson. 2009. *Reagan's Secret War: The Untold Story of His Fight to Save the World from Nuclear Disaster*, New York: Crown Publishing Group.
17. Reagan's vision of Armageddon had developed since the time he was in Sacramento; see Cannon, *President Reagan*, 247–249.
18. For the most detailed, though critical, account of SDI program, see F. Fitzgerald. 2000. *Way Out There in the Blue: Reagan, Star Wars and the End of the Cold War*, New York: Simon and Schuster.
19. Wilentz, *The Age of Reagan*, 164.
20. Cited in Leffler, *For the Soul of Mankind*, 158.
21. www.thereaganfiles.com, NSC Meetings, NSC Meeting, 30 Nov. 1983, subject: Strategic Defense Initiative.
22. Ibid., NSC Meetings, NSC Meeting, 4 Dec. 1984, subject: US-Soviet Arms Control Objectives.
23. www.thereaganfiles.com, NSC Meetings, NSC Meeting, 10 Dec. 1984, subject: Discussion of Geneva format and SDI.
24. Ibid., NSC Meetings, NSC Meeting, 10 Dec. 1984, subject: Discussion of Substantive Issues for Geneva.
25. On the Pentagon's first reaction to the idea of launching SDI program, see Fitzgerald, *Way Out There in the Blue*, 196–206 and Powaski, *Return to Armageddon*, 30–31.
26. MX basing mode had been long debated within the NSC, where different possible options were examined; see for example: www.thereaganfiles.com, NSC Meetings, NSC Meeting, 18 Nov. 1982, subject: M-X Basing decision.
27. On the different attitudes about SDI and arms control negotiations existing within the Reagan administration, see Rhodes, *Arsenals of Folly*, 190 and 222–223 and Powaski, *Return to Armageddon*, 34.
28. RRL, National Security Decision Directives, box 1, folder NSDDs 171–180, 30 May 1985, NSDD 172.
29. On the questionable concept of 'enhanced deterrence', see: S.D. Drell, P.J. Farley and D. Holloway. 1984. 'Preserving the ABM Treaty: A Critique of the Reagan Strategy Defense Initiative', *International Security*, 9(2), 51–91.
30. www.thereaganfiles.com, NSC Meetings, NSC Meeting, 20 Sept. 1985, subject: Soviet Foreign Minister Shevardnadze's visit.
31. Rhodes, *Arsenals of Folly*, 187.
32. RRL, Exec. Secret. NSC System files, box 4, folder 8510141, 19 and 20 Nov. 1985, Memorandum of conversation, Reagan-Gorbachev Meeting in Geneva.
33. Ibid.
34. Ibid. Reagan had also repeated 'his inability to comprehend how, in a world full of nuclear weapons, it was so horrifying to seek to develop a defense against this awful threat, how an effort to reduce nuclear weapons could break down because of such an attempt'.

35. www.thereaganfiles.com, National Security Planning Group Meetings, NSPG Meeting, 3 Feb. 1986, subject: Arms Control – responding to Gorbachev.
36. Ibid., NSC Meetings, NSC Meeting, 1 July 1986, subject: Program Briefing on SDI.
37. Rhodes, *Arsenals of Folly*, 218–220.
38. RRL, Exec. Secret. NSC System files, box 6, folder 8690725, 11 and 12 Oct. 1986, Memorandum of conversation, Reagan-Gorbachev Meeting in Reykjavik.
39. Ibid.
40. Rhodes, *Arsenals of Folly*, 271.
41. www.thereaganfiles.com, Letters between Reagan and the Soviet Leaders, 1981 and 1989, letter from General Secretary M. Gorbachev to President Reagan, 15 Sep. 1986.
42. Ibid. Letters between Reagan and the Soviet Leaders, 1981 and 1989, letter from President Reagan to General Secretary M. Gorbachev, 10 Apr. 1987.

BIBLIOGRAPHY

B.F. Abrams. 2004. *The Struggle for the Soul of a Nation: Czech Culture and the Rise of Communism*, Lanham, MD: Rowman and Littlefield

R. Accinelli (ed.). 2006. *Normalization of U.S.-China Relations: An International History*, Cambridge, MA: Harvard University Press

D. Allen, R. Rummel and W. Wessels (eds). 1978. *European Political Cooperation: Towards a Foreign Policy of Western Europe*, London: Butterworth Scientific

H. Alphand. 1977. *L'étonnement d'être: journal, 1939–1973*, Paris: Fayard

M. Anderson and A. Anderson. 2009. *Reagan's Secret War: The Untold Story of His Fight to Save the World from Nuclear Disaster*, New York: Crown Publishing Group

J. Andréani. 2005. *Le Piège, Helsinki et la chute du communisme*, Paris: Odile Jacob

G.A. Andrianopoulos. 1991. *Kissinger and Brzezinski*, Macmillan: London

L. Armand. 1961. *Plaidoyer pour l'avenir*, Paris: Calmann-Lévy

L. Armand and M. Drancourt. 1968. *Le Pari Européen*, Paris: Fayard

V. Aubourg. 2003. 'Organizing Atlanticism: The Bilderberg Group and the Atlantic Institute, 1952–1963', in G. Scott-Smith and H. Krabbendam (eds), *The Cultural Cold War in Western Europe, 1945–1960*, London: Frank Cass, 92–105

———. 2004. 'Le groupe de Bilderberg et l'intégration européenne jusqu'au milieu des années 1960. Une influence complexe', in M. Dumoulin (ed.), *Réseaux économiques et construction européenne. Economic Networks and European Integration*, Brussels: Peter Lang, 411–430

J. Aunesluoma. 2008. 'Finlandisation in Reverse: The CSCE and the Rise and Fall of Economic Détente 1968–1975', in Bange and Niedhart (eds), *Helsinki 1975 and the Transformation of Europe*, New York: Berghahn Books, 98–112

B. Bagnato. 2003. *Prove di Ostpolitik: politica ed economia nella strategia italiana verso l'Unione Sovietica: 1958–1963*, Florence: L. S. Olschki

E. Bahr. 1996. *Zu Meiner Zeit*, Munich: Karl Blessing Verlag

J.A. Baker, III. 1995. *The Politics of Diplomacy: Revolution, War and Peace, 1989–1992*, New York: Putnam

Oliver Bange. 2004. *Ostpolitik und Détente: Die Anfänge 1966–1969* (unpublished manuscript, University of Mannheim)

————. 2008. 'An Intricate Web: Ostpolitik, the European Security System, and German Unification', in Bange and Niedhart (eds), *Helsinki 1975 and the Transformation of Europe*, New York: Berghahn Books, 23–38

————. 2008a. 'Ostpolitik as a Source of Intrabloc Tensions', in M.A. Heiss and S.V. Papacosma (eds), *NATO and the Warsaw Pact: Intrabloc Conflicts*, Kent, OH: Kent State University Press, 106–121

O. Bange and G. Niedhart (eds). 2008. *Helsinki 1975 and the Transformation of Europe*, New York: Berghahn Books

U. Bar-Noi. 2008. *The Cold War and Soviet Mistrust of Churchill's Pursuit of Détente, 1951–1955*, Brighton: Sussex Academic Press

F. Barbagallo. 2006. *Enrico Berlinguer*, Rome: Carocci

F. Barbagallo and A. Vittoria (eds). 2007. *Enrico Berlinguer, la politica italiana e la crisi mondiale*, Rome: Carocci

F. Baudet. 2001. 'The Origins of the CSCE Human Dimension Mechanism: A Case Study in Dutch Cold War Policy', *Helsinki Monitor*, 12(3), 185–96

V. Benda. 1986. 'Perspektivy politického vývoje v Československu a možná role Charty 77', *Informace o Chartě 77*, 11(4), 12–15

T. Benn. 1988. *Office Without Power: Diaries 1968–72*, London: Hutchinson

————. 1989. *Against the Tide: Diaries 1973–76*, London: Hutchinson

G. Bennet and K.A. Hamilton (eds). 1997. *Documents on British Policy Overseas*, Series III, Volume 2, *The Conference on Security and Cooperation in Europe, 1972–1975*, London: Routledge

E. Berlinguer. 1972. *Per un governo di svolta democratica*, Rome: Editori Riuniti

————. 1976. *La politica internazionale dei comunisti italiani 1975–76*, Rome: Editori Riuniti

————. 1977. *Austerità, occasione per trasformare l'Italia*, Rome: Editori Riuniti

————. 1979. *Per il socialismo nella pace e nella democrazia*, Rome: Editori Riuniti

————. 1985. *La crisi italiana. Scritti su "Rinascita"*, Rome: Editrice l'Unità

————. 2001. *Discorsi parlamentari (1968–1984)*, edited M.L. Righi, Rome: Camera dei Deputati

M.H. Bernhard. 1993. *The Origins of Democratization in Poland: Workers, Intellectuals, and Oppositional Politics, 1976–1980*, New York: Columbia University Press

S. Berstein and J.-F. Sirinelli (eds). 2006. *Les années Giscard. Valéry Giscard d'Estaing et l'Europe 1974–1981*, Paris: Armand Colin

M.R. Beschloss and S. Talbott. 1993. *At the Highest Levels: The Inside Story of the End of the Cold War*, Boston: Little, Brown

G. Bischof and S. Dockrill (eds). 2000. *Cold War Respite: The Geneva Summit of 1955*, Baton Rouge: Louisiana State University Press

U. Bitterli. 2004. *Golo Mann. Instanz und Aussenseiter. Eine Biographie*, Berlin: Kindler Verlag

J. Bitterlich. 1998. 'In memoriam Werner Rouget. Frankreichs (und Europas) Weg nach Maastricht im Jahr der deutschen Einheit', in W. Rouget (ed.), *Schwierige Nachbarschaft am Rhein: Frankreich-Deutschland*, Bonn: Bouvier

P. Blažek. 2002. 'Člen-korespondent ČSAV Jiří Hájek. Cesta z Ústředního výboru Komunistické strany Československa k Chartě 77 (1968–1976)', in A. Kostlán (ed.), *Věda v Československu v období normalizace (1970–1975)*, Prague: Výzkumné centrum pro dějiny vědy, 423–455

C. Bohlen. 1973. *Witness to History*, New York: Norton

L. Borhi. 2008. 'The International Context of Hungarian Transition, 1989: The View from Budapest', in F. Bozo et al. (eds), *Europe and the End of the Cold War: A Reappraisal*, London: Routledge, 78–92

P. Borruso. 2009. *Il PCI e l'Africa indipendente. Apogeo e crisi di un'utopia socialista (1956–1989)*, Florence: Le Monnier

J. Botts. 2006. 'Nothing to Seek and … Nothing to Defend: George F. Kennan's Core Values and American Foreign Policy, 1938–1993', *Diplomatic History*, 30(5), 839–866

F. Bozo. 1996. *Deux Stratégies pour l'Europe: De Gaulle, les États-unis et l'Alliance Atlantique 1958–69*, Paris: Plon

———. 2005. *Mitterrand, la fin de la guerre froide et l'unification allemande. De Yalta à Maastricht*, Paris: Odile Jacob

———. 2007. 'Mitterrand's France, the End of the Cold War and German Unification: A Reappraisal', *Cold War History*, 7(4), 455–478

———. 2008. 'The Failure of a Grand Design: Mitterrand's European Confederation (1989–1991)', *Contemporary European History*, 17(3), 391–412

———. 2008a. 'France, German Unification, and European Integration', in F. Bozo et al. (eds), *Europe and the End of the Cold War: A Reappraisal*, London: Routledge, 148–160

———. 2010. 'France, "Gaullism", and the Cold War', in M.P. Leffler and O.A. Westad (eds), *Cambridge History of the Cold War*, vol. 2, Cambridge: Cambridge University Press, 2010, 158–178

F. Bozo, M.-P. Rey, N.P. Ludlow and L. Nuti (eds). 2008. *Europe and the End of the Cold War: A Reappraisal*, London, Routledge

R. Braithwaite. 2010. 'Thatcher's Role as an Interpreter of Gorbachev 1984–1991', *Journal of European Integration History*, 16(1), 31–44

W. Brandt. 1963. *Koexistenz – Zwang zum Wagnis*, Stuttgart: DVA

———. 1976. *Begegnungen und einsichten: die Jahre 1960–1975*, Hamburg: Hoffmann und Campe

———. 1989. *Erinnerungen*, Frankfurt: Propyläen

———. 1992. *My Life in Politics*, New York: Viking

———. 2002. *Die Partei der Freiheit. Willy Brandt und die SPD 1972–1992*, edited K. Rudolph, Bonn: Dietz

———. 2003. *Die Entspannung unzerstörbar machen. Internationale Beziehungen und deutsche Frage, 1974–1982*, edited F. Fischer, Bonn: Dietz

———. 2005. *Ein Volk der guten Nachbarn. Außen- und Deutschlandpolitik 1966–1974*, edited F. Fischer, Bonn: Dietz

———. 2009. *Gemeinsame Sicherheit. Internationale Beziehungen und Deutsche Frage*, edited U. Mai, B. Rother and W. Schmidt, Bonn: Dietz

Brennerová, C. 1997. 'Ex oriente lux? Obrazy východní Evropy v poválečném Československu', in E. Hahnová (ed.), *Evropa očima Čechů*, Praha: Nakladatelství Franze Kafky, 131–143

D. Brinkley. 1992. *Dean Acheson: The Cold War Years 1953–1971*, New Haven and London: Yale University Press

———. 2007. *The Reagan Diaries*, New York: HarperCollins

A. Brown. 1998. 'Glasnost at the FCO', *Prospect*, 32(July), 68–69

————. 2008. 'The Change to Engagement in Britain's Cold War Policy: The Origins of the Thatcher-Gorbachev Relationship', *Journal of Cold War Studies*, 10(3), 3–47

M.D. Brown. 2009. 'Détente, British foreign policy and public opinion, 1969–75', paper presented at *Britain and the End of the Cold War*, conference organized by the Centre for Contemporary British History, University of London, 23–25 June 2009

————. 2006. *Dealing with Democrats: The British Foreign Office and the Czechoslovak Émigrés in Great Britain, 1939 to 1945*, Frankfurt am Main: Peter Lang

W.E. Brownlee and H.D. Graham (eds). 2003. *The Reagan Presidency: Pragmatic Conservatism and Its Legacies*, Lawrence: University Press of Kansas

W. Bundy. 1998. *A Tangled Web: The Making of Foreign Policy in the Nixon Administration*, New York: Hill and Wang

E. Burin des Roziers. 1985. 'Le non-alignement', in E. Barnavi and S. Friedlander (eds), *La politique étrangère du Général de Gaulle*, Paris: Presses Universitaires de France

W. Burr. 1999. *Kissinger Transcripts: The Top Secret Meetings with Moscow and Beijing*, New York: The New Press

A.E. Busch. 1997. 'Ronald Reagan and the Defeat of the Soviet Empire', *Presidential Studies Quarterly*, 27, 451–466

G.H.W. Bush and B. Scowcroft. 1998. *A World Transformed*, New York: Knopf

J. Callaghan. 1987. *Time and Change*, London: Collins

D. Calleo. 1994. 'De Gaulle and the Monetary System: The Golden Rule', in N. Wahl and R. Paxton (eds), *De Gaulle and the United States, 1930–1970: A Centennial Reappraisal*, Oxford: Berg

Camera dei Deputati. 1996. *Aldo Moro, Discorsi Parlamentari (1963–1977)*, vol. 2, Rome: Camera dei Deputati

L. Cannon. 2000. *President Reagan: The Role of a Lifetime*, New York: PublicAffairs

H. Carrère d'Encausse. 1978. *L'Empire éclaté: la révolte des nations en URSS*, Paris: Flammarion

A. Carter. 1992. *Peace Movements: International Protest and World Politics since 1945*, London: Longman

I. Chernus. 1999. 'Eisenhower: Turning Himself Toward Peace', *Peace and Change* 24(1), 62–74

A. S. Chernyaev. 1995. *Moia zhizn i moe vremia*, Moscow: Mezhdunarodnye Otnosheniia

————. 2000. *My Six Years with Gorbachev*, University Park: Pennsylvania University Press

A. Chernyaev, V. Veber and V. Medvedev (eds). 2006. *V Politbiuro TsK KPSS...Po zapisiam Anatolia Cherniaeva, Vadima Medvedeva, Georgiia Shakhnazarova (1985–1991)*, Moscow: Alpina Business Books

G. Chiarante. 2009. *La fine del PCI. Dall'alternativa democratica di Berlinguer all'ultimo Congresso (1979–1991)*, Rome: Carocci

M. Clarke. 1986. 'Britain and European Political Cooperation in the CSCE' in K. Dyson (ed.), *European Détente: Case Studies in the Politics of East-West Relations*, London: F. Pinter, 237–243

————. 1988. 'The Soviet Union and Eastern Europe', in P. Byrd (ed.), *British Foreign Policy under Thatcher*, Oxford: Philip Allan/St Martin's Press, 54–75

————. 1992. 'A British View', in R. Davy (ed.), *European Détente: A Reappraisal*, London: Sage Publications

J. Colville. 1987. *Fringes of Power: Downing Street Diaries, 1939–1955, volume II: October 1941–1955*, London: Sceptre

E. Conze. 1996. *Die Gaullistische Herausforderung*, Munich: Oldenbourg

D. Cook. 1973. 'The European Security Conference', *Atlantic Monthly*, 232(4), 6–12

M. Cox. 2007. 'Another Transatlantic Split? American and European Narratives and the End of the Cold War', *Cold War History*, 7(1), 121–146

————. 2009. 'Why Did We Get the End of the Cold War Wrong?', *British Journal of Politics and International Relations*, 11, 161–176

J. von Dannenberg. 2008. *The Foundations of Ostpolitik: The Making of the Moscow Treaty Between West Germany and the USSR*, Oxford: Oxford University Press

R. Davy. 1975. 'The CSCE Summit', *The World Today*, 31(September), 349–353

————. 2009. 'Helsinki Myths: Setting the Record Straight on the Final Act of the CSCE, 1975', *Cold War History*, 9(1), 1–22

B. Day. 1999. *The Velvet Philosophers*, London: Claridge Press

M. Debré. 1993. *Trois Républiques pour une France: mémoires tome IV*, Paris: Albin Michel

A. Deighton. 1998. 'Ostpolitik or Westpolitik? British Foreign Policy, 1968–75', *International Affairs*, 74(4), 893–901

J. Dienstbier. 1988. 'Mit den Augen eines Mitteleuropäers. Eine Strategie für Europa', *Neue Gesellschaft, Frankfurter Hefte*, 35(4)

Diskuse o východní politice (=Komentáře, č. 7). Prague: Samizdat, 1986–87.

S. Dockrill. 2002. *Britain's Retreat from East of Suez: The Choice Between Europe and the World?*, Basingstoke: Palgrave Macmillan

G.F. Domber. 2008. 'Rumblings in Eastern Europe: Western Pressure on Poland's Moves towards Democratic Rransformation', in F. Bozo et al. (eds), *Europe and the End of the Cold War: A Reappraisal*, London: Routledge, 51–63

J. Donnelly. 2003. *Universal Human Rights in Theory and Practice*, London: Cornell University Press

R.J. Donovan. 1956. *Eisenhower: The Inside Story*, New York: Harper and Brothers

D. Dowe (ed.). 1993. *Die Ost- und Deutschlandpolitik der SPD in der Opposition 1982–1989*, Bonn: Friedrich-Ebert-Stiftung

S.D. Drell, P.J. Farley and D. Holloway. 1984. 'Preserving the ABM Treaty: A Critique of the Reagan Strategy Defense Initiative', *International Security*, 9(2), 51–91

K. Drobantseva-Landau. 1999. *Akademik Landau. Kak My Zhili*. Moscow: Zakharov

K. Dubiński. 1990. *Magdalenka*, Warsaw: Sylwa

A. Dudek. 2004. *Reglamentowana rewolucja*, Kraków: Arcana Historii

G. Edwards. 1985. 'Human Rights and Basket III Issues: Areas of Change and Continuity', *International Affairs*, 61(4), 631–642

J. Ehrman. 2005. *The Eighties: America in the Age of Reagan*, New Haven, CT: Yale University Press

D.D. Eisenhower. 1948. *Crusade in Europe*, Garden City, NY: Doubleday

J.S.D. Eisenhower (ed.). 1978. *Letters to Mamie*, Garden City, NY: Doubleday

D. Eisermann. 1999. *Außenpolitik und Strategiediskussion. Die Deutsche Gesellschaft für Auswärtige Politik 1955 bis 1972*, Munich: Oldenbourg Verlag

R.D. English. 2000. *Russia and the Idea of the West: Gorbachev, Intellectuals and the End of the Cold War*, New York: Columbia University Press

Europäisches Netzwerk für den Ost-West-Dialog (ed.). 1987. *Das Helsinki-Abkommen mit wirklichem Leben erfüllen (1986)*, Berlin

M. Evangelista. 2002. *Unarmed Forces: The Transnational Movement to End the Cold War*, Ithaca, NY: Cornell University Press

B. Falk. 2003. *The Dilemmas of Dissidence in East-Central Europe*, Budapest: Central European University Press

B. Fall. 1977. 'The Helsinki Conference, Belgrade and European Security', *International Security*, 2(1), 100–105

L. Fasanaro. 2008. 'Eurocommunism: An East German Perspective', in L. Nuti (ed.), *The Crisis of Detente in Europe: From Vietnam to Gorbachev, 1975–1985*, London: Routledge, 244–255

D. Fascell. 1979. 'The Helsinki Accord: A Case Study', *Annals of the American Academy of Political and Social Science*, 442(March), 69–76

P. Favier and M. Martin Roland. 1996. *La Décennie Mitterrand*, vol. 3, Paris: Seuil

D. Felken. 1993. *Dulles und Deutschland. Die amerikanische Deutschlandpolitik 1953–1959*, Bonn and Berlin: Bouvier Verlag

P. Ferrari. 2007. *In cammino verso Occidente. Berlinguer, il PCI e la comunità europea negli anni '70*, Bologna: CLUEB

L.V. Ferraris. 1979. *Report on a Negotiation: Helsinki, Geneva, Helsinki 1972–75*, Alphen a/d Rijn: Sijthoff and Noordhoff

G. Fiori. 1992. *Vita di Enrico Berlinguer*, Rome: Laterza

B.A. Fischer. 1997. *The Reagan Reversal: Foreign Policy and the Ending of the Cold War*, Columbia, MO: University of Missouri Press

———. 2004. 'The United States and the Transformation of the Cold War', in O. Njolstad (ed.), *The Last Decade of the Cold War: From Conflict Escalation to Conflict Transformation*, New York: Frank Cass, 226–240

———. Fischer. Forthcoming. *Triumph? The Reagan Legacy and US Foreign Policy Today*

T. Fischer. 2009. *Neutral Power in the CSCE. The N+N States and the Making of the Helsinki Accords 1975*, Baden-Baden: Nomos

F. Fitzgerald. 2000. *Way Out There in the Blue: Reagan, Star Wars and the End of the Cold War*, New York: Simon and Schuster

D.S. Foglesong. 1999. 'Roots of "Liberation": American Images of the Future of Russia in the Early Cold War, 1948–1953', *International History Review*, 21(1), 57–79

Fondazione Istituto Gramsci. 2003. *Caro Berlinguer. Note e appunti riservati di Antonio Tatò a Enrico Berlinguer*, Turin: Einaudi

Foreign and Commonwealth Office. 1977. *Selected Documents Related to Problems of Security and Cooperation in Europe, 1954–77*, London: Her Majesty's Stationery Office

H. Froment-Meurice. 1998. *Vu du Quai*, Paris: Fayard

A. Fursenko (ed.). 2004. *Prezidium TsK KPSS, 1954–1964: Chernovye Protokol'nye Zapisi Zasedanii Stenogrammy*, Moscow: Rosspen

———— (ed.). 2004a. *Prezidium TsK KPSS, 1954–1964: Postanovleniya, 1954–1958*, Moscow: Rosspen

A. Fursenko and T. Naftali. 2006. *Khrushchev's Cold War*, New York: Norton

J.L. Gaddis. 2006. *The Cold War: A New History*, London: Penguin

L. Galambos (ed.). 1978. *The Papers of Dwight D. Eisenhower*, vol. XII, Baltimore: Johns Hopkins University Press

A. Gallus. 2001. *Die Neutralisten. Verfechter eines vereinten Deutschland zwischen Ost und West, 1945–1990*, Düsseldorf: Droste

J. Garnett. 1970. 'BAOR and NATO', *International Affairs*, 46(4), 670–681

R. Garthoff. 1994. *Détente and Confrontation: Soviet-American Relations from Nixon to Reagan*, Washington, DC: Brookings Institution

————. 1994. *The Great Transition: American-Soviet Relations and the End of the Cold War*, Washington, DC: Brookings Institution

R.L. Garthoff. 2004. 'The US Role in Winding Down the Cold War, 1980–90', in O. Njolstad (ed.), *The Last Decade of the Cold War: From Conflict Escalation to Conflict Transformation*, London: Frank Cass, 179–195

T. Garton Ash. 1993. *In Europe's Name: Germany and the Divided Continent*, London: Jonathan Cape

P. Gassert. 2006. *Kurt Georg Kiesinger 1904–1988. Kanzler zwischen den Zeiten*, Munich: DVA

R. Gates. 1996. *From the Shadows: The Ultimate Insider's Story of Five Presidents and How They Won the Cold War*, New York: Simon and Schuster

C. de Gaulle. 1970. *Discours et Messages*, multiple vols, Paris: Plon

————. 1971. *Memoirs of Hope: Renewal and Endeavor*, New York: Simon and Schuster

————. 1987. *Lettres, Notes et Carnets*, vol. 10, Paris: Plon

T. Geiger. 2008. *Atlantiker gegen Gaullisten: aussenpolitischer Konflikt und innerparteilicher Machtkampf in der CDU/CSU 1958–1969*, Munich: Oldenbourg

D. Geyer and D. Selvage (eds). 2007. *Soviet-American Relations: The Détente Years 1969–1972*, Washington DC: U.S. Government Printing Office

T. W. Gijswijt. 2007. 'Beyond NATO: Transatlantic Elite Networks and the Atlantic Alliance', in A. Wenger, C. Nuenlist and A. Locher (eds), *Transforming NATO in the Cold War: Challenges Beyond Deterrence in the 1960s*, London: Routledge, 50–63

V. Giscard d'Estaing. 1995. 'Le commencement de tout', *Politique internationale*, 68, 1–7

M. Glaab. 1999. *Deutschlandpolitik in der öffentlichen Meinung. Einstellungen und Regierungspolitik in der Bundesrepublik Deutschland 1949 bis 1990*, Opladen: Leske and Budrich

P. Glotz. 2005. *Von Heimat zu Heimat. Erinnerungen eines Grenzgängers*, Berlin: Econ

J.E. Goodby. 1998. *Europe Undivided: The New Logic of Peace in U.S.-Russian Relations*, Washington, DC: United States Institute of Peace

M. Gorbachev. 1994. *Le idee di Berlinguer ci servono ancora*, Rome: Sisifo

————. 1999. *Social Democracy on the Eve of the XXst Century*, Moscow: RAN

M. Gorbachev and Z. Mlynář. 2002. *Conversations with Gorbachev: On Perestroika, the Prague Spring, and the Crossroads of Socialism*, New York: Columbia University Press

P.-M. de la Gorce. 1969. *La France contre les Empires*, Paris: Editions Bernard Grasset

D. Gowland and A. Turner. 2000. *Britain and European Integration 1945–1998: A Documentary History*, London: Routledge

H.-J. Grabbe. 1983. *Unionsparteien, Sozialdemokratie und Vereinigten Staaten von Amerika 1945–1966*, Düsseldorf: Droste

R.J. Granieri. 2003. *The Ambivalent Alliance: Konrad Adenauer, the CDU/CSU, and the West, 1949–1966*, New York: Berghahn Books

———. 2009. 'Odd Man Out? The CDU/CSU, Ostpolitik, and the Atlantic Alliance', in T.A. Schwartz and M. Schulz (eds), *The Strained Alliance: U.S.-European Relations from Nixon to Carter*, New York: Cambridge University Press, 83–101

A. Grau. 2005. *Gegen den Strom. Die Reaktion der CDU/CSU-Opposition auf die Ost- und Deutschlandpolitik der sozial-liberalen Koalition 1969–1973*, Düsseldorf: Droste

D. Greenhill. 1992. *More by Accident*, York: Wilton

A.A. Gromyko. 1989. *Memories*, London: Hutchinson

I. Grudzinska Gross. 1998. *Letters from Freedom*, Berkeley: University of California Press

A. Guerra. 2009. *La solitudine di Berlinguer. Governo, etica e politica. Dal «no» a Mosca alla «questione morale»*, Rome: Ediesse

H. Haftendorn. 2008. 'The Harmel Report and its impact on German Ostpolitik', in W. Loth and G.-H. Soutou (eds), *The Making of Détente: Eastern and Western Europe in the Cold War, 1965–75*, London: Routledge, 103–116

J. Hájek. 1954. *Zhoubná úloha pravicových socialistů v ČSR*, Prague: Státní nakladatelství politické literatury

———. 1958. *Mnichov*, Prague: Státní nakladatelství politické literatury

———. 1958a. 'Historie Mnichova', *Nová mysl*, 12(9), 790–803

———. 1968. 'Pracovní text projevu J. Hájka, předneseného v Radě bezpečnosti OSN, s požadavkem plného obnovení svrchovanosti Československa (1968, 24. srpna, New York)', in J. Vondrová and J. Navrátil (eds), *Mezinárodní souvislosti československé krize 1967–1970: Prosinec 1967–červenec 1968, Prameny k dějinám československé krize 1967–1970, vol. 4/1*, Prague: Doplněk

———. 1968a. 'Vytváříme podmínky pro úspěch obrodného procesu. Úkoly československé zahraniční politiky', *Rudé právo*, 6

———. 1968b. 'Konstanty a nové prvky v zahraniční politice', *Nová mysl*, 22(8), 984–990

———. 1978. *Lidská práva, socialismus a mírové soužití*, Prague: Samizdat

———. 1982. 'Die Achtung der Menschenrechte als Bestandteil einer Friedenspolitik', *Osteuropa*, 42(3), 177–188

———. 1986. 'Helsinky a perspektivy vývoje k celoevropskému společenství', *Diskuse. Teoreticko-politický občasník*, (40), 1–11

———. 1987. *Begegnungen und Zusammenstöße. Erinnerungen des ehemaligen tschechoslowakischen Außenministers*, Freiburg im Breisgau: Herder

———. 1988. 'Lidská práva v kontextu problematiky míru', *Informace o Chartě 77*, 11(15), 7–10

————. 1990. 'Československo a Evropa. Historická poučení pro dnešek', *Mezinárodní politika*, (14), 6–9

————. 1991. 'Rok nové čs. zahraniční politiky', *Mezinárodní politika*, 1(15), 4–6

————. 1997. *Paměti*, Prague: Ústav mezinárodních vztahů

J. Hájek and V. Kadlec. 1987. 'Přestavba také u nás?', *Listy*, 17(2), 28–31

P. Hakkarainen. 2005. 'A Monolithic Bloc or Individual Actors? West German Perceptions of the Warsaw Pact in the CSCE Process, 1969–72', in M. Rostagni (ed.), *The Helsinki Process: A Historical Reappraisal*, Padua: Cedam, 63–73

————. 2008. 'From Linkage to Freer Movement: The FRG and the Nexus between Western CSCE Preparations and Deutschlandpolitik, 1969–72', in A. Wenger, V. Mastny and C. Nuenlist (eds), *Origins of the European Security System: The Helsinki Process Revisited, 1965–75*, London: Routledge, 164–182

K. Hamilton. 1999. 'The Last Cold Warriors: Britain, Détente and the CSCE, 1972–75', European Interdependence Research Unit, Oxford, Discussion Paper, EIUR/991, 1–27

————. 2007. 'Cold War by Other Means: British Diplomacy and the CSCE, 1972–1975', in W. Loth and G.-H. Soutou (eds), *The Making of Détente: Eastern Europe and Western Europe in the Cold War, 1965–75*, London: Routledge, 168–182

J.M. Hanhimäki. 2003. '"They Can Write it in Swahili": Kissinger, the Soviets, and the Helsinki Accords, 1973–1975', *Journal of Transatlantic Studies*, 1(1), 37–58

————. 2004. *The Flawed Architect: Henry Kissinger and American Foreign Policy*, New York: Oxford University Press

W.F. Hanrieder. 1995. *Deutschland, Europa, Amerika. Die Außenpolitik der Bundesrepublik Deutschland 1949–1994*, Paderborn: Schöningh

P. Hanson. 1985. 'Economic Aspects of Helsinki', *International Affairs*, 61(4), 619–629

J.L. Harper. 1994. *American Visions of Europe*, Cambridge: Cambridge University Press

C. Hauswedell. 1997. *Friedenswissenschaften im Kalten Krieg. Friedensforschung und friedenswissenschaftliche Initiativen in der Bundesrepublik Deutschland in den achtziger Jahren*, Baden-Baden: Nomos

V. Havel. 1985. *The Anatomy of a Reticence: Eastern European Dissidents and the Peace Movement in the West*, Stockholm: Charta 77 Foundation

————. 1999. 'Setkání s Gorbačovem (1987)', in V. Havel (ed.), *Spisy 4 – Eseje a jiné texty z let 1970–1989*, Prague: Torst, 960–962

D. Healey. 1990. *The Time of My Life*, London: Penguin

E. Heath. 1998. *The Course of My Life: My Autobiography*, London: Hodder and Stoughton

L. Hejdánek. 1986. '"Milánská výzva" a co je kolem', *Diskuse. Teoreticko-politický občasník*, (39), 1–22

K. Hildebrand. 1984. *Von Erhard zur grossen Koalition*, Stuttgart: Deutsche Verlags-Anstalt

C. Hill (ed.). 1996. *The Actors in Europe's Foreign Policy*, London: Routledge

S. Hoffmann. 1974. *Éssais sur la France: Déclin ou Renouveau?*, Paris: Éditions du Seuil

A. Hofmann. 2007. *The Emergence of Détente in Europe: Brandt, Kennedy and the Formation of Ostpolitik*, London: Routledge

A. Horne. 2009. *Kissinger, 1973: The Crucial Year*, New York: Simon and Schuster

G. Howe. 1994. *Conflict of Loyalty*, London: Pan Books

M. Hromádková and M. Rejchrt. 1980. 'Dopis Charty 77 prezidentovi republiky z 17.9.1980', *Informace o Chartě 77*, 3(14), 1–2

E.J. Hughes. 1963. *The Ordeal of Power: A Political Memoir of the Eisenhower Years*, New York: Atheneum

W. Isaacson. 1991. *Kissinger*, New York: Simon and Schuster

W.D. Jackson. 1999. 'Soviet Reassessment of Ronald Reagan, 1985–1988', *Political Science Quarterly*, 113(4), 617–644

T. Johnston. 2008. 'Peace or Pacifism? The Soviet "Struggle for Peace in All the World", 1948–1954', *Soviet and East European Review*, 86(7), 259–282

T. Judt. 2007. *Postwar: A History of Europe since 1945*, London: Pimlico

R. Kagan. 1999. 'The Revisionist: How Henry Kissinger Won the Cold War, or So He Thinks', *The New Republic*, 220(25), 38–48

R. Kagan and R. Cooper. 2008. 'Is Democracy Winning?', *Prospect*, 146 (May), 24–25

R.G. Kaiser. 1992. *Why Gorbachev Happened: His Triumph, His Failure, and His Fall*, New York: Simon and Schuster

R.G. Kaufman. 1992. 'Winston S. Churchill and the Art of Statecraft: The Legacy of Principled Internationalism', *Diplomacy and Statecraft*, 3(2), 159–187

C.W. Kegley, Jr. 1994. 'How Did the Cold War Die? Principles for an Autopsy', *Merhson International Studies Review*, 38, 11–41

G.F. Kennan. 1947. 'The Sources of Soviet Conduct', *Foreign Affairs*, 25(4), 566–582

———. 1958. *Russia, the Atom and the West*, London: Oxford University Press

———. 1967. *Memoirs*, vol. 1, Boston: Little, Brown

———. 1972. *Memoirs 1950–1963*, London: Hutchinson

———. 1983. *The Nuclear Delusion*, New York: Pantheon

P. Kenney. 2002. *A Carnival of Revolution: Central Europe 1989*, Princeton, NJ: Princeton University Press

H. Kissinger. 1957. *Nuclear Weapons and Foreign Policy*, New York: Doubleday

———. 1957a. *A World Destroyed: Metternich, Castlereagh and the Problems of Peace, 1812–1822*, Boston: Houghton Mifflin

———. 1979. *White House Years*, Boston: Little, Brown

———. 1982. *Years of Upheaval*, Boston: Little, Brown

———. 1985. *Observations: Selected Speeches and Essays 1982–1984*, London: Weidenfeld and Nicolson

———. 1999. *Years of Renewal*, New York: Simon and Schuster

H. Klitzing. 2007. *The Nemesis of Stability: Henry A. Kissinger's Ambivalent Relationship with Germany*, Trier: Wissenschaftlicher Verlag

L. Kołakowski. 1969. 'In Praise of Inconsistency', in Kołakowski, *Marxism and Beyond*, London: Pall Mall Publishers, 231–240

———. 1971. 'Hope and Hopelessness', *Survey*, 17(3), 37–52

E. Kolodziej. 1974. *French International Policy under De Gaulle and Pompidou: The Politics of Grandeur*, Ithaca, NY: Cornell University Press

M. Kopeček. 2003. 'Obraz vnitřního nepřítele – revizionismus na stránkách „Otázek míru a socialismu" v letech 1958–1969', in Z. Karník and M. Kopeček (eds), *Bolševismus, komunismus a radikální socialismus v Československu*, Prague: Dokořán

J. Kozlík, M.R. Křížková and A. Marvanová (eds). 1983. *Charta 77 o míru*, Prague: Samizdat

J. Křesťan. 2004. 'KSČ, Společnost pro hospodářské a kulturní styky s SSSR a obraz Sovětského svazu v prostředí české levicové inteligence (1925–1939)', in Z. Karník and M. Kopeček (eds), *Bolševismus, komunismus a radikální socialismus v Československu*, Prague: Dokořán

R. Kuisel. 1993. *Seducing the French: The Dilemma of Americanization*, Berkeley: University of California Press

J. Kuroń. 1977. 'Document on Contemporary Poland: Reflections on a Program of Action', *Polish Review*, 22(3), 51–69

J. Kuroń and K. Modzelewski. 1982. *Solidarność: The Missing Link? The Classic Open Letter to the Party*, London: Bookmark's Publishing Cooperative

H.J. Küsters and D. Hofmann (eds). 1998. *Deutsche Einheit. Sonderedition aus den Akten des Bundeskanzleramtes 1989/90*, Munich: R. Oldenburg

G.P. Kynin and J. Laufer (eds). 2003. *SSSR i Germanskii Vopros*, vol. 3, Moscow: Mezhdunarodnye Otnosheniya

J. Lacouture. 1986. *De Gaulle: vol. 3 Le Souverain*, Paris: Seuil

K. Larres. 1994. 'Preserving Law and Order: Britain, the United States, and the East German Uprising of 1953', *Twentieth Century British History*, 5(3), 320–350
———. 1995. 'Eisenhower and the First Forty Days after Stalin's Death: The Incompatibility of *Détente* and Political Warfare', *Diplomacy and Statecraft*, 6(2), 431–469

M. Lazar and S. Courtois. 1995. *Histoire du Parti Communiste Français*, Paris: PUF

M. Ledeen and W. Lewis. 1981. *Débacle. L'échec américain en Iran*, Paris: Albin Michel

M. Leffler. 2007. *For the Soul of Mankind: The United States, the Soviet Union and the Cold War*, New York: Hill and Wang

M. Lerner. 2008. '"Trying to Find the Guy Who Invited Them": Lyndon Johnson, Bridge Building, and the End of the Prague Spring', *Diplomatic History*, 32(1), 77–103

J. de Lespinois. 2001. *L'Armée de terre française: de la défense du sanctuaire à la projection*, Paris: L'Harmattan

P. Lettow. 2005. *Ronald Reagan and His Quest to Abolish Nuclear Weapons*, New York: Random House

W. Link. 2004. 'Détente German-Style and Adapting to America', in D. Junker (ed.), *The United States and Germany in the Era of the Cold War, 1945–1990, vol. 2: 1968–1990*, Cambridge: Cambridge University Press

E. Lipinski. 1976. 'An Open Letter to Comrade Edward Gierek', *Survey*, 22(2), 194–203

W. Lippmann. 1947. *The Cold War*, New York: Harper and Bros.
———. 1958. 'Mr. Kennan and Reappraisal in Europe'," *Atlantic Monthly*, 201(4), 33–37

F. Logevall. 1999. *Choosing War: The Lost Chance for Peace and the Escalation of War in Vietnam*, Berkeley: University of California Press

W. Loth. 2002. *Overcoming the Cold War*, London: Palgrave

———. 2007. 'Détente and European Integration in the Policies of Willy Brandt and Georges Pompidou', in N.P. Ludlow (ed.), *European Integration and the Cold War: Ostpolitik – Westpolitik, 1965–1973*, London: Routledge, 53–66

W. Loth and G.-H. Soutou (eds). 2008. *The Making of Détente: Eastern and Western Europe in the Cold War, 1965–75*, London: Routledge

N.P. Ludlow (ed.). 2007. *European Integration and the Cold War: Ostpolitik-Westpolitik, 1965–1973*, London: Routledge

P. Machcewicz. 2001. 'Poland 1986–1989: From "Cooptation" to "Negotiated Revolution"', *Cold War International History Project Bulletin*, no. 12–13, 93–128

M. MacMillan. 2006. *Seize the Hour: When Nixon Met Mao*, London: Random House

E. Mahan. 2002. *Kennedy, De Gaulle, and Western Europe*, New York: Palgrave Macmillan

P. Maillard. 2001. *De Gaulle et le Problème Allemand: Les leçons d'un grand dessein*, Paris: Guibert

N. Malcolm (ed.). 1994. *Russia and Europe: An End to Confrontation?*, London: Pinter

R. Marcowitz. 1998. 'Yalta and the Myth of the Division of the World,' in C. Buffet and B. Heuser (eds), *Haunted by History: Myths in International Relations*, Oxford: Berghahn Books, 80–91

J. Maresca. 1987. *To Helsinki: The Conference on Security and Co-operation in Europe, 1973–1975*, Durham, NC: Duke University Press

V. Mastny. 1986. *Helsinki, Human Rights, and European Security: Analysis and Documentation*, Durham, NC: Duke University Press

———. 1992. *The Helsinki Process and the Reintegration of Europe, 1986–1991: Analysis and Documentation*, New York : New York University Press

———. 2008. 'Eastern Europe and the early prospects for EC/EU and NATO membership', in F. Bozo, M.-P. Rey, L. Nuti, and N.P. Ludlow (eds), *Europe and the End of the Cold War: A Reappraisal*, London: Routledge, 235–245

V. Mastny and M. Byrne (eds.). 2005. *A Cardboard Castle? An Inside History of the Warsaw Pact, 1955–1991*, Budapest: Central European University

V. Mastny, A. Wenger. 2008. 'New Perspectives in the Origins of the CSCE Process' in Wenger, Mastny and Nuenlist (eds), *Origins of the European Security System: The Helsinki Process Revisited, 1965–75*, London: Routledge, 3–22

J. Matlock. 2004. *Reagan and Gorbachev: How the Cold War Ended*, New York: Random House

C. Mauriac. 1970. *Un autre de Gaulle: journal 1944–1954*, Paris: Hachette

D. Mayers. 1988. *George Kennan and the Dilemmas of US Foreign Policy*, New York: Oxford University Press

C. Meneguzzi Rostagni (ed.). 2005. *The Helsinki Process. A Historical Reappraisal*, Padua: Cedam

A. Michnik. 1981. 'What we Want to Do and What We Can Do', *Telos* 47(Spring), 66–77

————. 1985. *Letters from Prison and other Essays*, trans. by Maya Latynski, Berkeley: University of California Press

————. 1987. 'Gorbachev – as seen from Warsaw', *East European Reporter* 2(4), 32–34

M. S. Milosch. 2006. *Modernizing Bavaria: The Politics of Franz Josef Strauß and the CSU, 1949–1969*, New York and Oxford: Berghahn Books

W. D. Miscamble. 1992. *George F. Kennan and the Making of American Foreign Policy, 1947–1950*, Princeton: Princeton University Press

G. Mitrovich. 2000. *Undermining the Kremlin*, Ithaca: Cornell University Press

F. Mitterrand. 1986. *Réflexions sur la politique étrangère de la France*, Paris: Fayard

————. 1996. *De l'Allemagne, de la France*, Paris: Odile Jacob

D. Möckli. 2008. *European Foreign Policy during the Cold War*, London: Macmillan

V.M. Molotov. 1949. *Problems of Foreign Policy: Speeches and Statements, 1945–1948*, Moscow: Foreign Languages Publishing House

————. 1993. *Molotov Remembers: Inside Kremlin Politics*, Chicago: Ivan R. Dee

Lord Moran. 1968. *Winston Churchill, The Struggle for Survival, 1940–1955*, London: Sphere Books

M. C. Morgan, 'North America, Atlanticism, and the making of the Helsinki Final Act', in A. Wenger, V. Mastny and C. Nuenlist (eds), *Origins of the European Security System: The Helsinki Process Revisited, 1965–75*, London: Routledge

E. Morin. 1988. *Europa denken*, Frankfurt: Campus

J. Ney, 1969. *The European Surrender*, Boston, Little, Brown

G. Niedhart. 1995. 'Friedens- und Interessenwahrung. Zur Ostpolitik der F.D.P. in Opposition und sozialliberaler Regierung 1968–1970', *Jahrbuch zur Liberalismus-Forschung*, 7, 106–26

————. 2004. 'Frankreich und die USA im Dialog über Détente und Ostpolitik 1969–1970', *Francia. Forschungen zur westeuropäischen Geschichte*, 31(3), 65–85

————. 2004a. 'The East-West Problem as Seen from Berlin: Willy Brandt's Early Ostpolitik' in W. Loth (ed.), *Europe, Cold War and Coexistence 1953–1965*, London: Frank Cass, 285–296

————. 2008. 'Status Quo vs. Peaceful Change: The German Question during the ESC/CSCE Process' in Bange and Niedhart (eds). *Helsinki 1975 and the Transformation of Europe*, New York: Berghahn Books, 39–52

————. 2010. 'Der Ost-West-Konflikt. Konfrontation im Kalten Krieg und Stufen der Deeskalation', *Archiv für Sozialgeschichte* 50, 557–594

G. Niedhart and O. Bange. 2004. 'Die "Relikte der Nachkriegszeit" beseitigen: Ostpolitik in der zweiten außenpolitischen Formationsphase der Bundesrepublik Deutschland im Übergang von den Sechziger- zu den Siebzigerjahren', *Archiv für Sozialgeschichte* 44, 415–448

P. Nitze. 1989. *From Hiroshima to Glasnost: At the Center of Decision*, New York: Grove Weidenfeld

'Not to Lure the Wolves out of the Woods: An Interview with Jacek Kuroń', *Telos* 47(Spring 1981), 93–97

M. Nowojczyk. 1994. 'Economic Reform as an Ideology in Poland during the 1980s', *History of European Ideas*, 19(1–3), 317–323

L. Nuti (ed.). 2008. *The Crisis of Détente in Europe: From Helsinki to Gorbachev 1975–1985,* London: Routledge

S.J. Nuttall. 1992. *European Political Cooperation,* Oxford: Clarendon Press, New York: Oxford University Press

D. Oberdorfer. 1991. *The Turn: From Cold War to a New Era,* New York: Poseidon Press

J. Øhrgaard. 1997. 'Less than Supranational, More than Intergovernmental: European Political Cooperation and the Dynamics of Intergovernmental Cooperation', *Millenium – Journal of International Studies,* 26(1), 1–29

C. O'Neill. 2000. *Britain's Entry into the European Community: Report on the Negotiations of 1970–1972,* London: Frank Cass

D. Orlow. 1997. 'Ambivalence and Attraction: The German Social Democrats and the United States, 1945–1974', in R. Pomerin (ed.), *The American Impact on Postwar Germany,* Providence: Berghahn Books, 35–52

J. O'Sullivan. 2006. *The President, the Pope and the Prime Minister,* Washington: Regnery Publishing

J. van Oudenaren. 1992. *European Detente,* Durham, NC: Duke University Press

A. Paczkowski. 2003. *The Spring Will Be Ours: Poland and Poles from Occupation to Freedom,* University Park: Penn State University Press

A. Paczkowski and M. Byrne (eds). 2008. *From Solidarity to Martial Law: The Polish Crisis of 1980–1981,* Budapest: Central European University Press

M. Palmer. 1972. 'A European Security Conference: Preparation and Procedure', *The World Today,* 28 (January), 36–46

J.T. Patterson. 2005. *Restless Giant: The United States from Watergate to Bush v. Gore,* New York: Oxford University Press

V. Pechatnov. 1999. 'The Allies Are Pressing on You to Break Your Will...', Cold War International History Project, Working Paper 26

E.G.H. Pedaliu. 2007. 'Human Rights and Foreign Policy: Wilson and the Greek Dictators, 1967–1970', *Diplomacy and Statecraft,* 18(1), 185–214

R. Pells. 1997. *Not Like Us: Europeans and the USA,* New York: Basic Books

A. Peyrefitte. 1994. *C'était de Gaulle,* vol. 1, Paris: Fayard

———. 1997. *C'était de Gaulle,* vol. 2, Paris: Fayard

———. 2000. *C'était de Gaulle,* vol. 3, Paris: Fayard

S. Pisar. 1970. *Les Armes de la paix. L'ouverture économique vers l'Est,* Paris: Denoël

I. Poggiolini. 2005. 'Una partnership italo-britannica per il primo allargamento: convergenza tattica o comunanza di obiettivi (1969–1973)?', in F. Romero and A. Varsori (eds), *Nazione, interdipendenza, integrazione. Le relazioni internazionali dell'Italia (1917–1989),* Rome: Carocci, 333–353

S. Pons. 2001. 'L'Italia e il PCI nella politica estera dell'URSS di Breznev', *Studi Storici,* 42(4), 929–951

———. 2006. *Berlinguer e la fine del comunismo,* Turin: Einaudi

C. Pöthig. 2000. *Italien und die DDR. Die politischen, ökonomischen und kulturellen Beziehungen von 1949 bis 1980,* Frankfurt: Peter Lang

R.E. Powaski. 2000. *Return to Armageddon: The United States and the Nuclear Arms Race, 1981–1999,* New York: Oxford University Press

L.V. Pozdeeva, O.A. Rzheshevsky and Yu. A. Nikiforov (eds). 2006. *Nauchnoie Nasledstvo. Tom 33. Ivan Mikhailovich Maisky. Dnevnik Diplomata. London 1934–1943*, vol. 1, Moscow: Nauka

A. Preston and F. Logevall (eds). 2008. *Nixon in the World: American Foreign Policy, 1969–1977*, New York: Oxford University Press

Public Papers of the Presidents of the United States, Ronald Reagan, 1983, Washington, DC: Government Printing Office, 1984

A.E. Rabinovich. 2004; 'Evgeny Rabinovich: "Golos Sovesti Atomnogo Veka"', *Nestor* 4, 306–324

M. Rakowski. 1993. 'Journalist und politischer Emissär zwischen Warschau und Bonn', in F. Pflüger and W. Lipscher (eds), *Feinde werden Freunde. Von den Schwierigkeiten der deutsch-polnischen Nachbarschaft*, Bonn: Bouvier, 154–159

R. Reagan. 1990. *An American Life*, New York: Pocket Books

C. Reijnen. 2005. '"Hebben we een missie?" Over de Praagse Lente, de Koude Oorlog en Europa', *Nieuwste Tijd* 4(2/14), 15–24

R. Reißig. 2002. *Dialog durch die Mauer*, Frankfurt and New York: Campus

M.-P. Rey. 1991. *La tentation du rapprochement: France et URSS à l'heure de la détente (1964–1974)*, Paris: Publications de la Sorbonne

―――. 2003. 'Le Département International du Comité central du PCUS, le MID et la politique extérieure soviétique', *Communisme*, 74/75, 179–215

―――. 2004. '"Europe is our Common Home": A Study of Gorbachev's Diplomatic Concept', *Cold War History*, 4(2), 33–65

―――. 2004a. 'The Western Communist Parties in the Cold War, 1957–1968', in W. Loth (ed.), *Europe, Cold War and Coexistence, 1953–1965*, London: Frank Cass, 202–215

―――. 2008. 'The USSR and the Helsinki Process 1969–1975', in A. Wenger, V. Mastny and C. Nuenlist (eds), *Origins of the European Security System: The Helsinki Process Revisited, 1965–75*, London: Routledge, 65–81

―――. 2008a. 'France and the German Question in the Context of Ostpolitik and the CSCE, 1969–1974', in O. Bange and G. Niedhart, *Helsinki 1975 and the Transformation of Europe*, New York: Berghahn Books, 53–66

―――. 2008b. 'Gorbachev's New Thinking and Europe, 1985–1991', in F. Bozo et al., *Europe and the End of the Cold War: A reappraisal*, London: Routledge, 23–35

―――. 2010. 'De Gaulle, French Diplomacy, and Franco-Soviet Relations as Seen from Moscow', in C. Nuenlist, A. Locher and G. Martin (eds), *Globalizing de Gaulle: International Perspectives on French Foreign Policies, 1958–1969*, Lanham, MD: Lexington Books, 25–42

D. Reynolds. 2000. *One World Divisible: A Global History since 1945*, London: Allen Lane

R. Rhodes. 2007. *Arsenals of Folly: The Making of the Nuclear Arms Race*, London, New York: Simon and Schuster

M. Rifkind. 2005. 'Britain Restored in the World', in S. Roy and J. Clarke (eds), *Margaret Thatcher's Revolution*, London: Continuum Press, 25–36

T. Risse, S.C. Ropp and K. Sikkink (eds). 1999. *The Power of Human Rights: International Norms and Domestic Change*, New York: Cambridge University Press

G. Roberts. 2008. 'A Chance for Peace? The Soviet Campaign to End the Cold War, 1953–1955', Cold War International History Project, Working Paper 57

P. Robrieux. 1982. *Histoire intérieure du parti communiste français*, vol. 3, Paris: Fayard

A. Romano. 2007. 'The Nine and the Conference of Helsinki: A Challenging Game with the Soviets', in J. van der Harst (ed.), *Beyond the Customs Union: The European Community's Quest for Deepening, Widening and Completion, 1969–1975*, Brussels: Bruylant, 83–104

———. 2009. *From Détente in Europe to European Détente: How the West Shaped the Helsinki CSCE*, Brussels: Peter Lang

S. Romano. 1992. 'L'Europe de l'Atlantique à l'Oural: concepts et réalités', in Institut Charles de Gaulle (ed.), *De Gaulle en son siècle*, vol. 5, Paris: La Documentation française, 507

J. Roosevelt (ed.). 1962. *The Liberal Papers*, Garden City, NY: Doubleday

W. Rostow. 1982. *Europe After Stalin: Eisenhower's Three Decisions of March 11, 1953*, Austin: University of Texas Press

W. Rostow, et al. 1954. *The Dynamics of Soviet Society*, New York: Mentor Books

A. Rubbi. 1994. *Il mondo di Berlinguer*, Rome: Napoleone

K. Rudolph. 2004. *Wirtschaftsdiplomatie im Kalten Krieg. Die Ostpolitik der westdeutschen Großindustrie 1945–1991*, Frankfurt/Main: Campus

A. Sakharov. 1968. *Reflections on Progress, Peaceful Coexistence, and Intellectual Freedom*, New York: Norton

———. 1992. *Memoirs*, New York: Vintage

———. 1998. *Materialy konferentsii k 30-letiiu raboty A.D. Sakharova "Razmyshleniia o progresse, mirnom sosuschestvovanii i intellektualnoi svobode"*, Moscow: Prava Cheloveka

P. Salmon. 2008. 'The United Kingdom and German Unification', in F. Bozo et al. (eds), *Europe and the End of the Cold War: A Reappraisal*, London: Routledge, 177–190

P. Salmon, K. Hamilton and S. Twigge (eds). 2009. *Documents on British Policy Overseas, German Unification 1989–1990*, Series III, Volume VI, London: Routledge

D. Sassoon. 2001. 'La sinistra, l'Europa, il PCI', in R. Gualtieri (ed.), *Il PCI nell'Italia repubblicana*, Rome: Carocci, 223–249

M. Schaller. 2007. *Right Turn: American Life in the Reagan-Bush Era*, New York, Oxford University Press

W. Schmidt. 2001. *Kalter Krieg, Koexistenz und kleine Schritte. Willy Brandt und die Deutschlandpolitik 1948–1963*, Wiesbaden: Westdeutscher Verlag

———. 2003. 'Die Wurzeln der Entspannung: Der konzeptionelle Ursprung der Ost- und Entspannungspolitik Willy Brandts in den fünfziger Jahren', *Vierteljahrshefte für Zeitgeschichte*, 51, 521–563

K. Schönhoven. 2004. *Wendejahre. Die Sozialdemokratie in der Zeit der Großen Koalition 1966–1969*, Bonn: Dietz

T. Schreiber. 2000. *Les Actions de la France à l'Est, ou les Absences de Marianne*, Paris: Harmattan

T. Schwartz. 2003. *Lyndon Johnson and Europe: In the Shadow of Vietnam*, Cambridge: Harvard University Press

H.-P. Schwarz. 1991. *Adenauer. Der Staatsmann*, Stuttgart: Deutsche Verlags-Anstalt

P. Schweizer. 1996. *Victory: The Reagan Administration's Secret Strategy That Hastened the Collapse of the Soviet Union*, New York: Atlantic Monthly

R. Seidelmann. 1981. 'Die Sozialistische Internationale als Parteienbewegung und politischer Wegbereiter', *Europa-Archiv*, 36, 659–668

———. 1990. 'Die Sozialistische Internationale und Osteuropa', *Europa-Archiv*, 45

D. Senghaas. 1966. 'Unilateralismus und Gradualismus. Zur Strategie des Friedens', *Neue Politische Literatur*, 11, 1–15

D. Senghaas, et al. 1966a. 'Katechismus zur deutschen Frage', *Kursbuch*, 4, 1–54

J.-J. Servan-Schreiber. 1967. *Le Défi Américain*, Paris: Denoël

———. 1968. *The American Challenge*, New York: Athenaeum

G. Shakhnazarov. 2001. *S vozhdiami i bez nikh*, Moscow: Vagrius

M.D. Shulman. 1963. *Stalin's Foreign Policy Reappraised*, Cambridge, MA: Harvard University Press

G.P. Shultz. 1993. *Turmoil and Triumph: My Years as Secretary of State*, New York: Scribner

M. Siekmeier. 1998. *Restauration oder Reform. Die FDP in den sechziger Jahren. Deutschland- und Ostpolitik zwischen Wiedervereinigung und Entspannung*, Cologne: Janus

H.G. Skilling. 1981. *Charter 77 and Human Rights in Czechoslovakia*, London: Allen and Unwin

K.K. Skinner, A. Anderson and M. Anderson (eds). 2001. *Reagan, In His Own Hand*, New York: The Free Press

Y. Smirnov and V. Zubok. 1994. 'Nuclear Weapons After Stalin's Death: Moscow Enters the H-Bomb Age', *Cold War International History Project Bulletin*, 4(Fall), 1 & 14–18

K.E. Smith. 2004. *The Making of EU Foreign Policy: The Case of Eastern Europe*, Basingstoke: Palgrave Macmillan

S.B. Snyder. 2009. 'The Rise of the Helsinki Network: "A Sort of Lifeline" for Eastern Europe', in P. Villaume and O.A.Westad (eds), *Perforating the Iron Curtain: European Détente, Transatlantic Relations and the Cold War*, Copenhagen: Museum Tusculanum Press

———. 2011. *Human Rights Activism and the End of the Cold War: A Transnational History of the Helsinki Network*, Cambridge: Cambridge University Press

T. Snyder. 2003. *The Reconstruction of Nations*, New Haven, CT: Yale University Press

M.J. Sodaro. 1990. *Moscow, Germany, and the West from Khrushchev to Gorbachev*, Ithaca, NY: Cornell University Press

H. Soell. 2008. *Helmut Schmidt. Bd. 2: 1969-heute. Macht und Verantwortung*, Stuttgart: DVA

G.-H. Soutou. 1996. *L'alliance incertaine. Les rapports politico-stratégiques franco-allemandes 1954–96*, Paris: Fayard

———. 2000. 'La décision française de quitter le commandement intégré de l'OTAN (1966)', in H.-J. Harder (ed.), *Von Truman bis Harmel: Die Bundesrepublik Deutschland im Spannungsfeld von NATO und europäischer Integration*, Munich: Oldenbourg, 185–208

———. 2003. 'De Gaulle's France and the Soviet Union from Conflict to Détente', in W. Loth (ed.), *Europe, Cold War and Coexistence, 1953–1965*, London: Frank Cass, 178–189

———. 2006. 'L'anneau et les deux triangles: les rapports franco-allemands dans la politique européenne et mondiale de 1974 à 1981', in S. Berstein and J.-F. Sirinelli (eds), *Les années Giscard. Valéry Giscard d'Estaing et l'Europe 1974–1981*, Paris: Armand Colin, 45–79

———. 2007. 'President Pompidou, *Ostpolitik*, and the Strategy of Détente', in H. Haftendorn, G.-H. Soutou, S. Szabo and S. Wells (eds), *The Strategic Triangle: France, Germany, and the United States in the Shaping of the New Europe*, Washington, DC: Johns Hopkins UP and Woodrow Wilson Center Press, 229–257

———. 2008. 'Convergence Theories in France during the 1960s and 1970s', in W. Loth and G.-H. Soutou (eds), *The Making of Détente: Eastern and Western Europe in the Cold War, 1965–75*, London: Routledge, 25–48

———. 2008a. 'Staatspräsident Valéry Giscard d'Estaing und die deutsche Frage', in K. Hildebrand, U. Wengst and A. Wirsching (eds), *Geschichtswissenschaft und Zeiterkenntnis. Von der Aufklärung bis zum Gegenwart. Festschrift für Horst Möller*, Munich: Oldenbourg, 373–382

Sovetsko-Amerikanskie Otnosheniya, 1949–1952, Moscow: Materik, 2006

R.M. Spaulding. 1996. '"Reconquering Our Old Position": West German Osthandel Strategies of the 1950s', in V.R. Berghahn (ed.), *Quest for Economic Empire: European Strategies of German Big Business in the Twentieth Century*, Providence: Berghahn Books, 123–143

———. 1997. *Osthandel and Ostpolitik: German Foreign Trade Policies in Eastern Europe from Bismarck to Adenauer*, Providence: Berghahn Books

SPD. 1985. *Jahrbuch der Sozialdemokratischen Partei Deutschlands. 1984–1985*, Bonn: Vorwärts

——— 1988. *Jahrbuch 86/87*, Bonn: Vorwärts

SPD-Parteivorstand (ed.). 1989. *Materialien. Frieden und Abrüstung in Europa. Ergebnisse der gemeinsamen Arbeitsgruppe SPD-PVAP*, Bonn: Vorwärts

'Special forum: U.S.-Soviet Relations in the Era of Détente', *Diplomatic History*, 33(4), 2009

M. Spencer. 1995; '"Political" Scientists', *Pugwash Online*, http://www.pugwash.org/reports/pim/pim1.htm (accessed 15 Feb, 2009)

K. Spohr Readman. 2006. 'National Interests and the Power of "Language": West German Diplomacy and the CSCE, 1972–1975', *Journal of Strategic Studies*, 29(6), 1077–1120

'Spravka KGB SSSR na akademika L.D. Landau', *Istoricheskii arkhiv*, 3, 1993

J. Staniszkis. 1984. *Poland's Self-Limiting Revolution*, edited Jan T. Gross, Princeton, NJ: Princeton University Press

J. Stanke. 2001. 'Danger and Opportunity: Eisenhower, Churchill, and the Soviet Union after Stalin, 1953', Ph.D. dissertation, Emory University

C.G. Stefan. 2000. 'The Drafting of the Helsinki Final Act: A Personal View of the CSCE's Geneva Phase (September 1973 until July 1975)', *SHAFR Newsletter*, 31(2), 7–10

A. Stephanson. 1989. *Kennan and the Art of Foreign Policy*, Cambridge, MA: Harvard University Press

M. Stewart. 1980. *Life and Labour: An Autobiography*, London: Sidgwick and Jackson

F.J. Strauß. 1965. 'An Alliance of Continents', *International Affairs*, 42(2), 191–203

———. 1966. *The Grand Design: A European Approach to German Unification*, New York: Praeger

———. 1966a. *Entwurf für Europa*, Stuttgart: Seewald

———. 1968. *Franz Josef Strauß: Bundestagsreden*, edited L. Wagner, Bonn: Studio AZ

———. 1968a. *Herausforderung und Antwort: Ein Programm für Europa*, Stuttgart: Seewald

———. 1969. *Challenge and Response: A Program for Europe*, London: Weidenfeld and Nicolson

———. 1989. *Erinnerungen*, Berlin: Goldmann

C.L. Sulzberger. 1969. *A Long Row of Candles: Memoirs and Diaries [1934–1954]*, New York: Macmillan

J. Suri. 2003. *Power and Protest: Global Revolution and the Rise of Détente*, Cambridge, MA: Harvard University Press

———. 2007. *Henry Kissinger and the American Century*, Cambridge, MA: Harvard University Press

L. Szymanski. 1982. *Candle for Poland*, San Bernardino, CA: The Borgo Press

S. Talbott. 1984. *Deadly Gambits: The Reagan Administration and the Stalemate in Nuclear Arms Control*, New York: Alfred A. Knopf

A. Tatò (ed.). 1984. *Conversazioni con Berlinguer*, Rome: Editori Riuniti

P. Taylor. 1979. *When Europe Speaks with One Voice: the External Relations of the E.C.*, Westport, CT: Greenwood Press

H. Teltschik. 1991. *329 Tage. Innenansichten der Einigung*, Berlin: Siedler

M. Thatcher. 1993. *The Downing Street Years*, London: HarperCollins

D.C. Thomas. 2001. *The Helsinki Effect: International Norms, Human Rights, and the Demise of Communism*, Princeton, NJ: Princeton University Press

———. 2005. 'Human Rights Ideas, the Demise of Communism, and the End of the Cold War', *Journal of Cold War Studies*, 7(2), 110–141

C. Townshend. 1986. 'Northern Ireland', in R.J. Vincent (ed.), *Foreign Policy and Human Rights: Issues and Responses*, Cambridge: Cambridge University Press, 132–137

M. Trachtenberg. 1999. *A Constructed Peace: The Making of the European Settlement 1945–1963*, Princeton, NJ: Princeton University Press

'Turnir dlinoi v tri desiatiletiia. TsK KPSS – M.M. Botvinnik', *Istoricheskii arkhiv* 2 (1993)

M. Vaïsse. 1993. '"Une hirondelle ne fait pas le printemps"': La France et la crise de Cuba', in M. Vaïsse (ed.), *L'Europe et la Crise de Cuba*, Paris: A. Colin, 89–107

———. 1998. *La Grandeur. Politique étrangère du Général de Gaulle, 1958–1969*, Paris: Fayard

———. 2006. 'Avant-propos', in M. Vaïsse (ed.), *De Gaulle et la Russie*, Paris: CNRS Éditions

C. Valentini. 1992. *Berlinguer. L'eredità difficile*, Rome: Editori Riuniti

A. Varsori. 1998. *L'Italia nelle relazioni internazionali dal 1943 al 1992*, Rome: Laterza

H. Vedrine. 1996. *Les mondes de François Mitterrand. A l'Elysée, 1981–1995*, Paris: Fayard

P. Vittorelli. 1987. 'La Internacional Socialista por la paz en la ultima decada (1976–1986)', *Revista Internacional de Sociologia. International Review of Sociology. Internationale Zeitschrift für Soziologie*, 45(3), 443–460

Vneshnaya Politika Sovetskogo Souza: 1949 god, Moscow: Gospolitizdat, 1953

A. Vogtmeier. 1996. *Egon Bahr und die deutsche Frage. Zur Entwicklung der sozialdemokratischen Ost- und Deutschlandpolitik vom Kriegsende bis zur Vereinigung*, Bonn: Dietz

J. Vondrová and J. Navrátil (eds). 1995. *Mezinárodní souvislosti československé krize 1967–1970: Prosinec 1967–červenec 1968, Prameny k dějinám československé krize 1967–1970, vol. 4/1*, Prague: ÚSD–Doplněk

W. Wagner. 1971. 'Basic Requirements and Consequences of the Ostpolitik', *The Atlantic Community Quarterly*, 9(1), 20–33

M. Walker. 1993. *The Cold War and the Making of the Modern World*, London: Vintage

S. Wall. 2008. *A Stranger in Europe: Britain and the EU from Thatcher to Blair*, Oxford: Oxford University Press

D.C. Watt. 1978. 'Rethinking the Cold War: A Letter to a British Historian', *The Political Quarterly*, 49(4), 446–448

C. Weinberger. 1990. *Fighting for Peace*, New York: Warner Books

S.F. Wells, Jr. 2003. 'Reagan, Euromissiles, and Europe', in E. Brownlee and H. Graham (eds), *The Reagan Presidency: Pragmatic Conservativism and Its Legacies*, Lawrence: University of Kansas Press, 133–152

A. Wenger. 2004. 'Crisis and Opportunity: NATO's Transformation and Multilateralization of Détente, 1966–1968', *Journal of Cold War Studies*, 6, 22–74

A. Wenger and J. Suri. 2001. 'At the Crossroads of Diplomatic and Social History: The Nuclear Revolution, Dissent and Détente', *Cold War History*, 1(1), 1–42

A. Wenger, V. Mastny and C. Nuenlist (eds). 2008. *Origins of the European Security System: The Helsinki Process Revisited, 1965–75*, London: Routledge

H. Wentker. 2007. *Außenpolitik in engen Grenzen. Die DDR im internationalen System 1949–1989*, Munich: Oldenbourg

G. Wernicke. 1998. 'The Communist-Led World Peace Council and the Western Peace Movements', *Peace and Change*, 23(3), 265–311

O.A. Westad. 2004. 'Beginnings of the End: How the Cold War Crumbled', in S. Pons and F. Romero, *Reinterpreting the End of the Cold War*, London: Frank Cass
———. 2005. *The Global Cold War: Third World Interventions and the Making of Our Times*, Cambridge: Cambridge University Press

S. Wilentz. 2008. *The Age of Reagan: A History 1974–2008*, New York: HarperCollins

H. Wilford. 2003. *The CIA, the British Left and the Cold War: Calling the Tune?*, London: Frank Cass

P. Williams. 1985. 'Détente and US Domestic Politics', *International Affairs*, 61(3), 431–447

————. 1986, 'Britain, Détente and the CSCE', in K. Dyson (ed.), *European Détente: Case Studies in the Politics of East-West Relations*, London: F. Pinter, 221–236

H. Wilson. 1979. *Final Term: The Labour Government, 1974–1976*, London: Weidenfeld and Nicolson

K. Wilson. 1996. 'Governments, Historians, and "Historical Engineering"', in K. Wilson (ed.), *Forging the Collective Memory: Government and International Historians through Two Great Wars*, Oxford: Berghahn Books, 1–23

L.S. Wittner. 1993. *One World or None: A History of the World Nuclear Disarmament Movement Through 1953*, Stanford, CA: Stanford University Press

————. 1997. *Resisting the Bomb: A History of the World Nuclear Disarmament Movement, 1954–1970*, Stanford, CA: Stanford University Press

XV Congresso del PCI - Atti. Rome: Editori Riuniti, 1977.

N.I. Yegorova. 2003. '"Evropeiskaya Bezopasnost", 1954–1955gg: Poiski Novykh Podkhodov', in N.I. Yegorova and A.O. Chubar'yan (eds), *Kholodnaya Voina, 1945–1963gg: Istoricheskaya Retrospectiva*, Moscow: Olma-Press, 455–486

H. Young. 1999. *This Blessed Plot: Britain and Europe from Churchill to Blair*, London: Macmillan

J.W. Young. 1996. *Winston Churchill's Last Campaign: Britain and the Cold War, 1951–5*, Oxford: Clarendon Press

V. Zaslavsky. 2004. *Lo stalinismo e la sinistra italiana*, Milan: Mondadori

P. Zelikow and C. Rice. 1997. *Sternstunde der Diplomatie*, Berlin: Propyläen

V. Zubok. 2000. 'Gorbachev's Nuclear Learning', *Boston Book Review*, (April–May)

————. 2007. *A Failed Empire: The Soviet Union in the Cold War from Stalin to Gorbachev*, Chapel Hill: University of North Carolina Press

R. Zuzowski. 1992. *Political Dissent and Opposition in Poland: The Workers' Defense Committee "KOR"*, Westport, CT: Praeger

NOTES ON THE CONTRIBUTORS

FRÉDÉRIC BOZO is professor at the Sorbonne (University of Paris III, Department of European Studies). He was educated at the Ecole normale supérieure, at the Institut d'études politiques de Paris and at Harvard University. He received his doctorate from the University of Paris X - Nanterre (1993) and his habilitation from the Sorbonne - Paris III (1997). His publications include *Mitterrand, the End of the Cold War, and German Unification* (2009) and *Two Strategies for Europe: De Gaulle, the United States and the Atlantic Alliance* (2001). He has also co-edited *Europe and the End of the Cold War: A Reappraisal* (2008) and published articles in *Cold War History, Contemporary European History, Diplomatic History, Politique étrangère,* and *Survival*. He has a chapter in the recently published *Cambridge History of the Cold War* (Melvyn P. Leffler and Odd Arne Westad, eds).

MARTIN D. BROWN is associate professor of international history at Richmond, the American International University in London; a fellow of the Royal Historical Society and a member of the steering committee of the British-Czech-Slovak Historians' Forum. The primary focus of his recent research has been British foreign policy during the era of détente. He has just co-edited a collection of essays written by distinguished Central European historians entitled *Slovakia in History* (2011) for Cambridge University Press. His previous publications include *Dealing with Democrats: The British Foreign Office's Relations with the Czechoslovak Émigrés in Great Britain, 1939–1945* (2006). A Czech-language version was published in October 2008.

GREGORY F. DOMBER is assistant professor of history at the University of North Florida. He received his Ph.D. from the George Washington University in 2008 and was a Hewlett Postdoctoral Fellow at Stanford University's Center on Democracy, Development, and the Rule of Law in 2007–2008.

His dissertation, 'Supporting the Revolution: America, Democracy, and the End of the Cold War in Poland, 1981–1989', which surveys American policies to promote democracy through governmental and non-governmental channels, won the 2009 Betty M. Unterberger prize from the Society of Historians of American Foreign Relations. His scholarship on the international history of Poland's democratic transformation has appeared in a number of journals and edited collections.

CHRISTIAN DOMNITZ specializes in the contemporary history of Central Europe in the European context. He wrote his Ph.D. thesis about ideas of Europe in the communist bloc at the European University Viadrina (Frankfurt/Oder) and then worked at the Centre for Research on Contemporary History (Potsdam), the Warsaw German Historical Institute and the Institute for European History (Mainz). He has published articles and essays about the imagery of Europe east of the former 'Iron Curtain'. His earlier research deals with Czech-German relations. He is interested in comparative and relational approaches to the contemporary history of Europe. Amongst his publications are *Hinwendung nach Europa. Neuorientierung und Öffentlichkeitswandel im Staatssozialismus 1975–1989* (Forthcoming) and *Die Beneš-Dekrete in parlamentarischer Debatte. Kontroversen im Europäischen Parlament und im tschechischen Abgeordnetenhaus vor dem EU-Beitritt der Tschechischen Republik* (2007).

LAURA FASANARO is lecturer in history of international relations at the University of Rome III. Her research fields are contemporary European history, German history and the history of the Italian communist party. She is the author of a book on Franco-German relations after the two world wars, *Energia contesa, energia condivisa* (2008), and of various essays on the East German SED, the PCI and Italy's relations with the Atlantic Alliance. She also teaches at the Institute for International Education of Students (IES, Rome) and Umbra Institute (Perugia).

BETH A. FISCHER is on the faculty at the Munk School of Global Affairs at the University of Toronto. She specializes in international security, American foreign policy and decision-making. Fischer is the author of *The Reagan Reversal: Foreign Policy and the End of the Cold War* (1997) and has written extensively on the ending of the Cold War. In addition, she has published articles on psychology and foreign policy decision-making, intelligence analysis, the Cuban Missile Crisis and the international campaign to ban landmines. In 2002 Fischer was awarded a Nobel Fellowship for her work on conflict management and the ending of the Cold War. From 2000 to 2003 she was co-editor, with Margaret MacMillan, of *International Journal*,

Canada's leading journal on international affairs. Fischer is currently writing a book entitled *Triumph? The Reagan Legacy and American Foreign Policy Today.*

MARILENA GALA is senior lecturer in history of international relations at the School of Political Sciences of the University of Rome III. In 1998, she received her Ph.D. in history of international relations from the University of Florence. She was a public policy scholar (European Studies Program) at the Woodrow Wilson International Center in 2003 and 2010. Besides several articles, she has published *Il paradosso nucleare. Il Limited Test Ban Treaty come primo passo verso la distensione* (2002) and *John F. Kennedy. Il presidente diventato mito di tutte le nuove generazioni* (2004). She is currently writing a book on the evolution of transatlantic relations between détente and the end of the Cold War from the standpoint of European security.

THOMAS GIJSWIJT is assistant professor of American studies at Radboud University Nijmegen. He is the author of several articles on relations between the United States and Europe during the first decades of the Cold War and has written the first history of the Bilderberg Group. Provisionally entitled *Uniting the West: The Bilderberg Group, the Cold War and European Integration, 1952–1966*, it is due to be published by Routledge.

RONALD J. GRANIERI is currently visiting assistant professor of modern European and international history at Syracuse University. He is the author of *The Ambivalent Alliance: Konrad Adenauer, the CDU/CSU, and the West, 1949–1966* (2003) and is completing a book entitled *The Fall and Rise of German Christian Democracy: From Détente to Reunification.*

JUSSI M. HANHIMÄKI is professor and chair of international history and politics at the Graduate Institute of International and Development Studies in Geneva. The recipient of the 2002 Bernath Prize from the Society for Historians of American Foreign Relations, he was elected Finland Distinguished Professor by the Academy of Finland in 2006. His books include *The Flawed Architect: Henry Kissinger and American Foreign Policy* (2004); *United Nations: A Very Short Introduction* (2008) and *The Rise and Fall of Détente: American Foreign Policy and the Transformation of the Cold War* (2011).

JOHN L. HARPER is resident professor of American foreign policy and European studies at the Bologna Center of the Johns Hopkins University School of Advanced International Studies (SAIS). He is the author of *America and the Reconstruction of Italy* (1986); *American Visions of Europe:*

Franklin D. Roosevelt, George F. Kennan, and Dean G. Acheson (1994); *American Machiavelli: Alexander Hamilton and the Origins of U.S. Foreign Policy* (2004) and *The Cold War* (2011).

PIERS LUDLOW is a reader in the Department of International History of the London School of Economics. His research interests centre on the historical development of the European Community/Union, the Cold War, and transatlantic relations during the Cold War. His latest monograph was *The European Community and the Crises of the 1960s: Negotiating the Gaullist Challenge* (2006).

GARRET MARTIN is an editor-at-large at the European Institute based in Washington, DC. He has taught at the George Washington University in Washington, DC, and the University of Warwick in the UK. He obtained his Ph.D. from the London School of Economics and Political Science in 2006. His research focuses on France, the Cold War and the 1960s. He has published several articles in edited volumes, and more recently in the *Journal of Cold War Studies*. He also co-edited, with Christian Nuenlist and Anna Locher, the book *Globalizing de Gaulle: International Perspectives on French Foreign Policies, 1958–1969* (2010).

GOTTFRIED NIEDHART is professor emeritus of modern history at the University of Mannheim. He has published on English and German history and on the history of international relations, recently in particular on East-West relations during the era of détente. Together with Oliver Bange he edited *Helsinki 1975 and the Transformation of Europe* (2008).

ILARIA POGGIOLINI holds a tenured position as associate professor of international history at the University of Pavia. She is a partner of the Machiavelli Centre for Cold War Studies (CIMA), a member of the teaching staff of the Doctorate Program in International History at the University of Florence, SCR fellow at the European Study Centre, St Antony's College, University of Oxford and associate of the Transatlantic Relations Programme at LSE IDEAS, London School of Economics. Previously, she has been Jean Monnet professor at the University of Milan, lecturer at the University of Sassari and fellow of the Fulbright program, NATO, the Woodrow Wilson School (Princeton University), the British Council and St. Antony's College, Oxford. Her research activities and publications focus on post–WWII international peacemaking, especially the cases of Italy, Japan and Vietnam; political and diplomatic relations between Italy and the Allies in the 1940s and 1950s; British accession to the EEC and Ostpolitik in the 1970s and 1980s. She is presently working on nuclear policies in Britain since the 1970s and on the meaning of, and contemporary debate on, Euroscepticism among EEC/EU countries.

MARIE-PIERRE REY is professor of Russian and Soviet History and director of the Centre of Slavic Studies at the Sorbonne (Paris I). She was educated at the Ecole Normale Supérieure and received her doctorate (1989) and her habilitation (1997) from the Sorbonne. Her publications include *Alexandre Ier, le tsar qui vainquit Napoléon* (2009); *Le dilemme russe : la Russie et l'Europe occidentale d'Ivan le Terrible à Boris Eltsine* (2002); *De la Russie à l'Union soviétique, la construction de l'empire* (1994); *La Tentation du Rapprochement, France et URSS à l'heure de la détente, 1964–1974* (1991). She has also co-edited *Europe and the End of the Cold War: A Reappraisal* (2008) and *Les Russes de Gorbatchev à Poutine* (2005), and published many articles devoted to Russian and Soviet history, such as '"Europe is our Common Home": A Study of Gorbachev's Diplomatic Concept' in *Cold War History*, January 2004.

GEOFFREY ROBERTS was educated at North Staffordshire Polytechnic and the London School of Economics. He teaches history and international relations and is head of the School of History at University College Cork, Ireland. His books include *The Unholy Alliance: Stalin's Pact with Hitler* (1989); *The Soviet Union and the Origins of the Second World War* (1995); *The Soviet Union in World Politics, 1945–1991* (1998); *Victory at Stalingrad: The Battle that Changed History* (2002); *Stalin's Wars: From World War to Cold War, 1939–1953* (2006); and *Molotov: Stalin's Cold Warrior* (2011).

ANGELA ROMANO is Marie Curie fellow at LSE IDEAS. She is a scholar of the Machiavelli Center for Cold War Studies (CIMA) and a member of RICHIE (Réseau International de jeunes Chercheurs en Histoire de l'Intégration Européenne), and was Jean Monnet fellow (2009/10) at the Robert Schuman Centre for Advanced Studies, EUI. She received her Ph.D. in history of international relations from the University of Florence in 2006, where she has been adjunct professor of history of international organizations (2007/08) and lecturer of history of North America (2008/09). Dr. Romano's main research interests include the Cold War, transatlantic relations, external relations of the EC/EU and the CSCE process. Since 2004 she has presented papers at several international conferences and workshops in Europe, the U.S., Russia and Japan. She is author of *From Détente in Europe to European Détente: How the West Shaped the Helsinki CSCE* (2009) as well as several articles and chapters in edited volumes.

BERND ROTHER is a historian at the Federal Chancellor Willy Brandt Foundation in Berlin. He has edited multiple volumes relating to Brandt, including *Willy Brandt: Über Europa hinaus. Dritte Welt und Sozialistische Internationale* (2006) and *Willy Brandt: Gemeinsame Sicherheit. Internationale Beziehungen und deutsche Frage 1982–1992* (2009). He has also contributed chapters to multiple edited volumes, notably 'Between East and West – Social Democracy as an Alternative to Communism and Capitalism: Willy Brandt's Strategy as President of the Socialist International', in Leopoldo Nuti (ed.): *The Crisis of Détente in Europe: From Helsinki to Gorbachev, 1975–1985* (2009).

GEORGES-HENRI SOUTOU is professor emeritus at Paris-Sorbonne (Paris IV) University and member of the Institut de France. He belongs to the Diplomatic Archives Commission of the French Foreign Ministry. A member of the editorial board of several journals, including *Relations internationales* and *Revue historique des Armées*, he is co-editor of the *Revue d'histoire diplomatique*. He works on international history of the twentieth century, particularly the First World War, Franco-German relations and East-West relations after 1945. Besides numerous articles, he has published *L'Or et le Sang. Les buts de guerre économiques de la Première guerre mondiale* (1989); *L'Alliance incertaine. Les rapports politico-stratégiques franco-allemands, 1954–1996* (1996); *La Guerre de Cinquante Ans. Les relations Est-Ouest 1943-1990* (2001) and *L'Europe de 1815 à nos jours* (2007).

JACLYN STANKE is associate professor of history at Campbell University (Buies Creek, North Carolina). She received her Ph.D. in history from Emory University in 2001. Her field of research is the Cold War, and her most recent publications include articles on the Cold War and the American South as well as American popular perspectives on the Solidarity movement in Poland. She is currently working on a project documenting American popular culture and popular perspectives of the 1980s as the Cold War went from a deep freeze to a rather sudden end.

VLADISLAV M. ZUBOK is professor of history at Temple University, Philadelphia. He was born and educated in Russia and received his Ph.D. at the Institute for US and Canada Studies, the Academy of Science, Moscow. Among his numerous publications are the books *Inside the Kremlin's Cold War: From Stalin to Khrushchev* (1996), co-written with C. Pleshakov, and *A Failed Empire: The Soviet Union in the Cold War from Stalin to Gorbachev* (2007). Most recently, he published *Zhivago's Children: The Last Russian Intelligentsia* (2009).

INDEX